MCA
Microsoft Certified
Azure Administrator
Study Guide
Exam AZ-104

MCA
Microsoft Certified Associate
Azure Administrator
Study Guide
Exam AZ-104

Rithin Skaria

SYBEX®
A Wiley Brand

ISBN: 978-1-119-70515-4
ISBN: 978-1-119-70520-8 (ebk.)
ISBN: 978-1-119-70518-5 (ebk.)

Acknowledgments

Although the book bears my name as the author, many people contributed to its success and creation. I believe without their help and contribution this book wouldn't have been possible. Kenyon Brown was the acquisitions editor; he helped me to get the book started. Melissa Burlock, editorial assistant, was always available to help and answer my questions. Mahalingam M was the technical editor; he was very helpful in giving constructive feedback on the technical content and concepts; nevertheless, any mistakes that remain are my own. Kim was the copy editor, and Janet was the proofreader; they helped me to correct any grammatical mistakes, formatting issues, and typos. I would also like to thank my manager, Monty Pattan, for empowering and motivating me. Last but not least, I would like to extend my gratitude to my family, mentors, friends, colleagues, and everyone who helped directly or indirectly toward the success of this book.

About the Author

Rithin Skaria is a cloud evangelist with almost a decade of experience in managing and administering Azure, AWS, and OpenStack. He currently works at Microsoft as a Customer Engineer empowering customers to achieve more. His other works include *Linux Administration on Azure, Second Edition*; *Azure for Architects, Third Edition*; and *Migrating Linux to Microsoft Azure*. He can be reached at rithin@rithin.net. Connect with him on LinkedIn: @ rithin-skaria.

About the Technical Editor

Mahalingam M is an Azure Consultant and works with Enterprises to design and implement their solutions in Azure. He also assesses large-scale applications hosted on Azure and provides recommendations to optimize them. He started his journey on Azure five years back, and he is a certified Azure Solutions Architect Expert, Azure Security Engineer Associate, and Azure Administrator Associate. In addition to this, he is also a Microsoft Certified Trainer and delivers Workshops on Azure IaaS and PaaS.

Contents at a Glance

Contents

Table of Exercises

Introduction

Microsoft Azure is the public cloud offering from Microsoft, and it offers more data centers, security, and other services than any other cloud provider. As more organizations are moving their workloads to Azure, there is a high demand for professionals who are trained and certified on Azure. In this book, we will be focusing on Azure administration; the knowledge from this book will help you to manage and administer Azure infrastructure and also help you to pass the AZ-104: Microsoft Azure Administrator exam.

The AZ-104: Microsoft Azure Administrator exam is an associate exam targeting professionals interested in certifying their knowledge of implementing, managing, and monitoring the Azure infrastructure. Azure administrators are usually part of a team dedicated to certain tasks and responsibilities. These responsibilities include implementation, management, governance, and monitoring of an organization's cloud deployment.

This book is aligned to the official curriculum published by Microsoft, and the purpose of this book is to help you pass the AZ-104: Microsoft Azure Administrator exam. We are focusing on this exam because it covers all the tasks that are involved in the day-to-day life of an Azure administrator. You'll learn enough to get started deploying to workloads to Azure, and you'll learn how to administer, monitor, and manage these workloads. Even after you've taken and passed the AZ-104: Microsoft Azure Administrator exam, this book should remain a useful reference.

Don't just study the questions and answers! The questions on the actual exam will be different from the practice questions included in this book. The exam is designed to test your knowledge of a concept or objective, so use this book to learn the objectives behind the questions.

The AZ-104: Microsoft Azure Administrator Exam

Microsoft Azure was formerly known as Windows Azure until 2014. Internally the project was called Project Red Dog and was announced at Microsoft's Professional Developers Conference in 2008. Today, Microsoft Azure is one of the leading cloud providers, and many organizations have adopted it as part of the cloud transformation.

Though Azure started with just a handful of services, at present Microsoft Azure comprises numerous services such as compute, storage, network, identity, data management, and so on. As the number of services are increasing, customers are relying on the Azure platform. Getting certified on Microsoft Azure will bring more value to your résumé.

Why Become AZ-104: Microsoft Azure Administrator Certified?

There are several good reasons to get your AZ-104: Microsoft Azure Administrator certification.

Provides Proof of Professional Achievement   Certifications are quickly becoming status symbols in the IT industry. As many organizations are moving to the cloud, the demand for cloud skills is high. Employers are pushing their employees to get certified in Azure to support their cloud workloads. Every day, more people are putting the Azure Administrator Associate badge on their LinkedIn profile and résumé.

Increases Your Marketability   AZ-104: Microsoft Azure Administrator certification makes individuals more marketable to potential employers. Also, AZ-104: Microsoft Azure Administrator–certified employees might receive a higher salary base because employers won't have to spend as much money on vendor-specific training.

Provides an Opportunity for Advancement   Most raises and advancements are based on performance. AZ-104: Microsoft Azure Administrator–certified employees work faster and more efficiently. The more productive employees are, the more money they will make for their company; and, of course, the more money they make for the company, the more valuable they will be to the company. So, if employees are AZ-104: Microsoft Azure Administrator certified, their chances of getting promoted will be greater.

Raises Customer Confidence   As the IT community, users, small business owners, and the like become more familiar with the AZ-104: Microsoft Azure Administrator–certified professional moniker, more of them will realize that AZ-104: Microsoft Azure Administrator professionals are more qualified to work in their cloud environment than noncertified individuals.

How to Become AZ-104: Microsoft Azure Administrator Certified

The Microsoft certification is available to anyone who has experience implementing, managing, and monitoring Azure environment.

The exam is delivered by Pearson VUE, which is partnering with Microsoft. The exam can be taken at any Pearson VUE testing center or using OnVUE online delivery from your home or office. If you pass, you will get two badges. One is for the AZ:104 exam, and the other one is the Azure Administrator Associate badge. These badges will be emailed to you, and you can use Credly to claim them. Contact (877) 551-PLUS (551-7587) for Pearson VUE information.

Registration with Pearson VUE is completed online at https://docs.microsoft.com/en-us/learn/certifications/exams/az-104#certification-exams by clicking

Schedule Exam. You'll be asked for your name, mailing address, phone number, employer, when and where you want to take the test (i.e., which testing center), and your credit card number (arrangement for payment must be made at the time of registration).

Exam policies can change from time to time. We highly recommend that you check the Pearson VUE site for the most up-to-date information when you begin your preparing, when you register, and again a few days before your scheduled exam date.

Who Should Buy This Book

Anybody who wants to pass the AZ-104: Microsoft Azure Administrator exam may benefit from this book. If you're familiar with Azure fundamentals and would like to expand your knowledge to an administrator level, this book covers the material you will need to learn Azure administration, and it continues to provide the knowledge you need up to a proficiency level sufficient to pass the AZ-104: Microsoft Azure Administrator exam. You can pick up this book and learn from it even if you've never used Azure before, although you'll find it an easier read if you've at least casually used Azure in the past. If you're already familiar with Azure administration, this book can serve as a review and as a refresher course for information with which you might not be completely familiar. In either case, reading this book will help you to pass the AZ-104: Microsoft Azure Administrator exam.

This book was written with the assumption that you know the fundamentals of Azure (what it is, and possibly the role of services that are offered by Azure). I also assume that you know some basics about cloud computing in general, such as IaaS versus PaaS versus SaaS, how the cloud is beneficial, and so on. Chances are, you have used Azure in a substantial way in the past. I do *not* assume that you have extensive knowledge of Azure administration, but if you've done some Azure administration, you can still use this book to fill in gaps in your knowledge.

As a practical matter, you'll need an Azure subscription with which to practice and learn in a hands-on way. Neither the exam nor this book covers actually how the subscription is created. You may need to sign up for a Free Trial or an Azure for Students offer to create a subscription. Alternatively, if your organization has provided you with a Visual Studio subscription, you can use that to create a subscription. Please visit https://azure.microsoft.com/en-in/support/legal/offer-details to view the list of Azure offers.

Study Guide Features

This study guide uses a number of common elements to help you prepare. These include the following:

Summaries   The summary section of each chapter briefly explains the chapter, allowing you to easily review what was covered.

Exam Essentials   The exam essentials focus on major exam topics and critical knowledge that you should take into the test. The exam essentials focus on the exam objectives provided by Microsoft.

Chapter Review Questions   A set of questions at the end of each chapter will help you assess your knowledge and whether you are ready to take the exam based on your knowledge of that chapter's topics.

The review questions, assessment test, and other testing elements included in this book are *not* derived from the actual exam questions, so don't memorize the answers to these questions and assume that doing so will enable you to pass the exam. You should learn the underlying topic, as described in the text of the book. This will let you answer the questions provided with this book *and* pass the exam. Learning the underlying topic is also the approach that will serve you best in the workplace—the ultimate goal of a certification.

Additional Study Tools

This book comes with additional study tools to help you prepare for the exam. They include the following.

Go to www.wiley.com/go/sybextestprep, register your book to receive your unique PIN, and then once you have the PIN, return to www.wiley.com/go/sybextestprep and register a new account or add this book to an existing account.

Interactive Online Learning Environment and Test Bank

We've put together some really great online tools to help you pass the Microsoft Azure Administrator exam. The interactive online learning environment that accompanies the MCA Azure Administrator Study Guide provides a test bank and study tools to help you prepare for the exam. By using these tools you can dramatically increase your chances of passing the exam on your first try.

The online section includes the following:

Sample Tests

Many sample tests are provided throughout this book and online, including the Assessment Test, which you'll find at the end of this introduction, and the Chapter Tests that include the review questions at the end of each chapter. In addition, there are two bonus practice exams. Use these questions to test your knowledge of the study guide material. The online test bank runs on multiple devices.

Flashcards

The online text bank includes more than 100 flashcards specifically written to hit you hard, so don't get discouraged if you don't ace your way through them at first! They're there to ensure that you're really ready for the exam. And no worries—armed with the review questions, practice exams, and flashcards, you'll be more than prepared when exam day comes! Questions are provided in digital flashcard format (a question followed by a single correct answer). You can use the flashcards to reinforce your learning and provide last-minute test prep before the exam.

Glossary

A glossary of key terms from this book and their definitions are available as a fully searchable PDF.

Like all exams, the AZ-104: Microsoft Azure Administrator certification from Microsoft is updated periodically and may eventually be retired or replaced. At some point after Microsoft is no longer offering this exam, the old editions of our books and online tools will be retired. If you have purchased this book after the exam was retired or are attempting to register in the Sybex online learning environment after the exam was retired, please know that we make no guarantees that this exam's online Sybex tools will be available once the exam is no longer available.

Conventions Used in This Book

This book uses certain typographic styles to help you quickly identify important information and to avoid confusion over the meaning of words such as on-screen prompts. In particular, look for the following styles:

- *Italicized text* indicates key terms that are described at length for the first time in a chapter. (Italics are also used for emphasis.)

- A `monospaced` font indicates the contents of configuration files, messages displayed at a command prompt, filenames, text-mode command names, and Internet URLs.

- *Italicized monospaced text* indicates a variable—information that differs from one system or command run to another, such as the name of a client computer or a process ID number.

- **Bold monospaced text** is information that you're to type into the computer, for example at a shell prompt. This text can also be italicized to indicate that you should substitute an appropriate value for your system.

In addition to these text conventions, which can apply to individual words or entire paragraphs, a few conventions highlight segments of text.

 A note indicates information that's useful or interesting but that's somewhat peripheral to the main text. A note might be relevant to a small number of networks, for instance, or it may refer to an outdated feature.

EXERCISES

An exercise is a procedure you should try on your own computer to help you learn about the material in the chapter. Don't limit yourself to the procedures described in the exercises, though! Try other commands and procedures to really learn about Azure.

Exam Objectives

This book has been written to cover every Microsoft exam objective at a level appropriate to its exam weighting, shown here.

Subject Area	% of Exam
Manage Azure identities and governance	15–20%
Implement and manage storage	15–20%
Deploy and manage Azure compute resources	20–25%
Configure and manage virtual networking	25–30%
Monitor and back up Azure resources	10–15%
Total	100%

Objective Map

Objective	Percentage of exam	Primary chapter
Manage Azure identities and governance	15%–20%	
Identity: Azure Active Directory		Chapter 1
Compliance and cloud governance		Chapter 2
Implement and manage storage	10%–15%	
Azure Storage		Chapter 6
Deploy and manage Azure compute resources	25%–30%	
Azure Virtual Machines		Chapter 7
Automation, Deployment, and Configuration of Resources		Chapter 8
PaaS Compute Options		Chapter 9
Configure and manage virtual networking	30%–35%	
Virtual Networking		Chapter 3
Intersite connectivity		Chapter 4
Network Traffic Management		Chapter 5
Monitor and backup Azure resources	10%–15%	
Data Protection		Chapter 10
Monitoring resources		Chapter 11

Assessment Test

1. Which feature in Azure AD can be used to manage the devices and enforce organizational policies?

   A. Azure AD Domain Services

   B. Multifactor authentication

   C. Device access management

   D. Azure AD Join

2. Azure AD offers self-service options for users to reset their own password. What is this service called?

   A. Self-user password reset

   B. Self-service password reset

   C. Self-password reset

   D. User password reset

3. True or false: To use Azure AD, you need to create a Windows Server instance in Azure and install Active Directory Domain Services.

   A. True

   B. False

4. Which service in Azure is used to provide authorization for a user to access or manage a specific service?

   A. Azure policies

   B. Management groups

   C. Role-based access control

   D. Azure AD

5. You would like to limit your deployments to the East US region only. Which service should you use?

   A. Azure policies

   B. Resource locks

   C. Role-based access control

   D. Blueprints

6. You would like to group your resources based on the name of the person who created it. What is the easiest way to add this information to a resource?

   A. Azure policies

   B. Azure tags

   C. Azure resource locks

   D. Azure resource metadata service

7. Which service in Azure is responsible for establishing communication between virtual machines and the Internet?

    A. Route table

    B. VPN gateway

    C. Virtual network

    D. ExpressRoute

8. True or false: Network security groups can be used only to filter the traffic entering the subnet; we cannot filter the traffic hitting the network interface card.

    A. True

    B. False

9. True or false: Azure Firewall operates at layer 7.

    A. True

    B. False

10. If we peer networks that are part of different Azure regions, we call it _____.

    A. Cross-region peering

    B. Cross-regional peering

    C. Global virtual network peering

    D. Cross-global peering

11. You have hired a developer to work on a project, and the developer is working remotely. You have been requested to assist the developer in setting up VPN connectivity to the Azure environment. What type of connection should you set up for the developer?

    A. Site-to-site

    B. Site-to-user

    C. ExpressRoute

    D. Point-to-site

12. You have been requested to set up a low-latency connectivity between two virtual networks. Which solution will you select?

    A. Site-to-site connection

    B. VNet-to-VNet connection

    C. Point-to-site connection

    D. VNet peering

13. Which load balancing solution should you use if you would like to load balance across any TCP or UDP protocols?

    A. Azure Load Balancer

    B. Azure Application Gateway

    C. Azure Front Door

    D. Azure Traffic Manager

14. You have three production web applications running on Azure App Service in the same region. You want to perform layer 7 load balancing between these web applications. Which load balancing solution should you use?

   A. Azure Load Balancer

   B. App Service Load Distributor

   C. Application Gateway

   D. Azure Traffic Manager

15. You need a DNS load balancing solution. What solution should you deploy?

   A. Azure Load Balancer

   B. App Service Load Distributor

   C. Application Gateway

   D. Azure Traffic Manager

16. Which storage service should you select for backup, archiving, and disaster recovery scenarios?

   A. Blob Storage

   B. Table Storage

   C. File Storage

   D. Queue Storage

17. Which storage service should you select to create a network file share in Azure?

   A. Blob Storage

   B. Table Storage

   C. File Storage

   D. Queue Storage

18. Which of the following storage redundancy offers the highest durability? (Select all that apply.)

   A. LRS

   B. ZRS

   C. GRS

   D. GZRS

19. Azure Virtual Machine is an example of a(n) _____ service.

   A. Infrastructure-as-a-Service

   B. Platform-as-a-Service

   C. Function-as-a-Service

   D. Software-as-a-Service

20. _____ can be used to connect to Azure VMs.

   A. SSH

   B. WinRM

   C. HTTP

   D. Webhook

21. RDP can be used to connect to Windows VMs, and it uses the _____ port for communication.

   A. UDP/3389

   B. TCP/3389

   C. TCP/3387

   D. UDP/22

22. An ARM template is written in _____ format.

   A. XML

   B. HTML

   C. JSON

   D. HCL

23. _____ can be used to store values in ARM templates.

   A. Parameters

   B. Variables

   C. Constants

   D. Resources

24. True or false: Incremental mode is the default deployment mode for ARM templates.

   A. True

   B. False

25. _____ defines the compute resources provisioned for running Azure App Service.

   A. App Service Plan

   B. Deployment slots

   C. Hybrid mode

   D. App Service Environment

26. True or False: App Service supports autoscaling from the Basic plan onward.

   A. True

   B. False

27. _____ is an example of a managed Kubernetes cluster.

   A. Container Instances

   B. Kubernetes Instances

   C. Container Kubernetes Service

   D. Azure Kubernetes Service

28. Which service offers the easiest way to run containers in Azure?

    A. Container Instances

    B. Virtual Machines

    C. Docker host

    D. Azure Kubernetes Service

29. True or false: Recovery Services Vault can be used to back up Azure VMs only.

    A. True

    B. False

30. True or false: Azure Backup supports both Windows and VMs.

    A. True

    B. False

31. Which service can be used for infrastructure disaster recovery in the case of regional failures?

    A. Azure Backup

    B. Microsoft Backup Server

    C. Azure Site Backup

    D. Azure Site Recovery

32. Log Analytics uses _____ for querying the datasets.

    A. SQL

    B. KQL

    C. CQL

    D. DQL

33. You can store your notification preferences for alerts using _____

    A. Notification groups

    B. Messaging group

    C. Action groups

    D. Alert groups

34. All data collected by Log Analytics is stored in _____.

    A. An Azure Storage Account

    B. Data Explorer

    C. Workspace

    D. Azure Monitor

Answers to Assessment Test

1. D. Azure AD Join offers device management. Refer to Chapter 1.

2. B. The self-service password reset service can be used by users to reset their own password with the help of authentication methods configured by cloud administrators. Refer to Chapter 1.

3. B. Azure AD is a cloud-managed identity and access management solution. You don't need to install ADDS or manage virtual machines in Azure to use Azure AD. In fact, these are two different services. Refer to Chapter 1.

4. C. Role-based access control (RBAC) is responsible for managing authorization. Refer to Chapter 2.

5. A. Azure policies are used to limit deployments to the East US region. This can be achieved by using the Allowed Locations policy. Refer to Chapter 2.

6. B. Resource tags can be used to logically organize the resources in your environment. We can add metadata to our resources including the owner name, cost center, department, etc. Refer to Chapter 2.

7. C. A virtual network enables virtual machines to connect to the Internet securely. Refer to Chapter 3.

8. B. Network security groups (NSGs) can be used to filter traffic at both the subnet and NIC level. Refer to Chapter 3.

9. A. Azure Firewall is a layer 7, or Application layer, firewall. Refer to Chapter 3.

10. C. If we peer networks that are part of different Azure regions, we call it global VNet peering. You can establish peering from Azure public cloud regions to China cloud regions as well. However, you cannot peer Azure public cloud and government cloud regions. You can establish peering between the same regions in a government cloud. Refer to Chapter 4.

11. C. Point-to-site (P2S) helps in connecting individual devices to the Azure virtual network. Using P2S, you can connect the developer workstation to the Azure virtual network. Refer to Chapter 4.

12. D. VNet peering offers the lowest latency as the traffic is via the Microsoft backbone network. Refer to Chapter 4.

13. A. Azure Load Balancer is a L4 load balancer that supports any TCP/UDP protocols. Refer to Chapter 5.

14. C. Application Gateway supports App Services as a backend and L7 load balancing. Refer to Chapter 5.

15. D. Azure Traffic Manager is the DNS load balancing solution. Refer to Chapter 5.

16. A. Azure Blob Storage is the object storage service offered by Microsoft that can be used for backup, archiving, and disaster recovery storage scenarios. Refer to Chapter 6.

17. C. Network file shares can be created using the Azure File service, and this can be accessed via the SMB protocol. This file share can be mounted to multiple VMs or on-premises machines, which is ideal for sharing files across machines. Refer to Chapter 6.

18. C, D. Both GRS and GZRS offer 99.9999999999999999 percent durability over a given year. Refer to Chapter 6.

19. A. Azure VM is an example of an infrastructure-as-a-service (IaaS) service. Refer to Chapter 7.

20. A. SSH can be used to connect, manage, and administer Azure VMs. Refer to Chapter 7.

21. B. By default, RDP uses TCP/3389 for establishing communication to Azure Windows VMs. However, this port can be configured to a different one if needed. Refer to Chapter 7.

22. C. ARM templates are written in JSON format. Refer to Chapter 8.

23. B. Variables are used to hard-code certain values to keywords in ARM templates so that they can be reused throughout the template. Refer to Chapter 8.

24. A. Incremental mode is the default mode of deployment for ARM template deployment unless you override the mode. In incremental mode, Azure Resource Manager will not alter any resources that are already present in the target resource group. The resources that are declared in the template will be added to the existing resources in the resource group. Refer to Chapter 8.

25. A. App Service Plan is responsible for providing the compute resources for the application to run. Refer to Chapter 9.

26. B. Autoscaling is available from the Standard plan onward. The Basic plan doesn't support autoscaling; however, manual scaling is supported. Refer to Chapter 9.

27. D. Azure Kubernetes Service is a completely platform-managed cluster. Using AKS, you can easily create Kubernetes clusters in Azure and deploy your applications. Refer to Chapter 9.

28. A. Azure Container Instances offers the easiest way to run containers in Azure without the need to manage any VMs or infrastructure. Refer to Chapter 9.

29. B. Recovery Services Vault supports System Center DPM, Windows Server, Azure Backup Server, and other services from on-premises along with Azure VMs.

30. A. You don't require any agents for backing up virtual machines running in Azure, and Azure Backup provides native support for Windows and VMs. Refer to Chapter 11.

31. D. Azure Site Recovery is a business continuity and disaster recovery (BCDR) solution for protecting your infrastructure against regional failures. Refer to Chapter 10.

32. B. Kusto Query Language is used to query the dataset stored in Azure Log Analytics. Refer to Chapter 11.

33. C. An action group is a collection of notification preferences that can be reused in multiple alerts. The notifications and actions that you define inside the action group will be executed when the alert is fired. Refer to Chapter 11.

34. C. Each workspace is an environment that will be used for the ingestion Azure Monitor logs. The connected sources, configuration, and repository are managed per workspace. Refer to Chapter 11.

Chapter

1

Identity: Azure Active Directory

MICROSOFT EXAM OBJECTIVES COVERED IN THIS CHAPTER:

✓ **Manage Azure Active Directory (Azure AD) objects**

- **Create users and groups**

- **Manage user and group properties**

- **Manage device settings**

- **Perform bulk user updates**

- **Manage guest users**

- **Configure Azure AD Join**

- **Configure self-service password reset**

With the recent cloud transformation, the number of organizations migrating to the cloud has drastically increased, and security has become one of the primary concerns. In on-premises, the IT administrator and security administrators controlled the overall security of the organization. When it comes to the cloud, the traditional methods we are accustomed to should be replaced by modern identity and access management tools.

In Microsoft Azure, Azure Active Directory is a cloud-based directory and identity management service. Though the name looks like the Active Directory that we use on our on-premises Windows Servers for identity and access management, this one is completely different and takes access management to the next level. As an administrator, you will be working with Azure Active Directory day in and day out for various administrative tasks, including user management, group management, password reset, joining, registering your devices to Azure AD, and so on. Although these are basic tasks, sometimes administrative tasks include complex integrations such as single sign-on (SSO), multifactor authentication (MFA), and conditional access. From an exam standpoint, fulfilling the basic tasks is more than enough; however, having knowledge of the complex configurations will help you progress in your career.

Azure Active Directory

As mentioned in the introduction of this chapter, Azure AD is Microsoft's cloud-based identity and access management (IAM) solution. Azure AD is an especially useful solution for IT admins, developers, and subscribers of various Microsoft solutions (such as Microsoft 365, Dynamics 365, and Azure). Primarily, Azure AD deals with helping employees to sign-in to various resources such as O365, M365, Dynamics, Azure, etc. However, the integration does not stop here; you can integrate Azure AD as the IAM solution for third-party applications and your internal applications as well. Developers are constantly working on integrating Azure AD as the IAM solution because of the increased reliability it provides. Since this book is about Azure administration, we will focus on how Azure AD is intended to help IT admins.

Benefits

Let's explore the different benefits of Azure AD and why organizations should consider Azure AD as the IAM solution.

SSO to Cloud and On-Premises Applications   Having too many credentials for different applications increases the complexity and results in a higher chance of human error because an SSO solution will help users to sign in to all cloud applications, on-premises applications, and devices using their corporate credentials. Azure AD is not only meant for Microsoft Stack, but for thousands of SaaS applications such as Dropbox, ServiceNow, DocuSign, etc.

Easily Extend On-Premises Active Directory to the Cloud   When organizations move from on-premises to the cloud, there is a need to synchronize the users with the cloud. Otherwise, users will end up with two credentials, one for on-premises and another one for the cloud. To avoid this scenario and to provide a seamless SSO experience, Azure AD allows administrators to synchronize users, groups, passwords, and devices across both on-premises and the cloud. This is accomplished using a tool called Azure AD Connect that needs to be installed on your on-premises domain controller or any other domain-joined server with Windows Server 2012 or later, and it will help with the synchronization.

Cross-Platform Support   Regardless of what platform the user is using, be it iOS, Android, Windows, Linux, or macOS, the sign-in experience is going to be the same, and the users can sign-in to their applications using their work credentials.

Increase Security of Your On-Premises Applications   You can use the Azure AD Application Proxy service to access your on-premises applications via a secured remote access. The best part is you do not have to expose any additional ports on your on-premises firewalls; the access is managed by application proxy endpoints. The access can be tightened using multifactor authentication and conditional access policies.

Better Monitoring and Data Protection   Azure AD amplifies the overall security posture of your environment by providing unique identity protection features. Azure AD Identity Protection comprises several features including suspicious sign-in activity, risk alerts, etc. These triggers can be further integrated with conditional access policies to make business decisions. In addition to these capabilities, administrators can leverage security reports, sign-in activities, and potential vulnerability reports that are available off the shelf without the need to deploy any additional components.

Self-Service Capabilities   If you have worked as an IT administrator, you know most of the calls to the help desk will be regarding password resets. Azure AD offers a feature called Self-Service Password Reset by which users can reset their own passwords with the help of an authentication method such as phone, email, security questions, or a combination of these. IT admins need to enroll users into the SSPR program before they can use this feature. Enrolling is also self-serve, and the user will be prompted to verify the authentication methods. Enabling SSPR in your environment can elevate the security and reduce help-desk engagements.

If you are using Office 365, Azure, or Dynamics 365 in your environment, knowingly or unknowingly you are interacting with Azure AD to complete the authentication process.

We have been talking about Azure AD for a while now, and it is time that we understand the concepts that are part of Azure AD.

Concepts

Understanding the various terminologies that are related to Azure AD is the first step in learning Azure AD. The following are the Azure AD concepts:

Identity   An object that can interact with Azure AD and get authenticated is called an *identity*. A user is an exceptionally good example of an identity; to get authenticated, a user will present the username and password to Azure AD. Upon receiving these credentials, Azure AD will substantiate and confirm if the authentication was successful. Servers and applications can also use their identity to authenticate with Azure AD; since these can be authenticated, they are also called *identities*. When it comes to servers or applications, they use certificates or secrets for completing the authentication.

Account   Any identity that has data associated with it is called an *account*. For example, if we take a user named John Doe, the user will have different data attributes associated to it such as user principal name, sign-in name, manager name, department, etc. All the data associated to the user identity will make the identity an account. Since identity is required for mapping these attributes, you cannot have an account without an identity. The account can be on-premises as well as in the cloud.

Azure AD Account   Usually known as work or school accounts, these accounts are provisioned in Azure AD or via other cloud services such as Office 365, etc. The data associated to these identities is stored in Azure AD and can be used to log in to services that use Azure AD as the authentication provider.

Azure Subscription   This is the container created in Azure to separate billing and environments. An account can have multiple subscriptions that can be used to create isolated environments and billing boundaries. Each subscription you create will be mapped to a tenant, and it is always a one-to-one mapping. You can always move subscriptions across tenants if you have a multitenant environment.

Azure AD Tenant/Directory   The term *tenant* means a single instance of Azure AD denoting a single organization. When you sign up for any Microsoft cloud service (Azure, O365, etc.), a dedicated instance of Azure AD is provisioned for you. There will be a unique name associated to this tenant that will have the suffix `onmicrosoft.com` and a unique ID assigned to the tenant called the *tenant ID*. An organization can create multiple directories/tenants for creating disparate environments or realms with different users and groups.

Now that we are familiar with the concepts related to Azure AD, the next question you will have in your mind is how Azure AD is different from Active Directory Domain Services.

Azure AD vs. Active Directory Domain Services

You might have already worked or heard about Active Directory Domain Services (AD DS) in your on-premises environment. If you have not heard about AD DS, this is a deployment of the Active Directory service/role on Windows Server. The server can be a physical or virtualized one. The primary focus of AD DS is to work as a directory service. There are several other components of Active Directory that get installed along with the directory service such as Active Directory Lightweight Directory Service (AD LDS), Active Directory Federation Services (AD FS), Active Directory Certificate Services (AD CS), and Active Directory Rights Management Service (AD RMS). You can also implement AD DS in Azure by installing the Active Directory Domain Services role on your Windows virtual machines deployed in Azure. This is not a recommended scenario unless you have a special scenario that requires AD DS deployment; for all other scenarios, Azure AD is recommended.

At first look, AD DS and Azure AD may look the same and both can be used for authentication and offer directory services; however, there are some differences in the way things work under the hood. The key point to understand here is if you install the AD DS role on an Azure Windows virtual machine, it is not equivalent to Azure AD. A lot of beginners have this misconception and assume both are the same. Well, that is wrong. The following are some of the key differences that make Azure AD different from AD DS:

Hierarchy   A flat structure is used by Azure AD to represent or provision the users and groups. Therefore, organizational units (OUs) and Group Policy objects (GPOs), which exist in AD DS, do not exist in Azure AD.

Federation Services   Azure AD supports Federation Services as an authentication method, and you can further integrate with third-party providers such as Twitter, Facebook, etc. On the other hand, in the case of AD DS, we can set up federation with another domain controller or forest only, and third-party integration is not supported.

Lack of LDAP   In AD DS, we used a protocol called LDAP to query users, groups, or objects in Active Directory. In the case of Azure AD, since this is an HTTP/HTTPS-based service, we will be using the REST API for querying instead of LDAP.

Lack of Kerberos   AD DS deployment uses Kerberos authentication; however, Azure AD uses HTTP/HTTPS protocols like SAML, OpenID Connect for authentication, OAuth for authorization, and SAML. Developers can choose any of these communication protocols while they design security for their applications.

Management   Azure AD is a managed service, and it is an underlying infrastructure; the availability is managed by Microsoft. If AD DS is deployed on an Azure Windows virtual machine, the configuration, management, virtual machine patching, updates, upgrades, and other maintenance tasks should be taken care by the end customer.

Azure AD: Licensing

You have seen that Azure AD offers a lot of add-on features more than legacy identity and management solutions. These features come with a price, and not all organizations need all these features. Licenses are categorized based on the number of premium features it supports. There are four editions of Azure Active Directory.

Azure Active Directory Free   As the name implies, this is the free version of Azure Active Directory and offers minimal features such as user management, group management, Azure AD Connect for syncing on-premises identities, basic reporting, SSO, SSPR, etc. If you have not purchased any Azure AD license, this is going to be your default edition.

Azure Active Directory Microsoft 365 Apps   If you have O365, this edition of Azure AD is automatically provisioned for you. Besides the features offered by Azure AD Free, this edition offers additional functionalities such as IAM for Microsoft 365 Apps, branding, MFA, etc.

Azure Active Directory Premium P1   Azure AD Premium P1 offers all the capabilities of Azure AD Free and some additional premium features that can increase the overall security of your environment. Dynamic groups, self-serve group management, Microsoft Identity Manager, and password writeback are some of the additional features offered by Azure AD Premium P1.

Azure Active Directory Premium P2   This is the top edition of Azure AD and offers all features in the P1 and Azure AD Free editions; additionally, Identity Protection and Identity Governance are offered.

Table 1.1 provides a quick comparison of all editions of Azure AD and the features offered by each edition.

TABLE 1.1   Comparison of Azure AD Editions

Feature	Free	Microsoft 365 Apps	Premium P1	Premium P2
Directory objects	500,000	Unlimited	Unlimited	Unlimited
Single sign-on	Unlimited	Unlimited	Unlimited	Unlimited
Core identity and access management	✓	✓	✓	✓
Business-to-business collaboration	✓	✓	✓	✓
Identity and access management for Microsoft 365 apps	✗	✓	✓	✓
Hybrid identities (password writeback)	✗	✗	✓	✓
Advanced group access management	✗	✗	✓	✓
Conditional access	✗	✗	✓	✓
Identity protection	✗	✗	✗	✓
Identity governance	✗	✗	✗	✓

The pricing of Azure AD licensing can be reviewed on the Azure AD pricing page.

`https://azure.microsoft.com/en-us/pricing/details/active-directory`

In addition to these editions, if you already have an Office 365 E3/E5 license, then you can use the premium features of Azure AD, and you do not have to pay for these licenses separately. P1 is included in E3, and P2 is included in E5, respectively.

Since you have the basic understanding of the editions of Azure AD and how they are different from a traditional Active Directory deployment, let's talk quickly about custom domains in Azure AD.

Custom Domains in Azure AD

Every tenant will have two properties that make it unique from other tenants created by other organizations (tenant ID and the tenant initial domain). By default, when you create a tenant, there will be a default domain that will look like `<yourdomainname>.onmicrosoft.com`. This initial domain cannot be changed or deleted once the tenant is provisioned. Because of the uniqueness of this domain name, sometimes you will not get the domain name that you are looking for. For example, when you try to sign up for a Gmail or Outlook mailbox, you get an option to choose a username. Though you have a choice, username allocation works based on the availability of the username. Sometimes you might try to get an email with your name, and you might end up with Gmail suggesting some usernames having random numbers because the one you asked for is not available. The same concept applies to the initial domains as well; if the name you request is taken, then you must append some letters or numbers to make the name unique.

 If the tenant was created while you signed up for the Azure subscription using your email address, then Microsoft Azure uses your email address and considers that as the initial domain name. You can create additional domains, and at that point you will get an option to choose the initial domain name. Refer to the "Managing Multiple Directories" section in this chapter to understand multitenant environments.

The problem with this approach is that all the users you create will have this initial domain assigned to their username. Since you have added letters and numbers to make it unique, this initial domain is hard to remember and not user friendly. To resolve this issue, you can use custom domains in Azure AD.

Using custom domains, you can use your domain that you created with the domain registrar. Adding custom domains requires you to validate and prove to Azure that you own the domain. This verification can be completed by adding a TXT/MX record to your DNS domain. The value for this DNS record will be given by Azure. When you add a domain to Azure AD, it will be unverified. After you add the DNS record to your DNS zone, you can initiate the verification request, and Azure AD will start querying your domain to verify if the value given by Azure is returned as the answer for the DNS query. Once the record is returned, Azure AD will mark the domain as verified, and you will be able to use the domain when you create users. You can have multiple domains and keep one of them as your primary.

Nevertheless, this is not a daily task for the administrators, and this is a one-time setup. In the future, if more domains need to be linked, then you may have to repeat the verification process. This topic is not part of the exam; however, understanding custom domains will help you set up your test environment with a custom domain. In this chapter, the exercises will have a custom domain name instead of the onmicrosoft.com domain name. I hope that this quick introduction of custom domains will help you understand why your test environment has an onmicrosoft.com domain and the exercises have a proper domain name.

If you would like to add your custom domain to Azure AD, please follow the process outlined in this documentation:

https://docs.microsoft.com/en-us/azure/active-directory/
fundamentals/add-custom-domain

On that note, we will start with users and groups in Azure AD.

Users and Groups

Users and groups are the primary objects of every IAM solution, and Azure AD also has a user and group management system, which is the backbone for access management. You have seen what an account is; just to refresh what we discussed; an account is an identity that has data associated to it. In Azure AD, you have user accounts and group accounts for managing users and groups. Let's get started with user accounts and see the operations that are available for administrators.

User Accounts

As the name suggests, user accounts consist of user identities, which will be used by users to log in to services such as Azure, O365, Dynamics 365, SaaS applications, and other third-party applications that are integrated with Azure AD.

You should create a subscription for testing all labs in this book. You can create a Free Trial subscription. If you are using your personal email address to sign up for the subscription, a new tenant will be automatically provisioned for you. All operations can be performed on that tenant.

Now that you know what a user account is, it is time to see how you can see users in our directory.

Viewing User Accounts

If you are working on a new directory that was set up for testing the exercises in this book, then you won't have any additional users apart from the account that you used to sign up for the subscription. However, in a production environment, there will be hundreds of users. As an administrator, you will be asked to verify if the account exists in Azure AD or get information about a particular user. Hence, knowing how to view user accounts is particularly important in an IT admin's daily job. We will follow a step-by-step process to view the users in your directory, as shown in Exercise 1.1.

EXERCISE 1.1

Viewing Users in Your Directory

1. Open your browser (Microsoft recommends that you use the latest version of your favorite browser) and navigate to the Azure portal, which is available at https://portal.azure.com.

2. A sign-in screen will be presented to you. Sign in using the email address that you used to create the subscription. The data you enter (username and password) will be sent to Azure AD. If the credentials are correct, then you will be logged in.

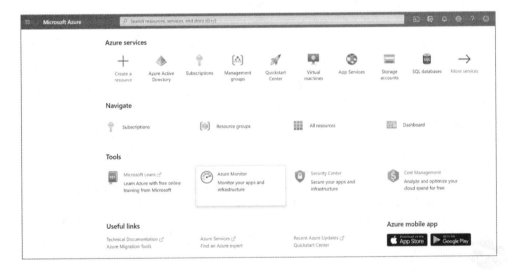

3. Now that you are in the Azure portal, you can click the hamburger icon at the top-left corner and click Azure Active Directory.

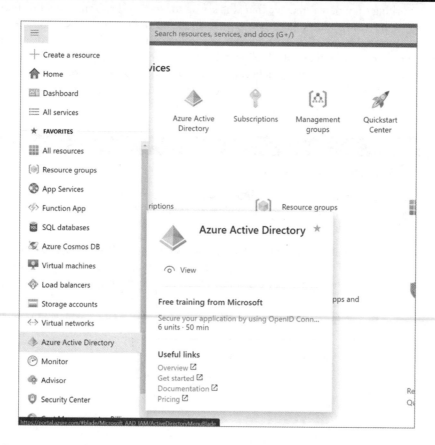

4. Selecting Azure Active Directory will take you to the Overview blade of Azure Active Directory. This blade gives you some idea about certain aspects of your Azure AD such as the tenant ID, tenant name, primary domain associated to your tenant, edition of Azure AD, and number of users, groups, applications, and devices. If you scroll down, you will see more information such as your account, Azure AD connect, secure score, etc. The graphic here shows the overview of the tenant that is used for the demonstration.

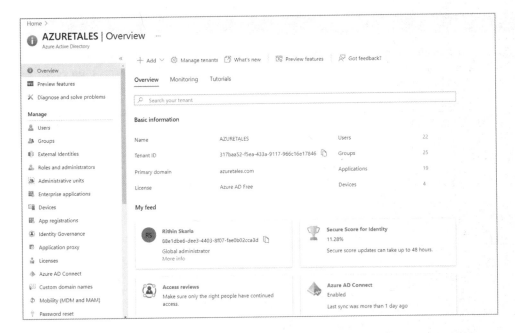

If you take a close look at the graphic, you can see at the top the option that will let you create, manage, and delete tenants. These options are quite useful if you are managing a multi-tenant environment. One thing to note here is that deleting a tenant requires you to cancel all active Azure subscriptions that are part of the tenant. You cannot delete a tenant when there is an active Azure subscription associated with that tenant. Since we are working on user management, let's shift our focus to the Users blade under the Manage section.

5. Once you click the Users blade, you will be presented with the All Users view. Your view might be different from what is shown here as it is displaying the users in the demo tenant.

6. If you click any user, you will be presented with the details of the user such as name, user principal name, job title, department, manager, etc., along with the creation date and last sign-in date.

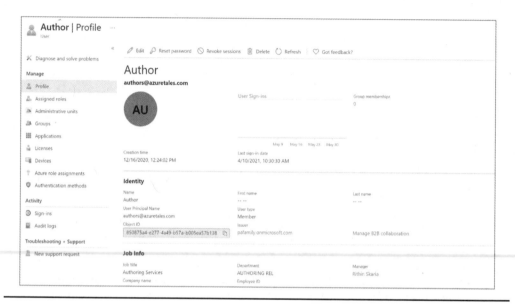

In this section you saw how to view the existing users in the directory and find the details of a user. Now that you know how to find a user in the directory, let's see how to add a new user to the directory.

Adding Users

In an enterprise environment, user insertion happens frequently, and cloud administrators are responsible for this. Whenever a new employee joins the organization, administrators are required to create their account, add the necessary licenses, complete their profile, set up their initial password, etc. In this section, we will add users from the Azure portal to understand the user insertion process. Before we start the exercise, it is important you know the user types that are available in Azure AD. There are three types of users in Azure AD.

Cloud Identities   As the name implies, these are identities that are created in Azure AD and exist only in Azure AD. In the upcoming exercise, we are going to create a user called John Doe in Azure AD. This user is going to be a cloud identity as the user will exist only in Azure AD. Another point to note here is that the user can be part of another Azure AD as in an Azure AD of another organization. For instance, assume that there is a company abc.onmicrosoft.com with a user called Jane Doe. Jane Doe can be added to another company's Azure AD, say, xyz.onmicrosoft.com, through an invitation process also known as *business-to-business collaboration*. In this case, Jane Doe is a cloud identity of `abc.onmicrosoft.com` and she is added to `xyz.onmicrosoft.com` for collaboration. When Jane's account is deleted from her primary directory (`abc.onmicrosoft.com`), her presence in the other directory is not automatically removed; we have to perform this action manually.

Directory Synchronized Identities   As mentioned earlier, one of the features in Azure AD is that you can synchronize your on-premises Active Directory to Azure AD. If you have an identity that is synchronized, then you will see Yes in the Directory Synced column for the user in the All Users view (Figure 1.1).

FIGURE 1.1   Distinguishing directory synchronized users

Guest Users   These are accounts that exist outside of Azure. These include Microsoft accounts (earlier known as Live accounts) or accounts from other identity providers and accounts from other organizations. The identities are not part of your organizational Azure AD; they need to be invited to your tenant for collaboration. These accounts will be shown as Guest if you look at the User Type value of the user (refer to Figure 1.1). Once the collaboration is no longer required, you can delete these accounts from your user list, and the access will be revoked.

Additionally, we need to keep a couple of points in mind while managing users.

- You must be a Global Administrator of the tenant to manage the users. This is one of the Azure AD roles that we will discuss later in this chapter. The Global Administrator role is like a superuser role and should be granted to users who need to manage all aspects of Azure AD. There are other roles like User Administrator who can manage the users, but this can be used only for managing non-admin accounts.

- While creating a username, the name and password are the only mandatory options. You have two choices with password. First, you can let the system generate a password for the user. The second option is to bring your own password. In both cases, the user will be asked to change the password during the first sign-in, and as an administrator, you should be finding a way to securely share the password with the new user. The commonly used method is to email the new user's manager.

- Even though the users can be deleted (will be covered in the "Deleting and Modifying Users" section), you can restore these users within 30 days from the deletion date.

Now that we are clear about the different user types and key points, let's create users in Azure AD, as shown in Exercise 1.2.

EXERCISE 1.2

Creating Users in Azure AD

1. Navigate to the All Users blade inside Azure Active Directory. You can follow the steps 1–5 of Exercise 1.1 to reach the All Users blade.

2. Once you are in the All Users blade, you can click the New User option.

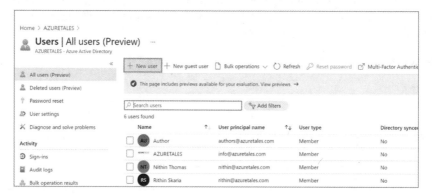

3. Selecting New User will display a window to input details of the new user you intend to create. You will be presented with two options, Create User and Invite User.

4. Selecting Create User will help you create a cloud identity that will exist only in Azure AD. On the other hand, if you select Invite User, you can invite a person from another Azure AD or a person who doesn't have an Azure AD account (Guest user) via an invitation process. In this exercise, we will choose Create User as our plan is to create a cloud identity user type.

5. Here the username, name, and password are the mandatory fields. You can fill in the fields First Name, Last Name, Department, Job Title, Contact Info, Profile Picture, etc., if you'd like; they are optional. In the previous graphic, you can see that we have left Password as "Auto-generate password," which means that the system will generate the password for the user. You can see the password by enabling the Show Password option.

6. Since we have filled the mandatory fields, we can click Create to provision the user. Within a couple of seconds, you will get a notification that the user is created, and the new user will be visible in your All Users blade.

You have successfully created a new user in the Azure AD. As of now, we have covered two exercises where you are viewing and adding users to Azure AD. As an administrator, your responsibility does not stop here; in your daily tasks you will be asked to delete users when someone leaves the organization, modify user attributes when they move to a different department, or change their location. To give you the idea of how to delete and modify users, let's head to the next section.

Deleting and Modifying Users

As mentioned in the previous section, whenever someone gets promoted, moves to a different department, or changes their work location, these details need to be updated on the user profile. Though these fields are not mandatory, they will be important in understanding more details about the user. Assume that there are two John Does in your organization—one works for HR and the other one works for IT. Adding department details here will help the administrator to perform the operations on the right user. In Exercise 1.3, we are going to modify the user we created in Exercise 1.2 and then delete the user.

Modifying and Deleting Users

Let's perform the update process on the user we created in Exercise 1.2. The tasks we have here are as follows:

- Reset the password of the user to a new password.
- Change the department of the user to HR.
- Add the employee ID as 1322.
- Verify the user details.
- Delete the user.

   The first step here is to navigate to the All Users blade as we have done in Exercise 1.1; you can follow these steps to update the user attributes:

1. From the All Users blade, select the user John Doe by clicking the name; that will take you to a screen similar to the following one.

2. Since our first task here is to reset the password, you can click Reset Password, and you will be asked to confirm whether you want to proceed with the reset process. You must click again the Reset Password option, which will be visible in the right corner of the screen. To reset a user's password, you need to be the Global Administrator. User Administrators, Helpdesk Administrators, and Password Administrators can also reset the passwords of non-administrative accounts. However, User Administrators, Helpdesk Administrators, and Password Administrators cannot reset the password of a Global Administrator. Password reset of the Global Administrator can be done only by another Global Administrator.

3. Confirming the reset password option will display a temporary password on the screen. This needs to be changed on the first sign-in after the reset as this is a temporary password and an administrator is responsible for sending this password securely to the user.

4. Now that you have reset the password, the next task is to update the department and employee ID. If you recall, we skipped these optional fields while creating the user, and it is time now to update them. To edit the user details, you can click the Edit button, which is on the left side of the Reset Password button.

5. Clicking the Edit button will enable all the text boxes. Once you have updated the information, you can click Save. You can update all information except the object ID, which is a unique ID assigned to every identity by Azure AD.

6. After saving the details, if you go back to user profile, you will be able to see that all the data you entered is populated to the user profile.

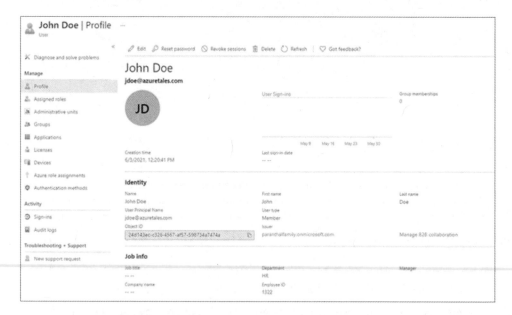

7. From this graphic, we confirmed that the department details and employee ID have been added to the user profile. The next task is to delete the user. Assume that John Doe is leaving the organization and you have to deprovision his account. In the graphic, you can see that there is a Delete button next to the Reset Password button. Clicking Delete will ask for your confirmation.

8. Click Yes, and John Doe's profile will be deleted. However, this is not a permanent delete action. All deleted users can be viewed from the Deleted Users blade.

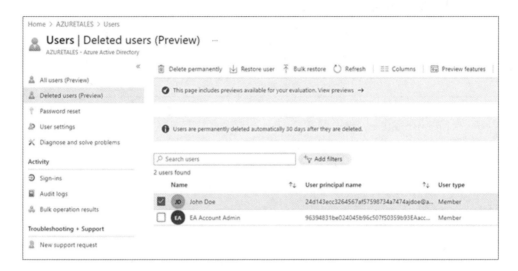

9. You will have 30 days from the deletion date if you want to restore the user, using the Restore option. You can also delete the user immediately by selecting the Delete Permanently option instead of waiting for 30 days.

 All these actions can be also performed from the Office 365 Admin panel, PowerShell, or CLI if required.

In Exercises 1.1, 1.2, and 1.3 you have seen how an administrator can view, add, modify, or delete users. Performing these tasks one by one from the portal is not a great idea if you have a large user base. All the actions that you have seen in the previous exercises can be performed in bulk. In the next section, you will learn how administrators can leverage bulk operations available for user accounts.

Bulk Operations

In an enterprise environment, new users are added, updated, or deleted in bulk. Performing these actions one by one for each user is a hectic task, and there is a higher chance of human error. You need to automate these tasks and should be able to perform these tasks in bulk. Azure AD provides bulk operations by which you can create, invite (for guest users), delete, and download users in your directory. These bulk actions are achieved via uploading a CSV file with the details. This file template will be available for download from Azure Portal itself. In the next exercise, you will use a bulk operation to create nine users (all Avengers characters) in a single shot, and once they are visible on the portal, you will perform a bulk delete operation. See Exercise 1.4.

EXERCISE 1.4

Performing Bulk Operations

1. Navigate to the All Users blade. If you are not able to recall the steps to reach the All Users blade, please follow steps 1–5 of Exercise 1.1.

2. Select Bulk Operations and then select Bulk Create.

3. Selecting Bulk Create will let you download a CSV template. You need to download the template, fill in the details, and upload it to Azure AD for processing. Azure will prompt you with the steps.

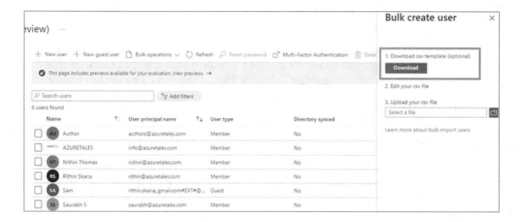

4. Once the file is downloaded, you can open it in Microsoft Excel and fill in the details. The headers will be auto populated; some of them are required, while some are optional. The fields that are required will have a [Required] tag in the header. The required fields are Name, Username, Initial Password, and Block Sign In. Fill in the template, as shown here.

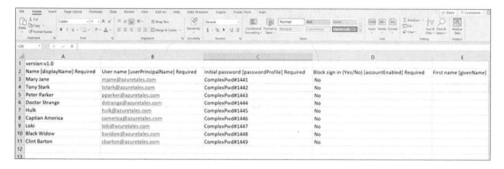

5. You can fill the optional details if required; however, it is mandatory to fill in the required fields; otherwise, the validation will fail.

6. Let's upload the file to Azure AD and see if we got it correct. You can use the upload option shown in step 3. If you closed the window after downloading the CSV file, you can click Bulk Operations ➤ Bulk Create and the upload window will be shown again. If the file is uploaded successfully, you will see a message on the screen. Once the file is uploaded, click Submit.

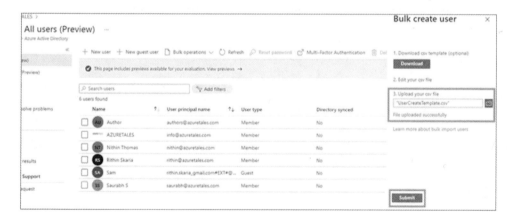

EXERCISE 1.4 *(continued)*

7. As soon as you click Submit, the status will change to "In Progress." If the format is correct, then you will get a "Succeeded" message.

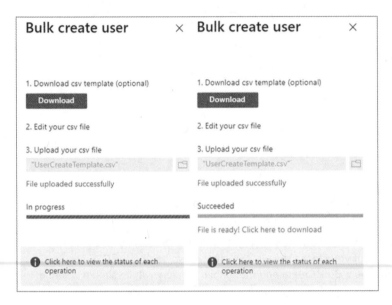

8. You can also verify the status of any bulk operation by navigating to the Bulk Operation Results blade. You will be able to troubleshoot from this blade if you get an error during the bulk operation.

9. Since our bulk operation was successful, let's confirm if the users are visible in the All Users blade.

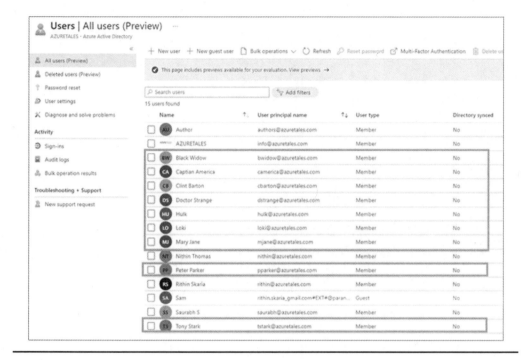

Similarly, you can perform bulk delete and bulk invite operations by downloading the corresponding CSV and uploading them back to Azure AD. Speaking about invitations, let's see how external users can be invited to your tenant for collaboration.

From the Deleted Users blade, you can perform bulk delete and restore operations if required.

Inviting Users

In the "Adding Users" section, we discussed several types of users. If you recall, we talked about Guest accounts (Microsoft accounts and users from external Azure ADs). These users need to be invited to your tenant. Recipients can redeem the invitation and join your tenant for collaboration.

In the All Users blade, you have an option to add a new Guest user. Clicking New Guest User will redirect you to a screen similar to Figure 1.2.

FIGURE 1.2   Inviting users

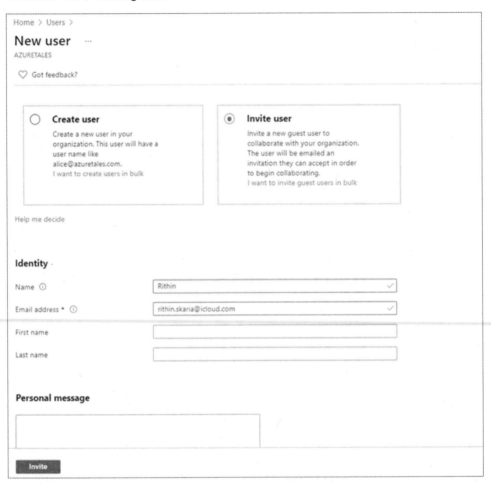

    You can also add a guest user by clicking New User and then selecting the Invite User radio button instead of Create User.

The only email address is the mandatory field, and you can even customize the personalized message. By clicking Submit, this message will be appended to the email invitation, which will be triggered to the recipient, as shown in Figure 1.3.

A sample invitation has been added for your reference (refer to Figure 1.4).

These users can be easily spotted in the All Users blade by looking at the User Type column. You can further add a filter in the blade as shown in Figure 1.5 to list all the Guest users in your tenant.

FIGURE 1.3   Customizing the invite

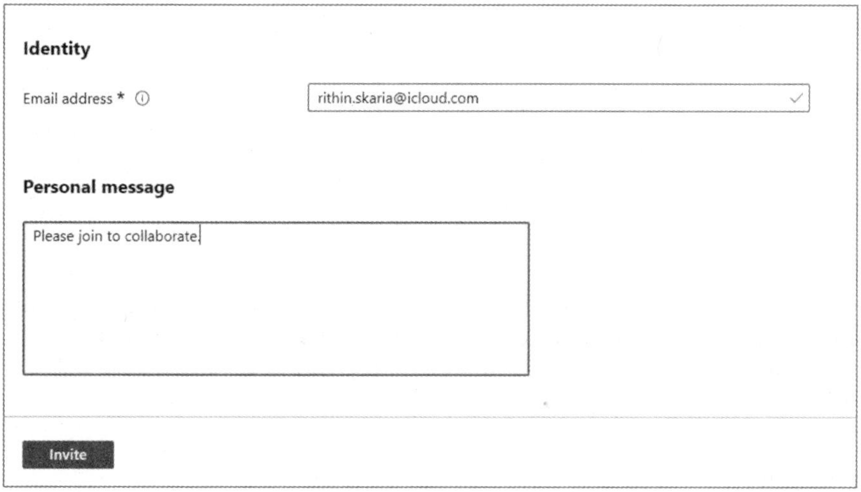

Identity

Email address * ⓘ

rithin.skaria@icloud.com   ✓

Personal message

Please join to collaborate.

Invite

FIGURE 1.4   Invitation for Guest user

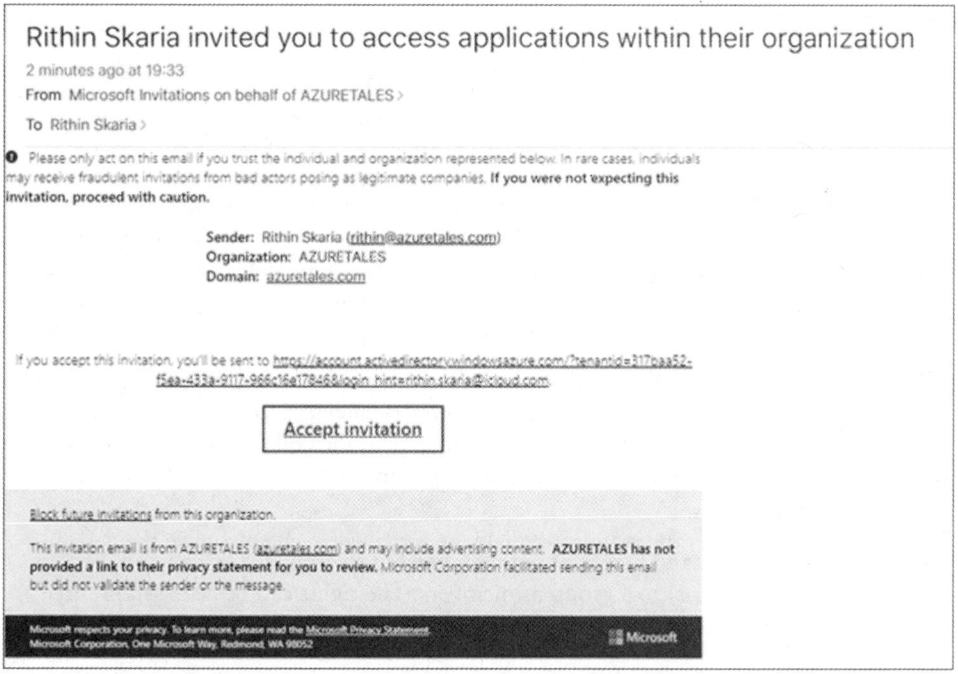

Rithin Skaria invited you to access applications within their organization

2 minutes ago at 19:33

From Microsoft Invitations on behalf of AZURETALES ›

To Rithin Skaria ›

❶ Please only act on this email if you trust the individual and organization represented below. In rare cases, individuals may receive fraudulent invitations from bad actors posing as legitimate companies. **If you were not expecting this invitation, proceed with caution.**

Sender: Rithin Skaria (rithin@azuretales.com)
Organization: AZURETALES
Domain: azuretales.com

If you accept this invitation, you'll be sent to https://account.activedirectory.windowsazure.com/?tenantid=317baa52-f5aa-433a-9117-966c16e178468login_hint=rithin.skaria@icloud.com

Accept invitation

Block future invitations from this organization.

This invitation email is from AZURETALES (azuretales.com) and may include advertising content. AZURETALES has not provided a link to their privacy statement for you to review. Microsoft Corporation facilitated sending this email but did not validate the sender or the message.

Microsoft respects your privacy. To learn more, please read the Microsoft Privacy Statement.
Microsoft Corporation, One Microsoft Way, Redmond, WA 98052   ▦ Microsoft

FIGURE 1.5   Filtering Guest users

So far, you have been working on user accounts and different operations that administrators can perform for managing users. Basic administrative tasks are limited not only to user management but can include group management as well. In the next section, we will talk about group accounts in Azure AD.

Group Accounts

When it comes to access management, applying permissions or roles to each user one by one is cumbersome, so to solve this complexity, we have groups in Azure AD. We can group users to create group accounts and then apply the permissions or roles to the group so that all members of the group get that access. Group accounts make access management easier. You can also synchronize groups from on-premises to the cloud, the same as with users.

Azure AD allows you to create two types of groups, security groups and Microsoft 365 Groups. Let's understand the differences between these types.

Security Groups   Groups play an inevitable role in access management. Security groups can be used to control access to resources easily. For instance, you can create a security group called All HR and give access to all HR-related resources. As an administrator, the advantage here is you do not have to manage individual access; this can be controlled at the group level. Security groups require the Azure AD administrator to perform management actions.

Microsoft 365 Groups   Microsoft 365 groups serve the same purpose as security groups; however, they provide additional capabilities such as access to a shared mailbox, shared calendar, SharePoint, and more. You can extend the collaboration and provide access to external users as well. Unlike security groups, both users and admins can use Microsoft 365 groups.

Another point to understand here is about membership to groups. You can add users as well as groups (nested groups) to a group as members. The rights can be accessed in three diverse ways, as follows:

Assigned   This one is straightforward; this will let you add users (or groups) to the group as members. This type of addition is also known as *direct membership*.

Dynamic User   Group memberships are controlled using member attributes; using them we can dynamically add or remove users from a group. For example, you can have a rule like if the department of a user is HR, then that user should be added to the group All HR. Here Azure constantly reviews user attributes. If a new user is added with the department as HR, then Azure will add that user to the All HR group. Similarly, when someone leaves the department, Azure automatically removes the user from the group. This is especially useful for administrators, as they do not have to remove or add access whenever a new user is added or removed; but they must make sure that the attributes are added to the user correctly.

Dynamic Device   This is applicable only in the case of security groups and is like the dynamic user concept. The primary difference is that instead of looking at the user attributes, here you are looking at the device attributes. You can register or join our devices to Azure AD, and based on the device attributes, the group membership can be controlled; we will cover AD Join later in this chapter.

Now that you are familiar with the membership types, let's go ahead and perform some hands-on tasks related to groups.

Viewing Groups

In Exercise 1.5, you will see how you can view groups in Azure AD.

> If you are using a new setup, chances are you might not see any groups in your environment. This is fine; the purpose of the exercise is to make you understand how you can reach the Groups blade.

EXERCISE 1.5

Viewing Groups in Azure AD

1. At this point, you should be familiar with the navigation in the Azure portal and how to reach the Azure Active Directory blade. Right below the Users option that you used earlier, you will be able to see Groups. Clicking Groups will take you to All Groups.

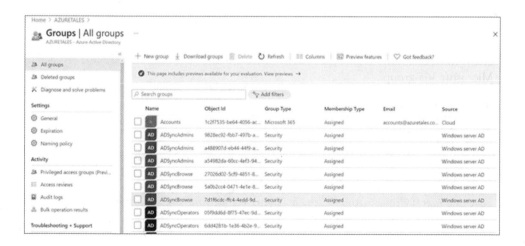

EXERCISE 1.5 *(continued)*

2. If you take a close look at the graphic, you can see that this list provides a lot of insights about the listed groups. For example, you can see the group type (Security Group or Microsoft 365 Group), membership type (Dynamic or Assigned), group email (shown only for Microsoft 365 as there will be a shared mailbox), and source (synchronized from Windows Server AD or the cloud). These details are extremely useful in managing the groups and in understanding the properties of a group.

3. Clicking any of the groups (you can skip this step if you do not have any groups in your environment) will give you a plethora of details about the group such as how many members are there, list of owners, group membership, device membership, etc.

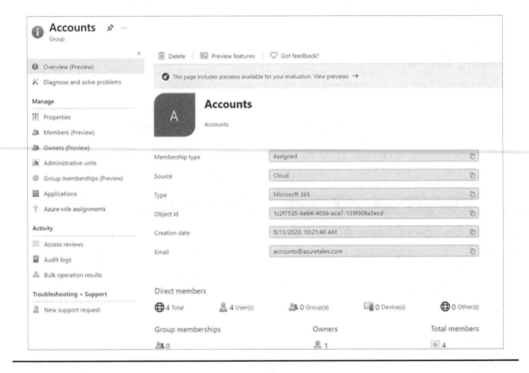

Now that you know how to navigate to the Groups blade and find a group, let's move on and see how you can add a new group.

Adding Groups

In this section, we will cover how you can add a new security group and Microsoft 365 group. In addition, you will see how you can work with dynamic rules and direct membership to these groups. Especially in Exercise 1.6, you will create a security group called Avengers and add the users we created in Exercise 1.4 via direct membership.

EXERCISE 1.6

Adding Security Groups to Azure AD

1. Navigate to the Groups blade by following the steps mentioned in Exercise 1.5, and you will be able to see New Groups option.

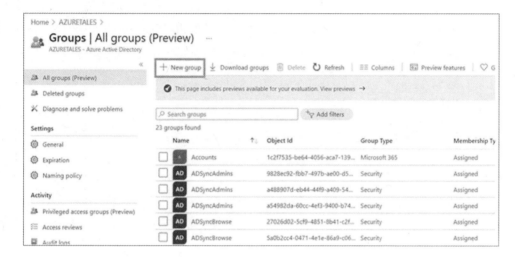

2. Since our first task is to create a security group, you can see that we have selected the following options:

   a. **Group type:** Security (as we need to create a security group).

   b. **Group name:** Avengers (as we are going to add the Avengers users here).

   c. **Group description:** This field is optional; if you need to add a description about the group, feel free to add it.

   d. **Azure AD roles can be assigned to this group:** Yes, this setting needs to be enabled if you plan to assign roles to this group from an access management perspective.

   e. **Membership type:** Assigned (as we are going to perform direct assignment).

EXERCISE 1.6 *(continued)*

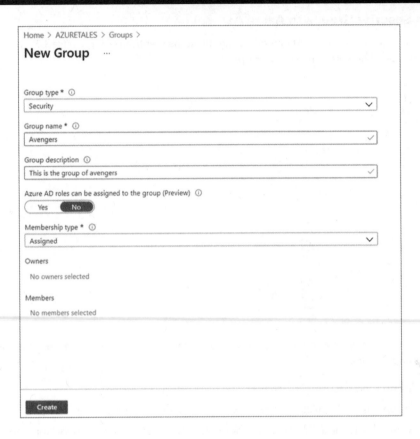

f.   **Owners:** You can select the owners for the group. This set of users will manage the group such as adding or removing users. You can search users, and add once you are done, click Select.

g.   Members: This is the set of users who will be part of the group; we will select all users that we need in the group. Once they are selected, click Select to add members to the group.

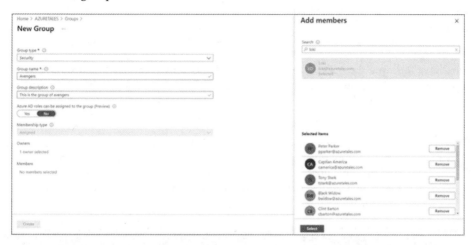

3.   The new group window will now show the number of users you selected as owners and members. The next step is to click Create and create the group.

EXERCISE 1.6 *(continued)*

4. Navigate to All Groups and search for *Avengers*; you will be able to see the new group you created for our Avengers. Clicking the group name will reveal the properties of the group.

If you have followed these steps, then you have successfully completed the exercise to create a security group. Now let's focus on Microsoft 365 groups and dynamic users in Exercise 1.7.

Security groups can also be created with dynamic memberships support-ing both dynamic users and devices; we are going to use Microsoft 365 and dynamic users for demonstration purposes only. You can apply the same logic with security groups and dynamic users, if needed.

EXERCISE 1.7

Adding Microsoft 365 Groups in Azure AD

In the previous exercise, we created security groups. It is time that we take the exercise to the next level by creating a Microsoft 365 group and adding users dynamically based on rules.

1. Before you create the group, you need to add some new users using the bulk create method. If you cannot recall the process, perform the steps in Exercise 1.4 to accom-plish bulk creation. The following is a sample file used for creation and note that here we are using the usageLocation and department headers to add the usage location and department of the users. These attributes will later be used to build our dynamic rules. Upload the file and create the users before you create the group.

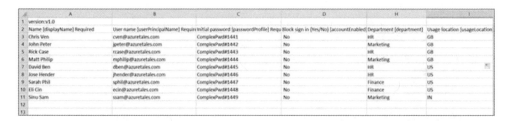

	A	B	C	D	H	I
1	version:v1.0					
2	Name [displayName] Required	User name [userPrincipalName] Requir	Initial password [passwordProfile] Requi	Block sign in [Yes/No] [accountEnabled]	Department [department]	Usage location [usageLocation]
3	Chris Ven	cven@azuretales.com	ComplexPwd#1441	No	HR	GB
4	John Peter	jpeter@azuretales.com	ComplexPwd#1442	No	Marketing	GB
5	Rick Case	rcase@azuretales.com	ComplexPwd#1443	No	HR	GB
6	Matt Philip	mphilip@azuretales.com	ComplexPwd#1444	No	Marketing	GB
7	David Ben	dben@azuretales.com	ComplexPwd#1445	No	HR	US
8	Jose Hender	jhender@azuretales.com	ComplexPwd#1446	No	HR	US
9	Sarah Phil	sphil@azuretales.com	ComplexPwd#1447	No	Finance	US
10	Eli Cin	ecin@azuretales.com	ComplexPwd#1448	No	Finance	US
11	Sinu Sam	ssam@azuretales.com	ComplexPwd#1449	No	Marketing	IN
12						
13						

2. As you performed in Exercise 1.6, you need to reach the New Group window and add properties as follows:

    a. **Group type:** Microsoft 365 (as we need to create a Microsoft 365 group).

    b. **Group name:** All HR (a group for all users whose department is HR).

c. **Group email address**: This is a required field as all Microsoft 365 groups should have an email address. You can add something like "all-hr" and the domain will be auto populated based on your tenant domain.

d. **Group description**: This field is optional; if you need to add a description about the group, feel free to add it.

e. **Membership type**: Dynamic User (as we are going to use dynamic queries to add users).

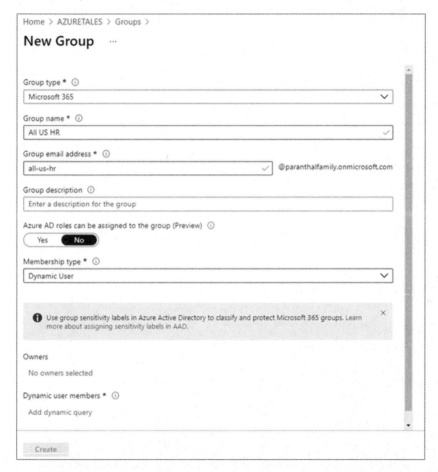

f. Owners can be selected in the same fashion as we did in the case of security groups (refer to Exercise 1.6 step 2.f).

g. The next option is to define the dynamic query for the user. If you take a closer look at the previous graphic, at the bottom you can see there is an option to add a dynamic query. Click that, and you will be taken to the dynamic membership rules editor.

h. Based on the properties you are selecting, corresponding rules are created. In our example, we are adding the property "department" EQUALS "HR." We can add more expressions by clicking Add Expression.

i. Azure Portal will automatically generate the rule syntax based on our selection. The rule syntax for what we selected here is user.department -eq "HR". Once you have verified the rules, click Save to save the rule.

3. Wait for a couple of minutes, and the members of the group will be automatically added based on the rule you configured.

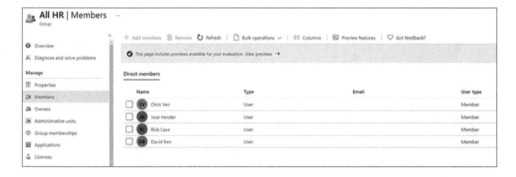

4. Let's try to create another group called India Marketing where we will set up the rule using an additional expression. The final syntax will be (user.department -eq "Marketing") and (user.usageLocation -eq "IN"), as shown here.

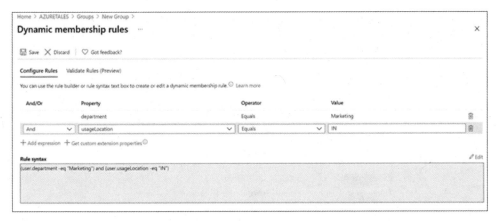

5. You will see that the members matching the rule are added to the Members blade.

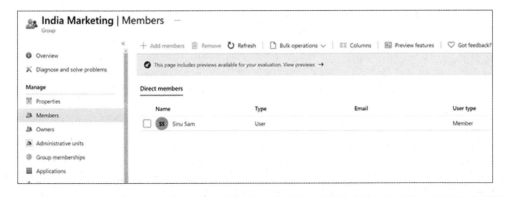

If you completed both the exercises, by now you know how to create security groups and Microsoft 365 groups. Now let's see how to delete or modify the existing groups.

Deleting Groups

Deleting groups is a straightforward process; however, you need to perform this action with caution because deleting a group in production may cause serious repercussions on access management. Some scenarios where you will need to delete a group include the following:

- You selected the wrong group type while creating the group. This selection cannot be modified after creation; the only option is to delete the group and re-create the group with the right type.

- You have a duplicate group.

- You no longer need the group in your environment.

If you want to delete a group, you can navigate to Azure Active Directory ➤ Groups ➤ All Groups and open the group you want to delete. Clicking the Delete button as shown in Figure 1.6 will delete the group.

FIGURE 1.6   Deleting group

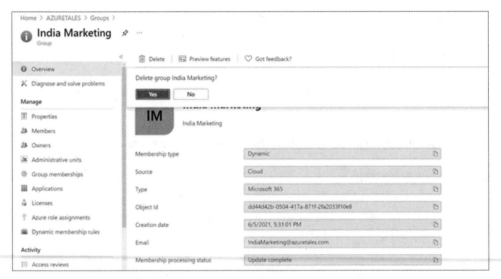

Updating details in a group is no different than updating the user properties. You can add or remove users any time from security groups or Microsoft 365 groups with an assigned membership type. However, in dynamic membership groups, you cannot manually add or remove users. The member management is completely managed by dynamic rules that you create. Azure gives you the option to modify the dynamic rules of your existing group without the need to re-create the group.

Now that are familiar with the user and group accounts in Azure AD, we will talk about the roles in Azure AD.

Azure AD Roles

Azure AD roles are used to manage the permissions that can be assigned to users. You can assign roles to users so they can perform certain actions such as resetting user passwords, assigning, or removing licenses, adding, or removing users, etc.

More than 50+ built-in roles are available in Azure AD so you can follow the principle of least privilege and assign users the permission that they need to complete the tasks given to them. Azure AD roles make sure that the users are not over-privileged or under-privileged with the permissions given to them. For example, if you want to give a user the permission to create/manage groups, create/manage groups settings such as naming and expiration policies, and view groups activity and audit reports, then Groups Administrator is the right role that can be assigned to the user.

Here is the complete list of roles available in Azure AD:

```
https://docs.microsoft.com/en-us/azure/active-directory/roles/
permissions-reference
```

You can assign roles to the users from the Users ➤ Assigned Roles blade. At the time of authoring this book, assigning roles to groups is in preview. If you would like to know more about this preview feature, refer to this document:

```
https://docs.microsoft.com/en-us/azure/active-directory/roles/
groups-concept
```

We will cover more about Azure AD roles when we discuss role-based access control in Chapter 2, "Compliance and Cloud Governance."

We talked about managing users and groups and assigning roles to them. In an enterprise environment, not only users but devices used by users need to be managed and monitored. Azure AD Join helps you to make sure that the devices used by the users follow the organizational standards. Let's discuss Azure AD Join.

Azure AD Join

Single sign-on is one of the features offered by Azure AD. You can use SSO on devices, apps, and services from anywhere in the world. Joining devices to Azure AD assures the corporate devices are protected and that they follow the compliance standards set by the organization. Users can bring their own devices and join them to Azure AD, and administrators can make sure that these devices also follow the standards of your organization. Now, we will look at the benefits of Azure AD Join.

Benefits

Azure AD Join has the following benefits:

Single Sign-On   This is the primary feature of AD Join; you can sign-in to any of your applications and services without a username and password prompt. The best part is it is not necessary to connect to the domain network to use SSO.

Enterprise Client Roaming   The settings are synchronized across devices that are joined to Azure AD.

Microsoft Store for Business   Joining your device and signing-in to the store with work or school accounts gives you a customized catalog of applications that are shared by your organization.

Windows Hello   This provides you with biometric authentication using facial recognition or fingerprints to access corporate resources and sign-in to devices. The devices should have hardware that supports Windows Hello to use this feature.

Block Access Administrators can enforce policies and devices that do not meet the requirements can be easily blocked.

Let's see what connection options are offered by Azure AD Join.

Connection Options

You can connect your devices to Azure AD using the following options:

Register to Azure AD Registration creates an identity for the device, and this identity can be used for authentication. Whenever a user signs in, the identity of the device can be used for authentication. Administrators have the right to enable or disable this identity.

Join to Azure AD Joining to Azure AD provides the same features as registration and additionally changes the local state of the device. With a change of local state, users can sign in to their device using their work or school account. Joining is more like an extension to the registration process.

Combining the registration process with Microsoft Intune (it is a mobile device management [MDM] solution) will help you create conditional policies using the device attribute. Using this combo, you can block devices that do not follow the organizational compliance standards. For example, you could block all devices that are using Windows XP or Windows 7 and make Windows 10 the prerequisite for accessing corporate resources.

You could join your device to Azure AD by going to your Windows 10 Settings ➤ Accounts ➤ Access To Work Or School. Signing in with your work or school account will connect your device to the Azure AD domain, and you can sign in to corporate resources using SSO. Figure 1.7 shows how a connected device looks.

FIGURE 1.7 Connecting a device to Azure AD

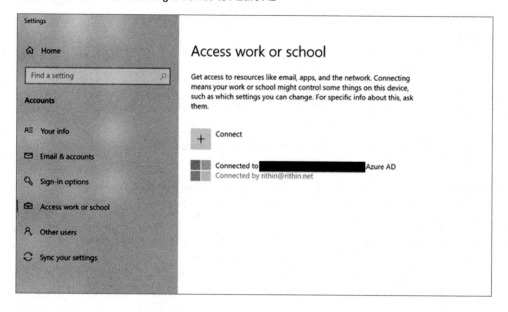

All the devices that are connected to Azure AD can be explored from the Azure Active Directory ➤ Devices blade. This blade will show OS information, OS version, join type, and owner of the devices that are joined (refer to Figure 1.8).

FIGURE 1.8   Listing all devices connected to Azure AD

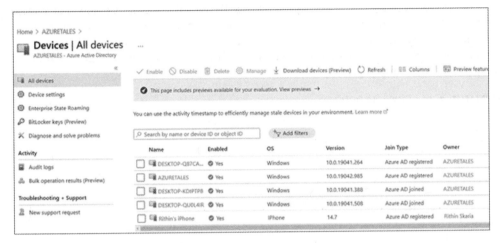

Now we will talk about a lifesaver for administrators: self-service password reset. Using self-serve options reduces the incoming requests to the IT help desk so administrators can utilize their time for more productive work.

Self-Service Password Reset

If you have worked at an IT help desk, you know most of the calls are for user password reset. Self-service password reset (SSPR) allows users to reset their passwords using a set of authentication methods set by the cloud administrators. Self-service password reset is always enabled to administrators to avoid lock-out scenarios. Admins need to use two authentication methods for password reset.

Enabling SSPR

Cloud administrators need to enable SSPR options for users or groups as this option is not enabled by default. To enable this feature, you need to have the Global Administrator role in the tenant.

SSPR can be enabled from Azure Portal ➤ Azure Active Directory ➤ Password Reset. SSPR provides three options (refer Figure 1.9).

- **None:** SSPR is not enabled.
- **Selected:** SSPR is enabled for selected groups.
- **All:** SSPR is enabled for all users in the tenant.

Once SSPR is enabled, users need to register for SSPR. Azure will automatically redirect users to the registration page on first sign-in after SSPR is enabled. Users can always navigate to `https://aka.ms/ssprsetup` to set up their authentication methods or to change them in the future. For example, you might have registered with one phone number when you enrolled for SSPR, but you changed your phone number. In this case, you can change it by going to the SSPR setup page.

FIGURE 1.9   Enabling SSPR

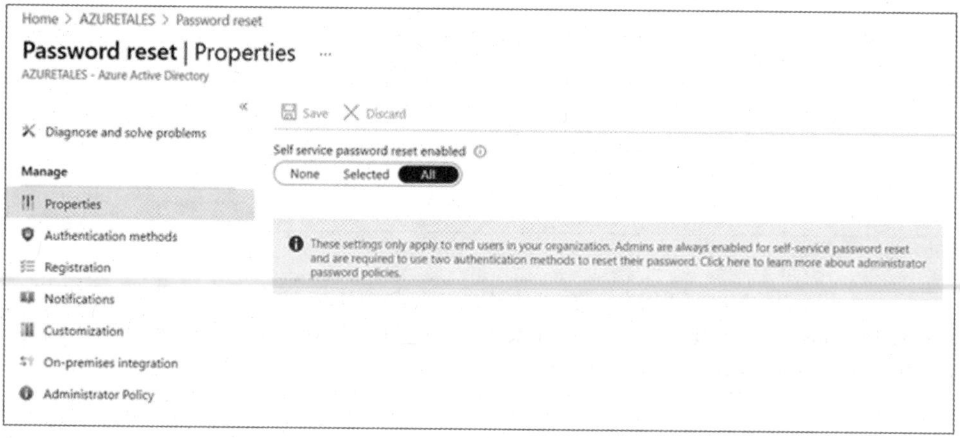

Registered users can always reset the password from the sign-in page by clicking "Can't access your account?" as shown in the Figure 1.10.

It is not necessary that you navigate to Azure Portal to click "Can't access your account?"; you can navigate to any sign-in page that uses Azure AD login like Office 365, Dynamic 365, SharePoint, etc.

Users can also navigate to the reset page directly by going to `https://aka.ms/sspr`. This is an alias for the following:

`https://passwordreset.microsoftonline.com`

Now that you are familiar with SSPR setup, let's see what authentication methods are available for the users and how administrators can control these methods.

Authentication Methods

The administrator can choose the number of authentication methods required to reset the password and the number of methods available for users.

FIGURE 1.10   Initiating password reset

For a successful reset operation, you require at least one authentication method. Nevertheless, it is always better to have a secondary method. For example, if you set up SSPR with an email method, and if the user has no email access, then the user will not be able to reset the password. Here, it is better to have a second option like a mobile phone so that the user can receive the code as a text message and complete the authentication.

Methods available include the following:

- Email notification
- Text message to mobile phone
- Text message to office phone
- Mobile app notification
- Mobile app code
- Security questions

In the case of security questions, the administrator can decide how many questions need to be registered and how many of them need to be answered to reset the password. Nonetheless, security questions are considered less secure as the answers to these questions can be guessed if the intruder or hacker knows the user personally. Attackers can also collect answers for these questions via social engineering.

Authentication methods can be configured from Azure Portal ➤ Azure Active Directory ➤ Password Reset ➤ Authentication Methods (refer to Figure 1.11).

FIGURE 1.11   Configuring SSPR authentication methods

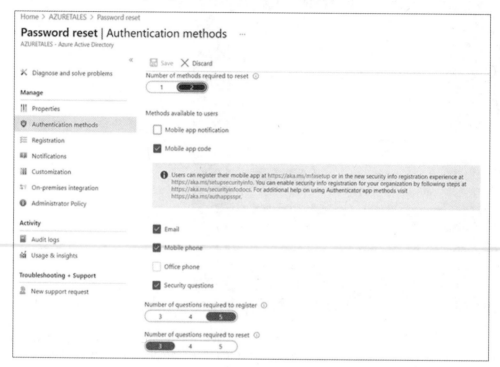

So far, we concentrated on a single-tenant environment; in real-world scenarios there will be different tenants, and admins are responsible for the management of these tenants. Let's see why we need multiple directories and what benefits it provides.

Managing Multiple Directories

Each tenant represents an organization, and it is a fully independent resource. Every tenant that you create is logically separated from other tenants that you manage in a multitenant environment. Even if you are the common administrator for all these tenants, there will not be any parent-child relationship between these tenants or directories. Resource independence, administrative independence, and synchronization independence are there between the tenants.

Resource independence is when you create or delete a resource in one tenant; this action will have no impact on any other resource in another tenant. However, there is a small exception that we discussed in the case of cloud identities from external AD. By default, Azure AD doesn't delete Guest users when they are deleted from their home tenant; however, we can set this up manually.

Administrative independence is when a non-admin user (say the user's name is John) of tenant A creates a new tenant, say tenant B.

- John will be the Global Administrator of the tenant B as he created the new tenant. The user will be added as a user from external AD. Here it says external AD, because John is not from tenant B but from tenant A.

- Administrators of tenant A have no control over tenant B. If the users of tenant A need to access or manage tenant B, then John must invite these users to tenant B and give the necessary role. One thing to note here is that if the admins of tenant A takeover John's account, they can access tenant B.

- Adding or removing an admin role in one tenant will not affect the role of the user in the other tenant. Here we're not removing the user; we are adding or removing the Azure AD roles, which will have no impact on the other tenant, and all roles the user has in the other tenant will be retained.

When it comes to synchronization independence, you can set up independent synchronization on each Azure AD.

With that, we have covered all the topics that are within the scope of the exam.

Summary

In this chapter, we talked about the identity and access management solution in Azure: Azure Active Directory. We started the chapter looking at the benefits of Azure AD, and then we examined how Azure AD is different from the traditional Windows Server Active Directory deployment.

As we progressed, we spoke about Azure AD licensing and how administrators can set up custom domains. After that, we learned about user accounts and group accounts. This is a major element of this chapter; understanding user and group management is crucial for cloud administrators. If you are not confident with identity and access management, there can be a chance of security flaws. Security issues are not something welcomed in an organization as they can cause damage to the reputation of the organization, especially when you are dealing with customer data. Along with the impact on the reputation, this can also lead to revenue loss. As an administrator, you should excel in the identity and access management field.

Then we spoke about Azure AD roles and how administrators should put emphasis on the principle of least privilege. Several other key ideas were reviewed including AD Join and SSPR. You learned about the advantages of incorporating these features in your environment.

Toward the end of the chapter, we covered multitenant environments and the independence they provide in terms of administration, resources, and synchronization.

Like with security, implementing governance and compliance is crucial in setting up the environment. In the next chapter, we will cover governance and compliance.

Exam Essentials

Understand Active Directory.   Understand the purpose, benefits, and concepts related to Azure Active Directory. Along with that, recognize the key differences between different editions of Azure AD and the relevance of custom domains.

Know user and group management.   Understand the different types of users who can be created in Azure AD. Know how these users can be viewed, updated, or deleted when required using portal and via bulk operations. Also, know how these users can be added to groups. In group management, focus on security groups and Microsoft 365 groups with dynamic users and assigned users.

Understand Azure AD Roles.   Understand the relevance of Azure AD roles and how these are used to control the access and permissions of users and groups in Azure AD.

Know Azure AD Join.   Recognize the differences between Azure AD Join and Azure AD register.

Understand SSPR.   You need to understand how SSPR is configured for users and how the authentication methods are configured for users.

Understand a multitenant environment.   Understand the independence provided by tenants while you are managing multiple directories.

Review Questions

1. Your users want to enable single sign-on to devices, apps, and services across all devices that are compliant with your organizational standards. Per your company, all devices should be protected, and users can use only their work or school account. Also, as an administrator, you should be able to disable their device in the case of a compromise. What should you do? (Select one.)

   A. Join the device to Windows Active Directory

   B. Install BitLocker and enable High Security Protocol

   C. Register the device to Azure AD

   D. Join the device to Azure AD

2. You are a user administrator, and one of the global administrators reached out to you to reset their password. Which of the two following ways can be used to reset the password of the global administrator?

   A. User administrator can elevate access and reset password

   B. Redirect the user to self-service options

   C. Reset the password from the profile of the user and share via secured channel

   D. Ask user to contact another global administrator

3. You are setting up self-service password reset for your users. Which of the following is not a validation method?

   A. Fax to office number

   B. A text or code to the office phone

   C. Security questions

   D. Email notification

4. Your organization would like to collaborate with a freelancer for project work. The project manager has sent the agreement to the freelancer, and they accepted it. As an administrator, you need to add this Microsoft account to the tenant for granting access. If you add this user to the tenant, which type of user will be created?

   A. Cloud identity

   B. Guest user

   C. Directory synchronized identity

   D. User-assigned managed identity

5. Which of the following facts about Azure AD is not correct?

   A. Azure AD uses HTTP/HTTPS communication.

   B. Azure AD has a flat hierarchy.

   C. Azure AD can be queried through LDAP.

   D. Federation Services is supported by Azure AD.

6.   You are the Global Administrator of the tenant, and one of the users in the tenant who has a Compliance Administrator role creates a new tenant. What would be the role of the user who created the tenant in the new tenant?

A.   Compliance Administrator

B.   User role (no role will be assigned)

C.   Cross Tenant Administrator

D.   Global Administrator

7.   You have an on-premises application, and you would like to give access to the application for cloud identities in your Azure AD. Your security team said that they cannot expose the application to the public Internet. How can you enable access in this case?

A.   Use a load balancer and send to on-premises

B.   Leverage Azure AD Application Proxy

C.   Use conditional access

D.   Enable PIM

8.   You created a new tenant with the initial domain name `microteamengineering` `.onmicrosoft.com`. Your company already has a domain called `MTE.com`. When you create users, the usernames have the initial domain name. You decide to use the custom domain feature of Azure AD and add your domain. The domain stays unverified, and you cannot use the domain while creating users. What should have been done to use the domain in Azure AD?

A.   Purchase a domain certificate before using the domain

B.   Enroll in Intune services and register the domain

C.   Work with your domain registrar and enable Azure AD integration

D.   Add TXT/MX records given in Azure AD for proving the ownership of domain

9.   You are the Global Administrator and trying to use the identity governance feature in Azure AD; however, the feature is grayed out. You are using a Premium P1 license. What could be the reason for this?

A.   Purchase Premium P2 license

B.   Contact Microsoft Support to enable this feature

C.   Only Identity Governance Administrators can use this feature

D.   Enroll your device to the identity governance program

10.   You are editing the details of a user in your Azure AD. Which of the following fields cannot be changed?

A.   Manager

B.   Object ID

C.   User Principal Name

D.   Name

11. Your organization shared a list of 35 users to be deleted, and you want to delete users easily and in a trackable fashion. Which feature should you use?

    A. Select the users and use the Delete Users option in the Users blade

    B. Write an LDAP query and execute a bulk delete

    C. Manually delete each user

    D. Leverage a bulk delete operation

12. Deleted users from Azure AD can restored within _____ days.

    A. 10

    B. 90

    C. 30

    D. 180

13. You need to group devices in your environment based on device attributes. Which type of group and assignment should you choose?

    A. Security group with dynamic devices

    B. Microsoft 365 group with dynamic devices

    C. Microsoft Device Management service

    D. GPO in on-premises AD

14. You have the following users in your environment:

    User 1: Marketing department and location is US

    User 2: HR department and location is US

    User 3: Marketing department and location is UK

    User 4: HR department and location is India

    You created a dynamic rule using this syntax: `(user.department -eq "HR" or user.usageLocation -eq "GB") and (user.usageLocation -ne "US")`. Which users will be part of the group?

    A. User 1, User 2, User 3, and User 4

    B. User 1, User 2, and User 4

    C. User 2 and User 4

    D. User 3 and User 4

15. You are planning to host a SharePoint site to share content only within the users of your environment. You need to set up a group for the admins to have a shared calendar and mailbox to collaborate. Which type of group should they go for?

    A. Security group with mailbox enabled

    B. Microsoft 365 group

    C. Microsoft Exchange group

    D. SharePoint mailbox group

16. You are the Office 365 administrator of your organization, and you created Microsoft 365 groups with dynamic users from the Office 365 Admin panel. You have been asked by your Azure AD Global Administrator to synchronize these groups with Azure AD for management purposes. How can you achieve this?

    A. Use the Azure AD Connect tool and synchronize users and groups with Azure AD.

    B. Use Office 365 connector for Azure AD and sync users.

    C. All users and groups in Office 365 are automatically synchronized with Azure AD.

    D. You cannot synchronize users; you need to re-create them on Azure AD.

17. After joining devices in your organization to Azure AD, you would like to enable facial recognition and biometric authentication for Windows 10 devices with supported hardware. Which feature of Windows 10 should be used for this?

    A. Intune

    B. Windows Hello for Business

    C. Authenticator app for Windows 10

    D. The Azure portal

18. You are assigning Azure AD roles. Which role will allow the user to manage all the groups in your tenant and be able to assign other administrator roles?

    A. Global Administrator

    B. Password Administrator

    C. Security Administrator

    D. Compliance Administrator

19. Identify which of the following statements about Azure AD is not correct.

    A. Azure AD uses HTTP and HTTPS communications.

    B. Azure AD uses Kerberos authentication.

    C. There are no organizational units (OUs) or Group Policy objects (GPOs) in Azure AD.

    D. Azure AD includes Federation Services.

20. You are Azure AD administrator, and your developers are asking you to block users from a certain country, and also if the users are from the United States, they require MFA before accessing the application. Which feature of Azure AD should you use to accomplish this?

    A. Identity protection

    B. Application Proxy secure endpoint

    C. Privileged identity management

    D. Conditional access

Chapter

2

Compliance and Cloud Governance

MICROSOFT EXAM OBJECTIVES COVERED IN THIS CHAPTER:

✓ **Manage subscriptions and governance**

- **Manage subscriptions**
- **Manage resource groups**
- **Manage costs**
- **Apply and manage tags**
- **Configure Azure policies**
- **Configure resource locks**
- **Configure management groups**

✓ **Manage role-based access control (RBAC)**

- **Create a custom role**
- **Provide access to Azure resources by assigning roles at different scopes**
- **Interpret access assignments**

As organizations migrate to the cloud, there can be a lot of confusion and misconceptions. Cloud governance and compliance is all about a set of rules that you need to comply with while you are creating, migrating, or managing resources in the cloud. These rules vary from organization to organization. For example, a government organization may have strict rules that they need to follow when they run a business in the cloud. On the other hand, a private company will have liberal rules compared to the government one. Ideally, these rules are no different than the ones you have on-premises; the only difference is that in the cloud you will be using Microsoft Azure as the platform instead of your on-premises servers.

A lack of rules or controls will create issues with your data privacy, security, and cost, as well as efficiency. With on-premises, you controlled the entire infrastructure, and the perimeter was secured using firewalls and other security devices. In the cloud, you won't have complete control over the network, so you need to be aware of the vulnerabilities and the best practices or offerings provided by Azure to resolve them.

Common rules that are followed in organizations are related to data residency, compliance policies like PCI-DSS if you are dealing with customer credit card information, budgeting for cost optimization, and security services to ensure that there are no vulnerabilities that can be exploited by hackers. Compliance and governance cannot be achieved in a single day; this is a continuous process. The policies and procedures need to be tweaked and evolved as you notice room for improvement. Also, sometimes you need to expand the rules to accommodate new services.

Concisely, cloud compliance is all about setting up rules by which you will be continuously monitoring and amending relevant controls for cost optimization, improving efficiency, and eradicating security risks.

We will cover all the topics that are part of the exam objectives; however, the order of topics has been changed to bring continuity and improve flow. We will start with subscriptions and governance and then move on to role-based access control.

Let's start with Azure regions because regions not only give flexibility to customers to deploy in multiple locations across the globe but also perform a critical role in data residency requirements.

Azure Regions

Microsoft Azure comprises datacenters that are located across the globe. At the time of authoring this book, Azure has more than 60 regions, and there are more in the pipeline. This global presence makes Azure the cloud provider with the highest number of regions.

Also, this omnipresence gives customers the ability to choose the regions that are right for them. If you are wondering what an Azure region is, a *region* is a geographical area on the planet comprising at least one datacenter, but usually multiple. The datacenters are isolated from each other in close proximity and connected to each other via low-latency networks, enabling faster and seamless communication.

East US, Brazil South, UK South, India West, and Australia Central are some examples of Azure regions. Figure 2.1 shows the list of public regions available for Azure at the time of authoring this book.

FIGURE 2.1   Azure regions

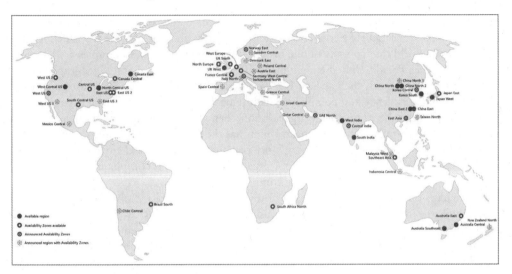

Let's understand some key points about regions.

Facts

The following are some of the facts related to regions:

- Regions offer flexibility for customers to deploy resources to regions that are close to their customers.
- Regions ensure data residency for customers.
- Regions offer compliance and resiliency options.
- When you deploy a resource in Azure, in most cases you will be asked to choose a region.
- Certain services are region specific, and the availability is limited to some regions when they are launched. Gradually, Microsoft will expand the service to other regions.

- Services like Azure AD, Azure Traffic Manager, and Azure DNS do not require a region. The region for these resources will be shown as Global in the Azure portal.

- Each Azure region is paired with another region within the same geography to form regional pairs.

Understanding these facts will help you plan your resource deployment, choose a region, and understand why you are not able to find a specific service in a region. Let's shift our focus to regional pairs, which is an important concept in Azure.

Regional Pairs

As you already know, each region consists of one or more datacenters that are in close proximity and connected via a low-latency network. Now, an Azure *geography* is defined as an area of the world that consists of one or more Azure regions. Some examples are United States, India, Asia Pacific, United Kingdom, etc. If we take the United States geography, it consists of several regions such as East US, West US, Central US, etc. So, an Azure geography ensures the data residency and compliance requirements are met. If you are an organization working with a US government organization, then you cannot store data outside of the United States. Similarly, the European Union has the General Data Protection Regulation (GDPR) where organizations cannot store personal data of the EU citizens outside EU member states. As an administrator, if your organization is GDPR compliant, you can pick a geography that is within the EU and stay compliant.

Azure pairs one region with another region within the same geography. Regional pairs play a vital role in business continuity and disaster recovery (BCDR). Whenever there is a planned update on the Azure platform, Azure rolls out the update sequentially across regional pairs. This guarantees that only one region in the regional pair is updated at a time and the other one can be leveraged for the recovery of the services if something goes wrong.

Figure 2.2 shows a graphical representation of regional pairs in Azure.

FIGURE 2.2 Graphical representation of Azure regional pairs

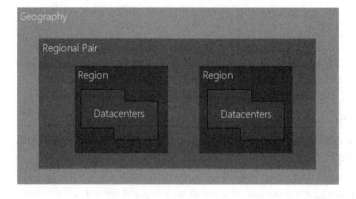

The following are some of the focus points about Azure regional pairs:

Physical Separation   Three hundred miles is the preferred distance between datacenters that are part of the regional pair; however, this might not be feasible in certain geographies. This isolation will diminish the probability of both regions being affected at the same time due to outages caused by natural disasters, power outages, etc.

Replication   Services like storage accounts provide georedundant storage (GRS). Using GRS, your data will be replicated to the paired region and thus provide reliability.

Recovery Order   If a mass outage happens, Microsoft will prioritize the recovery of one region out of every regional pair.

Serialized Updates   Azure planned updates are rolled out sequentially to the regions in a region pair. As the update is not done simultaneously, even if something goes wrong, one of the regions in the region pair can be used for recovery.

Data Residency   As the regions in a regional pair are part of the same geography, customers can get the benefit of regional pairs without breaking any of the data residency policies.

- All region pairs have regions from the same geography; the only exception is Brazil South, and the paired region for Brazil South is South Central US. South Central US is part of the United States geography. However, the South Central US paired region is not Brazil South.

- All region pairs are paired in both directions. One exception here is West India. West India's pair is South India; however, South India's secondary region is Central India.

Understanding regional pairs and incorporating them into your infrastructure will help you architect highly available solutions with business continuity in Azure. The complete list of Azure region pairs and how services can leverage regional pairs is available here:

`https://docs.microsoft.com/en-us/azure/best-practices-availability-paired-regions`

With that, we will move on to Azure accounts and subscriptions.

Azure Accounts and Subscriptions

We covered Azure AD concepts in Chapter 1, "Identity: Azure Active Directory," where we defined an Azure subscription as a logical unit for setting up a resource boundary, environment boundary, and billing boundary. Every subscription will have an account that is attached to it. This account can be a work or school account or an account that Azure AD trusts. If you don't have a work or school account, you can use a Microsoft account to use Azure. The reason behind this is that Azure AD trusts Microsoft accounts. Let's learn more about Azure accounts and subscriptions.

Azure Accounts

Subscriptions will always be mapped to an account. Any identity that is part of Azure AD or a directory trusted by Azure AD is referred to as an Azure account. It could be a work or school account that is created in Azure; you already saw in Chapter 1 how users can be added to Azure AD. Also, it could be a Microsoft account that is trusted by Azure. If you use your personal account, then you will be creating a Microsoft account and using that as the Azure account.

When you sign up for an Azure account using your work or school account, all subscriptions will be created in the Azure AD that your account is part of. If you are using a personal account, then Azure will automatically create an Azure AD tenant during the account creation process.

Azure Subscriptions

We already discussed the boundaries of Azure subscription sets in terms of resources, environment, and billing. In Azure, billing is done per subscription, and this is charged based on the type of subscription you have. We will cover some of the common types of subscriptions that you will be using for personal, development, and production workloads.

The user who created the Azure account is called the Account Administrator, and a user can have multiple subscriptions inside an account. Reasons for having multiple subscriptions may include environment isolation, project isolation, etc. In Figure 2.3, you can see that the Azure account has multiple subscriptions; these subscriptions are created to separate the workloads in these environments.

FIGURE 2.3   Types of Azure subscriptions

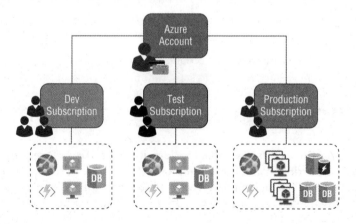

By default, only the account administrator will have access to the newly created subscription. If you would like to grant access to others, then you can use the classic administrator role or role-based access control (RBAC). As we are not using classic resources anymore, Microsoft recommends that you use RBAC for granting access to users and external partners to your Azure resources.

There are multiple channels from which you can get an Azure subscription. Now, we will look at these channels and how each one of these is different.

Getting a Subscription

You can get a subscription from multiple channels. You might not be eligible for all the subscriptions listed here; the eligibility is dependent on the terms and conditions of the respective offers.

Enterprise Agreements (EAs)   EA customers will sign an agreement with Microsoft or Microsoft Partners and make an up-front monetary commitment to Azure. All usage incurred will be charged against the monetary commitment; when the commitment expires, the customer will start receiving invoices. You can make the prepayment again and continue using the services. The advantage of using EAs is that they offer more discounts than other offers as the customer is paying the amount up front. If your organization is looking for massive deployments in Azure and requires 99.95 percent monthly SLA, then an EA is the best option.

Web Direct   In web direct, customers can directly go to the Azure website and purchase a new subscription. If you prefer, you can sign up for a Free Trial subscription and upgrade if you are interested in continuing the service. You won't be charged until you upgrade the subscription from Free Trial to Pay-As-You-Go. Once you upgrade, as the name implies, you will be charged as per the charges mentioned in the Azure public-facing documents. There are no discounts available for you in this case, and you will require a credit card to sign up for this subscription.

Reseller   Using the Open Licensing program, customers can buy tokens from resellers and sign up for an Azure-in-Open subscription. As a customer, you can buy a token for any amount you need; the charges incurred will be taken from this amount. When the amount is exhausted, you need to buy a new token and refill your account to avoid service interruption. This works like a prepaid cellular plan.

Partners   You can purchase an Azure subscription from partners, and they can help you with the cloud transformation. The partners will be your first point of contact for any Azure-related concerns as the agreement is signed between the partner and the customer. These types of subscriptions are called cloud solution provider (CSP) subscriptions, and every month you'll receive an invoice from your partner based on your usage. Microsoft doesn't play any role in the invoice generation as you don't have any direct billing relationship with Microsoft. CSP subscriptions offer more discounts compared to the Pay-As-You-Go subscriptions and are ideal for organizations that don't have the budget to make the up-front monetary commitment for an EA.

This is not the complete list of offers that are supported by Azure. There are other offers that come with credits for MSDN subscribers and Visual Studio subscribers. You can see all the available offers here:

`https://azure.microsoft.com/en-in/support/legal/offer-details`

Now that you have an idea about the common offers, let's see how the metering or usage is done in these subscription offers.

Subscription Metering

All offers provided by Azure are meant for unique needs and requirements. For people who want to test the services there is a Free Trial, for students there is Azure for Students, and finally for enterprise deployments we have different paid subscription offers like EA, Pay As You Go, etc., which provide service level agreements (SLAs). The most commonly used subscription types are these:

- Free subscription
- Pay-As-You-Go
- Enterprise Agreement
- Azure for Students

Azure Free Subscription   You can get a $200 credit to spend on any Azure service for the first 30 days. You have to upgrade your Free Trial if you exhaust your credits or when you complete the trial period (whichever happens first). Along with the credit, you will get selected popular Azure services free for the first 12 months and 25+ services always free. However, this benefit will be applied only if you upgrade to a paid subscription. Signing up for a Free Trial will require a credit card; this is only for the verification purposes, and you will not be charged unless you upgrade to the paid subscription.

Azure Pay-As-You-Go Subscription   Once you upgrade your Free Trial subscription, your subscription will be converted to a Pay-As-You-Go (PAYG) subscription. In PAYG, you will be receiving invoices monthly based on your consumption. However, this will not be from the first to the last of the month; the billing cycle is dependent on what date you started the PAYG usage. PAYG is ideal for individuals to small businesses; even some large organizations use PAYG. However, there are no discounts applied like with EAs.

Azure Enterprise Agreement   Customers can buy cloud services and software licenses under one single agreement. These customers are also eligible for discounts on services, licenses, and software assurance. The targeted audience for this is enterprise organizations. Customers need to pay the cost upfront to Microsoft as a monetary commitment, and the consumption will be deducted from this prepayment.

Azure for Students   As the name suggests, this subscription is ideal for students who want test or develop solutions in Azure for learning purposes. Students will receive $100 as a credit that is valid for 12 months. Along with the credit, there will be free services that users can leverage. Students need to verify their student status using a university email address to activate this subscription. Also, Azure for Students doesn't require a credit card.

So far, you have seen the different offer types that are available in Azure and how customers can choose one that suits their needs. You have also seen how usage is computed in each offer; now you will see how you can leverage Azure Cost Management in monitoring and optimizing cloud expenditure.

Azure Cost Management

Controlling your cloud expenditure is part of cloud governance, and you need tools to properly see the breakdown of the costs and track them. Azure Cost Management is the go-to tool for performing your billing administrative tasks and for monitoring costs. Opening Cost Management in the Azure portal will show some charts that explain your cloud spending, as shown in Figure 2.4.

FIGURE 2.4   Azure Cost Management views

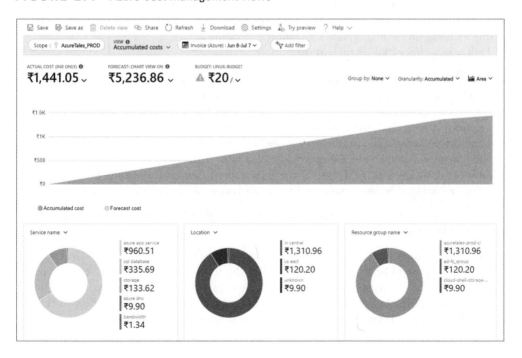

Additionally, Azure Cost Management provides the following features:

- Users can create budgets, and alerts can be triggered if the threshold is crossed.
- Usage reports can be exported to a storage account for auditing purposes based on a schedule.
- You can forecast future costs using predictive analytics.
- You can ingest your AWS costs and analyze them on Azure.
- Azure Cost Management can be integrated with Azure Advisor.
- You can track Azure reservation usage and calculate potential savings.
- You can track Azure Hybrid Benefit discounts.
- Azure Cost Management has richer APIs that can be integrated with third-party tools for visualization.
- Azure Cost Management has a Power BI connector for the easy export of data to Power BI dashboards (supported for EA/MCA customers only).

Administrators can leverage all the aforementioned features to improve the cost monitoring and cost optimization. Now, we will discuss some features that you can use to plan and control your cloud expenditure.

Plan and Control Expenses

If you navigate to Cost Management + Billing ➤ Cost Management in the Azure portal, you will see the tools that are required for planning and controlling your expenses. We are primarily focusing on the highlighted tools shown in Figure 2.5.

Let's take a closer look at each of these tools.

Cost Analysis   This blade can be used for viewing and analyzing your cloud spending. There are different views (built-in views and custom views can be created), filters, and grouping options available in Cost Analysis that can be leveraged by administrators to perform a deep analysis of the cost. You can also decide the granularity and the timeframe for analysis. Timeframe options include monthly, quarterly, yearly, or even custom for customization. Figure 2.4 shows what the Cost Analysis blade looks like. You can export your Azure usage data to a storage account based on a schedule. These CSV files can be leveraged by third-party analytics and visualization tools for creating dashboards.

Cost Alerts   You can configure alerts that will notify administrators if the cost crosses the set threshold.

Budgets   Every project has budget constraints, and the Budgets feature in Cost Management will help organizations to meet this financial accountability. You can set up thresholds and trigger alerts using action groups when the usage exceeds a certain percentage of the budget set. You can also integrate budgets with automation workflows to shut down VMs automatically when the spending exceeds a certain limit.

FIGURE 2.5   Azure Cost Management highlighting tools

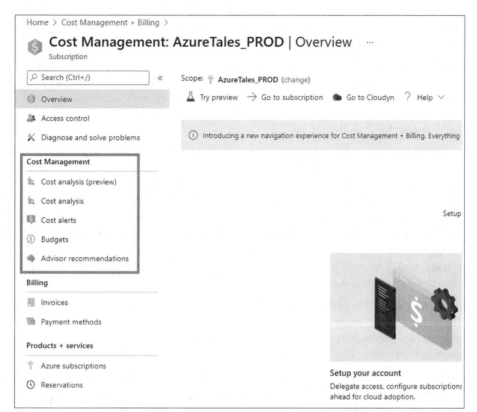

Advisor Recommendations   These recommendations are generated from Azure Advisor based on your usage. Azure Advisor uses machine learning on your usage to generate these recommendations. These recommendations include reservation purchases and downsizing underutilized VMs. You can directly remediate these issues and make your cloud more cost-effective.

Incorporating these tools in your environment can improve the cost planning and optimization.

Cost Saving Techniques

There are a set of services or techniques administrators can use to get the best out of their infrastructure.

Reservations   Reserved instances (RIs), or reservations, can be used by customers to save costs on selected services. Selected services include Azure Virtual Machine, SQL

Database, Azure Cosmos DB, Azure SQL Managed Instance, and other services. You can pay for a one-year or three-year term for these services upfront or in a monthly manner. For certain services, Microsoft has extended the term to five years. Purchasing reservations will reduce the costs up to 72 percent over the Pay As You Go rates.

Azure Hybrid Benefit   You can bring your own Windows Server or SQL Server or Linux licenses to use on Azure Virtual Machine, Azure SQL Database, and Azure Managed Instances. If you have already purchased licenses with software assurance, you don't have to pay for these licenses in Azure. Combining RI and Azure Hybrid Benefit can increase the savings.

Azure Credits and Dev/Test Subscriptions   It's always recommended that you choose the right subscription to host your workloads. If you are testing or developing solutions, there are subscriptions with free credit that can be utilized rather than deploying your solutions in a production subscription and paying invoices. For example, if you are a Visual Studio Subscriber (Enterprise/Professional), you can get a subscription with free credits that gets renewed every month. If you have an EA, then you can use an EA Dev/Test subscription for testing and development. EA Dev/Test rates are cheaper than the production EA subscription. Similarly, Pay As You Go customers can purchase PAYG Dev/Test for development and testing purposes.

Azure Regions   The prices of Azure services vary from region to region; you can always deploy to a region that has a lower cost to save your spending. However, make sure that this decision is not affecting the performance or data residency requirements (if there are any).

Budgets   You already learned about budgets in the "Plan and Control Expenses" section. Having a budget will help you get notified whenever you are crossing the limits assigned to you; you can also take necessary actions to remediate this. Budgets plays a crucial role in accounting and cost tracking.

Pricing Calculator   In Azure, there are hundreds of services, and each service has several pricing tiers. It's not possible for an administrator or an architect to remember all these pricings and calculate them. Using the Pricing Calculator, you can estimate the cost of any service in Azure. You can export it to Excel to share with your stakeholders or directly share the link for estimation. The Pricing Calculator can be accessed here:

```
https://azure.microsoft.com/en-in/pricing/calculator
```

We will now move on to resource groups.

Resource Groups

A resource group is a container used for the logical organization of resources in Azure. These resources may be part of the same solution or based on any grouping that you prefer. Some organizations prefer to keep all services that are part of a solution in a single resource group. For example, say you are hosting a payroll application that has a virtual machine, SQL database, and storage. You can group these resources so that you can manage the lifecycle of them together. Some organizations prefer to keep resources of the same type together, for example, all virtual machines in a single resource group or all databases in a single resource group. This strategy would help them to manage the access to all virtual machines or databases easily.

Resource groups make it easy to deploy, delete, or update resources in bulk. Instead of performing operations on these resources one by one, you could directly perform the action on the resource group, and all resources that are part of the resource group are updated with the action. Assume you have 135 services deployed to your subscription and now your management is asking you to delete these 135 services. You could select all services from the portal or write a script in PS/CLI to delete the resources. Another easier workaround is to delete the resource group so that all the resources are deleted. This is not an action that is recommended in a production environment, as this delete action cannot be reversed, and the deleted services cannot be recovered. It's recommended that you are cautious and vigilant before deleting a resource group.

A resource group contains the metadata about the resources that are part of the resource group. You can have resources from different regions be part of the same resource group; however, the metadata about these resources will be stored in the region of the resource group. An example is if the location of your resource group is East US and you have a couple of VMs from West US that are part of the resource group. Another is if the East US region is facing an outage and you are making any changes to the VM. Even though the VMs are from West US, the metadata cannot be updated as the East US (region of the resource group) is facing an outage.

Now we will see how you can manage (create, list, open, and delete) a resource group from the Azure portal; see Exercise 2.1, Exercise 2.2, and Exercise 2.3.

EXERCISE 2.1

Creating a Resource Group from the Azure Portal

1.   Sign in to the Azure portal.

2.   Select Resource Groups and click Create.

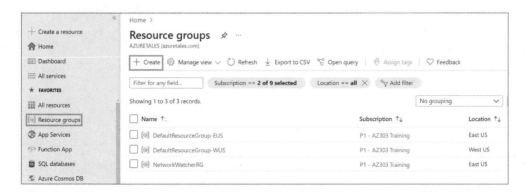

EXERCISE 2.1 *(continued)*

3. Input the following values:

    ▪ **Subscription**: Select your subscription.

    ▪ **Resource Group**: Enter a name for the new resource group.

    ▪ **Region**: Select the region for the resource group such as East US, India Central, UK South, etc.

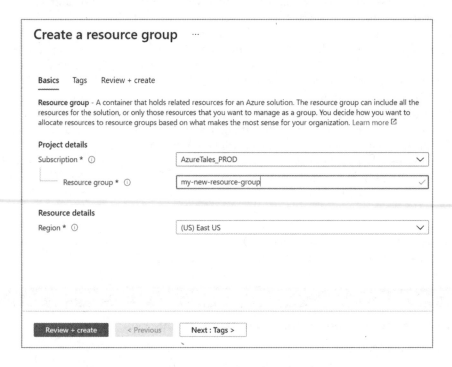

4. Clicking Review + Create will take you to the validation phase.

5. Once the validation is done, you will see the Create button. Click Create, and your resource group will be created.

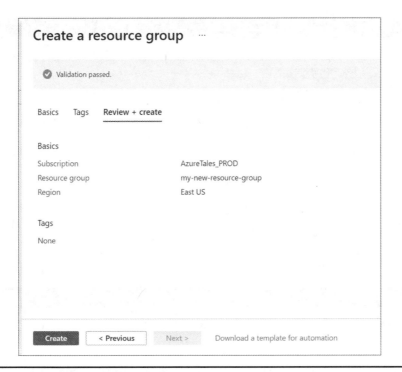

Listing Resource Groups from the Azure Portal

1. Sign in to the Azure portal.

2. Select the Resource Groups blade, and you will be able to list all the resource groups in your subscription. You have already seen how to list the resources groups; if you can't recall, refer to Exercise 2.1, step 2, to see the resource groups (if there are any).

3. You can open any resource group by clicking the name of the resource group. If the resource group is a new one, it will be empty. You will see a Create Resources button to add resources to the resource group.

EXERCISE 2.2 *(continued)*

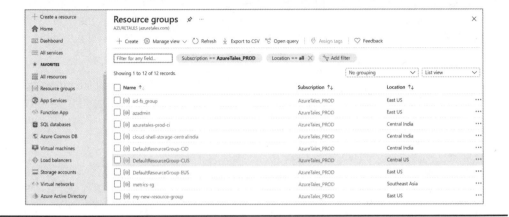

EXERCISE 2.3

Deleting Resource Groups from the Azure Portal

1. Sign in to the Azure portal.

2. Select the Resource Groups blade, and you will be able to list all resource groups in your subscription.

3. Open the resource group you would like to delete. Once you are inside the resource group, you will be able to see the Delete Resource Group option that can be used to delete the resource group. You need to enter the name of the resource group to confirm the deletion as this action cannot be undone.

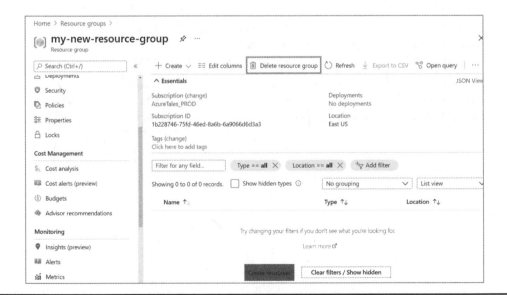

So far, we used the Azure portal to perform the management actions. You can also use Azure PowerShell or the Azure CLI to perform the same tasks. As of now, you can delete only one resource group at a time from the Azure portal. By using scripting, you can perform the management actions in bulk. It's recommended that you refer to the documentation to learn how to use one of the scripting languages if you prefer to automate your actions in bulk.

In Figure 2.6, you can see that we have created the resource group using the `New-AzResourceGroup` command along with the location and name parameters, listing resource groups using the `Get-AzResourceGroup` command, and finally deleting one of the resource groups using the `Remove-AzResourceGroup` command.

FIGURE 2.6   Managing resource groups using PowerShell

```
PS /home/rithin> New-AzResourceGroup -Name my-sample-rg -Location "East US"

ResourceGroupName : my-sample-rg
Location          : eastus
ProvisioningState : Succeeded
Tags              :
ResourceId        : /subscriptions/1b228746-75fd-46ed-8a6b-6a9066d6d3a3/resourceGroups/my-sample-rg

PS /home/rithin> Get-AzResourceGroup | Ft

ResourceGroupName               Location        ProvisioningState Tags TagsTable ResourceId
-----------------               --------        ----------------- ---- --------- ----------
cloud-shell-storage-centralindia centralindia   Succeeded                       /subscriptions/1b228746-75fd-46ed-8a6b-6a9066d6d3a3/resourceGrou…
DefaultResourceGroup-CID        centralindia    Succeeded                       /subscriptions/1b228746-75fd-46ed-8a6b-6a9066d6d3a3/resourceGrou…
azuretales-prod-ci              centralindia    Succeeded                       /subscriptions/1b228746-75fd-46ed-8a6b-6a9066d6d3a3/resourceGrou…
DefaultResourceGroup-CUS        centralus       Succeeded                       /subscriptions/1b228746-75fd-46ed-8a6b-6a9066d6d3a3/resourceGrou…
DefaultResourceGroup-EUS        eastus          Succeeded                       /subscriptions/1b228746-75fd-46ed-8a6b-6a9066d6d3a3/resourceGrou…
azadmin                         eastus          Succeeded         {}            /subscriptions/1b228746-75fd-46ed-8a6b-6a9066d6d3a3/resourceGrou…
ad-fs_group                     eastus          Succeeded                       /subscriptions/1b228746-75fd-46ed-8a6b-6a9066d6d3a3/resourceGrou…
my-new-resource-group           eastus          Succeeded         {}            /subscriptions/1b228746-75fd-46ed-8a6b-6a9066d6d3a3/resourceGrou…
my-sample-rg                    eastus          Succeeded                       /subscriptions/1b228746-75fd-46ed-8a6b-6a9066d6d3a3/resourceGrou…
metrics-rg                      southeastasia   Succeeded                       /subscriptions/1b228746-75fd-46ed-8a6b-6a9066d6d3a3/resourceGrou…
NetworkWatcherRG                southeastasia   Succeeded                       /subscriptions/1b228746-75fd-46ed-8a6b-6a9066d6d3a3/resourceGrou…
PS /home/rithin> Remove-AzResourceGroup -Name my-sample-rg

Confirm
Are you sure you want to remove resource group 'my-sample-rg'
[Y] Yes  [N] No  [S] Suspend  [?] Help (default is "Y"): Y
True
```

Similarly, you can perform the command using the Azure CLI, as shown in Figure 2.7. With that, we will move on to the next topic, which is management groups.

Management Groups

When we were discussing accounts and subscriptions, you saw that an account can have multiple subscriptions. If you think of it from an organizational perspective, there will be multiple accounts, and there will be multiple subscriptions meant for different environments and workloads. Using management groups, you can logically group subscriptions. This way, management groups offer a new scope above the subscriptions, which can be used for granting access, assigning policies, and analyzing costs.

FIGURE 2.7   Managing resource groups using the Azure CLI

```
rithin@Azure:~$ az group create -n my-sample-rg -l "East US"
{
  "id": "/subscriptions/1b228746-75fd-46ed-8a6b-6a9066d6d3a3/resourceGroups/my-sample-rg",
  "location": "eastus",
  "managedBy": null,
  "name": "my-sample-rg",
  "properties": {
    "provisioningState": "Succeeded"
  },
  "tags": null,
  "type": "Microsoft.Resources/resourceGroups"
}
rithin@Azure:~$ az group list -o table
Name                                Location        Status
----------------------------------  --------------  ---------
cloud-shell-storage-centralindia    centralindia    Succeeded
DefaultResourceGroup-CID            centralindia    Succeeded
azuretales-prod-ci                  centralindia    Succeeded
DefaultResourceGroup-CUS            centralus       Succeeded
DefaultResourceGroup-EUS            eastus          Succeeded
azadmin                             eastus          Succeeded
ad-fs_group                         eastus          Succeeded
my-new-resource-group               eastus          Succeeded
my-sample-rg                        eastus          Succeeded
metrics-rg                          southeastasia   Succeeded
rithin@Azure:~$ az group delete -n my-sample-rg
Are you sure you want to perform this operation? (y/n): y
rithin@Azure:~$ []
```

All access or policies assigned to the management group will be inherited to the sub-scriptions that are part of the management group. We will cover how access and policy management is performed later in this chapter. Figure 2.8 shows a sample hierarchy where management groups are used.

Management groups enable administrators to do the following:

- They can logically group subscriptions into different containers.

- They can apply policies and access a set of subscriptions easily.

- Cost management can be scoped at the management group level for tracking the costs of multiple subscriptions in a single shot.

- Budgets can be created at the management group level, which is ideal for teams and projects having multiple subscriptions.

Management groups can be created from the Azure portal, PowerShell, and the CLI. There will be a default management group that will be provisioned along with your tenant called the *root management group*. All new management groups will be created as children of this root management group.

Creating a management group is a straightforward process you can perform by searching and navigating to management groups in the Azure portal. You can click Add (refer to Figure 2.9) to add a new management group. In Figure 2.9, you could also see a couple of management groups created for demonstration purposes.

FIGURE 2.8   Understanding management groups

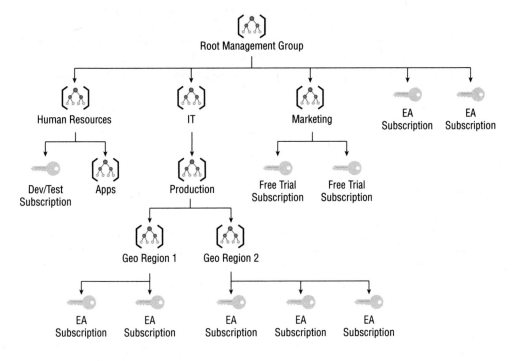

FIGURE 2.9   Creating management groups

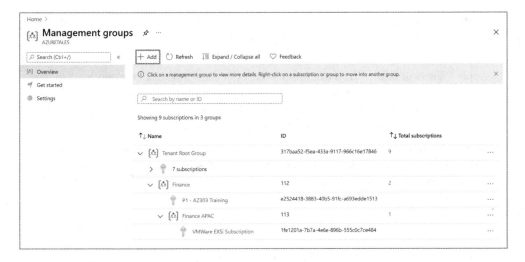

Two parameters are required while you create a management group. The first one is Management Group ID; this identifier is used to denote the management group when you want to run commands against the management group. Second, you need to add a display name, which will act like a friendly name for your management group. Whenever you are making PowerShell, Azure CLI, or REST API calls, you will be using the identifier to point to the management group. Management Group ID cannot be modified once the management group is created.

While discussing management groups, you read that it can be leveraged to apply policies and grant access easily on a larger scope. Now, we will see what these policies are and what role they play in governance.

Azure Policy

You can create, assign, and manage policies using the Azure Policy service. To ensure that the organizational standards and compliance controls are met, you can enforce rules and affect your resources using policies. Azure Policy constantly runs evaluations or scans on your resources to make sure they are compliant. If not, these will be reported in a well-presented dashboard for administrators to act on as required.

Azure Policy can stop new resources from breaking the compliance requirements. However, the existing resources will still be evaluated and reported if they are noncompliant, and we can remediate the noncompliance. Azure Policy cannot delete resources that are noncompliant.

Key features of Azure Policy include the following:

Compliance and Enforcement   You can leverage the built-in policies or build custom policies to ensure that the compliance requirements are met. Since the policy is enforced, users will not be able to deploy resources that break your policies.

Apply Policies at Scale   You can apply policies at the management group level so that the policy is inherited to all subscriptions that are part of the management group. Even if you add a new subscription to the management group, the policy is automatically inherited. Thus, you can make sure all existing and new subscriptions stay compliant.

Mitigation and Remediation   Since the resources are continuously evaluated by Azure Policy whenever there is deviation from the compliance policies, administrators can remediate and make sure your environment is 100 percent compliant. The remediation can be automated as well.

There are lot of built-in policies that come with the Azure Policy service. Nevertheless, administrators can always build custom policies to match your organizational requirements. Some of the use cases of Azure policies are as follows:

- Control the resource types that your organization can deploy to Azure. This policy can stop users from deploying expensive services like ExpressRoute, Cosmos DB, etc., unless an exception is provided.

- Restrict the deployment of virtual machines to a specific set of SKUs. This will help in controlling users from creating expensive VM SKUs, thus avoiding billing impact.

- Limit the deployment of resources to selected regions only. This will help in meeting your data residency requirements.

- Enforce required tags and its value to resources during deployment. We haven't covered resource tags yet; once we cover them, you will get an idea about the purpose of tags and the advantage of this policy.

- Audit that Azure Backup service is enabled for all virtual machines. This will ensure that Azure Backup service is enabled, which can be useful to recover VMs from catastrophic failures.

Let's see how we can implement a policy in Azure.

Implementing Azure Policy

Implementing an Azure policy comprises three main parts. We will start with the policy definition, policy assignment and scoping, and policy evaluation.

Policy Definition

There are many built-in policies, and users can write custom policies. You can see built-in policies by navigating to Azure Portal ➤ Policy ➤ Definitions. You need to add a filter to see the built-in policies, as shown in Figure 2.10.

FIGURE 2.10 Listing built-in policy definitions

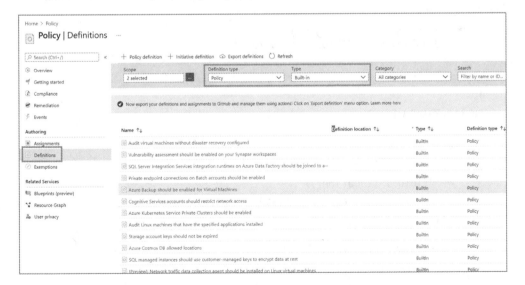

The definition is a JSON manifest that describes what action will be taken by the policy if it's assigned. The policy contains the condition and effect. The condition is what you evaluate to verify whether the effect needs to be applied or not. If the condition matches the declaration you made, the effect action will be taken. The following is a sample policy definition:

```
{
  "properties": {
    "displayName": "Allowed locations",
    "policyType": "BuiltIn",
    "mode": "Indexed",
    "description": "This policy enables you to restrict the locations
your organization can specify when deploying resources. Use to enforce
your geo-compliance requirements. Excludes resource groups, Microsoft.
AzureActiveDirectory/b2cDirectories, and resources that use the 'global'
region.",
    "metadata": {
      "version": "1.0.0",
      "category": "General"
    },
    "parameters": {
      "listOfAllowedLocations": {
        "type": "Array",
        "metadata": {
          "description": "The list of locations that can be specified when
deploying resources.",
          "strongType": "location",
          "displayName": "Allowed locations"
        }
      }
    },
    "policyRule": {
      "if": {
        "allOf": [
          {
            "field": "location",
            "notIn": "[parameters('listOfAllowedLocations')]"
          },
          {
            "field": "location",
            "notEquals": "global"
          },
          {
```

```
        "field": "type",
        "notEquals": "Microsoft.AzureActiveDirectory/b2cDirectories"
      }
    ]
  },
  "then": {
    "effect": "deny"
  }
 }
},
"id": "/providers/Microsoft.Authorization/policyDefinitions/e56962a6-4747-
49cd-b67b-bf8b01975c4c",
"type": "Microsoft.Authorization/policyDefinitions",
"name": "e56962a6-4747-49cd-b67b-bf8b01975c4c"
}
```

This policy is used to restrict the locations where your organization users can deploy resources. In the condition we have mentioned that if the location selected is not part of the list of allowed locations or global, then the effect action should be taken. You can see the effect as "deny," which means if the selected location is not part of the list of allowed locations, then the deployment will be denied. Having these built-in policies helps the administrators to apply these policies without the need to invest time in writing new policies.

These are examples of policy definitions:

- Allowed Locations specifies the locations allowed for deployments and restricts deployment to other regions.

- Allowed Locations for Resource Groups specifies the locations allowed for resource groups.

- Allowed Virtual Machines SKUs allows you to select a set of VM SKUs that your organization users can deploy.

Now that we found the policy that we need to apply, we will discuss policy scope.

Policy Assignment and Scope

When we discussed management groups, you saw that management groups can be used as a scope for policy assignment and for granting access. Policy scope is defined as the process of determining which subscriptions, resource groups, and resources for which the policy should be enforced. Supported scopes include management groups, subscriptions, and resource groups.

Policy assignment is the process of assigning a policy definition to a specific scope, say, management groups, subscriptions, or resource groups. In the same definition blade, you will see an Assign option, as shown in Figure 2.11.

FIGURE 2.11   Assigning a policy

Once you click Assign, you will be taken to the assignment process, and you will get the option to select the scope. Clicking the blue rectangle (refer to Figure 2.12) will show the available scopes including management groups, subscriptions, and resource groups. Based on the scope that you select, the policy will be assigned. After assignment, it takes around 30 minutes to generate the evaluation report. If you would like to assign your custom policy at the management group level, you should create the policy with the management group scope.

FIGURE 2.12   Selecting a policy scope

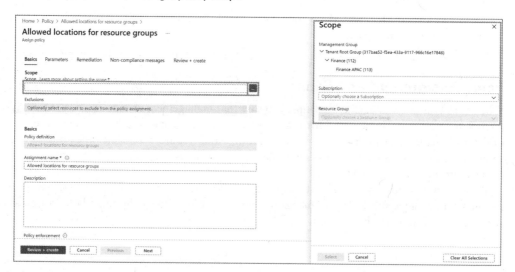

In Exercise 2.3, you will see the end-to-end assignment and evaluation process.

Policy Evaluation

After assigning the policy, the existing resources in your scope is reviewed to see if there are any noncompliant resources. Azure Policy offers a dashboard in which you can see the overall compliance of any selected scope and remediate any compliance issues.

Figure 2.13 exhibits a sample dashboard and overall compliance and noncompliant resources in the demo environment. The dashboard can be accessed from Policy ➤ Overview or the Policy ➤ Compliance blade.

FIGURE 2.13   Evaluating policies

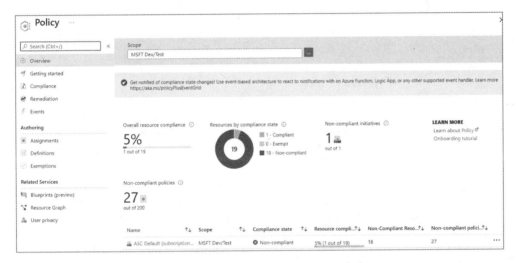

In Exercise 2.3, you will see the end-to-end creation, assignment, and evaluation process of Azure policies. In the exercise, you will create a custom policy called "G series VMs are not allowed." This policy will enforce a rule that G series VMs cannot be deployed to the scope. This helps in stopping users from creating expensive VMs like the G series.

EXERCISE 2.3

Implementing a Custom Policy

1. Sign-in to the Azure portal.

2. Search for *Policy* and open the Policy blade.

3. Navigate to the Definitions blade and click Policy Definition.

EXERCISE 2.3 *(continued)*

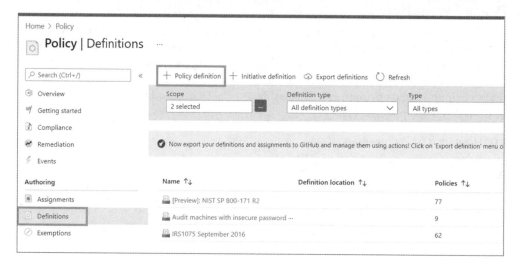

4. In the next window, you need to provide the details such as the definition location, name of the policy, description of the policy, and finally definition itself. The following are the values you can give for completing this exercise:

    ▪   **Definition location**: Select the management group or subscription where you would like to save the new policy definition. Here we are selecting a subscription for saving the definition. You can select your subscription. If you are planning to use this policy for a management group, then you should choose the management group as the location. Policies defined at the subscription level cannot be assigned to management groups.

    ▪   **Name**: Specify a name for the policy that will be displayed in the policy list. Since we are creating the policy for blocking the deployment of G series VMs, you can give the name as "G series VMs are not allowed."

    ▪   **Description**: This will be useful for other users to understand what this policy is about. Giving a good description is always recommended. In this case, we can add the description as **Use this policy to block the deployment of G series VM.**

    ▪   **Category**: You could specify to which category this new policy should be added. There are built-in categories for every service; if you want, you can create a new category altogether. This will be useful for filtering policies under a specific category while searching for policies. For the time being, you can mark the category as General.

    ▪   **Policy Rule**: We have two options here; either you can import a policy definition from GitHub, or you can write in the Azure portal itself using the editor. In this demo, we will add the policy definition in the Azure portal. You can copy and add the following definition to the policy rule:

```
{
    "policyRule": {
```

```
"if": {
"allOf": [{
"field": "type",
"equals": "Microsoft.Compute/virtualMachines"
},
{
"field": "Microsoft.Compute/virtualMachines/sku.name",
"like": "Standard_G*"
}
]
},
"then": {
"effect": "deny"
}
}
}
```

5. Once the values are entered as shown here, you can click Save to save the definition.

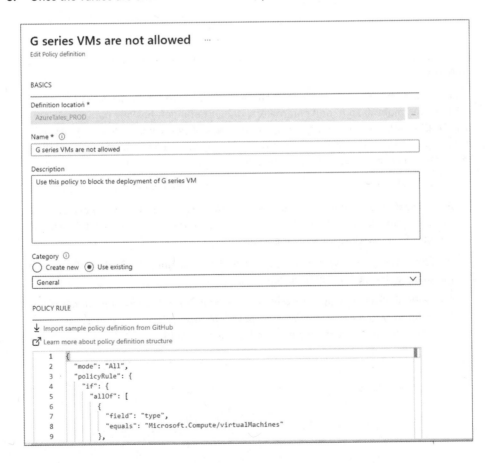

6. Now that you have created the custom policy, it will be added to the definitions within a few seconds. You can confirm if the policy is created by filtering using the type as Custom. Since you do not have numerous custom policies, this filtering is enough. In a production environment, there will be multiple custom policies, and you can leverage the category and search options to narrow down the search. Also, make sure that the scope is the same as the definition location you selected while creating the custom policy.

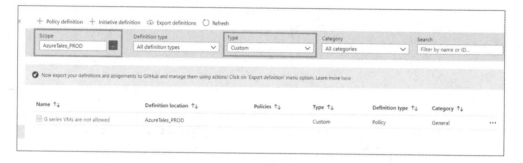

7. Selecting the custom policy will give you the option to assign, edit, duplicate, delete, and export the definition. You can proceed with the assignment process by clicking Assign.

8. In the assignment window, our policy only requires input to the Basics tab. In some policies, you might need to add parameters. If your definition has any parameters as in listOfAllowedLocations, which we saw in the case of "Allowed locations" policy, is an example of a parameter. Our current policy does not have any parameters. On the Basics tab, you can add the following details:

    -   **Scope:** This is the scope where you would like to apply the policy.

    -   **Exclusions:** If you would like to exclude any resources from the policy evaluation, that exception can be added here. Even if the resource is noncompliant, it will not be reported as we have passed the exclusion.

    -   **Assignment Name:** Give a friendly name for your assignment. By default, it will be the name of the policy you have selected.

    -   **Description:** You could add a description about the reason for assigning this policy. In the future, if another administrator looks into this assignment, they should be able to understand the rationale behind this assignment.

- **Policy Enforcement**: If this is set to Disabled, compliance evaluation will be available; however, the user will not be denied from creating a resource. We can keep it as Enabled as we need to deny users from deploying G series VMs.

- **Assigned By**: This is the name of the user who is assigning the policy. The default value is the sign-in name of the user who is assigning this policy. This is useful if you are using a generic admin email for assigning policies and you want to mention your name for letting others know who assigned the policy.

9. After adding the details, clicking Review + Create will create the assignment. Once the policy is assigned, you will get a message that it will take up to 30 minutes to run the evaluation and render the compliance dashboard.

10. In most cases, you can see that the policy will kick in within 15 minutes.

11. Trying to create a G/GS series will fail during the validation with the error message stating RequestDisallowedByPolicy.

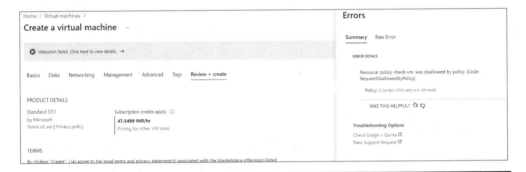

This was the end-to-end process from the creation, scoping, assignment, and validation of the policy. Here, we have used a custom policy; you could also use built-in policies for testing.

Now, we have used a single policy and its action on the scope. Think of a scenario where you have multiple policies defined by your organization. If the numbers are exceedingly high, assigning them one by one and managing them is going to be a tedious task for an administrator. Here comes the role of policy initiatives; in the next section, we will cover initiatives.

Implementing Initiatives

Using initiatives, you can chain or combine multiple policies, assign them on a scope, and manage them without hassle. Like policies, you can use the built-in initiatives, or you can produce a custom initiative. The concepts related to policies such as assignment, scoping, definition, and evaluation are also applicable in the case of initiatives.

If we navigate to Policy ➤ Definition and filter the definition type as Initiative, you will be able to see all the built-in initiatives. In the list (refer to Figure 2.14), if you take a closer look at the column Policies, you will be able to see the number of policies that are part of the initiative. For example, notice the IRS1075 September 2016 initiative comprises of 62 policies. Some initiatives will have fewer policies, while others will have 150+ policies.

FIGURE 2.14   Listing initiative policies

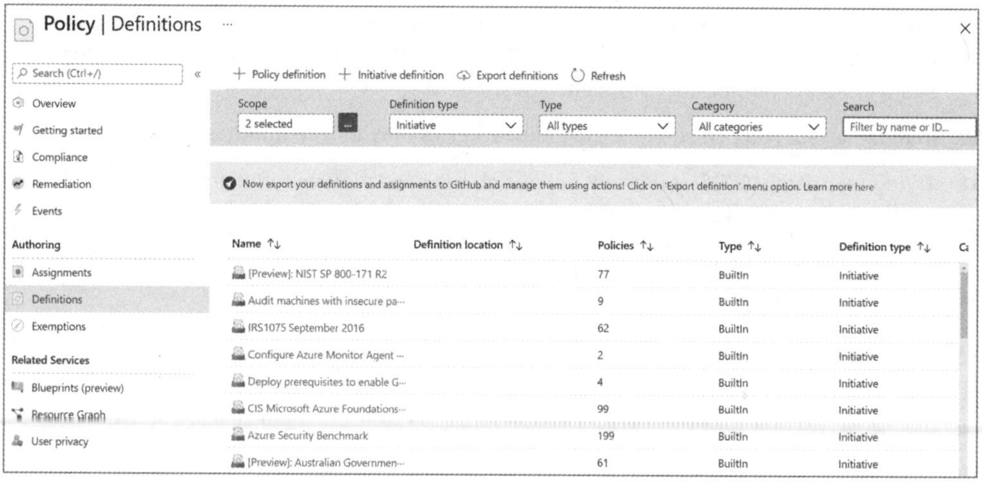

The built-in initiatives are available for all popular compliance standards such as ISO, FedRAMP, PCI, NIST, etc., and several region-based standards. Having these initiatives built-in can help organizations to easily attain these standards without wasting time.

If you open any of the initiatives, you will be able to see the list of policies that are chained to the initiative. For example, search for *Azure Security Benchmark* and open the initiative by clicking the name. This initiative comprises 199 policies at the time of authoring this book. Opening the initiative gives the list of policies that are part of the initiative (refer to Figure 2.15). Also, it gives you the option to assign, duplicate, or export the definition.

Creating a new initiative definition follows the same process of creating a policy definition. If you noticed in the graphic in Exercise 2.3, step 3, next to policy definition there is a button to create an initiative definition as well. Clicking this button will take you through the process of chaining or combining the policies and creating the initiative. The assignment and scoping work exactly the same way as policies. If you are familiar with the workflow of policies, you can easily implement initiatives.

The next topic we are going to cover is role-based access control.

FIGURE 2.15 Inspecting the initiative policy

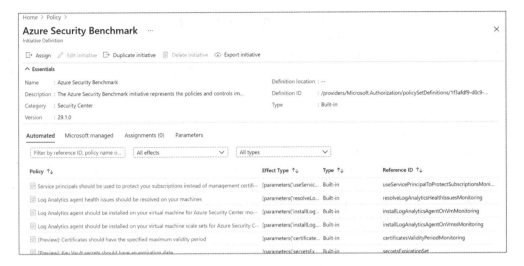

Role-Based Access Control

Role-based access control (RBAC) is used for the access management of cloud resources. This is a critical function for any organization as we do not want unauthorized users to access our resources. You can follow the principle of least privilege and assign RBAC roles to different users to accomplish their daily tasks.

RBAC has built-in roles that provide fine-grained access management of resources. Also, if you want to write a custom role based on your organizational need, RBAC supports custom roles.

The following are some of the use case scenarios of Azure RBAC:

- Allow a user to perform all actions on resources

- Allow a group to manage virtual machines

- Allow a user to work as a help-desk agent and open cases with Microsoft Support

- Allow an application to manage IP addresses

Using RBAC, you can separate out duties within your organization (e.g., Network Admins, Virtual Machine Admins, Billing Admins) and grant them the necessary permissions to perform their respective administrative tasks. Rather than giving unrestricted access to everyone, you could limit the actions that are allowed using RBAC.

Now we will discuss the concepts related to RBAC.

Concepts

Understanding these concepts will help you utilize RBAC more effectively. Also, as an administrator, you should be familiar with these concepts. Without knowing these concepts, it will be hard to assign access in an efficient manner.

RBAC assignment is all about the three Ws (who, what, and where): in simple terms, to whom you want to give the permission (who), the set of permissions you are providing (what), and the scope to which this role is assigned (where). Let's comprehend these concepts.

Security Principal (Who)

The security principal represents an object in Azure AD (user, group, service principal, or managed identity) that is requesting access to the resources. When you assign a role, you get to choose the security principal to which you want to assign the permissions.

If you assign a role to a group, all members of that group will automatically inherit that role as long as they are part of the group. The security principal represents an identity to which you can assign permissions.

Role Definition (What)

As we discussed in the case of Azure Policy, each role in RBAC has a corresponding definition called the *role definition*. The role definition will contain a collection of permissions that can be performed by any security principal to which you assign the role.

This definition is defined in a JSON file. The fields that are included in the manifest are name, ID, and description. Apart from these, you will see a set of allowable permissions (Actions), denied permissions (NotActions), and scope for the role.

You can use PowerShell or the Azure CLI to extract the manifest of any role. For example, there is a role called Owner that will give complete read, write, and permissions to delegate access to another user on the assigned scope. In Figure 2.16, you can see that we are using the PowerShell command `Get-AzRoleDefinition -Name Owner` to see the definition of the role. Also, piping the output to `ConvertTo-Json` will show you the definition in JSON format.

Similarly, in Azure CLI, you can use `az role definition list --name Owner` to see the same output. In the CLI, you will directly get the JSON output (refer to Figure 2.17).

When we discuss custom roles, you will learn how you can reuse this definition to create new roles in Azure.

Scope (Where)

Scope is not an unfamiliar word for us. You saw this term when we discussed management groups and policies. In RBAC, scope is used to define where exactly the security principal should have the permissions described in the definition.

Allowed scopes include management groups, subscriptions, resource groups, and resources. Unlike policies, you can have resource-level permissions. The access given to a higher scope is inherited by all child scopes.

FIGURE 2.16   Viewing the definition of a role using PowerShell

```
PS /home/rithin> Get-AzRoleDefinition -Name Owner

Name            : Owner
Id              : 8e3af657-a8ff-443c-a75c-2fe8c4bcb635
IsCustom        : False
Description     : Grants full access to manage all resources, including the ability to assign roles in Azure RBAC.
Actions         : {*}
NotActions      : {}
DataActions     : {}
NotDataActions  : {}
AssignableScopes : {/}


PS /home/rithin> Get-AzRoleDefinition -Name Owner | Convertto-json
{
  "Name": "Owner",
  "Id": "8e3af657-a8ff-443c-a75c-2fe8c4bcb635",
  "IsCustom": false,
  "Description": "Grants full access to manage all resources, including the ability to assign roles in Azure RBAC.",
  "Actions": [
    "*"
  ],
  "NotActions": [],
  "DataActions": [],
  "NotDataActions": [],
  "AssignableScopes": [
    "/"
  ]
}
```

FIGURE 2.17   Viewing the definition of a role using the Azure CLI

```
rithin@Azure:~$ az role definition list --name Owner
[
  {
    "assignableScopes": [
      "/"
    ],
    "description": "Grants full access to manage all resources, including the ability to assign roles in Azure RBAC.",
    "id": "/subscriptions/1b228746-75fd-46ed-8a6b-6a9066d6d3a3/providers/Microsoft.Authorization/roleDefinitions/8e3af657-a8ff-443c-a75c-2fe8c4bcb635",
    "name": "8e3af657-a8ff-443c-a75c-2fe8c4bcb635",
    "permissions": [
      {
        "actions": [
          "*"
        ],
        "dataActions": [],
        "notActions": [],
        "notDataActions": []
      }
    ],
    "roleName": "Owner",
    "roleType": "BuiltInRole",
    "type": "Microsoft.Authorization/roleDefinitions"
  }
]
```

Assignment

Combining the service principal (who), role definition (what), and scope (where) forms the assignment. In other words, the action of attaching a role definition to a security principal at a specific scope is called *role assignment*.

As an administrator, you will be creating the assignments to grant users access to particular scopes. The action mentioned in the role definition can be performed by these users as long as they have access to the scope.

Figure 2.18 illustrates how the security principal, role definition, and scope are combined to create a role assignment.

FIGURE 2.18   Role assignment process

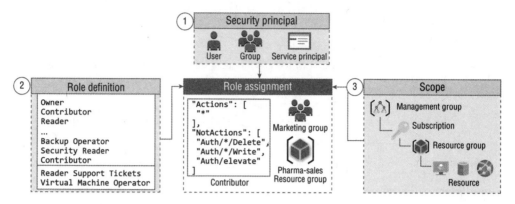

Now that you are familiar with the concepts, let's learn the fundamental roles for RBAC.

Azure RBAC Roles

In this section, we will discuss the fundamental roles that every administrator should know. Additionally, we will cover the key differences between Azure AD roles, Azure RBAC roles, and custom roles.

Fundamental RBAC Roles

Azure provides 100+ built-in roles meant for providing granular access to each service; however, memorizing all these roles is not possible. These fundamental roles are useful in scenarios where you want to give full access or read-only access to a specific scope. If the fundamental roles or built-in roles are not able to meet your requirements, then you will go with the custom roles. There are four Azure fundamental roles that you should be aware of.

Owner   Has full access to the scope to which this is assigned; also as an Owner you can delegate access to other users. For example, you as Owner can assign Owner or any other role to another user.

Contributor   Has the same level of resource permissions as Owner; however, Contributor cannot delegate access to others.

Reader   Assigns a read-only role.

User Access Administrator   Can delegate access to other users; however, this role cannot manage any resources.

A common dilemma that everyone has is how the Azure AD roles are different from Azure RBAC roles and where exactly the classic roles fit. Let's understand the differences between these concepts.

Azure Classic Roles vs. Azure RBAC Roles vs. Azure AD Roles

If you are new to Azure, you will find it a little confusing to understand the distinct roles in Azure and how they are different. When Azure was released, the RBAC roles were not there. We had something called the *classic* subscription administration roles. There were three roles, and they were used to manage resources and access. The following are the classic roles:

Account Administrator   The user who signs up for the Azure subscription is the Account Administrator. By default, the user will have access to the billing as well as to the service management. There will be only one Account Administrator for a subscription.

Service Administrator   The Account Administrator can delegate the service administration to another user. If the Account Administrator and Service Administrator are two different users, then the Account Administrator will be managing the billing aspects of the subscription, and all resource management will be carried out by the Service Administrator. The Service Administrator role is similar to the Owner role we have in RBAC. There will only be one Service Administrator for a subscription.

Co-administrators   Co-administrators can manage all aspects of resources the same way as Service Administrators; however, Co-administrators cannot delegate access. For example, if you are a Co-administrator, you cannot add another person as a Co-administrator. This action can be done only by a Service Administrator. The Co-administrator role is similar to the Contributor role in RBAC.

These classic roles were assigned at the subscription level, and the idea of scoping was not there in the earlier days. This caused a lot of security concerns as we were not able to give fine-grained access to resources. For example, if you wanted to assign a role to a user for managing virtual machines, there was no customized role at that time. The lowest privilege that you could assign was the Co-administrator role. Since this classic role is defined at the subscription level, the user would end up getting access to all resources. Due to this drawback, Azure produced RBAC when it introduced Azure Resource Manager (ARM). The rest is history; administrators can customize roles, fine-tune the access, and assign them at different scopes.

Now we will shift our focus to Azure AD roles. In Chapter 1 you saw that Azure AD roles are for managing the resources in Azure AD. This is where the difference between Azure AD and Azure RBAC lies. Azure AD roles are created to manage the users, groups, domains, and other objects that are part of Azure AD. Table 2.1 will explain the key differences between these roles.

TABLE 2.1   Comparing Classic, RBAC, and Azure AD Roles

Aspect	Azure Classic Roles	Azure RBAC Roles	Azure AD Roles
Access	Manages access to Azure resources. Microsoft recommends using Classic roles only for the management of Classic resources.	Manages access to Azure resources.	Manages access to Azure AD resources like users, groups, domains, and other objects.
Scope	Scope is limited to subscription scope.	Scope can be defined at multiple levels, starting from management groups, subscriptions, resource groups, and resources.	Scope is limited to tenant level.
Role management	Can be managed from the Azure portal and Accounts Portal (reaching EOL).	Can be managed from Azure Portal, Azure CLI, Azure PowerShell, ARM templates, SDKs, and REST API.	Can be managed from the Azure portal, Microsoft 365 Admin Center, Microsoft Graph API, and Microsoft Azure AD PowerShell module.
Custom roles	Not Supported.	Supported.	Supported.

Figure 2.19 shows where each of the roles is related and how they fit into the bigger picture.

At this point you are aware that Azure RBAC supports custom roles. In the next section, we will talk about custom roles and how they are created.

Custom RBAC Roles

Using custom RBAC roles, we can create fine-tuned roles that match your organizational needs. This customization offered by Azure RBAC is a boon for administrators. We can combine multiple roles and create a single role, or we can take a built-in role as a baseline and customize that. In next exercise, we will create a custom role using PowerShell.

FIGURE 2.19   Role comparison

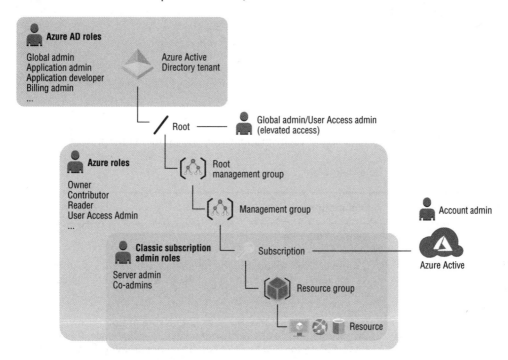

We can always build from scratch or clone a role and modify it. It's easy to clone and modify a role as there will be minimal chances of syntax errors as the structure is cloned from an existing role. To explain the components of the JSON definition, we will take the Owner as an example. We have already seen how to extract the JSON when we discussed role definition.

```
{
  "Name": "Owner",
  "Id": "8e3af657-a8ff-443c-a75c-2fe8c4bcb635",
  "IsCustom": false,
  "Description": "Grants full access to manage all resources, including the
ability to assign roles in Azure RBAC.",
  "Actions": [
    "*"
```

```
  ],
  "NotActions": [],
  "DataActions": [],
  "NotDataActions": [],
  "AssignableScopes": [
    "/"
  ]
}
```

Table 2.2 explains the meaning of each component in the JSON manifest.

TABLE 2.2   Azure Role Definition

Properties	Explanation
Name	Name of the role.
Id	Unique ID used to identify the role. When we create a custom role, we will leave this field blank, and Azure will automatically assign a unique ID to the role.
IsCustom	This flag denotes if the role is a custom role or not. Here we used Owner role, this is obviously not a custom role; hence, this flag is set to false (or BuiltInRole). If you are creating custom role, make sure this flag is set to true (or CustomRole).
Description	Description of the role.
Actions	Set of specific management operations that the role allows to perform.
NotActions	Set of actions that are excluded from allowed actions.
DataActions	Set of data operations that are allowed by the role.
NotDataActions	Set of data actions that are excluded from allowed data actions.
AssignableScopes	Set of scopes where the role is available for assignment.

The aforementioned properties are shown only in Azure PowerShell. When you are using the Azure Portal, Azure CLI, or REST API, the property names will be slightly different. However, you can easily figure them out. The following is the list of properties shown in the Azure portal, Azure CLI, or REST API:

roleName

name

```
type
description
actions []
notActions []
dataActions []
notDataActions []
assignableScopes []
```

In the definition, we can define what operational actions are allowed. Operations are specified in the format {Company}.{ProviderName}/{resourceType}/{action}. The {action} denotes the set of operations that you can perform on a resource type. For example, if you need to grant read access to virtual machines, then the string format will be Microsoft.Compute/virtualMachines/read. At this point, do not worry about how we derived this string. During the exercise, you will see an easy way to derive these operation strings. Table 2.3 shows the set of actions available.

TABLE 2.3 Supported Actions

Action String	Explanation
*	Grants access to all operations
read	Enables read operation (GET)
write	Enables write operations (PATCH or PUT)
action	Custom operations (POST)
delete	Allows delete operation (DELETE)

To complete this exercise, you need to be an Owner or User Access Administrator.

In Exercise 2.4, you will create a role called Virtual Machine Supporter. This role should be able to start/stop VMs and manage support cases. Let's get started.

EXERCISE 2.4

Creating a Custom Role Using PowerShell

1. Sign in to the Azure portal and open the cloud shell; then switch to PowerShell. You can also use a local shell if you have installed the Az PowerShell module.

2. In the cloud shell, you can use the command Get-AzRoleDefinition | FT Name. This command will list all the roles available in Azure. You need to pick a role that is closer to the role that you want to create. If you are unsure, then go with the Owner role.

3. Now you need to understand the operations that you want the user to have access to. In our case, we need permission to start or stop VMs. Every resource has a resource provider that is responsible for all operations that we are performing on the resource. The resource provider for virtual machine is `Microsoft.Compute`. If you would like to see the resource providers and resource types supported, you can use the PowerShell command `Get-AzResourceProvider | FT`. As shown here, you can see the virtual machine is part of `Microsoft.Compute` resource provider.

```
PS /home/rithin> (Get-AzResourceProvider) | ft

ProviderNamespace              RegistrationState ResourceTypes
-----------------              ----------------- -------------
Microsoft.Batch                Registered        {batchAccounts, batchAccounts/pools, batchAccounts/certificates, operations…}
Sendgrid.Email                 Registered        {accounts, operations}
Microsoft.AlertsManagement     Registered        {resourceHealthAlertRules, alerts, alertsSummary, smartGroups…}
Microsoft.Migrate              Registered        {projects, migrateprojects, assessmentProjects, moveCollections…}
Microsoft.OffAzure             Registered        {VMwareSites, HyperVSites, ServerSites, ImportSites…}
Microsoft.MachineLearningServices Registered     {workspaces, workspaces/onlineEndpoints, workspaces/onlineEndpoints/deployments, workspaces/batchE
Microsoft.ChangeAnalysis       Registered        {operations, resourceChanges, changes}
Microsoft.Blueprint            Registered        {blueprints, blueprints/artifacts, blueprints/versions, blueprints/versions/artifacts…}
Microsoft.Maintenance          Registered        {maintenanceConfigurations, updates, configurationAssignments, applyUpdates…}
Microsoft.GuestConfiguration   Registered        {guestConfigurationAssignments, software, softwareUpdates, softwareUpdateProfile…}
Microsoft.ResourceHealth       Registered        {availabilityStatuses, childAvailabilityStatuses, childResources, events…}
Microsoft.DomainRegistration   Registered        {domains, domains/domainOwnershipIdentifiers, topLevelDomains, checkDomainAvailability…}
Microsoft.Network              Registered        {virtualNetworks, virtualNetworks/taggedTrafficConsumers, natGateways, publicIPAddresses…}
Microsoft.Authorization        Registered        {roleAssignments, roleDefinitions, classicAdministrators, permissions…}
Microsoft.Storage              Registered        {deletedAccounts, locations/deletedAccounts, storageAccounts, operations…}
Microsoft.Security             Registered        {operations, securityStatuses, tasks, secureScores…}
Microsoft.Compute              Registered        {availabilitySets, virtualMachines, virtualMachines/extensions, virtualMachineScaleSets…}
Microsoft.PolicyInsights       Registered        {policyEvents, policyStates, operations, asyncOperationResults…}
```

4. The VM related actions are part of the `Microsoft.Compute/virtualMachines` namespace. We need to find the operations available for this provider. The operations can be found using the command `Get-AzProviderOperation "Microsoft .Compute/virtualMachines/*"`. As shown here, you can see the operations required for viewing, starting, and powering off the VMs, namely, `Microsoft .Compute/virtualMachines/read`, `Microsoft.Compute/virtualMachines/ start/action`, and `Microsoft.Compute/virtualMachines/ powerOff/action`.

```
PS /home/rithin> Get-AzProviderOperation "Microsoft.Compute/virtualMachines/*" | ft

Operation                                                              OperationName                                              ProviderNam
                                                                                                                                  espace
---------                                                              -------------                                              -----------
Microsoft.Compute/virtualMachines/read                                 Get Virtual Machine                                        Microsoft …
Microsoft.Compute/virtualMachines/write                                Create or Update Virtual Machine                           Microsoft …
Microsoft.Compute/virtualMachines/delete                               Delete Virtual Machine                                     Microsoft …
Microsoft.Compute/virtualMachines/start/action                         Start Virtual Machine                                      Microsoft …
Microsoft.Compute/virtualMachines/powerOff/action                      Power Off Virtual Machine                                  Microsoft …
Microsoft.Compute/virtualMachines/reapply/action                       Reapply a virtual machine's current model                  Microsoft …
Microsoft.Compute/virtualMachines/redeploy/action                      Redeploy Virtual Machine                                   Microsoft …
Microsoft.Compute/virtualMachines/restart/action                       Restart Virtual Machine                                    Microsoft …
Microsoft.Compute/virtualMachines/retrieveBootDiagnosticsData/action   Retrieve boot diagnostic logs blob URIs                    Microsoft …
Microsoft.Compute/virtualMachines/deallocate/action                    Deallocate Virtual Machine                                 Microsoft …
Microsoft.Compute/virtualMachines/generalize/action                    Generalize Virtual Machine                                 Microsoft …
Microsoft.Compute/virtualMachines/capture/action                       Capture Virtual Machine                                    Microsoft …
Microsoft.Compute/virtualMachines/runCommand/action                    Run Command on Virtual Machine                             Microsoft …
Microsoft.Compute/virtualMachines/convertToManagedDisks/action         Convert Virtual Machine disks to Managed Disks             Microsoft …
Microsoft.Compute/virtualMachines/performMaintenance/action            Perform Maintenance Redeploy                               Microsoft …
Microsoft.Compute/virtualMachines/reimage/action                       Reimage Virtual Machine                                    Microsoft …
Microsoft.Compute/virtualMachines/login/action                         Log in to Virtual Machine                                  Microsoft …
Microsoft.Compute/virtualMachines/loginAsAdmin/action                  Log in to Virtual Machine as administrator                 Microsoft …
Microsoft.Compute/virtualMachines/installPatches/action                Install OS update patches on virtual machine               Microsoft …
Microsoft.Compute/virtualMachines/assessPatches/action                 Assess virtual machine for available OS update patches     Microsoft …
Microsoft.Compute/virtualMachines/cancelPatchInstallation/action       Cancel install OS update patch operation on virtual machine Microsoft …
```

5. You are done with the first set of permissions required for the virtual machines. Now you need to find the operations required for managing support tickets. If you list the resource providers, you can see that `Microsoft.Support` is responsible for support tickets. Since you need all operations under this name space, you can set operations to a wildcard by adding an asterisk as in `Microsoft.Support/*`.

6. To summarize, our role should have the following operations to match our requirements:

   - `Microsoft.Compute/virtualMachines/read`: Getting the virtual machine

   - `Microsoft.Compute/virtualMachines/start/action`: Operation to start VM

   - `Microsoft.Compute/virtualMachines/powerOff/action`: Operation to power off VM

   - `Microsoft.Support/*`: All actions related to support tickets

7. Now you need to clone a built-in role and modify the JSON with the permissions in which you are interested. Clone the Owner role using the PowerShell command `Get-AzRoleDefinition -Name Owner | ConvertTo-JSON > role.json`. This command will export the definition to a file `role.json` and will be saved in your cloud shell or local directory depending on which one you are using.

8. You need to edit the JSON file and customize it. If you are using a local shell, you can use any text editor like Visual Studio Code, Sublime, or even Notepad. In the cloud shell, there is a built-in editor that you can use. You can invoke the code editor in the cloud shell by using the command code followed by the filename. In our case, we are using `code role.json`.

```
PowerShell ∨   ⏻  ?  ⚙  ⎘  ⎗  {}  ⤓
                                              role.json
 1  {
 2    "Name": "Owner",
 3    "Id": "8e3af657-a8ff-443c-a75c-2fe8c4bcb635",
 4    "IsCustom": false,
 5    "Description": "Grants full access to manage all resources, including the ability to assign roles in Azure RBAC.",
 6    "Actions": [
 7      "*"
 8    ],
 9    "NotActions": [],
10    "DataActions": [],
11    "NotDataActions": [],
12    "AssignableScopes": [
13      "/"
14    ]
15  }
16

PS /home/rithin> code role.json
```

9. After making the modifications, you can hit Ctrl+S and then Ctrl+Q to quit the editor. The following is the modified version of the file:

```
{
"Name": "Virtual Machine Supporter",
"Id": "",
"IsCustom": true,
"Description": "Read, start and stop VMs. Create and manage support tickets",
"Actions": [
  "Microsoft.Compute/virtualMachines/read",
  "Microsoft.Compute/virtualMachines/start/action",
  "Microsoft.Compute/virtualMachines/powerOff/action",
  "Microsoft.Support/*"
],
"NotActions": [],
"DataActions": [],
"NotDataActions": [],
"AssignableScopes": [
  "/subscriptions/<yourSubscriptionID>"
]
}
```

10. You have the modified JSON file, and now you can create a new role using the New-AzRoleDefinition command. For this exercise, you can run New-AzRoleDefinition -InputFile ./role.json, and the output will be similar to the graphic shown here:

```
PS /home/rithin> New-AzRoleDefinition -InputFile ./role.json

Name             : Virtual Machine Supporter
Id               : 6c662093-c522-443e-a007-d1ec4d1099f9
IsCustom         : True
Description      : Read, start and stop VMs. Create and manage support tickets
Actions          : {Microsoft.Compute/virtualMachines/read, Microsoft.Compute/virtualMachines/start/action,
                   Microsoft.Compute/virtualMachines/powerOff/action, Microsoft.Support/*}
NotActions       : {}
DataActions      : {}
NotDataActions   : {}
AssignableScopes : {/subscriptions/1b228746-75fd-46ed-8a6b-6a9066d6d3a3}
```

11. Navigate to Azure Portal ➢ Subscriptions ➢ Select Your Subscription. Click Access Control (IAM) and switch to the Roles tab. If you search for *Virtual Machine Supporter* with the Type = CustomRole filter, you will be able to see the custom role you just created.

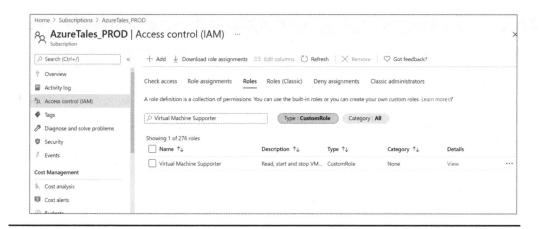

In this exercise you created a new custom role in Azure using Azure PowerShell. You can also create roles from the Azure portal, which is easier compared to performing the same steps from PowerShell. However, understanding PowerShell is really useful if you are scripting and creating roles on the go. You can use the same JSON file in the Azure portal or add permissions one by one by exploring each of the resource providers. If you are interested in testing it using the Azure portal, you can refer to the following:

https://docs.microsoft.com/en-us/azure/role-based-access-control/
custom-roles-portal

Now that we have created the custom role, let's see how this role can be assigned to our users.

Role Assignment

You already saw what a role assignment is theoretically when we studied the concepts related to Azure RBAC. In this section, you will be reusing the custom role you created in the previous exercise and assigning that role to a user. Once it's assigned, you will sign in as the user and verify the permissions you have given are correct and working as expected. See Exercise 2.5.

EXERCISE 2.5

Assigning Roles from the Azure Portal

1. Sign in to the Azure portal using the Owner credentials.

2. You will create a new resource group and a VM to evaluate the role. Since we have not discussed virtual machines yet, you can execute the following commands in Cloud Shell to create a VM.

EXERCISE 2.5 *(continued)*

3. You need a resource group that can be created using the following command. Assume that you need the user to manage only this resource group, so the scope of the assignment should be the resource group.

   ```
   New-AzResourceGroup -Name VMGroup -Location EastUS
   ```

4. You will create a VM for testing purposes using the following command. The password should be between 8 to 123 characters and should have any of three out of four complexity requirements: have upper characters, have lower characters, have a digit, have a special character. You will be asked to provide the username and password for the VM once you execute the command:

   ```
   New-AzVM -Name server-1 `
     -ResourceGroupName VMGroup `
     -Image UbuntuLTS `
      -Credential (Get-Credential)
   ```

5. You will be able to see the progress in the shell, and once the VM is created, you will see confirmation.

6. Exit the cloud shell. Navigate to Resource Groups and open the new resource group you created called VMGroup.

7. Click the Access Control (IAM) blade. In every scope (management group, subscription, resource group, resource) you will see this blade; any changes you make in this blade will be inherited to all child items.

8. Click Add and select Add Role Assignment.

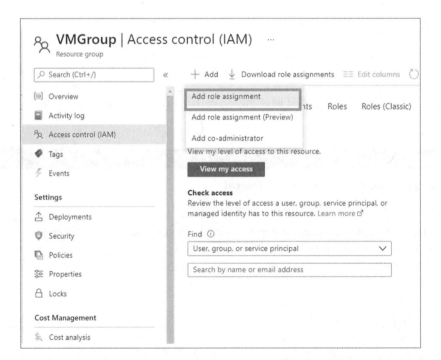

9. In the side pane, you can select the Virtual Machine Supporter role and search for a user in your environment. If you do not have another user in your environment, refer to Exercise 1.2 and create another user before proceeding. The option Assign Access To will help you filter your search results. By default, the value is set to the user, group, or service principal. This means if you search, Azure will list the user, group, or service principal that matches your query. You can change this default choice to the user-assigned managed identity to filter the user-assigned managed identities.

10. Search a user and select the user; the moment you start typing in the name Azure will start showing the matches. In this demo environment, user Doctor Strange has been selected. You can select one of the users present in your environment. Click Save to save the assignment.

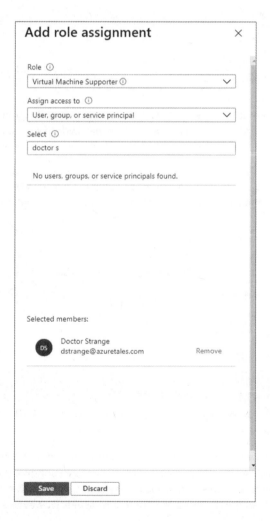

EXERCISE 2.5 *(continued)*

11. Navigate to the Role Assignments tab, and you will be able to see the assignment.

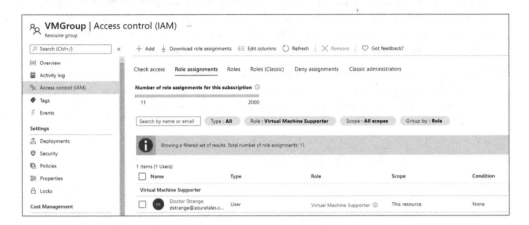

12. Open an incognito window and sign in as the user you selected. If you do not remember the password, you can always reset the password as we discussed in Chapter 1. Once signed in navigate to the Virtual Machines blade (or search for *Virtual Machines*).

13. You should be able to see the VM you created in step 4. Click the VM name and try to delete the VM using the Delete button. Click OK to confirm the deletion.

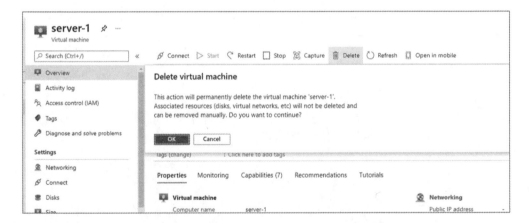

14. You will get an error message stating that you do not have enough permissions to delete the VM. This is because, in our custom role, we have not given the permission to delete. The only permission this role has is to view, start, or stop VMs. You could try to start or stop the VM, and that will work without any issues. However, any other operations will fail.

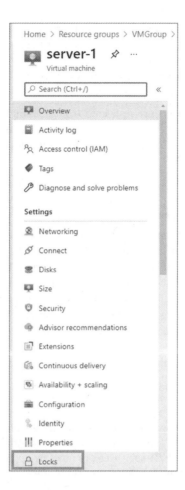

15. You can try working with support tickets if needed and see what the Virtual Machine Supporter role you created can do.

This Role Assignments blade can be used to see the existing assignments, add new assignments, and delete the assignments. Concisely, we created a custom role and tested the role using role assignment. On that note, we are winding up RBAC. The next topic we are going to cover is resource locks.

Resource Locks

Sometimes performing actions without caution will lead to accidental deletion or modification of mission-critical workloads that you have in your environment. In Azure, administrators can use locks to lock a subscription, resource group, or resource from getting deleted or modified. The lock will override any permission that is granted to you via RBAC. For example, even if you are the owner of the subscription, if the resource is locked, your permissions will be limited based on the lock set.

There are two lock levels: `CanNotDelete` and `ReadOnly`. In the Azure portal, you will see these as Delete or Read-only, respectively.

- **CanNotDelete** means that users are restricted from deleting the resource; however, the resource can be modified. For example, if the CanNotDelete lock is applied to a virtual machine; users can start, stop, or update the VM properties. However, they will not be able to delete the VM.

- **ReadOnly**, as the name suggests, means you will be able to read the resource; deletion or modification of the resource is not permitted. Even if you have an Owner role, if this lock is applied to a resource, your permissions will be limited to that of a Reader role.

Locks also follows inheritance as you saw in the case of RBAC and Azure Policy. For instance, if you apply a lock to the subscription, the lock will be inherited to the resource groups and resources that are associated with the subscription. In other words, if you apply a lock to a parent scope, all resources under that scope inherit the lock.

One thing to keep in mind here is locks apply only to control plane actions; they cannot prevent changes that are happening in the data plane. Control plane operations are any API calls made to `https://management.azure.com`, and the data plane operations are operations executed to a blob or any storage service. When you execute an action on a storage blob, for instance, you will be sending the API calls to the following:

```
https://<storageAccountName>.blob.core.windows.net
```

The aforementioned links will not be accessible via a browser as these are meant for API calls and would require authentication headers for a proper response. These URLs are used by applications to accomplish Azure management actions programmatically.

Similarly, you can apply locks to these databases, preventing accidental deletion or modification of the resource. However, a user can still log in to the database and amend the data stored in the database. It is especially important to understand the differences between data plane operations and control plane operations. In Microsoft documentation, scenarios are given for you to consider before applying locks. You can refer to the following:

```
https://docs.microsoft.com/en-us/azure/azure-resource-manager/
management/lock-resources?tabs=json#considerations-before-
applying-locks
```

To create or delete locks, you need to be Owner or User Access Administrator. If you are using custom roles, then `Microsoft.Authorization/*` or `Microsoft.Authorization/locks/*` should be there in your actions section.

Let's see how we can add lock to a resource in Azure. The process works the same way for any scope where you want to assign a lock.

Configuring Locks

From the Azure portal, you can add/delete locks by following the instructions in this section. You can also add/delete locks from Azure PowerShell, the Azure CLI, ARM templates, and the REST API.

The first step in assigning a lock is to understand which scope you want to apply the lock to. For example, if you would like to add a lock to the virtual machine we created Exercise 2.5, navigate to the Virtual Machine blade and click the VM name. In the Settings blade of your selected scope (resource, resource group, or subscription), you can see Locks, as shown in Figure 2.20.

FIGURE 2.20   Navigating to Locks

Now you can add a lock by clicking the Add button (refer to Figure 2.21). You could also see lock buttons for the subscription and resource group to which the selected resource belongs, in case you want to add the lock at a higher level.

FIGURE 2.21   Listing locks

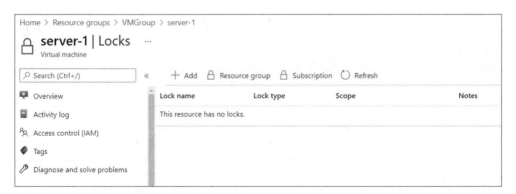

After clicking Add, you have to give a name to the lock, select the type of lock, and a note for other administrators to understand why you added this lock (see Figure 2.22). Even though the note is an optional field, adding a note is always considered as a best practice. Once you are done, click OK to set the lock.

FIGURE 2.22   Adding locks

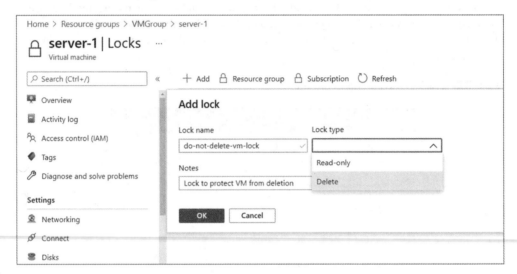

Once added, you can see the lock listed. You can always edit and change the lock type or delete the lock if needed (refer to Figure 2.23).

FIGURE 2.23   Managing locks

In this case, we added a Delete lock. You can try start, stop, and delete the VM and see what the outcome is. Similarly, you can remove the lock and add a read-only option and then try to start or stop the VM. The Delete lock will let you modify the VM (start, stop, or update), but you cannot delete the VM. On the other hand, read-only will not let you stop, start, or delete the VM as it prevents you from making changes to the resource.

Resource Tags

Resource tags can be used to logically organize the resources in your environment. Each tag comprises a key-value pair, where you will be adding a name and a corresponding value. For example, if your key or name for the tag is Environment, you could have different values like Production, QA, Development, or Testing. Adding these tags will help you understand which environment a resource belongs to. These tags are reusable, which means you do not have to create them for each resource. Once the tag is created, you can use it with applicable resources.

Use Cases

There are several use cases for tags; the following are some examples:

- You can group and filter your resources using tags. If you navigate to the All Resources blade, in real-world environments there will be thousands of resources. Tags can be used to filter resources across different regions and resource groups. Here tags can be leveraged for filtering (refer to Figure 2.24).

FIGURE 2.24 Sorting resources using tags

- In Azure Cost Management, you can use tags to see the cost of resources to which the tag is assigned (see Figure 2.25). This is useful if you have the tag Environment with the values Production, QA, and Development; using the tag, you can easily identify the cost related to production, QA, and development resources.

- When you download the usage report for your Azure consumption via REST API or from the portal, these tags will be present there are well. As this is a CSV file, you can easily apply filters and analyze the consumption.

FIGURE 2.25   Analyzing cost using tags

- If you are using Power BI connectors to create Azure consumption dashboards, then you can analyze the consumption using tags.

- Not all resource tags are available in Azure Cost Management. You can check the list of supported resources here:

  ```
  https://docs.microsoft.com/en-us/azure/azure-resource-
  manager/management/tag-support
  ```

- Tags applied to resource groups will not be shown in Azure Cost Management because Azure charges you at the resource level. Tags at the resource group level are logical organization only. Also, tags applied at the resource group level are not inherited to resources by default.

- Tags at the resource group level can be applied to resources using Azure Policy. Refer to this website:

  ```
  https://docs.microsoft.com/en-us/azure/governance/
  policy/tutorials/govern-tags#modify-resources-to-
  inherit-the-costcenter-tag-when-missing
  ```

Applying Tags

As mentioned earlier, tags can be applied at the subscription, resource group, or resource level. You can always search for *Tags* in the Azure portal, and the portal will list all tags that are there in your environment, as shown in Figure 2.26.

FIGURE 2.26   Listing tags

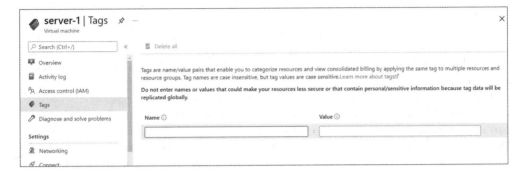

You can add tags by navigating to any resource and click Tags, as shown in Figure 2.27.

FIGURE 2.27   Adding tags to resources

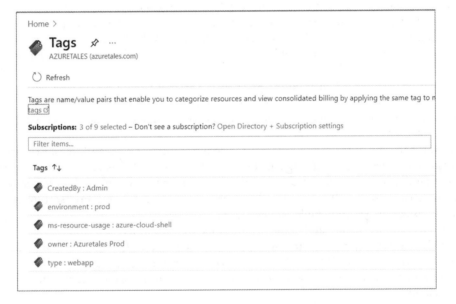

If you click the Name box, the portal will list all the tags that are currently available. If the tag is new, you can simply type in the name and it will be added. If you are selecting an existing key or name, the corresponding values are automatically displayed. If you want to add a new value, you can type that in. New tags that are added will take around 24 hours to reflect in Azure Cost Management for cost analysis. Also, any usage prior to the tag addition will not be included in the analysis. Azure Cost Management can display the usage only after tag addition if you are filtering using tags.

Summary

In this chapter, we discussed compliance and governance in the Azure cloud. We looked at a list of services that are responsible for bringing in compliance and governance. We started this chapter with Azure regions, as they are particularly important in maintaining data residency and data sovereignty.

Then we discussed Azure accounts and subscriptions and the several types of subscriptions offered by Azure based on your organizational requirements. Another key part of governance is running your workloads in a cost-optimized manner, so for this we looked at Azure Cost Management. Along with Cost Management, we saw how to plan the expenditure and what the optimization techniques are for controlling your cloud spending. The next topic of discussion was resource groups and how they help in the logical grouping of resources for access management, policy assignments, cost management, and lifecycle management. We also covered management groups, which can be used to logically group subscriptions. This grouping enables administrators to manage policies and access at a higher level than managing at the individual subscription scopes.

Azure Policy was the next service we discussed and the role it plays in keeping your environment in compliance with your organizational standards. We saw how we use the built-in policies and write custom policies to match your requirements. Also, if your organization wants to chain policies and assign them as a single unit, they can leverage initiatives. After Azure Policy, we talked about RBAC, which is responsible for access management in Azure. We covered the concepts related to Azure and how to make an assignment. In the exercise we created a custom role by cloning an existing role and assigned a user for assessing the role.

Towards the end of the chapter we covered resource locks and resource tags. Resource locks help in preventing accidental deletion or modification of the resources that are there in your production environment. On the other hand, resource tags are used for logically organizing the resources. We saw several use cases of tags including resource sorting, cost analysis, usage analysis, and building dashboards.

Throughout this chapter and in the previous one we used different mediums to manage Azure like the Azure portal, Azure PowerShell, and the Azure CLI. There are additional tools such as ARM templates, SDKs, and the REST API. In Chapter 3, "Virtual Networking," we will see what management tools are available for administrators to manage their Azure cloud.

Exam Essentials

Understand Azure accounts and subscription.   Understand how the sign-up process works and the different offers available for users based on their organizational needs. Along with that, understand the concepts of regions and regional pairs in subscriptions.

Understand resource groups and management groups.   Be able to understand the use case scenarios of resource groups and how they can be used as the scope for cost management, policy assignment, and role assignments. Also, understand the concept of management groups and how they fit into the hierarchy. Know the relation between management groups, subscriptions, and resource groups.

Learn about Azure Cost Management.   Understand how to use Azure Cost Management and the add-on features such as cost alerts, recommendations, budgets, and exports. Get acquainted with the cost planning and optimization techniques.

Understand how Azure Policy works.   Learn the concepts related to Azure Policy including policy definition, policy scope, and policy assignment. Also, learn the difference between policies and initiatives.

Know Azure role-based access control.   Understand Azure RBAC definition, scope, and assignment. Learn the fundamental built-in roles and how to create custom roles.

Learn resource locks.   Learn how critical resources can be protected from accidental deletion or modification using resource locks.

Understand resource tags.   Understand the use-case scenarios of tags and how these can be added to your resources in Azure.

Review Questions

1. Your organization has requested that you find a way to apply policies and create budgets across several subscriptions you manage. What should you do?

   A. Use Azure Cost Management billing groups

   B. Use resource groups

   C. Use management groups

   D. Use tags

2. Your organization started to use Azure tags. For tracking costs, you have been asked to create a solution that can be used to validate if the tags are present during the resource creation. What should you do?

   A. Use RBAC and assign the Tag Validator role

   B. Use Azure policies

   C. Email all users to ensure that the tags are added using AD groups

   D. Create a resource validation rule

3. Your company financial controller wants to be notified whenever the company is exceeding 50 percent of the money distributed for their cloud expenses. Which solution should you use?

   A. Create Azure reservation and save costs

   B. Apply a policy to notify when the threshold is reached

   C. Sign in to the Azure Pricing Calculator and set the organization threshold

   D. Create a budget in the Azure Cost Management and set the threshold

4. Your organization has several policy requirements that need to be enforced. What is the easiest method to enforce these policies?

   A. Create an initiative

   B. Create a group policy

   C. Create a resource group

   D. Create a management group

5. Your organization is using management groups. Under the root management group, you have management groups for Marketing, Finance, and HR. Each of these management groups has a nested management group, namely, NA, EMEA, and APAC denoting the region of operation. If the head of EMEA Marketing needs access to cost analysis, at which scope would you assign the appropriate role? Your assignment should make sure that the user has access to subscriptions that are created in the future as well.

   A. Root ➤ Marketing ➤ EMEA

   B. Root ➤ Marketing

   C. Marketing ➤ EMEA

   D. EMEA ➤ Subscription

6. You have three virtual machines (VM-A, VM-B, and VM-C) in a resource group. Your team hires a new employee. The new employee must be able to modify the settings on VM-C, but not on VM-A and VM-B. Your solution must minimize administrative overhead. What should you do?

    A. Assign the user the Contributor role on the resource group.

    B. Assign the user the Contributor role on VM-C.

    C. Move VM-C to a new resource group and assign the user to the Contributor role on VM-C.

    D. Assign the user to the Contributor role on the resource group and then assign the user to the Owner role on VM-C.

7. You would like to classify resources and billing for different departments like Finance and Marketing. The billing needs to be consolidated across multiple resource groups, and you need to ensure everyone complies with the solution. What should you do? (Choose two.)

    A. Create tags for each department

    B. Create a billing group for each department

    C. Create an Azure policy

    D. Add the groups into a single resource group

8. You would like to stop users from deleting resources in the production subscription. Which of the following solutions should you use?

    A. Add a CanNotDelete lock to the subscription scope

    B. Add a CanNotDelete lock to the resource group scope

    C. Add a ReadOnly lock to the subscription scope

    D. Add a ReadOnly lock to the resource group scope

9. Which of the following facts about policy is incorrect?

    A. A policy can evaluate resources and ensure compliance.

    B. A policy can restrict user access to resources.

    C. A policy can validate deployments and deny them if deployment does not match the organizational standards.

    D. A policy can have exclusions during the assignment.

10. Which of the following commands can be used to export the Owner role definition and display it as JSON? (Select two.)

    A. `Get-AzRoleDefinition -Name "Owner"`

    B. `Export-AzRoleDefinition -Name "Owner" -Format-JSON`

    C. `Get-AzRoleDefinition -Name "Owner" | ConvertTo-JSON`

    D. `az role definition list --name Owner`

11. Which of the following facts about Azure tags is not true? (Select two.)

    A. Tags applied at the resource group level are inherited to resources in the resource group automatically.

    B. Tags applied can be used to filter resources and resource groups.

    C. Tags added to the resource group level can be used for cost analysis.

    D. Tags can be enforced using Azure policies.

12. Which of following is not a use-case scenario for locks?

    A. Locks can be applied to subscription, resource group, and resource levels.

    B. Read-only locks can restrict deletion and modification of resources.

    C. Locks can be used to avoid accidental changes to the data plane.

    D. Read-only makes a user with the Owner role equivalent to the Reader role on the applied scope.

13. A new member joined your team, and you were asked by your manager to assign a role to the new user. This new user should be able to assign access to other users within your subscription, and at the same time, the user shouldn't be able to modify any resources.

    A. Assign the User Access Administrator role at the subscription scope.

    B. Assign the Contributor role at the subscription scope.

    C. Create a custom role as this role is not available.

    D. Create a managed identity.

14. User A has the following access given at different scopes:

    Subscription scope: Owner role

    Resource Group A: Contributor

    Database inside resource group A: Reader

    What permission will the user have on the database?

    A. Reader role as it's directly assigned to the database.

    B. Contributor role as resource group role is inherited.

    C. Owner role as subscription role gets inherited to underlying resources.

    D. You cannot assign a role to an individual resource when you give permissions at the subscription scope.

15. You are trying to deploy a virtual machine, and during the validation phase the deployment fails. You have Owner permission on the resource group to which you are trying to deploy the virtual machine. What could be the reason for this?

    A. You need to have the Virtual Machine Owner role to create virtual machines.

    B. Check the error message and verify if there are any policy restrictions.

    C. You need to have the Owner role at the subscription level.

    D. Contact the Global Administrator.

16. You are using Power BI dashboards to analyze your cloud spending. Which of the following out-of-the-box solutions can be leveraged? (Select two.)

A. Use the Azure Cost Management API or Cost Management connector

B. Use Exports to export to a storage account that can be used by Power BI

C. Copy the dashboard link from the Azure portal and add to Power BI

D. Share dashboards from Azure Cost Management to Power BI

17. If a user signs up for a subscription, what are the default roles assigned to the user? (Select two.)

A. Owner

B. Service Operator

C. Account Administrator

D. Service Administrator

18. Who can change the service administrator?

A. User Access Administrator

B. Service Administrator

C. Account Administrator

D. Owner

19. Which of the following can be used to optimize virtual machine cost? (Select two.)

A. Azure Reservations

B. Azure Container Instances

C. Azure Kubernetes Service

D. Azure Hybrid Benefit

20. Which section of the role definition can be used to define the set of data actions that are not permitted?

A. `DataActions`

B. `NullDataActions`

C. `NotAllowedDataActions`

D. `NotDataActions`

Chapter

3

Virtual Networking

MICROSOFT EXAM OBJECTIVES COVERED IN THIS CHAPTER:

✓ **Implement and manage virtual networking**

  ▪ **Create and configure virtual networks**

  ▪ **Configure private and public IP addresses**

  ▪ **Configure user defined routes**

  ▪ **Implement subnets**

  ▪ **Configure service endpoints on subnets**

  ▪ **Configure private endpoints**

  ▪ **Azure DNS**

✓ **Secure access to virtual networks**

  ▪ **Create security rules**

  ▪ **Network Security Groups**

  ▪ **Implement Azure Firewall**

Networking is the fundamental building block of cloud infrastructure. Once the workloads are migrated from on-premises to the cloud, organizations require the same networking functionality as they had on-premises. Some customers do not prefer to keep their workloads Internet facing as it a security threat; some workloads also need network isolation. Microsoft Azure offers a plethora of networking resources that can help you replicate the topologies you had on-premises.

Without proper networking, your servers cannot communicate with each other or with on-premises users, and servers cannot connect to the cloud. Also, if the network is not secured, you stand vulnerable to attacks. Therefore, as an administrator, you should be well versed with the networking concepts and how to implement networking technologies. In this chapter, we will focus on the networking concepts and techniques to secure your virtual network. In the upcoming chapters, we will cover how to implement a hybrid architecture and high availability using load balancing in Microsoft Azure.

Virtual Networks

Whenever you are implementing infrastructure, the first thing you should think about isn't virtual machine; it's the network. As mentioned earlier, the network is the fundamental building block that enables communication and requires the most planning. In Azure, virtual networks represent your own network in the cloud. Working with the Azure VNet service is similar to working with a traditional network in your on-premises; however, there are some additional benefits that virtual networks bring to the table. These benefits include scalability, availability, and network isolation.

With VNet, you can do the following:

- Establish a private connection between the Azure virtual machines and other Azure services

- Extend your on-premises architecture to the cloud for hybrid solutions

- Link with other virtual networks in the same region or different regions for private communication

- Enable virtual machines to connect with the Internet securely

Now that you have had a quick introduction to virtual networks, let's go ahead and learn about some concepts related to the Azure VNet service.

VNet Concepts

The following are the concepts related to the Azure VNet service.

Address Space

The term *address space* might not be new for administrators who handle on-premises networking. In on-premises, you manage address spaces with the CIDR block. The same concept appears in the cloud as well. In Azure, using public and private (RFC 1918) addresses, you must specify an address space for your virtual network whenever you create one. The IP address for your resources will be assigned from this address space. For example, if you deploy a VM to the virtual network with the address space 172.16.0.0/16, then Azure will assign an IP address from this address space to your VM, say 172.16.0.4.

Whenever you create a virtual network, you are required to have an address space associated to it. Also, it's a best practice that your address space doesn't overlap with other address spaces that you have in your organization. This could lead to a conflict when you are connecting the virtual networks to each other or when setting up hybrid connections.

Subnets

Another concept from traditional networking is a *subnet*. Using subnets, you create one or more subnetworks by segmenting your virtual network. Once the virtual network is segmented, then you can deploy resources to the specific subnet. Subnetting helps in segmenting addresses or different workloads and also enhances the address allocation efficiency. At the subnet level, you can configure network security groups (NSGs) to secure your workloads. We will discuss NSGs later in this chapter.

For example, you can create a virtual network with address space 172.16.0.0/16 and then segment the network to subnetworks like 172.16.0.0/24, 172.16.1.0/24, and so on. Then you could use the first subnet 172.16.0.0/24 for your frontend and use the second subnet 172.16.1.0/24 for your databases.

The CIDR block for the subnet is decided based on how many hosts or servers you want to deploy to the subnet. It's recommended that your subnets not cover the entire address space of the virtual network. You can plan ahead and reserve some IP addresses for your future use when your infrastructure is expanding.

Regions

In the Chapter 2, "Compliance and Cloud Governance," you learned what Azure regions are and what role they play in resource deployment and data residency. In the case of virtual networks, they are always scoped to a single region or location. Nevertheless, this doesn't stop you from connecting with other networks that are in other regions. You could implement solutions such as virtual network peering and VPN gateways to establish connectivity between virtual networks in different regions. In fact, you can establish communication with virtual networks that are part of different subscriptions. We will discuss peering and gateways in Chapter 4, "Intersite Connectivity."

When you create a virtual network in Azure, you will get an option to choose the region. Depending on the region you choose, the virtual network will be deployed to the respective region, and the virtual machines deployed to the virtual network will also fall under the same region. If you want to move a virtual network deployed in one region to another region, you need to use Azure Resource Mover feature.

Subscription

When we discussed concepts related to Azure Active Directory, you learned that an Azure subscription creates a billing boundary and a resource boundary. In the case of networking, a subscription acts like a home for the network. In a subscription, you can have multiple virtual networks scoped to different regions. This linkage to the subscription helps in billing the organization for different networking-related charges.

For example, if you have a virtual network with the name VNet-1, then the resource ID will be as follows:

```
/subscriptions/<subscriptionId>/resourcegroups/<resouceGroupName>/
providers/Microsoft.Network/virtualNetworks/VNet-1
```

Figure 3.1 shows how these concepts are related and how they fit into the bigger picture.

FIGURE 3.1   Understanding virtual networks

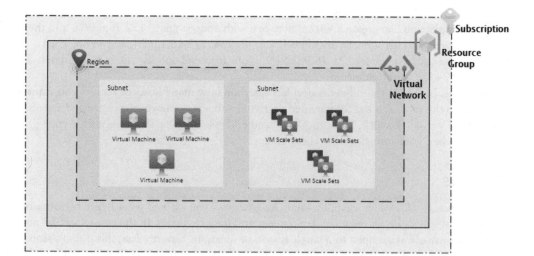

Now you will take a look at the IP addressing methods available in Azure.

IP Addressing

When you create a virtual network, an address space is required, and the resources you deploy to the virtual network will obtain the IP address from this address space. Resources will be using this IP address to communicate with the resources within the virtual network and other resources in Azure, on-premises, and the Internet. The communication is accomplished with the help of two types of IP addresses, namely, public IP addresses and private IP addresses. Before you learn about private and public IP addresses, let's understand the available allocation methods for these IP addresses.

Static and Dynamic Addressing

IP addresses can be assigned or allocated in two ways, statically or dynamically. In on-premises, we had a similar concept of fixed IP addresses for our resources; a static IP address is the same logic. With statically assigned IP addresses, the IP addresses do not change. If you don't opt for static allocation, the IP address will be dynamically allocated. Dynamic allocation does not reserve the IP address, and once your server is restarted, the IP address will be gone, and you will be assigned a new IP address. Having said that, you can use DNS labels to get a static addressing type of experience. While using DNS labels, Azure will make sure that even if the IP address changes, the DNS record will always point to the current IP address.

Though dynamic IP address allocation with DNS labels can help tackle changing IP addresses, static IP allocation is recommended for the following scenarios:

- Apps or services that require a static IP address for IP address–based security models

- TLS/SSL certificates linked to a specific IP address

- Firewalls that are using IP-based filtering rules

- Domain controllers or DNS servers

Understanding these allocation methods is particularly important for an administrator, as you should be able to decide which one is ideal for your workloads. Now let's learn about the difference between private and public IP addresses.

Private IP Addresses

Private IP addresses are used for facilitating private communications within your Azure resources and with on-premises resources if you are using a VPN or ExpressRoute connection. Private IP addresses can be associated with a network interface card (NIC) of the virtual machines, internal load balancers, and application gateways. We will cover load balancers and application gateways in Chapter 4. For the time being, understand that these are load balancing solutions used to maintain high availability.

Dynamic and static allocation is supported by Azure. When you create a virtual network, the address space you use denotes the private IP address space, and when you create a resource such as a VM, then a private IP address from the associated subnet is assigned to the resource. In the case of dynamic assignment, the next available IP address from the subnet range is assigned to the resource. This process is similar to the DHCP process you saw on-premises where IP addresses are allocated dynamically using a DHCP server. Dynamic assignment is the default method.

When it comes to static assignment, you can pick an IP address from the address range of the subnet and assign it to your resource. The point to note here is you should make sure that the IP address is not assigned to any other resource. Nevertheless, Azure will stop you from using an IP address already allocated to another resource.

In Exercise 3.1, you will see how you can create a virtual network using the Azure portal.

EXERCISE 3.1

Creating Virtual Networks

1. Sign in to the Azure portal and search for *Virtual Networks*.

2. Click the Create button to take you through the creation process.

3. In the first section, fill in these inputs:

   ▪ **Subscription:** Select your subscription.

   ▪ **Resource Group:** Select an existing resource group or create a new one.

   ▪ **Name:** Enter the virtual network name.

   ▪ **Region:** Your virtual network will be scoped to this region.

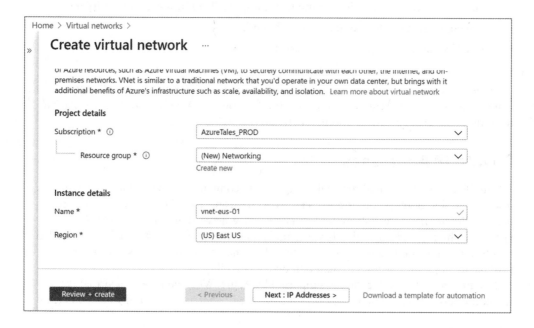

4. Click Next : IP Addresses >. This will take you to the section to define the address space and subnet.

5. By default, Azure will add an address space based on the virtual networks that you have in the region. You can remove this address space by clicking the trash icon, or you can add multiple address spaces to the virtual networks.

6. When it comes to subnets, Azure will add a subnet named *default* to the virtual network, and you can add more subnets or modify the default one as required.

Create virtual network ⋯

Basics   **IP Addresses**   Security   Tags   Review + create

The virtual network's address space, specified as one or more address prefixes in CIDR notation (e.g. 192.168.1.0/24).

IPv4 address space

10.1.0.0/16 10.1.0.0 - 10.1.255.255 (65536 addresses)	🗑
192.168.0.0/16	✓ 🗑

⚠ Address space '192.168.0.0/16 (192.168.0.0 - 192.168.255.255)' overlaps with address space '192.168.0.0/16 (192.168.0.0 - 192.168.255.255)' of virtual network 'server-1'. Virtual networks with overlapping address space cannot be peered. If you intend to peer these virtual networks, change address space '192.168.0.0/16 (192.168.0.0 - 192.168.255.255)'. Learn more ☐

☐ Add IPv6 address space ⓘ

The subnet's address range in CIDR notation (e.g. 192.168.1.0/24). It must be contained by the address space of the virtual network.

+ Add subnet   🗑 Remove subnet

☐ Subnet name	Subnet address range	NAT gateway
☐ default	10.1.0.0/24	-
☐ workload	192.168.1.0/24	-

---

7. Click Review + Create, and your request will be validated. Once the validation is passed, you can click Create to create the resource.

In Exercise 3.1, you created a virtual network with address spaces 10.1.0.0/16 and 192.168.0.0/16. You also added two subnets, 10.1.0.0/24 and 192.168.1.0/24. When you deploy a supported resource like a virtual machine, internal-facing load balancer, etc., you can select this virtual network and corresponding subnet. The resource will then obtain an IP address from the subnet address range. The addresses that are part of the virtual network and subnet are private IP addresses. Once they are assigned to a resource, you can specify whether you need a static assignment or dynamic assignment.

Virtual networks can be created from Azure PowerShell and the Azure CLI as well. Using the code in Exercise 3.2, you will be able to create a virtual network from Azure PowerShell.

EXERCISE 3.2

Creating Virtual Networks Using Azure PowerShell

1. Open your cloud shell or local shell. If you are using the local shell, make sure you are signed in to Azure.

2. The first step in the process is to create a virtual network using the New-AzVirtualNetwork command. You need to pass in the resource group name, location, name of the virtual network, and address space as parameters. We will be storing the output of this command to a variable so that you can use reuse it during the subnet creation. You can use appropriate values as per your environment.

   ```
   $vnet = New-AzVirtualNetwork -ResourceGroupName Networking -
   Name vnet-eus-02 -Location eastus -AddressPrefix 172.16.0.0/16
   ```

   You can verify if the virtual network is created using the Get-AzVirtualNetwork command along with the name of the virtual network.

   ```
   Get-AzVirtualNetwork -Name vnet-eus-02
   ```

3. The next step is to create a subnet. Use values as appropriate.

   ```
   $subnet = Add-AzVirtualNetworkSubnetConfig -Name subnet-01
   -AddressPrefix 172.16.1.0/24 -VirtualNetwork $vnet
   ```

4. Once the subnet is created, you can associate the subnet to the VNet using the following command:

   ```
   $subnet | Set-AzVirtualNetwork
   ```

5. If you run the Get-AzVirtualNetwork command again, then you will see that the subnet you created is associated to your newly created virtual network.

Let's take a quick glance at public IP addresses and understand where they are used.

Public IP Address

Public IP addresses are associated with a virtual machine NIC, public load balancer, VPN gateways, application gateways, and any other resource that can be accessed from the Internet. Here also we can choose the allocation method to be static or dynamic. However, the availability of allocation methods depends on which SKU of public IP address we are using. The SKU is more like a pricing tier, where you will find different prices based on which SKU you are selecting. Let's quickly compare the SKUs available for public IP addresses to understand the key differences. The available SKUs are Basic SKU and Standard SKU; Table 3.1 shows the differences between them. You can always upgrade from Basic SKU to Standard SKU.

TABLE 3.1   Understanding Public IP SKUs

Feature	Basic SKU	Standard SKU
IP assignment	Static or dynamic	Static
Security	Open by default	Closed to inbound traffic and secured by default
Resources supported	VM NIC, VPN gateways, application gateways, and public load balancers	VM NIC, application gateway, and public load balancer
Redundancy offered	Not zone redundant	Zone redundant

Now let's perform an exercise to create a public IP address; see Exercise 3.3.

EXERCISE 3.3

Creating Public IP Addresses

1. Sign in to the Azure portal and search for *Public IP addresses*. From the Public IP Addresses window, click Create.

2. Set IP Version to IPv4 or IPv6 or Both. Depending on which IP version you require, you can select that. Selecting Both would create both IPv4 and IPv6 addresses.

3. As you saw earlier, you can set the SKU to Basic or Standard depending on the requirements.

4. Set the tier to the regional tier.

5. Input the name of the public IP address. This will be a friendly name for you to identify the IP address.

6. Next is the assignment; you can choose Static or Dynamic. If the SKU is Standard, then the option will be grayed out as Standard SKU supports only Static IP.

7. You can also add a DNS label. This is an optional field; it is mostly used when the allocation is Dynamic.

8. You can leave the routing preference and idle timeout with the default values. The routing preference determines how your traffic routes between Azure and the Internet, and idle time out helps you configure the minutes to keep a TCP or HTTP connection open without relying on clients to send keep-alive messages.

9. Other than these fields, you need to select the subscription, resource group, and location for the public IP address. If you select Standard SKU, then you will get an option to choose the availability zone as well.

Home > Public IP addresses >

Create public IP address   ⋯   ✕

IP Version * ⓘ
◉ IPv4 ◯ IPv6 ◯ Both

SKU * ⓘ
◉ Standard ◯ Basic

Tier
◉ Regional ◯ Global

IPv4 IP Address Configuration

Name *
[   ]

IP address assignment
◯ Dynamic ◉ Static

Routing preference ⓘ
◉ Microsoft network ◯ Internet

Idle timeout (minutes) * ⓘ
◯── [4]

DNS name label ⓘ
[   ]
                                                                                    .eastus.cloudapp.azure.com

Subscription *

[**Create**]   Automation options

10. Once the appropriate values are selected, you can click Review + Create to validate
    the deployment. If the validation was successful, click Create to create the public
    IP address.

Once the public IP address is created, you can associate the IP address with any of the
supported resources. This IP address will be Internet facing, and users can access the associated service over the Internet using this IP address. Having a public IP address that is open to
the Internet leaves an attack vector and makes your workloads vulnerable. You need to use
network security groups to control the traffic inbound and outbound to our resources. In the
next section, we will cover network security groups and how they can be used to secure your
workloads in the cloud.

Network Routes

Network routes or route tables have existed in traditional networks for an exceptionally
long time. The routes that are part of the route table decide how to direct a packet to the
destination or, in other words, determine which is the next hop the resource should communicate to in order to reach the final destination. In Azure, we are using the same concept to direct network traffic between virtual machines, the Internet, and the on-premises
infrastructure.

There are two types of network routes in Azure: system routes and user-defined routes (UDR). Packets are always evaluated against these rules to route them to the destination. If there are no matching rules, then the packet is dropped. Let's learn about the types of network routes.

System Routes

Whenever we create a VM, the VM will be able to communicate with the Internet without setting up any routes. In AWS, we need to create different gateways like NAT Gateway or Internet Gateway to facilitate the connection from a VM to the Internet. However, in Azure this is enabled by default with the help of system routes.

The traffic between virtual machines, the Internet, and the on-premises infrastructure are routed using the system routes. Scenarios where system routes are used for packet routing include the following:

- When you deploy multiple VMs to the same subnet, the communication between these VMs is done using system routes.

- The communication between VMs in different subnets in the same virtual network.

- Access to the Internet from VMs.

- ExpressRoute and site-to-site connections via VPN gateway.

For example, if you have a virtual network named vnet-01 that has two subnets, frontend-subnet and database-subnet, you will have a web server deployed to frontend-subnet and a database deployed to database-subnet. The server in frontend-subnet will be able to communicate with the database in database-subnet without setting up any rules or gateways. This communication is facilitated by the system routes. Also, the servers will be able to talk to the Internet to download the system updates or to check the Internet time without setting up any gateways. This communication is also achieved by using system routes. One thing to note here is the communication from the Internet to the servers is always blocked using the network security groups.

The system routes are stored in a routing table and with the help of these routes the traffic can be routed with the virtual networks, the Internet, and the on-premises infrastructure. Users can always override these rules and stop any of the communications that come as part of the system route. Let's understand how users can override these and come up with custom routes.

User-Defined Routes

Using system routes, Azure automatically handles all packet routing. As mentioned earlier, users can always override these routes using user-defined routes (UDRs). To give an example of routing, assume we have three subnets inside a virtual network. The subnets are the public subnet, DMZ subnet, and private subnet. In the DMZ subnet, assume that we have a network virtual appliance (NVA). NVAs are VMs that can optimize our networks with routing and firewall capabilities. Our goal is to make sure that all traffic coming from the public subnet should be routed to the NVA before it gets routed to the private subnet. The reason for this is that a public subnet contains workloads that are Internet facing, and a private subnet contains workloads that are not exposed to the Internet, such as databases, application logic, backend servers, etc. By default, the communication from the public subnet is allowed to the private subnet; however, we need to make sure that the traffic is filtered before it reaches the private subnet. This will help us to protect the private workloads, as all traffic is matched against the rules that you have set up in the NVA. If there is any attack or malicious traffic, NVA will take care of it. Now, the question is, how can we implement this? As you can see in Figure 3.2, we have used the routing table with UDR to accomplish this task. By default, the traffic from the public subnet to the private subnet is allowed, but using UDR, you are forcing the packets to go through the NVA.

FIGURE 3.2   Routing architecture

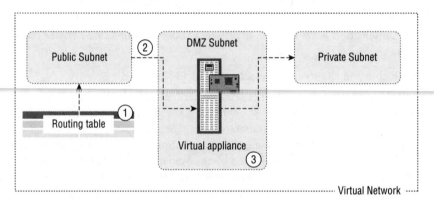

UDR will help you create custom routes, and you can specify which is the next hop for the packet. In the previous example, the next hop was NVA. The hop can be a virtual network, VPN gateway, virtual appliance, or the Internet. You can associate the same route table to multiple subnets; however, a subnet can be associated to a single route table at a time. Creating route tables will not incur any charges, and these are free of cost.

The following are the steps to force the traffic to route through the NVA:

1. Create a routing table.

2. By adding a custom route, you can direct the traffic from a public subnet to the NVA.

3. Finally, associate the route table to the subnet.

Let's perform a hands-on exercise to understand how these steps can be performed on the portal. You will create a routing table, add a custom route, and finally associate the route table to the subnet. See Exercise 3.4.

EXERCISE 3.4

Creating a Route Table

1. Sign in to the Azure portal and create a virtual network with the address space 172.17.0.0/16. You can review Exercise 3.1 for instructions on how to create a virtual network. The virtual network will have three subnets: public (172.17.1.0/24), DMZ (172.17.2.0/28), and private (172.17.3.0/24).

2. The next action is to create a routing table, and the process is straightforward. Search for *route tables* in the Azure portal, and click Create. You have to provide a name for the routing table and select a subscription, a resource group, and the location.

3. You can also decide if you want to use virtual network gateway route propagation by enabling Propagate Gateway Routes. The routes from on-premises are added to the route table automatically for all subnet network interfaces with virtual network gateway route propagation enabled.

4. Clicking Review + Create will submit the template and create the route table.

Now that you have created the route table, you need to add the route. The routing table is a collection of routes. As mentioned earlier, each route will be evaluated before directing a packet. If no matching routes or rules are found, then the packet is dropped. In Exercise 3.5, you will create a UDR by which the packets are routed via NVA in a DMZ subnet to the private subnet.

EXERCISE 3.5

Creating a Custom Route

1. Sign in to the Azure portal and search for *route tables*. In the list of route tables, you will be able to see the route table that you created in Exercise 3.4. Click the route table name.

2. Click Routes under Settings and then click Add to add a new route.

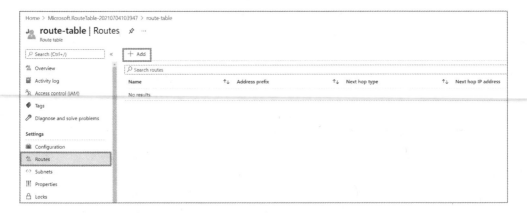

3. Now you need to add the route details. You need to add the name to the route. Since you are creating this route to send traffic to a private subnet via NVA, you should give it a meaningful name like "ToPrivateSubnet".

4. The address prefix should be the address space of the private subnet. This is the destination IP address range where the route applies. In our case, the value is 172.17.3.0/24.

5. The next hop type is going to be virtual appliance as you need to route via NVA. Once you select the virtual appliance, you will be asked to input the IP address of the NVA. Since you haven't deployed any NVA, you can give an IP address that's in the address range of the DMZ subnet. We picked the DMZ subnet because that's where our NVA is deployed. Let's assume the IP address of NVA is 172.17.2.4 and provide it in the Next Hop Address box.

6. If you have followed the instructions correctly, then your route configuration will be similar to the following graphic.

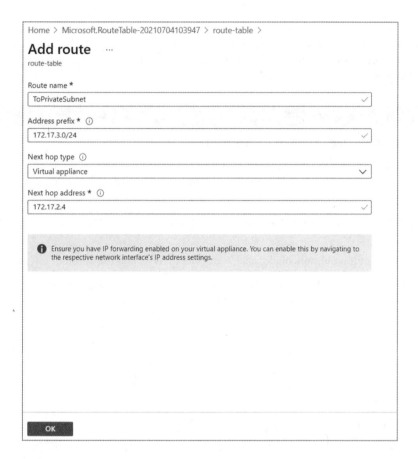

7. After confirming the details, you can click OK, and the route will be added to the Routes blade of the routing table.

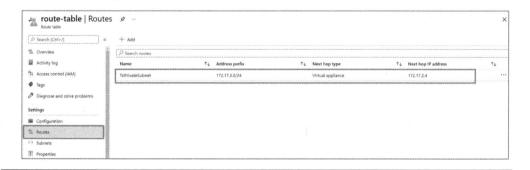

In short, this route will be applied to the private subnet with the address range 172.17.3.0/24, and all traffic heading to any addresses within the address range will be sent to the next hop IP address, which is the IP address of the NVA. The last step in our action plan is to associate the public subnet with the routing table we created. As we already discussed, routing tables can be reused because we associate with multiple subnets; however, each subnet can be associated to zero or one route table at a time. In Exercise 3.6, you will associate the routing table to the public subnet.

EXERCISE 3.6

Associating a Routing Table to a Subnet

1. Sign in to the Azure portal and search for *route tables*. In the list of route tables, you will be able to see the route table that you created in Exercise 3.4. Click the route table name.

2. Navigate to Subnets, which is right below the Routes blade that you used in Exercise 3.5.

3. Once you are in the Subnets blade, click Associate to associate the subnet.

4. As shown here, you will be able to associate the subnet by selecting the virtual network and the corresponding subnet. Click OK to confirm the association.

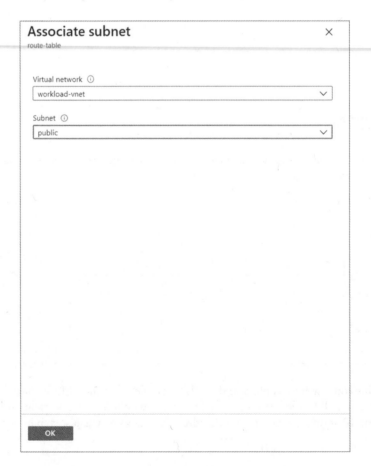

5. You will be able to see the subnet added to the Subnet blade. Also, if you navigate to the Overview blade, you will be able to see both the route and subnet listed.

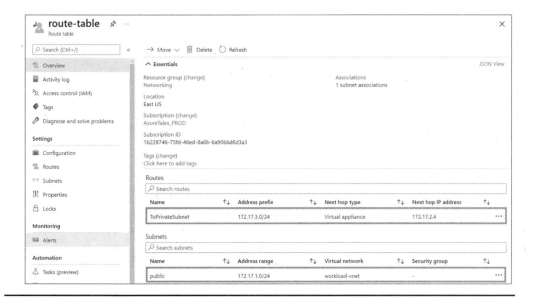

With that we have accomplished our mission. If you take a closer look at the graphic from Exercise 3.5, step 6, you can see there is a banner. As the banner says, you need to enable IP forwarding on the NVA to forward the traffic to the destination. Since you haven't created the NVA, you don't have to worry about this. However, in a real-world implementation of this scenario, you need to ensure that IP forwarding is enabled.

As you saw in the case of other services, Azure PowerShell and the CLI can also be used to manage and configure routes. If required, you can implement the steps using PowerShell or CLI. On that note, we will move on to the next topic, which is service endpoints.

Service Endpoints

The identity of a virtual network can be provided to the Azure service by using service endpoints. Many services support virtual network access, and with the service endpoint enabled, you can access these services in a secure manner. The communication from your virtual network to the Azure service is done via the Microsoft backbone network. For example, you can have a virtual machine deployed to a virtual network, and you can also have a storage account. On the storage account firewall, you need to allow the communication from the virtual network that the VM belongs to. Using a service endpoint, the VM will be able to communicate with the storage service securely using its private IP address as the source IP address, as shown in Figure 3.3.

FIGURE 3.3   Understanding service endpoints

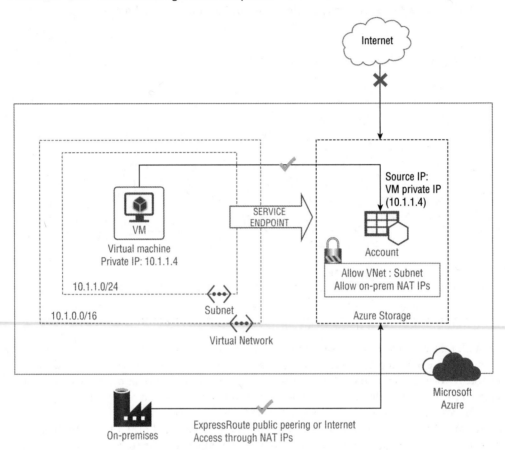

Sometimes your virtual network address spaces might be overlapping, and it's difficult to identify the traffic just based on the IP addresses. Chances are that the traffic is originating from a virtual network that has the same address space as of the virtual network that is supposed to access the service. The service endpoint mitigates this issue by creating an identity for your virtual network and sharing it with the Azure services. All you need to do is to add a virtual network security rule, and your resources will stay secured. This rule completely eliminates the public Internet access to the resources where service endpoints are added and allows only traffic originated from the virtual network. The key point here is that service endpoints can be used for secure communications only from the Azure virtual network; on-premises to Azure services is not supported.

Supported Services

Adding a service endpoint to a virtual network is an effortless process and several services including Azure Cosmos DB, KeyVault, Service Bus, SQL, Storage Accounts, and Azure Active Directory are supported. Let's understand the list of supported services.

- **Azure Storage:** This is supported in all Azure regions and is generally available. Using this endpoint, you can establish an optimal route to the Azure Storage service. You can associate up to 100 virtual network rules to each storage account.

- **Azure SQL Database and Azure Synapse Analytics (formerly Azure Data Warehouse):** Service endpoints can be used to communicate with the databases in Azure SQL Database or databases in Azure SQL Data Warehouse in a secure manner. These endpoints are added to the firewall of the database to enable access from the subnets. This is generally available in all Azure regions.

- **Azure Database for PostgreSQL and MySQL servers:** This enables you to communicate from your virtual network to PostgreSQL and MySQL servers deployed in Azure. Generally this is available in all Azure regions.

- **Azure Cosmos DB:** Using service endpoints, you can let the resources deployed in your virtual network communicate with the Cosmos DB. This is supported in all Azure regions.

- **Azure Key Vault:** This is available in all Azure regions. By enabling service endpoints, you can limit the communication to the key vault. Only requests from the allowed subnets are permitted to access the key vault; the rest of the requests will be denied.

- **Azure Service Bus and Event Hubs:** Service endpoints for Service Bus and Event Hub facilitates secure access to messaging capabilities from workloads such as virtual machines that are deployed in the virtual network.

 It may take up to 15 minutes for the service endpoints to come up after adding them to a service. Each service has its own documentation page stating the steps for enabling service endpoints.

When you are using service endpoints, the traffic will still hit the supported services on their public endpoints, and the source of the traffic will be a private IP from the virtual network. If you would like to access these services using their private IP addresses, then you should consider using a private link. In the next section, we will cover private links.

Private Endpoint

By implementing private endpoints, Azure PaaS services will get a private IP address on your virtual network. As the service is assigned with a private IP address, whenever you send traffic to a PaaS resource, the traffic always stays within your virtual network. Private endpoints can be used to connect Azure PaaS using a private link. A private link is a global service and has no regional restrictions. Figure 3.4 shows a classic example of using a private link where the VM is trying to access the database via a private connection.

FIGURE 3.4 Understanding a private link

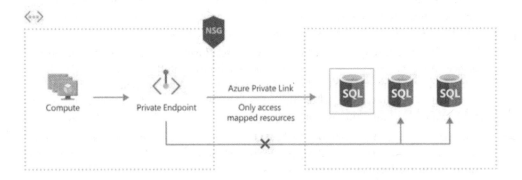

In the case of both service endpoints and private endpoints, you are restricting the connections to our services only from the resources in our virtual network. Also, the traffic between your service and the virtual network is always transmitted via the Microsoft backbone network. There is no need for the packets to go over the Internet.

The following are the features offered by a private link:

- **Private connectivity:** You can connect to resources over a Microsoft network that are deployed in different Azure regions. As no public Internet is involved in these connections, a complete private connectivity is established.

- **Hybrid connections and peered networks:** You can access the resources that are connected via private links from on-premises infrastructure via VPN or ExpressRoute connections. If the resources are deployed in cloud, you can use peered networks as well. As the network is hosted by Microsoft, you don't need to set up public peering or Internet gateways. This is not possible in the case of service endpoints.

- **Enhances security:** The access is limited to only selected resources and eliminates a data exfiltration threat.

- **Seamless integration:** Since the PaaS resources get an IP address from the virtual network, the connectivity will be seamless and with low latency.

Private links can be created from the private link center. The private link center gives a centralized place to manage your private connections and endpoints. The private link center can be accessed from the Azure portal by searching for *private link* (see Figure 3.5).

With that, we will move on to the next topic, Azure DNS.

FIGURE 3.5   Accessing a private link center

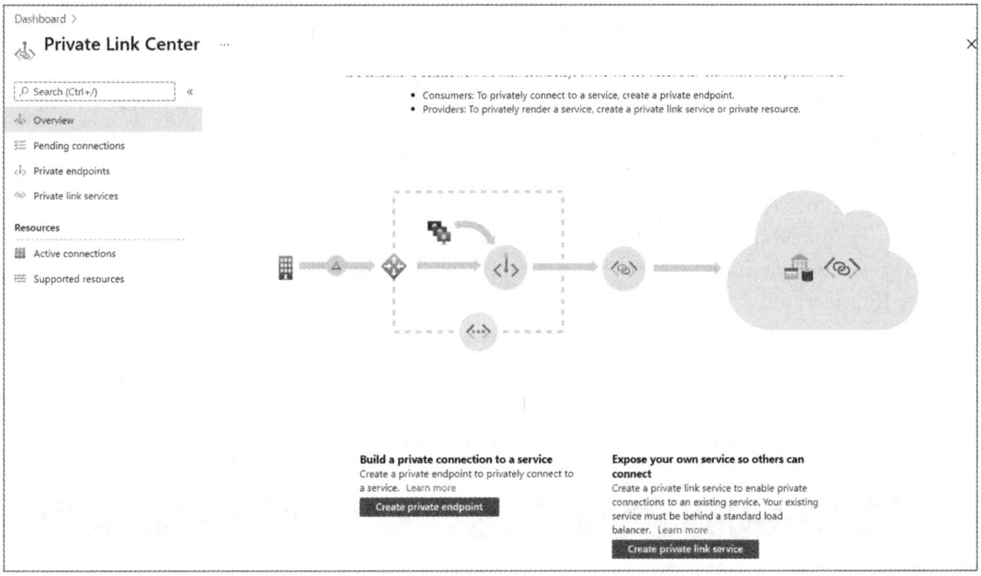

Azure DNS

We are familiar with the DNS servers that we used to administer on-premises. Some organizations used Windows Server as the server for hosting DNS zones, while others used BIND-based solutions. There are other third party-solutions that are used to manage DNS zones and records. In Azure, Azure DNS is used to host DNS zones for providing name resolution. By using Azure DNS, we will be able to manage zone and records in the same way we used to do in on-premises; however, the only difference is that everything is managed from the Azure portal. You don't have to navigate to any servers to manage your zones; all your zones are available in the Azure portal for you to manage.

Using Azure DNS, you cannot buy domains; if you would like to purchase domains, you can use App Service Domains or purchase them from any domain registrar. Once the domain is purchased, you can delegate the purchased domain to Azure, and the records can be managed from the Azure portal. Let's take a look at the benefits of using Azure DNS:

- **Reliability and performance**: Whenever you make a DNS query, the resolution is done by the nearest DNS server as Azure DNS uses anycast networking. Since the request is served by the closest server, the latency is incredibly low and thus ensures higher performance. Also, the domains are hosted in the global network of DNS server. If one server is not responding, the request will be served by another server ensuring reliability.

- **Security**: You can use RBAC, locks, and activity logs to control access, stop accidental deletion or modification, and track changes that happen to DNS zones.

- **Ease of use:** Azure DNS is a one-stop solution for managing DNS records of your Azure services and also for your external resources. As the integration is done to the Azure portal, the management of the zones and records is easy.

- **Private domains:** Azure DNS supports private domains that can be used for name resolution of your virtual network resources using your own custom domain rather than using the DNS names provided by Azure.

- **Alias records:** Another notable feature is the support of alias records. Alias records can be created for referencing resources such as Azure CDN, Azure public IP addresses, or Azure Traffic Manager profiles. The advantage here is that even if the public IP address changes, Azure will make sure that the DNS records are automatically updated with the new IP addresses.

In Exercise 3.7, you will see how you can create a DNS zone in Azure. Creating a DNS zone in Azure will let administrators manage the DNS records. You will be provided with a set of name servers that can be used by your clients for performing the name resolution. Let's see how you can create a DNS zone from the Azure portal.

EXERCISE 3.7

Creating an Azure DNS Zone

1. Sign in to the Azure portal and search for *DNS zones* and click DNS Zones. You will also get a private DNS zone, which is another topic altogether. For this demonstration, you need DNS zones.

2. Click Create, and the Azure portal will take you through the create wizard.

3. To create a zone, you need to provide the subscription name, resource group, name of the zone, and location of the resource group. The location gets automatically selected based on the resource group you select and doesn't allow you to modify the location. If the Create New resource group is selected, it will prompt you to select a location. Additionally, there will be an option that says "This zone is a child of an existing zone already hosted in Azure DNS." This option is used if you have a parent zone in Azure DNS and would like to add a child domain. In our case, this is our first domain, so there is no need to check this box.

4. Once you are done, click Review + Create to start the validation. After validation, click Create to create the zone.

5. Navigate back to DNS zones once the zone is created. Click the zone name to display the records and name servers.

Record Management

Azure DNS supports all common DNS record types including A, AAAA, MX, CAA, CNAME, PTR, SOA, SRV, and TXT records. You are familiar with these records as they are used in traditional DNS servers as well. The categorization is done based on the data stored on each of these records. For example, A records map a name to an IPv4 address, and AAAA records map a name to an IPv6 address. Similarly, each of the record types has its own use-case scenarios.

Record sets are also supported in Azure; these are useful in cases where you would like to create more than one DNS record in a single shot referencing a given name and type. For instance, say you have two web servers with IPv4 addresses 137.12.11.1 and 137.12.11.2. You would like to map both of these IP addresses to the A record www.mydomain.com. In this case, you don't have to create two DNS records; instead, you can create a DNS record set with the name as www under the zone mydomain.com and add both IP addresses to the same set. Using this all related IP addresses/aliases can be managed under a single record, and this offers ease of management for administrators.

While creating records, you can also specify the time-to-live (TTL). This value specifies how long the clients can cache this record before contacting the DNS server again for resolving the query. By default, this value is set to 3600 seconds or 1 hour. Since we are using records set, the TTL is set for the entire record, not for individual records. The value for TTL can be from 1 second to 2,147,483,647 seconds.

Wildcard records are also supported by Azure DNS. As we used to add wildcard using *
in on-premises, we can add wildcards by setting the record name as *. You can also use wildcards as a leftmost label, say *.foo. All records matching this expression will be returned by
the name servers.

Next, in Exercise 3.8, you are going to add records to the zone you have created.

Adding Records to an Azure DNS Zone

1. Sign in to the Azure portal and search for *DNS zones* and click DNS Zones. Select the
    DNS zone you created in Exercise 3.7.

2. Click + Record Set to add a record set. You need to provide the name, type, TTL, and
    value for the record set. In this demonstration, you are creating an A record, and you
    can provide the values shown here.

3. After the record is added, it will be available in the records list.

4. Now you can open the nslookup utility if you are using a Windows computer or the
    dig utility if you are using a Mac/Linux computer to query the record. You need to
    copy the name of any name server and run the queries pointing to that name server to
    obtain results. In the graphic shown here, the dig utility is used to query the record,
    and we got the response as 1.1.1.1 as we saved in our DNS zone. The syntax for dig is
    dig @nameserver <record> <record-type>.

```
⟦  riskaria dig @ns1-04.azure-dns.com. www.myzoneinazure.com

; <<>> DiG 9.11.3-1ubuntu1.11-Ubuntu <<>> @ns1-04.azure-dns.com. www.myzoneinazure.com
; (2 servers found)
;; global options: +cmd
;; Got answer:
;; ->>HEADER<<- opcode: QUERY, status: NOERROR, id: 14976
;; flags: qr aa rd; QUERY: 1, ANSWER: 1, AUTHORITY: 0, ADDITIONAL: 1
;; WARNING: recursion requested but not available

;; OPT PSEUDOSECTION:
; EDNS: version: 0, flags:; udp: 1232
;; QUESTION SECTION:
;www.myzoneinazure.com.          IN      A

;; ANSWER SECTION:
www.myzoneinazure.com. 3600     IN      A       1.1.1.1

;; Query time: 123 msec
;; SERVER: 40.90.4.4#53(40.90.4.4)
;; WHEN: Thu Jul 08 11:43:14 IST 2021
;; MSG SIZE  rcvd: 66
```

From this activity, you learned how to use Azure DNS zones to host our zones and add records. These records will be available if you point the query to one of the name servers of the zone. This process is equivalent to you creating a DNS zone in a Linux or Windows server and querying the server to resolve the record. While we were searching for DNS zones in the Azure portal, we saw there is another option called *private DNS zones*. Let's see what private DNS zones is.

Private DNS Zones

As mentioned earlier, Azure DNS can be used to provide name resolution using the Microsoft infrastructure. In Exercise 3.7 and Exercise 3.8, you created a zone and added records for query validation. The zone we hosted in that exercise is an Internet-facing DNS zone because we were able to query the zone from our local computer and resolve the names by pointing to one of the Azure name servers. Azure DNS also supports private zones, which will help in providing DNS service to your virtual network.

Using Azure Private DNS, the resources in your virtual network will be able to use the DNS service for name resolution. By default, Azure makes dynamic DNS updates to a zone that is provided by Azure. However, using a custom domain in lieu of an Azure-provided domain will simplify the DNS names and design the record names as per your organizational standards. Azure private zones can be used by virtual machines deployed in the virtual network as well as by the connected networks. In Exercise 3.9, we will create a private DNS zone and understand how we can link a virtual network to the zone.

EXERCISE 3.9

Creating a Private DNS Zone and Validating Resolution

1. Sign in to the Azure portal and search for *DNS Zones* and click Private DNS Zones.

2. The creation parameters are the same as the public domain that you created earlier. You need to fill in the subscription, resource group, name of the domain, and location of the resource group (if you are creating a new resource group). Refer to the graphic shown here to view the parameters.

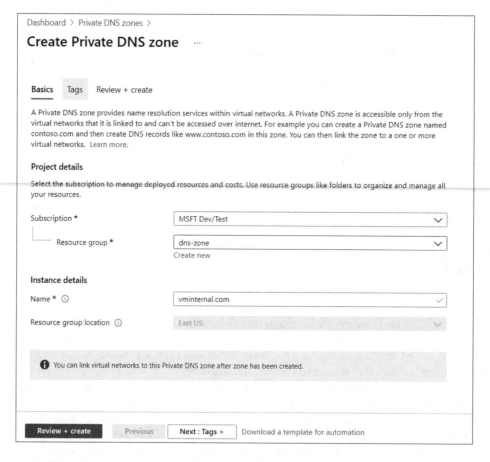

3. Once you have filled in the parameters, click Review + Create to start the validation. After validation, click Create to create the zone.

4. Now you need a VM and virtual network to test the DNS resolution. To speed up the process, let's use Azure PowerShell from the cloud shell to create the virtual network and virtual machine. You can use the same commands from Exercise 3.2.

5. Once you have created the virtual network and subnet following the steps mentioned in Exercise 3.2, let's create a VM using the following command in the Azure cloud shell (use a resource group name and VM name as per your environment).

```
New-AzVM -ResourceGroupName dns-zone `
-Name vm-01 -Location 'East US' `
-VirtualNetworkName vnet-eus -SubnetName subnet-01 `
-Image UbuntuLTS -Credential (Get-Credential)
```

6. You will be asked to provide the username and password for the VM; once that is shared, your VM will be deployed. Note the public IP address returned by the shell; we will use this later to connect to the VM.

7. Now it's time to link the virtual network to the DNS zone you created in step 2. Navigate to Private DNS Zones and click the zone you created.

8. Navigate to Virtual Network Links and click Add.

9. To create a link, you need to provide the name of the link and select the virtual network to which you want to create the link. There is also an option for enabling autoregistration. Enabling this will help in Dynamic DNS updates whenever virtual machines are connected to the network. There is another option called I Know The Resource ID Of The Virtual Network. If you have the resource ID of the virtual network, then you can directly specify that instead of specifying the virtual network. For now, we will go with the default option and select the virtual network manually. Once you have filled in the information, click OK to create the link.

EXERCISE 3.9 *(continued)*

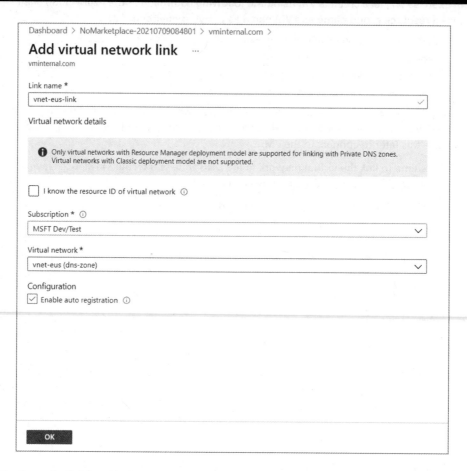

10. Once the link is added, you will be able to see it in the list of virtual networks that are linked. You need to click the Refresh button next to the Add button and make sure that the link status is completed before you perform the next step.

11. Navigate to the Overview blade of the private DNS zone, and you will be able to see that an A record for the VM created is added to the zone. Create another A record, say with a value of *backend* and an IP address of 1.1.1.1. You can provide any value and IP address, as this is for testing only. Adding a record set is the same process outlined in Exercise 3.8.

12. Once the record is added, navigate to the cloud shell and SSH to the VM using the command ssh username@IP. You need to replace the username with the username that you provided during the VM creation and replace the IP address with the public IP address of the VM that we noted earlier.

13. After logging in to the VM, try `ping backend.vminternal.com` where `vminter-nal.com` is the private DNS zone you created and `backend` is the A record.

14. You can see that the name is resolved to the IP address and the ping is working.

```
PowerShell ∨   ⏻  ?  ⚙  ⎘  ⎘  {}  ⎘
rithin@vm-01:~$ ping backend.vminternal.com
PING backend.vminternal.com (1.1.1.1) 56(84) bytes of data.
64 bytes from one.one.one.one (1.1.1.1): icmp_seq=1 ttl=53 time=1.10 ms
64 bytes from one.one.one.one (1.1.1.1): icmp_seq=2 ttl=53 time=0.978 ms
64 bytes from one.one.one.one (1.1.1.1): icmp_seq=3 ttl=53 time=1.23 ms
64 bytes from one.one.one.one (1.1.1.1): icmp_seq=4 ttl=53 time=1.24 ms
64 bytes from one.one.one.one (1.1.1.1): icmp_seq=5 ttl=53 time=1.24 ms
64 bytes from one.one.one.one (1.1.1.1): icmp_seq=6 ttl=53 time=1.10 ms
^C
--- backend.vminternal.com ping statistics ---
6 packets transmitted, 6 received, 0% packet loss, time 5007ms
rtt min/avg/max/mdev = 0.978/1.151/1.247/0.102 ms
```

This proves that the virtual network link added to the private zone is working and the virtual machine is using the private DNS zone for name resolution. You can create another VM in the same virtual network, and the record will get automatically registered to the zone. You can link multiple virtual networks to the same private zone and have all of them resolved by the private zone.

With that we have completed the topic of Azure DNS. The main takeaway is to understand how the Internet-facing zones are working and how the private zones work. On that note, we will move on to network security groups.

Network Security Groups

In quite simple terms, *network security groups* are a functionality in Azure used to filter and limit inbound and outbound traffic; in other words, they are similar to firewalls. An NSG is a collection of security rules that can be used to allow or deny inbound or outbound traffic. NSGs play a vital role in protecting VMs and other workloads that are deployed to a virtual network. Though we haven't covered virtual machines yet, it's good to have an understanding of NSG before we start talking about VMs. Each VM uses its network interface for communication with the resources in Azure, on-premises, and on the Internet. NSGs can be associated with a subnet, or a network interface based on your requirement. NSGs are reusable, which means you can have multiple NICs or subnet associations to a single NSG. NSGs operate at layer 4 of the OSI model.

NSG Concepts

Before we create an NSG, it's important to understand the concepts related to NSG. As mentioned earlier, NSGs can be associated with subnets or NICs; let's understand the purpose of these assignments and other concepts.

Subnets

Protected screened subnets can be created by assigning an NSG to subnets. You can protect all the workloads in a subnet by associating NSGs. Once you associate them, all traffic will be evaluated based on the rules you have added to the NSG. You can associate zero or one network security group to each subnet.

Network Interfaces

You can associate an NSG with the NIC of the virtual machine. All traffic that flows through the NIC will be evaluated based on the NSG rules. If you have an NSG associated with both subnet and NIC, then you will follow the effective NSG rules. We will cover the effective NSG rules in the next section. Each NIC can have zero or one NSG associated to it. When you create a VM, the NSG is automatically created with it and associated with the NIC, unless you specify another NSG.

NSG Rules

An NSG is a collection of security groups that can be used to filter inbound and outbound traffic of subnets and NIC. Whenever you create an NSG, there will be some default rules added by Azure to facilitate the virtual network traffic and load balancer traffic. Rules can be created by specifying the following parameters:

- **Name:** This is a friendly name given to the rule to identify the rule, which is unique.

- **Priority:** Priorities can be used to prioritize rules, and the value can be between 100 and 4096. The lower the value, the higher the priority. If you have a deny rule with priority 100 and an allow rule with priority 110, the deny action will be executed. This priority range doesn't apply for the default rules, and it gets automatically applied by Azure. Also, it's not possible to create two rules with the same priority.

- **Port:** Specify port numbers or a range of ports for both the source and the destination.

- **Protocol:** This can be Any, ICMP, TCP, and UDP.

- **Source:** This can be Any, IP addresses, application security groups, or service tag (a set of IP addresses maintained by Azure representing Azure services).

- **Destination:** This can be Any, IP addresses, or service tag (a set of IP addresses maintained by Azure representing Azure services).

- **Action:** This is to allow or deny traffic.

The rules are evaluated based on the priority value you assign to the rule. The lower the value, the higher the priority. For example, if you have a deny rule with a priority of 200 and an allow rule with priority 300, the deny rule will take effect as the lower value takes higher priority. There are two types of rules.

- **Inbound rules:** By default, there will be three inbound security rules (allow virtual network traffic, allow load balancer traffic, deny all other traffic) added to an NSG when you create NSG. All inbound traffic except the traffic from virtual network and Azure load balancer is not allowed. If you need to allow additional traffic, you need to add a respective rule. For example, if you are connecting to a Linux machine, you need to add an inbound rule to allow traffic on TCP port 22.

- **Outbound rules:** By default, there will be three rules: allow outbound traffic to the Internet and virtual network and deny all other traffic.

You will see how these rules can be implemented when you perform Exercise 3.10.

Associations

Once you create an NSG, from the Overview blade, you will be able to see the associations made to the NSG. Associations include subnet, NIC, and security rules. After creating the NSG, you will add rules that will be associated with the NSG. See Exercise 3.10.

EXERCISE 3.10

Creating NSG and NSG Rules

1. Sign in to the Azure portal and search for *Network Security Groups.* Once you are in Network Security Groups, click Create.

2. To create an NSG, you need the subscription name, resource group, name of the NSG, and region.

EXERCISE 3.10 *(continued)*

3. Once you have filled in the parameters, click Review + Create to start the validation. After validation, click Create to create the NSG.

4. After creating the NSG, navigate to the NSG you created. The Overview blade will show the associations and the rules (both inbound and outbound).

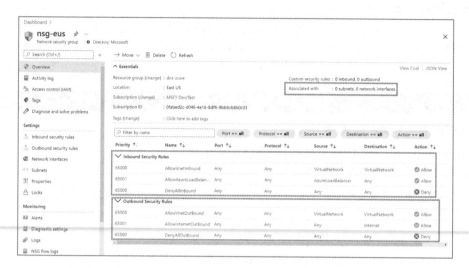

5. Click Inbound Security Rules and then Add to add a rule. As shown, you can add a rule by specifying the source, destination, port, protocol, action, priority, and name of the rule.

6. Similarly, you can create outbound security rules by navigating to the Outbound Security Rules blade.

7. Once the NSG rules are created, you can navigate to the Subnet or Network Interfaces blade to your associated NSG.

Now that you know how to create an NSG, add rules, and associate the NSG with subnets or NICs, you will look at the concept of effective rules.

NSG Effective Rules

If you are using NSGs at both the subnet and NIC level, the rules will be evaluated at both levels. For the traffic to be allowed, there should be an allow rule created at both the subnet and NIC levels. If any level doesn't have an allow rule, the traffic will be dropped. When you assign an NSG to a subnet, the rules will get applied to all NICs that are part of the subnet. You can override this inheritance and have a dedicated rule assigned to a NIC. When you apply NSG to both subnet and NIC, then effective rules come into the picture.

As mentioned earlier, each security rule will be evaluated independently when the NSG is applied to both the subnet and NIC levels. Incoming traffic will be first evaluated against the rules applied on the subnet level; if there is an allow rule, then the packet will be sent to the NIC. The rules set at the NIC level will be evaluated now, and only if there is an allow rule then the packet is allowed; otherwise, it will be dropped. Similarly, all outgoing traffic will be first evaluated against the NIC rules; if there is an allow rule, then the traffic is evaluated at the subnet level.

Having the ability to apply a rules subnet and NIC level reduces administrative overhead; rules at the subnet level can be always overridden by applying another set of rules at the NIC level.

Azure Firewall

Azure Firewall is a firewall-as-a-service offering from Microsoft Azure. It is a managed, cloud-based security solution that protects the workloads we have deployed in Azure virtual networks. Azure Firewall offers built-in high availability and scalability. Using Azure Firewall, we can create, enforce, and manage network policies across virtual networks and subscriptions. You might wonder why you need Azure Firewall when you have network security groups. The main difference is that NSG operates at layers 3 and 4 of the OSI layer; on the other hand, Azure Firewall works at layers 7 and 4. NSG is more of a traditional firewall, while Azure Firewall offers several features other than NSG.

Azure Firewall requires a dedicated subnet in your virtual network named Azure Firewall to deploy the firewall. A static public IP address will be assigned to the firewall, and all traffic will be routed via the firewall after evaluating the enforced rules. The Azure Firewall service is completely integrated with the Azure Monitor, which can be used for auditing, logging, and analytics.

The following are the features of Azure Firewall:

- **High-availability**: Azure Firewall provides built-in high availability, which means you don't have to deploy any additional infrastructure to the main high availability.

- **Zone redundant**: During deployment, you can span the firewall across availability zones to make the solution zone redundant.

- **Scalability**: Based on the traffic, Azure Firewall will scale in an unrestricted manner. This means you don't have to set up any scaling solutions.

- **Filtering rules**: Rules can be created or enforced based on FQDN and network parameters such as source IP address, destination IP address, protocol, and port.

- **Threat intelligence**: Traffic from/to malicious domains/IP addresses will be blocked by the firewall using threat intelligence. Threat intelligence feeds are managed by Microsoft.

- **Multiple public IP addresses**: Up to 100 public IP addresses can be associated with the Azure Firewall.

In the aforementioned list, you can see that Azure Firewall supports FQDN-based and IP-based filtering rules. Now, let's take a closer look at the different set of rules available in Azure Firewall for filtering the network traffic.

Azure Firewall Rules

In traditional firewalls that we had on-premises, we used to define rules for controlling the incoming and outgoing traffic from our infrastructure. Similarly, in Azure Firewall, we are using rules to filter and control the flow of traffic. Basically, there are three types of rules that you can set up in Azure Firewall. The default action set on the firewall is to block all the traffic, so if you have not created any rules, the firewall will block all incoming traffic. Let's explore the types of rules you can configure on the firewall.

NAT Rules

NAT rules are used to configure destination network address translation (DNAT) for translating and filtering the inbound traffic coming to our subnets. Using a NAT rule collection, you will be able to translate a public IP and port to a private IP and port. This is quite useful in publishing remote access protocols like SSH and RDP to the Internet.

To give an example, assume you have a Linux server with private IP address, say, 10.0.0.4, and the SSH server is available on port 22. Instead of exposing this port and IP to the Internet, you can create a NAT rule on the firewall. Using the public IP of the firewall and a random port, you can set up a NAT rule. Let's assume that the public IP address of the firewall is 52.172.11.16; using NAT rule you can redirect all traffic hitting port 5000 of the firewall to be translated to 10.0.0.4 and port 22. In short, translate 52.172.11.16:5000 to 10.0.0.4:22. In this way, you can translate the public IP address and port to a private IP address and port.

The configuration of a NAT rule will require the following parameters:

- **Name:** Unique name given to identify the rule.
- **Protocol:** TCP or UDP.
- **Source address:** To define the source of the traffic. It can be Internet, IP CIDR blocks, or specific IP addresses.
- **Destination address:** External IP address of the firewall you want to inspect for traffic.
- **Destination ports:** The port on which the rule will listen.
- **Translated address:** This is going to be the IP address of the service such as a virtual machine, load balancer, etc.
- **Translated port:** The port to which firewall routes the traffic after translation.

Recapping the example, our destination address was the public IP of the firewall, and the destination port was 5000. Similarly, the translated address was the private IP address of the VM, and the translated port was 22.

Network Rules

A network rule should be in place for any non-HTTP/S traffic to be allowed through the firewall. For a source to communicate with a destination deployed behind a firewall, you need to have a network rule configured from the source to the destination. If there is no rule that specifically calls out this incoming traffic, then it will be dropped. Let's take a look at the parameters that are required to set up a network rule; they will give you a better understanding.

- **Name:** Identifier to identify the rule.
- **Protocol:** TCP/UDP/ICMP/Any. Selecting will allow TCP, UDP, and ICMP.
- **Source address:** Address or CIDR block that represents the source.
- **Destination addresses:** Addresses or CIDR blocks that represent the source.
- **Destination port:** The destination port.

Looking at the parameters gives us a clear understanding of what you need to configure a network rule. If you take a closer look, you can see that we mentioned the source as the source address and destination as destination addresses. This means you have a sole source mapped to multiple destinations and have all of them in a single rule. Instead of writing so many rules, you can have a single rule that allows the traffic from a source to multiple destinations.

Application Rules

Application rules can be used to define the set of domain names that can be accessed by the resources deployed in the subnet. You will be defining these domain name as fully qualified domain names, and based on the domain names, the traffic is allowed. For example, you need to add domains like `windowsupdate.microsoft.com`, `download.windowsupdate.com`, `download.microsoft.com`, etc., to allow Windows update traffic from your subnet. You could also add wildcard entries for specifying the subdomains, for example, `*.windowsupdate.com`. Just like we did in the case of NAT rules and network rules, let's understand the parameters required to set up an application rule.

- **Name:** Friendly name given to identify the rule
- **Source addresses:** IP address of the source of traffic
- **Protocol and port:** HTTP/HTTPS protocol and the port numbers
- **Target FQDN:** The domain names you want to add to the rule

Rule Processing Order

When a packet hits the firewall, the packet will be inspected against the rules that we configured to decide if it's allowed or not. The rules are processed in the following order. The network rules will be evaluated first, and then the application rules are evaluated. Once a rule allows the traffic, no further evaluation is done. In other words, the evaluation stops when a matching allow rule is found; if none of the rule matches, then the traffic is dropped.

Since we have a clear understanding about the rules in the firewall, now we will present a scenario and see how the firewall can be implemented to secure the workload.

Implementing Azure Firewall

Azure Firewall implementation requires planning, and mostly the firewalls are placed in a central or hub virtual network, which is connected with other virtual networks using virtual network peering or VPN gateways. The Microsoft documentation gives an incredibly good representation of this architecture (refer to Figure 3.6).

If you look at the architecture, you can see that Azure Firewall acts as a crucial point for all communications happening from the Internet as well as on-premises. By default, all traffic from the Internet and on-premises is denied. Using the rules we discussed earlier, you will fine-tune our firewall and only allow the traffic that is required. You will be using NAT rules, application rules, and network rules to tailor a secured network. All known malicious IP and FQDNs are blocked by the Microsoft threat intelligence, so administrators need not set up any other security solution for blocking malicious traffic.

FIGURE 3.6   Demystifying the firewall architecture

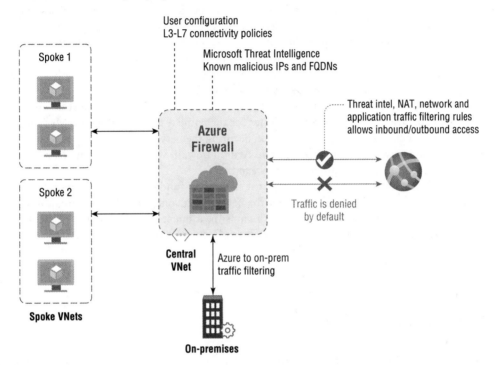

There is a full tutorial available in the Microsoft documentation for how to do the firewall implementation.

```
https://docs.microsoft.com/en-us/azure/firewall/tutorial-firewall-
deploy-portal-policy
```

Summary

The fundamental building block of infrastructure is networking, and in Azure we use virtual networks to implement networking. We discussed the concepts related to virtual networks and their role in the bigger picture. We covered IP allocation methods and types of IP addresses. Later, we discussed network routes and the purpose of system routes and user-defined routes. The system routes are responsible for all communications that happen between the resources inside a virtual network, as well as the communication from the virtual network to the Internet. Administrators can always override these system routes and define their own routing rules using UDR. UDR is useful if you are using NVA or Azure Firewall and you want to force the traffic to pass via NVA or Azure Firewall.

After covering routing, we covered service endpoints; they are used to establish a connection from your virtual network resources and other resources deployed in your subscription. The point to remember here is that the VMs will be able to communicate using their private IP address to the public endpoint of the service you want to connect. If you need the service to have a private IP address within the virtual network, then you need to implement a private link. Creating a private link will create a private IP address for the PaaS service as if it's deployed in the virtual network, the same as the VM.

Later, our discussion revolved around Azure DNS. You saw how you can host domains in Azure DNS and also set up private DNS zones for the name resolution of your VMs. Then, we shifted our focus to securing our network. Securing the network is primarily accomplished by using network security groups and Azure Firewall. We studied the implementation of both the resources and the difference between them.

Networking is a very vast topic, and we just started the fundamentals and some of the prerequisites. So far, we were talking about the networking configuration in Azure; however, in a hybrid cloud environment, administrators must be affluent in setting up intersite connectivity. By using intersite connectivity, you can extend your on-premises infrastructure to the cloud. In the next chapter, you will focus on setting up this hybrid environment and intersite connectivity using VPN gateways and ExpressRoute.

Exam Essentials

Understand virtual network and concepts.   Understand how the virtual networks are created and configured. Also, understand the concepts such as address spaces, subnets, regions, and subscriptions.

Understand private and public IP addressing.   You should be able to understand the difference between private and public IP addresses. Familiarize yourself with the allocation methods, static and dynamic. Understand how private and public IP addresses are created and managed in Azure.

Learn routing.   Learn the routing concepts in a virtual network. Get acquainted with the system routes and user-defined routes.

Learn service endpoints and private links.   Understand the key differences between service endpoints and private links. Understand how the end-to-end communication happens in both cases.

Understand Azure DNS.   Understand the use-case scenarios of Azure DNS and how clients can utilize Azure DNS zones for name resolution. Learn Azure private DNS zones and how you can link virtual networks to these zones for name resolution.

Learn to secure networks.   Securing a network is accomplished using network security groups and Azure Firewall. Understand NSG and how the effective rules are computed. Familiarize yourself with the implementation of Azure Firewall and the types of rules supported by Azure Firewall.

Review Questions

1. Your organization created an Azure DNS zone `firbish.com` and added an A record www that points to the IP address of your web server. Your on-premises clients are not able to resolve www.`firbish.com` to the right IP address. What should be done to achieve proper name resolution?

    A. Create an Azure private DNS zone

    B. Point the clients to one of the name servers of `firbish.com`

    C. Link the on-premises network to an Azure DNS zone

    D. Create a VPN connection to an Azure DNS

2. Your organization has created a virtual network in Azure with the address space as 192.168.0.0/23 and a subnet of 192.168.0.0/24. Your on-premises infrastructure uses the address space 192.168.1.0/24. Will there be any problem if you implement connectivity with your on-premises environment?

    A. Yes, the address spaces overlap.

    B. Yes, Azure DNS is not set up.

    C. No, we can implement connectivity to on-premises.

    D. No, the Azure environment is isolated from on-premises.

3. You are creating a web server in Azure using an Azure virtual machine. Your organization needs to reserve the IP address of the web server that will be shared with the clients across the Internet for accessing your website. Which type of IP should you use here?

    A. Private IP with dynamic assignment

    B. Public IP with dynamic assignment

    C. Private IP with static assignment

    D. Public IP with static assignment

4. You created a new VM in Azure and the VM was able to communicate with all other resources using a private IP in other subnets within the virtual network. Also, the VM was able to connect to the Internet without any additional configuration. How is this possible?

    A. Using the public IP address of the VM

    B. Using the Azure private DNS zone

    C. Using system routes

    D. Using a service endpoint

5. You are managing Azure DNS, you have a domain controller with hostname `dc.fir-bish.com`, and you would like this to resolve to 13.172.42.11. Also, there is an FTP server deployed on an Azure VM with the hostname `ftp.firbish.com`. You want `files.firbish.com` to resolve to `ftp.firbish.com`. Which records should you add to the Azure DNS zone?

A. A record for `dc.firbish.com` and CNAME for `files.firbish.com`

B. TXT record for domain controller and SRV record for FTP

C. DNS forwarders for redirecting requests

D. Redirect request to on-premises

6. You have created an Azure DNS zone called `firbish.com`. After creating the domain, you added the following records to the zone

- A : `dc.firbish.com` ➤ 13.172.13.11
- CNAME : `files.firbish.com` ➤ `ftp.firbish.com`
- TXT: @ ➤ ms1732
- MX: mailer ➤ `mail.firbish.com`

How long will it take these records to get propagated to the Internet name servers?

A. Records will be propagated within 72 hours.

B. Records will be propagated within 8 hours.

C. Records will not be propagated to the Internet name servers; resolution will be available only on Azure-provided name servers.

D. Resources will be updated instantly.

7. As an administrator, you are implementing service endpoints to access storage accounts from your VM in virtual network. Currently, all your VMs have a public IP address assigned to them, and the storage service also has a public endpoint. Which IP address will be used by a virtual machine for communication using a service endpoint?

A. Public IP address of the VM

B. Service endpoint IP

C. Private IP address of the VM

D. Gateway IP address

8. You have web server running inside a virtual network; this web server has a storage account connected in the backend to store customer data. You set up a service endpoint so that you can enable secure communication from the virtual machine to the storage account. However, the storage account is still accessed on the public endpoint. Your security team asked you to find a solution that can provide private IP addresses for the storage account and communicate with the VM over private IP addresses. Which solution would be recommended?

A. Enable private connections in service endpoints

B. Add a private endpoint and create a private link

C. Add virtual network integration for the storage account

D. Add a ReadOnly lock to the subscription scope

9. You are running three-tier applications that have front-end, middle tier, and backend applications all deployed to different subnets within a virtual network. Your security wants to restrict traffic directly flowing from the front end to backend, and only traffic from the middle tier should be allowed to the backend. How can you achieve this?

    A. Create user-defined routes

    B. Create NSG rules to deny and allow traffic

    C. Create a private link

    D. Add a firewall between the front end and backend to block traffic

10. Your organization created a private Azure DNS zone called `firbish.com`. The purpose of this zone is to provide name resolution for your Windows virtual machines deployed in the virtual network `eus-prod-vnet-01`. Which of the following steps should be performed for the virtual machines to resolve the records in the private DNS zone?

    A. Create a forwarder zone in Windows DNS server

    B. Change the DNS server by logging in to Windows VMs

    C. Enable auto registration to the zone

    D. Link the virtual network to the private DNS zone

11. You have the rules in Table 3.1 and Table 3.2 added to the subnet and NIC levels. You need to confirm if NTP traffic is allowed to NIC01.

TABLE 3.1 Subnet NSG Inbound Rules

Rule Name	Priority	Source/Service Tag: Port	Destination: Port	Action
Rule01	100	*:*	*:80, *:443, *:3389	Allow
Rule02	101	Internet: *	VirtualNetwork:22	Allow
Rule03	102	Internet:*	*:100-123	Allow

TABLE 3.2 NIC01 NSG Inbound Rules

Rule Name	Priority	Source/Service Tag: Port	Destination: Port	Action
NICRule01	110	*:*	*:100-123	Allow
NICRule02	105	Internet:*	*:80, *:443	Allow
NICRule03	101	Internet:*	*:100-143	Deny

A. Traffic is denied because of NICRule03.

B. Traffic is allowed because of Rule03.

C. Traffic is allowed because of NICRule01.

D. Traffic is denied because the NTP rule is not added.

12. You would like to allow traffic from Azure SQL to your virtual network. You have checked the IP addresses used by Azure SQL, and they keep changing as they are managed by Azure. You need to find a solution by which you can add the SQL service to NSG without the need to change the rule whenever Microsoft changes the IP address.

A. Open a support request and find the IP addresses that are permanent

B. Create a service endpoint

C. Allow the entire public address CIDR block used by Microsoft

D. Use service tags

13. You have deployed a Linux server to a subnet, and you also have a firewall added to the virtual network for securing the network. You need to make sure that the Linux server can communicate with the update repositories for updating the packages. How can you allow this traffic on the firewall?

A. Use a NAT rule

B. Use network rule

C. Use application rule

D. Use UDR

14. You are setting up Azure Firewall. Which type of rule should you add to the firewall to map the public IP address of the firewall, 13.72.11.25:5000, to the private IP address of a VM at 10.1.1.4:3389?

A. User-defined route rule

B. Security rule

C. NAT rule

D. Network rule

15. Your organization has implemented an NSG at the subnet and NIC levels. Your manager has asked you to confirm how the outgoing traffic from a virtual machine is evaluated and what the effective security rule is.

A. Traffic will be evaluated against the subnet NSG rules first and then with the NIC NSG rules.

B. Traffic will be evaluated against the NIC NSG rules first and then with the subnet NSG rules.

C. Traffic will skip the subnet NSG rules if the traffic is allowed in NIC NSG rules.

D. Traffic will skip NIC NSG rules as the rules from the subnet NSG rules are inherited to all NICs in the subnet.

16. Which one of the following is not a supported endpoint for a service endpoint?

   A. Azure Kubernetes Service

   B. Azure Cosmos DB

   C. Azure Key Vault

   D. Azure SQL Database

17. Which of the following statements about Azure service endpoints is not true?

   A. The service endpoint is applicable only for the virtual network deployed through Azure Resource Manager.

   B. The service endpoint doesn't require you to set up NAT or gateway devices for communication.

   C. The service endpoint uses the Microsoft backbone network.

   D. The service endpoint cannot be used to facilitate connection from on-premises resources to Azure resources.

18. Which protocols are supported in network security groups?

   A. TCP

   B. UDP

   C. ICMP

   D. All of the above

19. In which order are rules processed in Azure Firewall if you have application rule and network rule implemented in the firewall?

   A. Application rule, then network rule

   B. Skip application rule and evaluate network rule only

   C. Skip network rule and evaluate application rule only

   D. Network rule, then application rule

20. How many NSGs can be associated with a NIC? (Select all that apply.)

   A. 1

   B. 0

   C. More than 2

   D. More than 5

Chapter

4

Intersite Connectivity

MICROSOFT EXAM OBJECTIVES COVERED IN THIS CHAPTER:

✓ **Implement and manage virtual networking**

- Create and configure virtual networks, including peering

✓ **Integrate an on-premises network with Azure virtual network**

- Create and configure Azure VPN Gateway

- Create and configure Azure ExpressRoute

- Configure Azure Virtual WAN

Intersite connectivity means establishing connectivity between two sites. It's not necessarily that one is on-premises and the other is on the cloud. You can establish private connectivity between two Azure regions as well. Each region can be considered as a site and establish connectivity between them. You can broadly classify intersite connectivity as two types; one is Azure-to-Azure connectivity, and the second one is Azure to on-premises or any other cloud.

In Azure-to-Azure connectivity, you have two options: virtual network peering and VPN gateways. You will see how these are different and the implementation of these connectivity methods. In Azure to on-premises connectivity, you can have VPN and ExpressRoute for faster connections via dedicated lines. VPN gateways can also be used to establish a private connection between Azure and other cloud providers such as AWS, GCP, etc. For example, you need to have private connectivity from your Azure virtual machines to a set of EC2 instances deployed in AWS; using VPN gateways, you can establish this connection. One thing to note here is that you need to create the necessary resources in AWS to establish this connection.

Our goal in this chapter is to learn these methods and the implementation. Let's start with Azure-to-Azure connectivity.

Azure-to-Azure Connectivity

Azure-to-Azure connectivity refers to connectivity between two Azure virtual networks in the same region or different regions. For instance, say you have a set of virtual machines deployed in East US and you want to establish connectivity to another set of servers deployed in West Europe. Here the connection is established between two Azure regions. Also, it's not necessary that the connectivity is between two regions; it could be connectivity between resources in two different virtual networks created in the same region.

All resources deployed in a virtual network will be able to communicate with the Internet by default. This means the resource can initiate the connection to the Internet to get the time, download updates, etc. We already covered this in the previous chapter when we discussed system routes. For inbound connections, you need to set up public IP addresses or public load balancers. Regarding communication between Azure resources we have covered different methods such as deploying them to the same virtual network, service endpoints for communicating with Azure services, and private links for establishing a connection over a private IP address to Azure PaaS solutions. In this section, we are interested in communication between Azure resources deployed in two different virtual networks.

By default, each virtual network, regardless of whether they are in the same region or different regions, cannot communicate with each other unless you have one of the following methods established. Each virtual network will be an isolated network like you used to have on-premises. In on-premises, you used routers to connect two networks and enable communication; in Azure you have different methods available to enable this connection. Figure 4.1 shows each of the methods.

FIGURE 4.1   Reference architecture

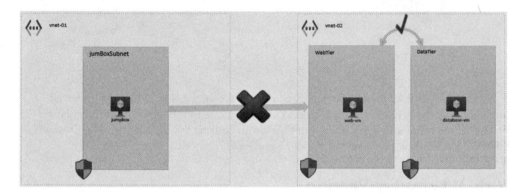

In Figure 4.1, you can see that the jumpbox VM deployed in the jumpBoxSubnet of vnet-01 cannot communicate with vnet-02. The vnet-02 has two subnets, WebTier and DataTier, each holding web-vm and database-vm, respectively. The web and database VMs are able to communicate with each other as they are in the same virtual network. Your goal is to let the jumpbox VM communicate with web-vm. (We are not taking the NSG into account. Let's assume that all ports are open for simplicity, though it's not an ideal configuration for production workloads.) We will start with the easiest and least secure method: the Internet.

Internet

As mentioned in the previous section, the Internet is the easiest, least secure, and least preferred implementation to connect two Azure sites or virtual networks. In this case, you can associate public IP addresses to your jumpbox VM and web-vm, and they will be able to communicate with each other over the Internet. This process is similar to deploying a VM with public IP addresses, and you connect from a local machine. Similarly, you can connect to web-vm and initiate a connection to the public IP address of the web-vm, or vice versa.

Opening the connectivity to the Internet opens a vector for attack. You could leverage firewalls or an NSG to filter the communication. However, the traffic needs to travel over the Internet, which adds risk. Your reference architecture needs to be modified to allow communication over the Internet (refer to Figure 4.2).

FIGURE 4.2   Communication over Internet

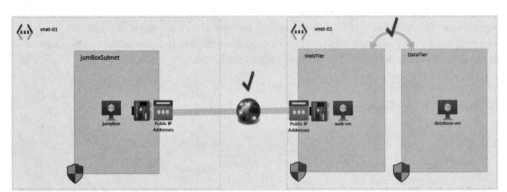

When we discuss communication between Azure resources, this is the least preferred method. In fact, it is not even considered as an option due to the security concerns. Nevertheless, it is good to know that there is an option to connect via the Internet. Next, we will talk about peering, which is one of the most preferred methods.

Virtual Network Peering

Though the Internet is the easiest and quickest way to connect resources in two virtual networks, it is never preferred by organizations as the traffic needs to go through the Internet, and the resources should have Internet-facing IP addresses. Since the Internet is out of the preference list, you have virtual network peering. This is one of the widely adopted methods to connect virtual networks because of its simplicity and ease of implementation. Enabling virtual network peering opens a channel for flawless connectivity between virtual networks. Once you establish the peering, the resources in the connected virtual networks will be able to communicate with each other as if they are part of the same virtual network.

Before you plan to set up peering, you need to make sure that you follow the best practices covered in Chapter 3, "Virtual Networking." To refresh your knowledge, let's go over them again.

- Avoid overlapping address spaces. Always make sure that the address spaces are not overlapping when you peer networks.

- Reserve some IP addresses for the future.

- Deploy larger virtual networks rather than deploying smaller ones. This reduces the management overhead. Also, if you need peering, this reduces the number of peering.

- Lastly, make use of NSG and allow only the traffic that is required.

Now that we have reiterated the best practices, let's dive deeper to understand more about peering. There are two types of peering: regional virtual network peering and global virtual network peering. Let's understand what the differences are between these types:

- **Regional virtual network peering:** If you peer networks that are in the same Azure region, you call it regional virtual network peering.

- **Global virtual network peering:** If you peer networks that are part of different Azure regions, you call it global virtual network peering. You can establish peering from an Azure public cloud region to China cloud regions as well. However, you cannot peer Azure public cloud and government cloud regions. You can establish peering between the same regions in the government cloud.

Figure 4.3 shows regional and global virtual network peering. In the figure, you can see that two virtual networks in East US with address spaces 10.0.0.0/16 and 192.168.0.0/16 are connected to each other via regional virtual network peering, as they are part of the same region. There is a third virtual network deployed in West US with the address space 172.16.0.0/16. This virtual network is peered with a virtual network in East US via global virtual network peering. It is called global virtual network peering as the virtual networks are located in two different regions.

FIGURE 4.3   Types of peering

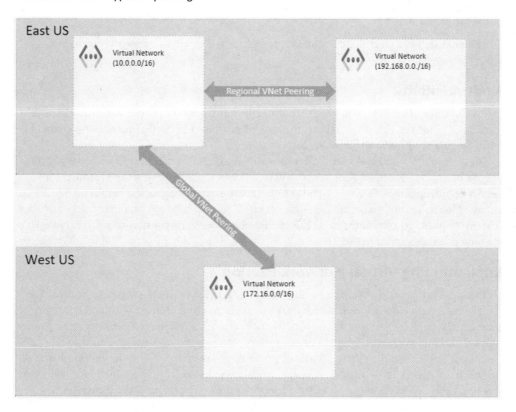

Now that you're familiar with the types of peering, let's take a moment to understand the benefits of peering.

Benefits

The following are the benefits of using peering for connecting your virtual networks:

- **Private network:** Peering uses a private network to send the traffic between peered networks. For communication, the Microsoft backbone network is used, and the public Internet is not required.

- **Low latency:** From a performance standpoint, peering offers a low-latency, high-bandwidth connectivity between the peered networks.

- **Easier implementation:** Implementing peering is easy and effortless.

- **Connectivity:** Once the networks are peered, the resources in the peered network will be able to communicate as if they were in the same network.

- **Seamless:** You can peer networks across Azure regions, Azure subscriptions, and even subscriptions across different tenants.

- **No downtime:** There will no disruption to the existing resources when you create peering.

The next step is to learn one of the key points related to virtual network peering: nontransitivity.

Nontransitivity

In your mathematics class, you probably studied what transitive property is: if A=B and B=C, then A=C. However, this is not true in the case of peering. That is the reason why virtual network peering is called *non-transitive*.

For example, if you have vnet-A peered with vnet-B and vnet-B peered with vnet-C, this doesn't mean that vnet-A is peered with vnet-C. If you would like to let the resources in vnet-A communicate with vnet-C, you should create an explicit peering between vnet-A and vnet-C. Hence, always make sure you have created peering between all the virtual networks that are required to communicate as the virtual network peering is non-transitive. Now let's see how peering is implemented.

Implementing Virtual Network Peering

Virtual network peering is similar to how you connect two network switches together. You need to connect a cable to each switch that you want to communicate with and configure them. In the implementation of virtual network peering, you need to create a peering connection on both networks you want to peer. In short, you need to implement a reciprocal connection to implement the peering. Luckily, in the Azure portal, opening the peering blade of one virtual network lets you create the reciprocal connection from the same blade. This way, you don't have to navigate to the other network to create the reciprocal connection.

When you are implementing cross-subscription peering, make sure that you have permissions on both subscriptions to manage the virtual network and the peering. In the case of cross-subscription and cross-tenant peering, the administrator of the peer network should at least grant you a Network Contributor role. Without this role, you will not be able to create a reciprocal connection on the other peer.

In Exercise 4.1, you will create two virtual networks in different regions, say, East US and West US. The virtual network vnet-01 is in East US, and vnet-02 is in West US. Both the virtual networks contain a default subnet with address ranges 172.16.0.0/24 and 192.168.0.0/24, respectively. In the default subnet of vnet-01, you have two VMs deployed. One VM is called the jumpbox-vm with a public IP address, and another VM is called vm-01 without the public IP address. In the default subnet of vnet-02, you have only a single VM vm-02 without a public IP address. Your goal is to establish peering between vnet-01 and vnet-02 so that you can connect to jumpbox-vm and then SSH to vm-01; from vm-01 you should be able to communicate with vm-02 using private IP addresses. You are using jumpbox-vm as an entry point to connect from the local machine to Azure. Figure 4.4 gives a high-level overview of the architecture.

FIGURE 4.4   Implementing virtual network peering

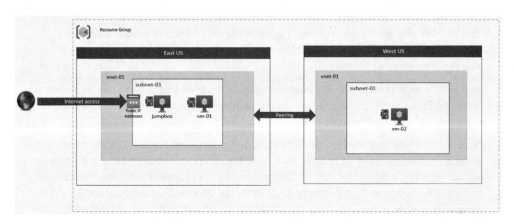

Setting up this infrastructure from scratch may take some time; you can use a PowerShell script in this GitHub repository to deploy the infrastructure shown in Figure 4.4.

```
https://github.com/rithinskaria/azure-infra/blob/main/peering.ps1
```

You can use your own username and password in the script by updating the variables or you can go with the default preconfigured values. All components will be deployed except the peering. You will create the peering in Exercise 4.1.

EXERCISE 4.1

Implementing Virtual Network Peering in the Azure Portal

1. If you have successfully run the PowerShell script, all resources will be deployed. SSH to the jumpbox using the public IP address of the VM. To find the public IP address, you can navigate to Azure Portal ➢ Virtual Machines ➢ jumpbox-vm. Look for the public IP address in the Overview blade. Alternatively, you can use the DNS name also for connecting to the VM.

EXERCISE 4.1 *(continued)*

2. You can use any terminal in your computer or the cloud shell to initiate a SSH connection to the VM. SSH can be initiated by running the command `ssh <username>@<public-ip>`.

3. You will be prompted to add the host to the list of allowed hosts. Continue by entering Y and hit Enter. Next, you will be prompted to enter the password; use the password you have used in the PowerShell script.

4. Now you are going to SSH to your vm-01 from jumpbox-vm. You need to find the private IP address of vm-01 to SSH. As vm-01 and jumpbox-vm are part of the same virtual network, they will be able to communicate via a private IP address. You can find the private IP address by navigating to Azure Portal ➤ Virtual Machines ➤ vm-01 ➤ Overview ➤ Properties. Once you have the private IP address, run `ssh <privateIP>` from the console to connect to vm-01. You don't have to specify the username as all your VMs use the same username.

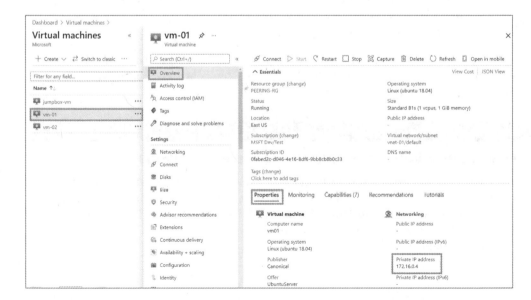

5. You will be asked the save the host signature and then enter the password. Once authenticated, you will be able to see that you are connected to vm-01. The following image is from Windows Terminal; depending on what SSH client you are using, the color schemes may vary.

```
rithin@jumpbox-vm:~$ ssh 172.16.0.4
The authenticity of host '172.16.0.4 (172.16.0.4)' can't be established.
ECDSA key fingerprint is SHA256:m39i1Wn+Ivruw/9zTOf0vyrUrnsdTc+pQqYlmn4bjJA.
Are you sure you want to continue connecting (yes/no)? yes
Warning: Permanently added '172.16.0.4' (ECDSA) to the list of known hosts.
rithin@172.16.0.4's password:
Welcome to Ubuntu 18.04.5 LTS (GNU/Linux 5.4.0-1051-azure x86_64)

 * Documentation:  https://help.ubuntu.com
 * Management:     https://landscape.canonical.com
 * Support:        https://ubuntu.com/advantage

  System information as of Sat Jul 17 07:40:56 UTC 2021

  System load:  0.08              Processes:          115
  Usage of /:   6.9% of 28.90GB   Users logged in:    0
  Memory usage: 29%               IP address for eth0: 172.16.0.4
  Swap usage:   0%

10 updates can be applied immediately.
3 of these updates are standard security updates.
To see these additional updates run: apt list --upgradable




The programs included with the Ubuntu system are free software;
the exact distribution terms for each program are described in the
individual files in /usr/share/doc/*/copyright.

Ubuntu comes with ABSOLUTELY NO WARRANTY, to the extent permitted by
applicable law.

To run a command as administrator (user "root"), use "sudo <command>".
See "man sudo_root" for details.

rithin@vm01:~$
```

6. Now, you need to find the private IP address of vm-02. You can follow the steps you performed for vm-01 to find the private IP of vm-02. If you used the PowerShell script, probably the private IP address would 192.168.0.4.

7. From the terminal, try `ping 192.168.0.4` and note the response. It's expected that you don't get any response as vnet-01 and vnet-02 is not configured to communicate with each other. You can exit out of ping by hitting Ctrl+C on your keyboard.

8. You will configure the peering now so that vm-01 can communicate with vm-02. For setting up the peering, navigate to the Azure portal and search for *virtual networks*. Click Virtual Networks, which will take you to the list of virtual networks in your subscription.

9. As mentioned in the introduction of this section, you can set up a connection from any one of the networks that you want to peer, and the reciprocal connection will be created on the other network.

10. Click vnet-01 and jump to the Peerings blade. Then click + Add to start the peering creation process.

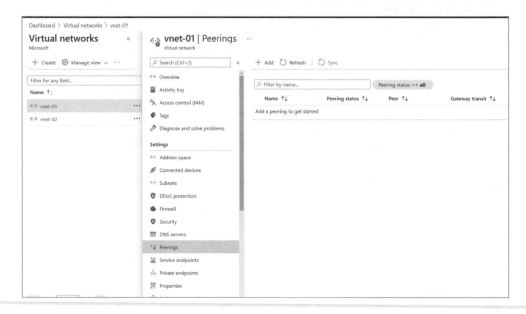

11. Provide the information as follows:

- **Peering link name:** This is a friendly name given to the link that you are creating in vnet-01. It's always recommended that you give names that you can use to understand the peering. For example, here you are connecting to vnet-01 to vnet-02. To recognize this connection, you can name it vnet-01-TO-vnet-02. This will help you recognize the connection in the future.

- **Traffic to remote virtual network:** This is for you to control whether you want to allow traffic from vnet-01 to vnet-02. In your case, you will set it to the default value, which is allow.

- **Traffic forwarded from remote virtual network:** This is for you to control what action needs to be taken on any traffic coming to vnet-01, which is forwarded by vnet-02. It is mentioned as forwarded because the origin of the traffic is not vnet-02. You will go with the default value allow.

- **Virtual network gateway or route server:** This option is used when you are dealing with dynamic routes. In your case, you will go with none, which is the default value.

- **Peering link name (remote virtual network):** You need to provide a name for the reciprocal connection, which will be created on vnet-02. For simplicity, let's call it vnet-02-TO-vnet-01.

- **Virtual network deployment model:** To select the classic or ARM network, you will select the Resource manager as we created vnet-02 as an ARM resource.

- **I know my resource ID:** If you know the resource ID of the remote network, then you can check this box and provide the resource ID. Let's keep it unchecked and select your vnet-02 by selecting the subscription.

- **Subscription:** You can select the subscription where your remote network (vnet-02) resides. This option will not be shown if you are going with the resource ID option.

- **Virtual network:** Once the subscription is selected, Azure will list all virtual networks in the subscription. Select the desired subscription from the drop-down. In your case, you will go with vnet-02.

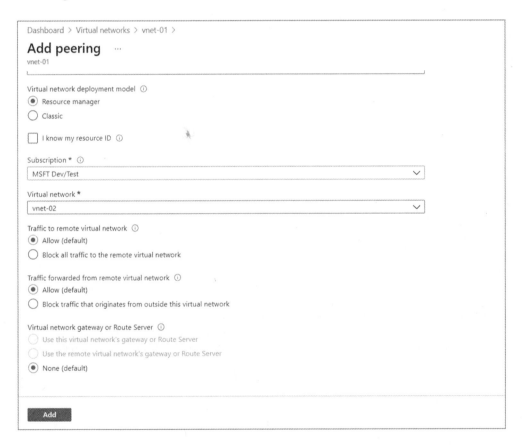

- Additionally, you will be asked to fill the traffic to the remote virtual network and forwarded traffic configuration. Set these values to the defaults. These are the properties of the peering link that will be created in vnet-02. In other words, here remote refers to vnet-01.

EXERCISE 4.1 *(continued)*

12. Once you provide the information, click OK to create the peering. You can see that two connections are getting created.

13. After 7 to 10 seconds, if you navigate back to the Peering blade, you can see the peering and the peering status as Connected. If you navigate to vnet-02 ➤ Peering, you will see the reciprocal connection also with the connected status.

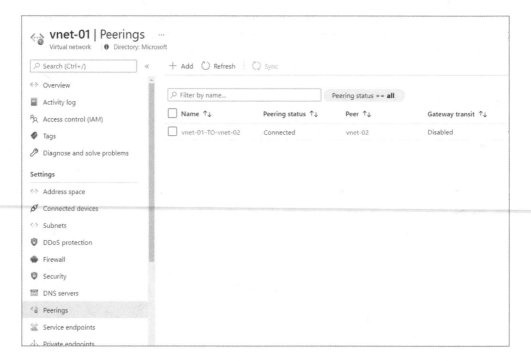

14. It's time to verify the peering. Switch back to the SSH terminal (or reconnect to vm-01 if you closed the connection) and try pinging the private IP address of vm-02 from vm-01. Unlike the last time, you will see that you are getting a ping response from the vm-02.

```
rithin@vm01:~$ ping 192.168.0.4
PING 192.168.0.4 (192.168.0.4) 56(84) bytes of data.
64 bytes from 192.168.0.4: icmp_seq=1 ttl=64 time=71.5 ms
64 bytes from 192.168.0.4: icmp_seq=2 ttl=64 time=60.7 ms
64 bytes from 192.168.0.4: icmp_seq=3 ttl=64 time=61.1 ms
64 bytes from 192.168.0.4: icmp_seq=4 ttl=64 time=61.0 ms
64 bytes from 192.168.0.4: icmp_seq=5 ttl=64 time=60.9 ms
64 bytes from 192.168.0.4: icmp_seq=6 ttl=64 time=61.1 ms
64 bytes from 192.168.0.4: icmp_seq=7 ttl=64 time=60.6 ms
^C
--- 192.168.0.4 ping statistics ---
7 packets transmitted, 7 received, 0% packet loss, time 6008ms
rtt min/avg/max/mdev = 60.618/62.474/71.594/3.735 ms
```

With the implementation of virtual network peering, the VM deployed in vnet-01 is able to communicate with VM deployed in vnet-02. The landscape and architecture of your network will change when there is a business requirement, so it's essential to know how you can modify the existing peering to accommodate the network changes.

Modify or Delete Virtual Network Peering

Modifying or deleting the virtual network peering will disrupt connectivity between the peered networks. You should have a valid business reason before you modify or delete the peering. Some scenarios where you modify or delete the peering include the following:

- The networks no longer require communicating with each other.
- Resources have been migrated to another virtual network, and the current peering is not required.
- You are implementing VPN/ExpressRoute connectivity between the virtual networks.
- New gateways were added to the network, and you plan to implement the gateway transit feature.
- You need to allow or block traffic from a certain peered network.

Modifying the peering is easy; you can navigate to one of the peered virtual networks and switch to the Peerings blade. In the Peerings blade, all peering connections will be listed. Clicking any of the connections will help you modify the properties such as traffic to the remote virtual network and traffic forwarded from the remote virtual network or route server. However, properties such as link names and the remote network cannot be changed. Similarly, you can navigate to the Peerings blade of the peered network to modify its properties, as shown in Figure 4.5.

Deleting virtual network peering can be also accomplished from the Peering blade. Find the peering you would like to delete and click the three dots in the far-right corner of the connection. You will be presented with the option to delete, as shown in Figure 4.6.

Once you click Delete, a confirmation window will pop up, and you need to select Yes. The connection that you have selected and the reciprocal connection in the other virtual network will be deleted in a single shot. Your resources in the virtual networks will no longer be able to communicate with each other.

Since you have completed virtual network peering, let's jump to the next method, which can be used to connect two Azure sites: a VPN gateway.

VPN Gateway

A virtual private network (VPN) gateway is popular for sending encrypted traffic between the Azure virtual network and on-premises datacenter over the public Internet. There is also another use case for these virtual network gateways, which is sending encrypted traffic between Azure virtual networks. In the previous section, you saw how you can implement virtual network peering and connect two virtual networks. Similarly, you can use virtual network gateways to connect two virtual networks for communication.

FIGURE 4.5   Modifying virtual network peering

Dashboard > Virtual networks > vnet-01 >

vnet-01-TO-vnet-02 ...
vnet-01

This virtual network
Peering link name
vnet-01-TO-vnet-02

Peering status
Connected

Peering state
Succeeded

Traffic to remote virtual network ⓘ
◉ Allow (default)
◯ Block all traffic to the remote virtual network

Traffic forwarded from remote virtual network ⓘ
◉ Allow (default)
◯ Block traffic that originates from outside this virtual network

Virtual network gateway or Route Server ⓘ
◯ Use this virtual network's gateway or Route Server
◯ Use the remote virtual network's gateway or Route Server
◉ None (default)

Remote virtual network
Remote Vnet Id
/subscriptions/0fabed2c-d046-4e16-8df6-9bb8cb8b0c33/resourceGroups/peering-rg/providers/Microsoft.Network/virt... ⎘

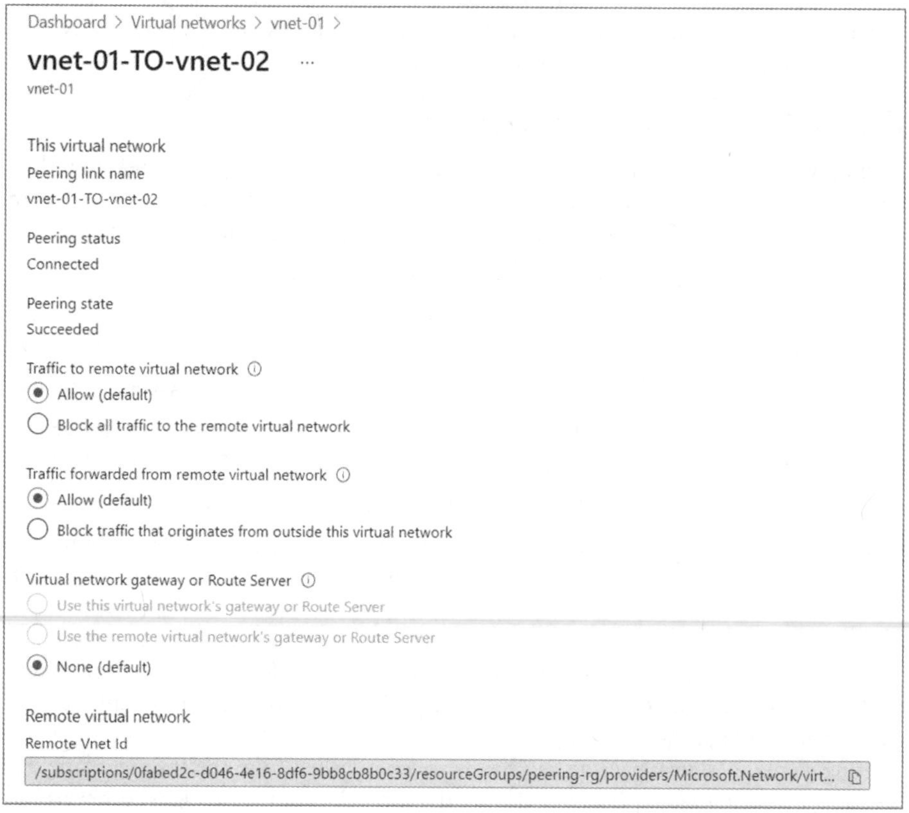

Each virtual network can have only one VPN gateway, and you can establish multiple connections to the gateway. Each connection shares the bandwidth allocated for the VPN gateways. The number of connections and bandwidth depends on which pricing tier of VPN gateway you are using. We will cover these pricing tiers later in this chapter. In Figure 4.7, you can see how two virtual networks are connected with the help of a VPN gateway.

A VPN gateway can be used to establish three types of connectivity.

- **Site-to-site (S2S):** Helps in connecting on-premises datacenter to cloud

- **Point-to-site (P2S):** Helps in connecting individual devices to an Azure virtual network

- **Virtual network-to-virtual network:** Establishes a connection between Azure virtual networks

FIGURE 4.6   Deleting virtual network peering

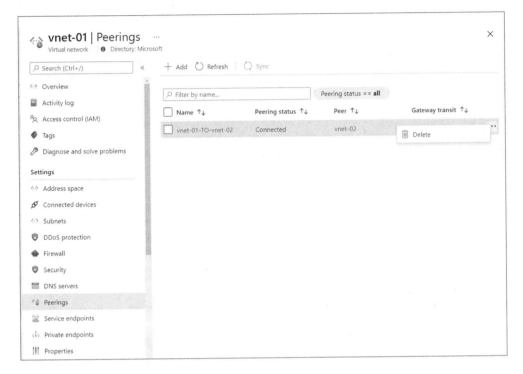

FIGURE 4.7   Virtual network-to-virtual network VPN connection

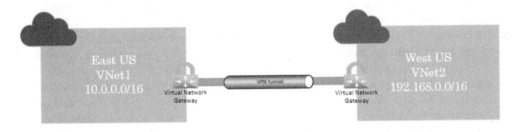

The first two types are exclusive for on-premises connectivity, and you are interested in the last connection type as you are covering Azure-to-Azure connectivity now. Virtual network-to-virtual network and site-to-site will appear similar in terms of implementation. However, the only difference is for a site-to-site connection; one end is Azure, and the other end is the on-premises datacenter. On the other hand, for a virtual network to virtual network, both ends are in Azure itself.

You need to create virtual network gateway to establish a VPN connection, and each virtual network gateway comprises two or more VMs managed by Azure. These VMs are deployed to a dedicated subnet within your virtual network called the *gateway subnet*. The VMs are managed by Azure, and you don't have the permission to customize or configure them. These VMs are responsible for maintaining the routing rules and running the gateway services. VPN gateways can also be deployed to availability zones; this can help you overcome connectivity issues when there are any zonal-level failures in an Azure region.

Before you deploy the gateway or establish a connection, it's vital to understand some of the concepts related to gateways such as types of gateways, pricing tiers, and high availability options. These topics are not applicable only to virtual network to virtual network communications, but also applicable while you set up on-premises connectivity. Let's start with the VPN gateway types.

VPN Gateway Types

When you create a VPN gateway, you need to select the VPN type. This selection is based on which type of connection is your end goal. For example, for establishing point-to-site connectivity, you need a route-based VPN type. This again depends on the type of hardware that you are using on-premises if you are going with a site-to-site connection. Let's take a look at these VPN types and understand how they differ.

- **Route-based VPN:** As the name suggests, the route-based VPN relies on the routing table or IP forwarding rules you configure to force the packets the respective tunnels interfaces. It's the responsibility of the tunnel interfaces to encrypt and decrypt traffic that comes in and out of the tunnel. Any to any traffic selectors are configured on the route-based VPNs.

- **Policy-based VPN:** Here also, as the name implies, the packets are routed based on the IPSec policies that you configured. The policies comprise the address prefix combinations based on your on-premises and Azure virtual network address spaces. Unlike route-based VPNs, the traffic selector is defined using an access list. There are certain limitations when it comes to policy-based VPN. As discussed, there are different pricing tiers of VPN, and policy-based VPN is not supported in the Basic SKU of the VPN gateway. Second, you can have only one tunnel, and your connections are limited to only site-to-site connections and certain configurations where you cannot control or modify the path the traffic will flow through. For most scenarios, you should prefer route-based VPNs.

With that you will move to the SKUs that are available for VPN gateways.

SKU

VPN gateway tiers are classified based on the number of connections, throughput, and features. You need to choose a tier or SKU based on the number of connections you require and throughput you desire. You will see a maximum number of connections that can be established for both P2S and S2S connections. Table 4.1 shows the different SKUs that are available for the VPN gateway along with the max connections and throughput.

TABLE 4.1   VPN Gateway SKUs

VPN Gateway Generation	SKU	S2S/Virtual Network to Virtual Network Tunnels	P2S SSTP Connections	P2S IKEv2/OpenVPN Connections	Agg: Throughput Benchmark
1	Basic	Max. 10	Max. 128	Not Supported	100 Mbps
1	VpnGw1	Max. 30	Max. 128	Max. 250	650 Mbps
1	VpnGw2	Max. 30	Max. 128	Max. 500	1 Gbps
1	VpnGw3	Max. 30	Max. 128	Max. 1000	1.25 Gbps
1	VpnGw1AZ	Max. 30	Max. 128	Max. 250	650 Mbps
1	VpnGw2AZ	Max. 30	Max. 128	Max. 500	1 Gbps
1	VpnGw3AZ	Max. 30	Max. 128	Max.1000	1.25 Gbps
2	VpnGw2	Max. 30	Max. 128	Max. 500	1.25 Gbps
2	VpnGw3	Max. 30	Max. 128	Max. 1000	2.5 Gbps
2	VpnGw4	Max. 30	Max. 128	Max. 5000	5 Gbps
2	VpnGw5	Max. 30	Max. 128	Max. 10000	10 Gbps
2	VpnGw2AZ	Max. 30	Max. 128	Max. 500	1.25 Gbps
2	VpnGw3AZ	Max. 30	Max. 128	Max. 1000	2.5 Gbps
2	VpnGw4AZ	Max. 30	Max. 128	Max. 5000	5 Gbps
2	VpnGw5AZ	Max. 30	Max. 128	Max. 10000	10 Gbps

The data in this table is copied from here:

https://docs.microsoft.com/en-us/azure/vpn-gateway/vpn-gateway-about-vpn-gateway-settings#benchmark

At the time of writing this book, these are the only SKUs available for VPN gateways. The SKUs that have *AZ* in the SKU name represent availability zone gateway SKUs; these SKUs can be deployed to availability zones and improve the high availability of your VPN gateway. Speaking of high availability, a VPN gateway is shipped with built-in availability. Let's understand how high availability is achieved in VPN gateways.

High Availability

When you create a VPN gateway, you will be asked to choose how to configure HA in the VPN gateways. There are two options by which you can implement HA in VPN gateways: active-standby and active-active. Now, you will see the HA configuration these models.

Active-Standby In Azure, each VPN gateway is configured in an active-standby configuration with the combination of two instances. During an event of any planned maintenance or unplanned interruptions to the active instance, Azure will automatically fail over to a standby instance. Once the failover is completed, the standby will resume all S2S and virtual network-to-virtual network connections. The IP address of the VPN gateway will remain the same. There will be a small interruption during the failover process. It takes about 1 minute, and in a worst-case scenario, it can go up to $1\frac{1}{2}$ minutes. The P2S connections' gateway will be disconnected during the failover process; clients will need to reconnect to the VPN as there will be a connection drop. Figure 4.8 shows how the active-standby configuration is set up for a virtual network-to-virtual network and on-premises gateway.

FIGURE 4.8 Active-standby configuration

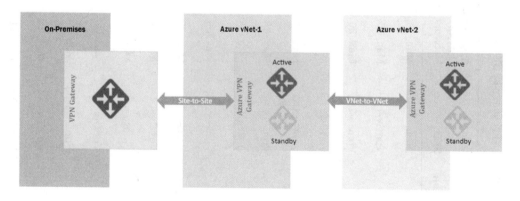

In Figure 4.8, you can see that a virtual network to virtual network connection is established using an active-standby configuration. You can set up on-premises high availability based on your requirements, and it's up to on-premises administrators to set that up. Active-standby is the default configuration whenever you create a VPN gateway; this can be changed to active-active by changing Enable Active-Active Mode to Enabled.

Active-Active   You can also configure active-active configuration in your VPN gateway, and in this configuration S2S connections will be established from both instances to your on-premises VPN device. In the case of a virtual network to virtual network connection and S2S connection, the tunnels will be established as shown in Figure 4.9.

FIGURE 4.9   Active-active configuration

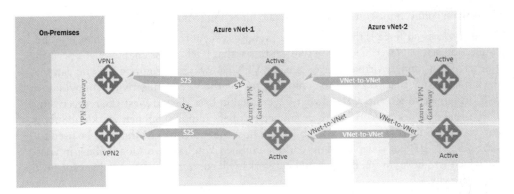

Here each instance will have its own public IP address on both sides of the virtual network. You need to let each instance know about the other two peers for establishing two tunnels. In the case of on-premises, you need to set up both of your VPN devices with the public IP addresses of the gateway instances.

In an active-active configuration, the traffic is routed concurrently through both tunnels. If a maintenance event or unplanned event occurs to one of the instances, the tunnel from that instance is terminated, and the communication will happen only through the other instance. This failover is automatic, and no intervention is required from your end.

I hope this gives you an understanding about the gateway high availability configuration. With that you will start setting up your virtual network-to-virtual network connectivity using VPN gateways.

Implementing Virtual Network-to-Virtual Network Connectivity Using VPN Gateways

To implement virtual network-to-virtual network connectivity, you need to go through a series of steps. These steps are relevant for establishing the connection. The following are the steps required:

- **Create virtual networks and subnets:** You need to set up your virtual networks and subnets to host the workloads.

- **DNS server:** This is an optional step; you can skip this if name resolution is not required.

- **Create gateway subnet:** Before you deploy the VPN gateway, you need to add a dedicated subnet to the virtual networks you want to connect. This subnet is for hosting the VPN gateway instances, and a CIDR block of /27 or /28 would suffice. The name of the subnet should be GatewaySubnet.

- **Create connection:** You need to create a connection from the VPN gateway.

The process outlined is the same for on-premises except there is a slight change in the connection setup. Nevertheless, you will get to see that later in this chapter. Let's perform an exercise to connect virtual networks using VPN gateways. In Figure 4.10, you can see the infrastructure that you need to deploy for testing the VPN connectivity. You will have two virtual networks, vnet-01 and vnet-02, created in East US and West US, respectively. The virtual network vnet-01 has three subnets, namely, jumpboxSubnet, workloadSubnet, and GatewaySubnet. The jumpboxSubnet will host the jumpboxVM that will be used to access the vm-01 that is deployed in workloadSubnet. You have workloadSubnet in vnet-02, which will host vm-02. Both virtual networks will contain a GatewaySubnet for hosting VPN gateway.

FIGURE 4.10   VPN demo infrastructure

You can deploy the resources shown in Figure 4.10 one by one because you have seen the deployment of each of these resources in the previous chapters except the VPN gateway. You can also use the PowerShell script added at the following location to deploy the infrastructure easily:

```
https://github.com/rithinskaria/azure-infra/blob/main/vpn-infra.ps1
```

If you have completed the infrastructure deployment, then you can start Exercise 4.2 to implement the VPN gateway connection. Once the PowerShell script is executed, it will return the FQDN to connect to the jumpboxVM and private IP addresses of vm-01 and vm-02, respectively. If you are deploying manually, please note these values as you need them during the exercise.

Implementing the Virtual Network to Virtual Network VPN in the Azure Portal

1. If you have successfully run the PowerShell script, all resources will be deployed. SSH to the jumpbox VM using the FQDN returned by the script.

2. From the jumpbox VM, SSH to vm-01 using the command `ssh 10.1.1.4`.

3. Once you are logged in to vm-01, try pinging vm-02. This will fail as you haven't set up any method to let these two virtual networks communicate with each other. In Exercise 4.1, you established the connectivity using peering, and here in this exercise, you will set up the connection using VPN gateways.

4. Let's deploy a VPN gateway to the GatewaySubnet of vnet-01 from the portal. Navigate to the Azure portal and search for *virtual network gateways*. Click Virtual Network Gateways; this will take you to the page where you can create the gateway.

5. Click + Create to start the creation process; the following inputs need to be provided:

   ▪ **Subscription:** Select the subscription where you have deployed the virtual networks.

   ▪ **Resource Group:** This will be automatically selected based on the resource group of the virtual network.

   ▪ **Name:** Provide a name for the VPN such as vpn-eus.

   ▪ **Region:** Set this as East US as vnet-01 is deployed in East US. You need to make sure that you select the same region as the virtual network.

   ▪ **Gateway Type:** VPN.

   ▪ **VPN Type:** Route-based.

   ▪ **SKU:** VpnGw1.

   ▪ **Generation:** Generation 1.

   ▪ **Virtual Network:** Select vnet-01; the gateway subnet will be automatically selected.

   ▪ **Public IP address:** Create a new public IP address.

   ▪ **Public IP address name:** Provide a name for the public IP address.

   ▪ **Enable active-active mode:** Disabled, as you are not configuring active-active mode.

   ▪ **Configure BGP:** Default value, disabled.

EXERCISE 4.2 *(continued)*

6. Once you have entered all the inputs, click Review + Create. This process will take 30 to 45 minutes.

7. In the interim, you can create the second gateway for vnet-02 in West US. Now, you will use PowerShell to create the gateway as you are already familiar with the process in the portal.

8. Create a public IP address using the following command:

```
$gwpip= New-AzPublicIpAddress `
-Name pip-vpn-wus `
-ResourceGroupName vpn-demo-rg `
-Location 'West US' `
-AllocationMethod Dynamic
```

9. Once the public IP is created, go ahead and create the VPN gateway by using the following command:

```
$vnet = Get-AzVirtualNetwork `
-Name vnet-02 `
-ResourceGroupName 'vpn-demo-rg'

$subnet = Get-AzVirtualNetworkSubnetConfig `
-Name 'GatewaySubnet' `
-VirtualNetwork $vnet

$gwipconfig = New-AzVirtualNetworkGatewayIpConfig `
-Name vpn-wus `
-SubnetId $subnet.Id `
-PublicIpAddressId $gwpip.Id

New-AzVirtualNetworkGateway `
-Name vpn-wus `
-ResourceGroupName vpn-demo-rg `
-Location 'West US' `
-IpConfigurations $gwipconfig `
-GatewayType Vpn `
-VpnType RouteBased `
-GatewaySku VpnGw1
```

10. As mentioned earlier, this deployment will also take 30 to 45 minutes to complete. Once the VPN gateway is deployed, you need to create the virtual network to virtual network connection.

11. Navigate to Virtual Network Gateways, select vpn-eus (gateway deployed in East US), and click Connections. Select + Add.

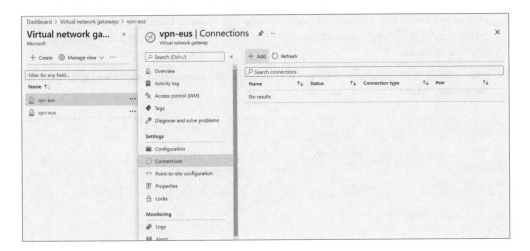

12. You need to add the connection details as follows:

    ■ **Name:** Name the connection. Since you are connecting from East US to West US, give a name like eus-to-wus.

    ■ **Connection Type:** This will be virtual network to virtual network, as you are connecting virtual networks.

    ■ **First virtual network gateway:** The East US gateway will be automatically selected, and you cannot modify this.

    ■ **Second virtual network gateway:** Select the virtual network gateway deployed in West US.

    ■ **Shared key (PSK):** This is a combination of letters and numbers, used to establish encryption for the connection. The same shared key must be used in both the virtual network gateways.

    ■ **Use Azure Private IP address:** Leave this unchecked, as this option is only available with AZ VPN SKUs.

    ■ **Enable BGP:** Leave this unchecked, as you are not using BGP.

    ■ **IKE Protocol:** Select IKEv2.

13. Once these details are filled in, click OK. You will be able to see that the connection is added, and it'll be in the updating state. Since you haven't configured the reciprocal connection on the West US gateway, soon the status will change to Unknown.

14. Navigate to the West US gateway and click Connections. In Connections, you will be able to see the eus-to-wus connection with a Not Connected status. Follow the same process outlined in step 12 and create a connection from the West US gateway to the East US gateway.

15. After adding the connection, within a few minutes, the connection status will change to the connected state for both connections.

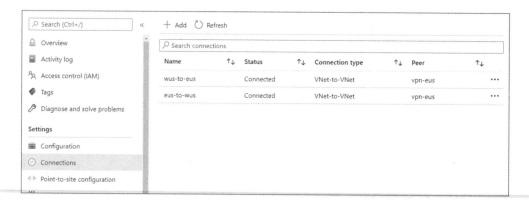

16. Now, you will SSH to jumpbox, and then from jumpbox VM you will SSH to vm-01.

17. From vm-01, try to ping the private IP address of vm-02, and the ping will work.

```
rithin@vm01:~$ ping 10.1.1.4
PING 10.1.1.4 (10.1.1.4) 56(84) bytes of data.
64 bytes from 10.1.1.4: icmp_seq=1 ttl=64 time=66.2 ms
64 bytes from 10.1.1.4: icmp_seq=2 ttl=64 time=65.3 ms
64 bytes from 10.1.1.4: icmp_seq=3 ttl=64 time=66.4 ms
64 bytes from 10.1.1.4: icmp_seq=4 ttl=64 time=66.9 ms
64 bytes from 10.1.1.4: icmp_seq=5 ttl=64 time=66.3 ms
64 bytes from 10.1.1.4: icmp_seq=6 ttl=64 time=69.0 ms
64 bytes from 10.1.1.4: icmp_seq=7 ttl=64 time=64.8 ms
64 bytes from 10.1.1.4: icmp_seq=8 ttl=64 time=65.0 ms
^C
--- 10.1.1.4 ping statistics ---
8 packets transmitted, 8 received, 0% packet loss, time 7010ms
rtt min/avg/max/mdev = 64.839/66.279/69.033/1.301 ms
```

If your gateways are in two different subscriptions, then you need to use PowerShell for establishing the connectivity. You can follow the steps mentioned here to connect the gateways:

https://docs.microsoft.com/en-us/azure/vpn-gateway/vpn-gateway-vnet-vnet-rm-ps

With that, you will move on to compare the virtual network peering and VPN gateway to understand the difference between these two implementations though they serve the same purpose.

Virtual Network Peering vs. VPN Gateway

From the two exercise you have performed, you can conclude that both virtual network peering and VPN gateways are used to facilitate virtual network communication. Both of them support the following connection scenarios:

- Virtual networks in different regions
- Virtual networks that are part of different Azure AD tenants
- Virtual networks deployed in different Azure subscriptions
- Virtual networks that use a mix of Azure classic and Azure Resource Manager deployment models

Similarities aside, let's see how these are different (refer to Table 4.2).

TABLE 4.2 Comparing Virtual Network Peering and VPN Gateway

Specification	Virtual Network Peering	VPN Gateway
Limits	Up to 500 virtual network peering per virtual network	One VPN gateway per virtual network, however, the maximum number of tunnels is SKU dependent
Pricing model	Ingress and egress cost	Hourly cost for the gateway and egress cost for the data transfer
Encryption	Encryption at software level is recommended	IPsec/IKE policies can be applied
Bandwidth limitations	No bandwidth limit	SKU dependent
Latency	Low latency	Higher latency compared to peering
Private connection	Yes, as the traffic is routed via Microsoft backbone network	Public IP is engaged
Transitivity	Nontransitive	If connected via VPN gateway and BGP is enabled, then transitivity works
Deployment time	Fast	30 to 45 minutes
Use case scenarios	Data replication, database failover, data backup	Scenarios where you need encryption, where it's not latency sensitive and high throughput is not required

We will pick one of the aforementioned scenarios based on your use-case scenarios. You also have another scenario, where you can combine the power of peering and the ability of the VPN gateway to connect to on-premises to form hub-spoke architectures. Later in this chapter, you will cover gateway transit and how the hub-spoke architecture can be leveraged. For now, you will wind up the Azure-to-Azure connectivity and move on to Azure to on-premises connectivity.

Azure to On-Premises Connectivity

Though the title says on-premises, this section is applicable for any Azure to AWS, GCP, or any other cloud provider as well. Nevertheless, going forward, we will use on-premises for explaining concepts. Basically, there are two ways to connect on-premises to Azure; one is VPN gateway, and the other one is ExpressRoute. Let's start with VPN gateways.

VPN Gateways

You saw one use-case scenario of VPN gateways when you implemented virtual network to virtual network connectivity; further, you can use VPN gateways to implement S2S and P2S connections as mentioned earlier. Along with S2S, you can also create P2S connections to your on-premises environment. Since we have already covered most of the details about VPN gateways in the previous section, let's go ahead and learn about the site-to-site implementation.

Implementing Site-to-Site Connections

You have already seen the different steps that are involved in the creation of a virtual network to virtual network connection. In the case of an S2S connection, you need to configure the on-premises device as well. Azure administrators will only create the necessary resources in Azure; then it's the responsibility of the on-premises network administrators to configure the local network gateway. Once the local network gateway is configured, then you can create the VPN connection. Figure 4.11 gives a high-level overview of the steps involved in creating an S2S connection.

FIGURE 4.11   Steps to configure S2S

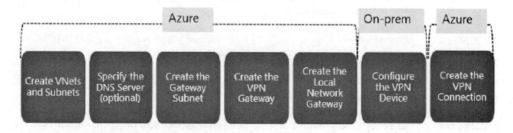

In the steps mentioned in Figure 4.11, you have already seen the relevance of the initial stages such as creating virtual networks and subnets, specifying the DNS server, creating the gateway subnet, and creating the VPN gateway. Here, you have a new stage to create a local network gateway. Since you are already acquainted with the initial steps, let's go ahead and understand the new steps that are involved in the S2S connection.

The local network gateway refers to the on-premises location. You create a reference resource called a *local network gateway* in Azure to specify your on-premises site. While creating the local network gateway, you will specify the address prefixes that are there in the on-premises network. You can search for local network gateways in Azure portal, as shown in Figure 4.12.

FIGURE 4.12   Navigating to the local network gateway

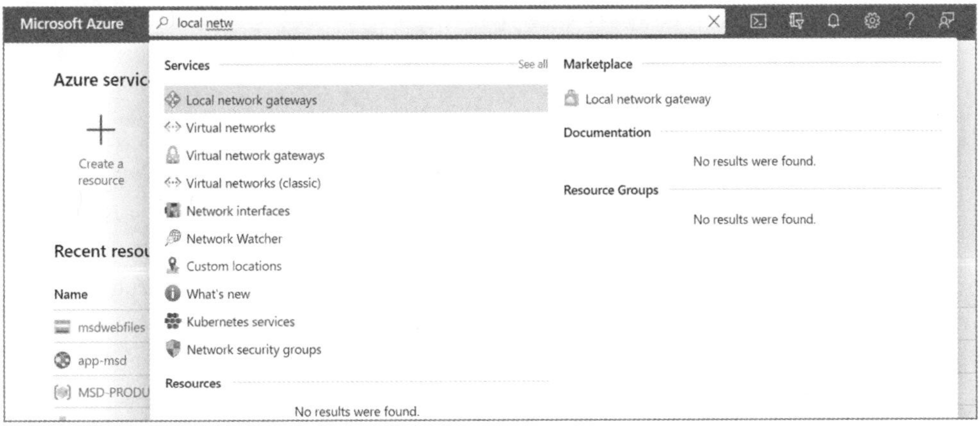

When you create the local network gateway, you need to provide inputs (refer to Figure 4.13). You can use either an IP address or an FQDN to specify your on-premises VPN device. Azure VPN gateway will be establishing connectivity to this device. Other than the IP address and address prefix, you will be asked to choose the subscription, resource group, and location for the resource.

Once the local network gateway is created, Azure knows the IP address or FQDN of your on-premises device. Now it's time to configure the on-premises device and configure it with the IP address of the Azure VPN gateway. There are a set of VPN devices that are compatible with the Azure VPN gateway. All well-known vendors like Cisco, Juniper, Barracuda Networks, and Ubiquiti have partnerships with Microsoft and helped in creating the list of supported devices. Certain devices may still work, even though they are not in the supported list of devices. You can contact the manufacturer for support and configuration of these devices.

FIGURE 4.13   Creating a local network gateway

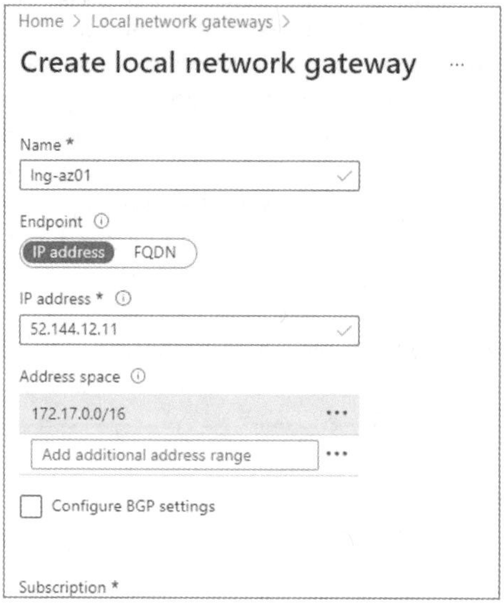

To configure the on-premises device, you need the following:

- **Shared key:** The shared key that you entered in the site-to-site connection. You added this key when you created the site-to-site connection in the VPN gateway.

- **Public IP of the VPN gateway:** The public IP address of the VPN gateway created in Azure.

With the aforementioned details, you will be able to set up your on-premises device. As of now, you created the local network gateway in Azure to let the Azure VPN gateway know the IP address of your on-premises environment. Similarly, in your on-premises environment, you added the key and public IP address of your Azure VPN gateway. Since both the gateways know each other, the only thing remaining is to create a connection between these two. This is the last stage of establishing a site-to-site connection.

As you did in the case of virtual network to virtual network connectivity, you need to navigate to the Connections blade of the VPN gateway to configure the S2S connection. The key difference here is that instead of choosing the connection type as virtual network to virtual network, you need to choose Site-to-Site (IPSec). After that you need to select the local network gateway and provide the key, as shown in Figure 4.14. Once you confirm all the details, click OK, and the connection will be initiated. If the on-premises configuration is made correctly, after a couple of minutes the connection status will change to the connected status.

If you know how to create the virtual network to virtual network connection, you can easily establish an S2S connection. The difference is, in the case of virtual network to virtual network, both the ends are virtual networks; however, in S2S one end is on-premises. To reference the on-premises site, you create a local network gateway in Azure. Then you will create a site-to-site connection in Azure referencing the local network gateway. The next step is to configure your on-premises device with the shared key and the public IP address of the Azure VPN gateway.

FIGURE 4.14   Creating a site-to-site connection

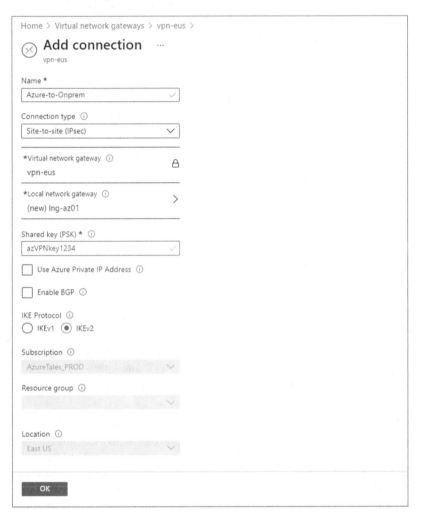

Implementing Point-to-Site Connections

At the time of writing this book, every nation in the world has been affected with the Covid-19 pandemic. The pandemic forced most of us to work from home. While working from home, you need to secure the method by which you can connect to your corporate resources.

Most of the organizations have configured the employee workstations or laptops with VPN so that the employees can connect to their corporate network securely. This is an example of a point-to-site connection. In the case of S2S connections, you create secure connections between two sites. All users in the on-premises environment will connect to their on-premises gateway. Since the on-premises gateway is connected to the Azure VPN gateway, users will be able to access Azure resources privately over a VPN. However, this will work only if the user is in the office or if they are connected to the on-premises network. What if the user is working remotely and is not present in the office? This is where you can leverage P2S connections.

Using a P2S connection, you can create a secure connection from an individual computer to an Azure virtual network over VPN. P2S is also an alternative to S2S connections if you have a limited number of users who want to connect to Azure and you don't have an on-premises equipment that supports S2S connections. The P2S connections are always initiated from the client machine. All clients need to download the VPN profile and install it on their device to establish the P2S connection.

Before Azure accepts P2S requests from the clients, authentication should be done first. There are three authentication types.

- Azure certificate

- RADIUS authentication

- Azure Active Directory

The availability of the authentication methods will depend on the VPN SKU. For example, Basic SKU only supports certificate authentication.

P2S connections support the following protocols:

- The OpenVPN protocol is a TLS VPN solution that supports Android, iOS (versions 11.0 and above), Linux, Windows, and macOS (versions 10.13 and above).

- Secure Socket Tunneling Protocol (SSTP) is also a TLS-based VPN protocol; however, the support is limited to Windows devices (Windows 7 and later).

- IKEv2 VPN is an IPSec VPN solution for macOS-based computers. macOS versions 10.11 and above are supported.

Since TLS uses 443, you don't need to open additional ports on your firewall. The selection of the protocol is based on the device support and your network configuration.

In Exercise 4.3, you will establish a P2S connection from your local machine to Azure. In Azure, you have a virtual network in the East US region with one VM added to the workloadSubnet and the GatewaySubnet for hosting the VPN gateway. The architecture can be reviewed in Figure 4.15. You can reuse the gateway that you created in Exercise 4.2. If you have deleted the resources or resource group, you can re-create the architecture using this PowerShell script:

```
https://github.com/rithinskaria/azure-infra/blob/main/
vpn-p2s-env.ps1
```

FIGURE 4.15   P2S architecture

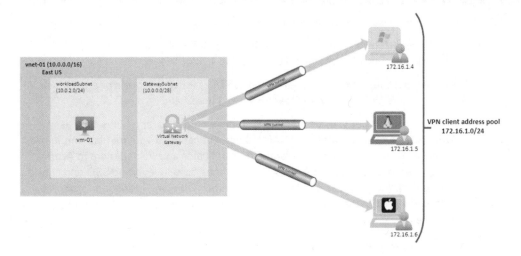

In Figure 4.15, you can see the P2S connection has been established to Linux, Windows, and macOS computers. You could also establish P2S connections to handheld devices and tablets. For the exercise, you will be connecting via a Windows machine and verify the connectivity to the VM. If you don't have a Windows machine, you can download the VPN profile for your OS. See Exercise 4.3.

EXERCISE 4.3

Implementing a P2S VPN in the Azure Portal

1. If you have successfully run the PowerShell script, all resources will be deployed. Navigate to the Azure portal and search for *Virtual Network Gateways*. Open the Virtual Network Gateways blade and select the gateway you created.

2. Go to the Point-to-Site configuration blade and click Configure Now.

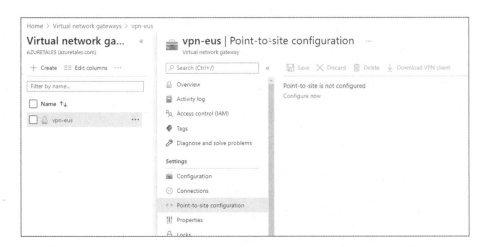

3.   The configuration window will come up with the fields to input the following values:

   ▪   **Address pool:** The pool from which addresses will be allocated to the P2S-connected clients. Let's set the value as 172.16.1.0/24.

   ▪   **Tunnel type:** You can choose OpenVPN or SSTP or IKEv2 protocols or any of their combinations. We will go with OpenVPN (SSL) here.

   ▪   **Authentication type:** You can configure multiple authentication types such as Azure AD, Azure certificates, and RADIUS authentication. If you are planning to use certificates, then you need to generate the certificates and upload them to Azure. In this exercise, you will use Azure AD as it will be easy to leverage SSO and connect to VPN. You need to provide the tenant information and grant admin consent. If you are not the global administrator of the tenant, then you cannot grant the access.

   You need to provide the following information:

   a.   **Tenant:** The endpoint should be added in the format `https://login.microsoftonline.com/{tenantId}`. You need to replace the `{tenantId}` with your tenant ID.

   b.   **Audience:** Since you are using Azure public, the audience is 41b23e61-6c1e-4545-b367-cd054e0ed4b4.

   c.   **Issuer:** The issuer is `https://sts.windows.net/{tenantId}`. You need to replace `{tenantId}` with your tenant ID.

   d.   Click Grant Administrator Consent For Azure VPN Client Application, and you will be redirected to a window similar to the one in the following graphic. Sign in using your Global Administrator credentials, grant consent, and accept the permissions. Once the consent is granted, you will be redirected back to the Azure portal.

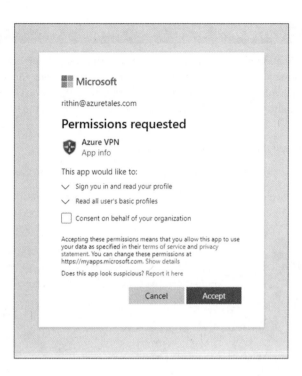

4. Once you fill in all the details, click Save to add the P2S configuration.

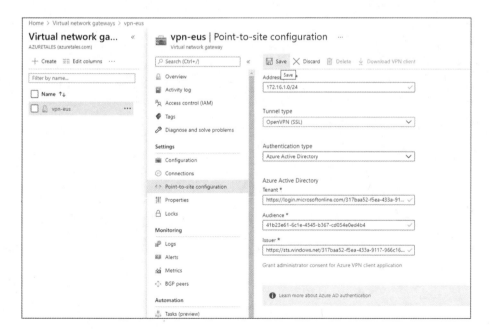

5. After getting notification that the gateway configuration is saved, refresh the page. You will be able to see the Download VPN Client option is available. Click the download button and download the ZIP file. Extract the files to a directory. The ZIP will contain two folders, Generic and AzureVPN. These directories contain the VPN profile and certificates.

6. Download and install the Azure VPN client from the Microsoft Store:

`www.microsoft.com/en-us/p/azure-vpn-client/9np355qt2sqb`

7. Open the Azure VPN client and add the profile using the Import option.

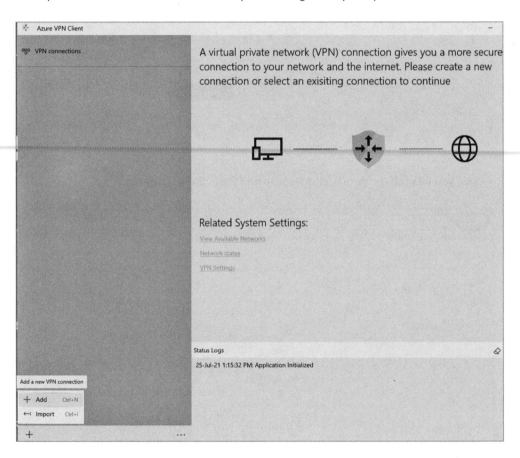

8. You will be asked to select the XML file that contains the VPN configuration. This file will be in your AzureVPN folder, named `azurevpnconfig.xml`. Selecting this file will import all the details.

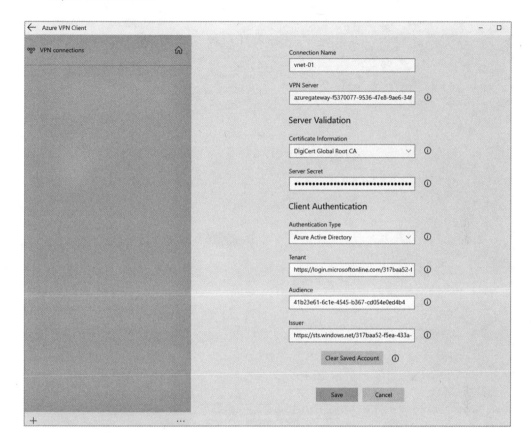

9. Click Save to save the configuration. Your VPN connection will be listed on the left side of the Azure VPN client. Click the Connect button to connect to the VPN and establish a P2S connection.

10. You will be asked to input the user credentials, you can use any user credentials from the tenant ID you have provided in the P2S configuration.

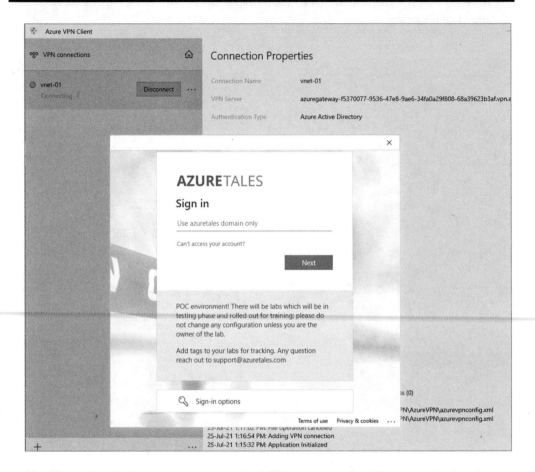

11. After authentication, you can see that the VPN is connected and the routes to virtual network are available to you. Let's go ahead and check if you can connect to the VM in the workloadSubnet using the private IP address. Run a ping from your local computer to check the private IP address of the VM, and the ping will be successful.

```
C:\Users\riskaria>ping 10.0.2.4

Pinging 10.0.2.4 with 32 bytes of data:
Reply from 10.0.2.4: bytes=32 time=245ms TTL=64
Reply from 10.0.2.4: bytes=32 time=243ms TTL=64
Reply from 10.0.2.4: bytes=32 time=244ms TTL=64
Reply from 10.0.2.4: bytes=32 time=243ms TTL=64

Ping statistics for 10.0.2.4:
    Packets: Sent = 4, Received = 4, Lost = 0 (0% loss),
Approximate round trip times in milli-seconds:
    Minimum = 243ms, Maximum = 245ms, Average = 243ms
```

With that, you have successfully established a connection from your client machine to an Azure virtual network using a P2S connection. Now that you are familiar with the VPN connections, let's go ahead and discuss ExpressRoute connections.

ExpressRoute Connections

Like VPN, ExpressRoute helps us to extend on-premises network into the Microsoft cloud. A connection provider facilitates the connection and can be used to establish connections to Microsoft cloud services, such as Microsoft Azure, Microsoft 365, and Dynamics 365. The public Internet is not involved in the case of ExpressRoute. Therefore, ExpressRoute connections offer faster speed, lower latency, security, and higher reliability compared to other connectivity models. Figure 4.16 shows an overview of an ExpressRoute connection from on-premises to the Microsoft cloud.

FIGURE 4.16   ExpressRoute connectivity

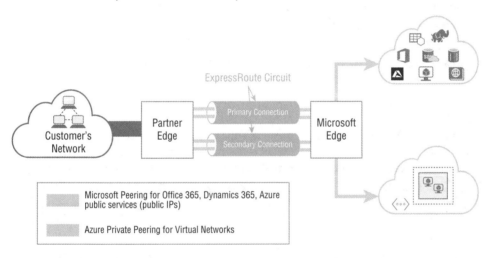

Using ExpressRoute, you can directly connect to the Microsoft cloud from your existing WAN. This connectivity can be established using a multiprotocol label switching (MPLS) VPN. This MPLS will be provided by the network provider. The bandwidth of the VPN gateway is limited to 10 Gbps; however, ExpressRoute provides bandwidth up to 100 Gbps. Because of this very high bandwidth, ExpressRoute is the perfect choice for scenarios such as data migration, data replication, and disaster recovery. ExpressRoute is also the best candidate for moving larger datasets from on-premises to Azure.

ExpressRoute is for extending an on-premises datacenter to the cloud. You can add additional compute and storage capacity to your existing datacenter using ExpressRoute. You can expand the infrastructure, which is ideal for scaling scenarios when required. Since the latency is much less, you don't need to negotiate on the network performance. As the traffic is not routed through the Internet, you can easily build hybrid applications without comprising performance or privacy. For example, you can deploy an application front end in Azure, and the backend datastore can be hosted on-premises for data compliance requirements. Here, you can use ExpressRoute to have private communication between the database and Azure servers. This traffic will be secured as it is not routed through the public Internet. Now that you have a fundamental idea about ExpressRoute, let's take a look at the advantages of ExpressRoute.

Benefits

The following are the benefits of ExpressRoute:

- **L3 connectivity:** ExpressRoute offers layer 3 connectivity. Microsoft leverages BGP to propagate the routes between your instances in Azure, on-premises network, and Microsoft public IP addresses. For different traffic profiles, multiple BGP sessions are created.

- **Redundancy:** Every circuit in ExpressRoute comprises an active-active configuration. This configuration includes two connections to the Microsoft edge routers from your network edge or provider network edge.

- **Access to Microsoft cloud:** ExpressRoute is not only for Azure, but you can also use it to connect to Microsoft 365 services and Microsoft Dynamics 365.

- **Cross-region connectivity:** You can use ExpressRoute to connect two Azure regions for establishing a low-latency, high-bandwidth connection.

- **ExpressRoute premium add-on:** Using the premium add-on feature, you can extend the connectivity across all regions.

- **ExpressRoute global reach:** You can enable the global reach to connect your on-premises sites using ExpressRoute. This is useful to establish low-latency connectivity between on-premises. The traffic will always traverse through Microsoft's network.

- **Choice of bandwidth:** You can purchase ExpressRoute circuits based on your bandwidth requirements. You can choose from 50 Mbps to 100 Gbps. It's recommended that you always check with your connectivity provider to verify if they can support this bandwidth.

- **Billing tiers:** ExpressRoute offers three different billing models that suit your connection requirements. You can pick any of the following models:

  - **Unlimited:** The billing is based on a monthly fixed charge. The ingress and egress data charges are included in the fixed fee and is free of additional cost.

  - **Metered:** There will be a monthly fee for the circuit. You will be charged per gigabyte for the egress data; however, the ingress is free of cost.

  - **Premium add-on:** This is ideal for customers who require a larger number of BGP routes, or more virtual network links per circuit can enable the premium add-on.

While we were discussing the benefits, we constantly used the term *circuit*. Since we haven't explained this concept yet, in the next section you will learn about ExpressRoute circuits and routing domains.

ExpressRoute Circuits

In ExpressRoute you establish a connection between your on-premises infrastructure and the Microsoft cloud with the help of a connectivity provider. The ExpressRoute circuit represents this connection. You can deploy multiple circuits as per your requirements, and these circuits can be connected to your on-premises with the help of different providers.

A service key is used to represent each circuit. This service is not a secret rather a standard GUID used to identify the circuit by the on-premises connectivity provider and Microsoft. If you are setting up ExpressRoute, this key will be shared with you and will be known to Microsoft and the connectivity provider. Each service key is mapped to an ExpressRoute circuit to preserve the uniqueness.

ExpressRoute has multiple peering options available. New ExpressRoute circuits include two independent peerings: private peering and Microsoft peering. However, existing peering may contain three peerings: Azure Private, Azure Public, and Microsoft. Independent BGP sessions and redundancy are implemented for each circuit. Between ExpressRoute and peering, the mapping is in the ratio 1:N where the value of N is from 1 to 3. This implies that each ExpressRoute circuit may have one, two, or all three peerings enabled. The bandwidth you opt for is shared across all the routing domains. Since we are discussing the routing domain, let's take a quick look at the peering in an ExpressRoute circuit.

ExpressRoute Peering

As mentioned in the previous section, each ExpressRoute circuit will have multiple peering or routing domains linked with it. Redundancy is incorporated into all the routing domains using an identical pair of routers; thus, high availability is ensured. You have three types of routing domains: Azure Private, Azure Public (not available in new circuits), and Microsoft.

Let's understand the differences between these routing domains.

Azure Private Peering   As the name suggests, Azure private peering is for services that are using Azure private IP addresses. In other words, resources that are in the deployed Azure virtual network can be accessed using Azure private peering. This helps in the extension of on-premises network to the cloud and communication using the private IP addresses. The connectivity is established in a bidirectional way, which means that the IaaS or PaaS solutions deployed in the virtual networks can communicate with on-premises resources on their private IP addresses. If you take a close look at Figure 4.16, you can see the private peering (blue color) is directed toward the virtual network resources.

Azure Public Peering (Deprecated)   In Figure 4.16, the red line represents Microsoft peering for O365, D365, and Azure public services. As stated earlier, Azure public peering is available only in the existing ExpressRoute circuits; any new circuits will have only Azure private and Microsoft peering. This is the reason why you are not able to see public peering in Figure 4.16.

Azure public peering is responsible for establishing connectivity between on-premises and Azure services that have public IP addresses (for example, Azure Storage). As this peering is dependent on the public endpoint, we call this Azure public peering.

In public peering, the traffic originated from the on-premises private IP address will be NAT by ExpressRoute before it reaches the public endpoint of Azure service. ExpressRoute uses its own NAT pool for providing IP addresses for the traffic coming from on-premises. Since this is not available for new ExpressRoute circuits, you will be using Microsoft peering to establish connectivity to Azure public services.

Microsoft Peering   Microsoft peering can be leveraged to enable connectivity from the on-premises infrastructure to Microsoft online services, which includes Azure PaaS services, Microsoft 365, and Dynamics 365. Though Microsoft 365 was created to be accessed securely over the Internet, rerouting the traffic over ExpressRoute is quite beneficial. The benefits include 99.95 percent SLA and predictability of the networking components. A dedicated connection to Microsoft 365 can be created with the help of ExpressRoute.

Since Azure public peering is not available for new ExpressRoute circuits, you can use Microsoft peering to establish connections to Azure PaaS solutions and services that have a public endpoint. In Figure 4.16, you can see that the Microsoft peering (red color) is connected to O365, D365, Azure Storage, Azure SQL, Azure Cosmos DB, etc. You can only connect to services that have public IP addresses; any resources that are deployed to a virtual network and have private IP addresses can use Azure private peering.

You can create a connection from on-premises to the Microsoft cloud in different ways. The connection type is determined depending on which connection model of ExpressRoute you are using. Let's shift your focus to connection models in ExpressRoute.

ExpressRoute Connection Models

The type of connection from on-premises to the Azure cloud using ExpressRoute is determined using the connection models. You have four models available: co-located at a cloud exchange, point-to-point Ethernet connection, any-to-any (IPVPN) connections, and ExpressRoute Direct. These offerings are provided by the connectivity provider, and you can pick the one that suits your requirement. Now, you will learn the difference between these connection models.

Co-located at a Cloud Exchange   This model is ideal if you are co-located in a facility with a cloud exchange. You can then order a virtual cross connection using your co-location provider's Ethernet exchange. Layer 2 cross connections and managed layer 3 cross connections are supported for establishing connectivity between the Microsoft cloud and your co-location facility.

Point-to-Point Ethernet Connections   Connectivity from on-premises to the Microsoft cloud can be established using point-to-point Ethernet links. Layer 2 connections and managed layer 3 connections are supported for establishing connectivity.

Any-to-Any (IPVPN) Networks   You can extend your on-premises by integrating your WAN with the Microsoft cloud. Once established, the Microsoft cloud will resemble another branch office in your WAN. Managed layer 3 connectivity is supported. ExpressRoute features and capabilities are the same across all the aforementioned connectivity models.

ExpressRoute Direct   ExpressRoute Direct offers the capability to use the peering location spread across the globe to connect with the Microsoft global network. An active-active connectivity with dual 100 Gbps or 10 Gbps connectivity is offered by ExpressRoute Direct. Further, it provides additional features such as faster ingestion of larger datasets to Azure Storage and Cosmos DB, isolation of connectivity, and granular allocation of circuit distribution within the organization.

With that we are concluding the Azure to on-premises section. Now you are familiar with the connectivity methods for establishing communication between Azure-to-Azure and Azure to on-prem. Let's combine all the methods we have studied so far to create an intersite connectivity architecture. This architecture is common in enterprise environments.

Intersite Connectivity Architecture

So far, you covered different connectivity methods by which you can establish connectivity between Azure-to-Azure and Azure to on-premises. When you explore enterprise environments, you will see that all three of these co-exist and work hand in hand to enable seamless intersite connectivity. Before you explore the architecture, it's important that you understand the concept of a gateway transit.

A gateway transit is a feature you enabled while you enable peering. To explain gateway transits in layman's terms, assume that you are booking a ticket from Singapore to Washington, DC. If you are taking British Airways, you need to get off at London, and board the next flight. Here London is a transit point, and Washington, DC, is your destination. You wanted to travel from Singapore to Washington, and in between you landed at the London airport. Nevertheless, you will reach your final destination. Gateway transit works the same way; you can utilize the gateway in the peered network as a transit point. From that transit point, your network traffic can travel to on-premises or any other location that is on the other side of the VPN gateway. When you configure gateway transit, you can communicate with resources that are outside the peered network. For example, you could establish connectivity from your peered network to the following:

- To on-premises via S2S
- To another virtual network

- To a client that is connected to P2S

- ExpressRoute connection

In all the aforementioned scenarios, the gateway transit will allow you to get access to the resources by sharing the gateway. This also helps in billing optimization; you don't need to add a gateway to all the networks for on-premises connectivity. Instead, you could add a gateway to a single virtual network and peer the rest of the virtual networks to the virtual network that has the gateway. As you enable gateway transit, all peered networks will be able to share the gateway and reach resources that are there on-premises. This architecture is known as a *hub-spoke architecture* (refer to Figure 4.17).

FIGURE 4.17   Hub-spoke architecture using a gateway transit

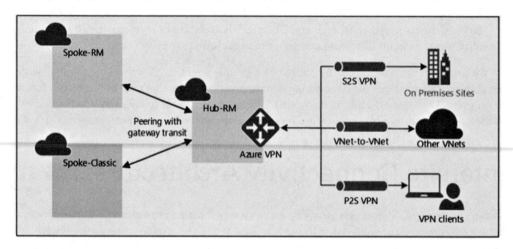

While creating the virtual network peering, you get the option to use the remote virtual network's gateway or route server. This can be enabled to activate the gateway transit feature, as shown in Figure 4.18. You need to make sure that the reciprocal connection is configured accordingly, and the remote network has a gateway deployed in it.

Now that you have a clear understanding about gateway transit, let's discuss the coexisting connections. In Figure 4.19 you can see peering, S2S connection, P2S connection, and ExpressRoute circuit, all of them coexisting in the same architecture.

Some of the inferences you can make from the figure include the following:

- Virtual networks Spoke-VNet-1, Spoke-VNet-2, and Spoke-VNet-3 are peered with the Hub-VNet. You have gateway transit enabled, which means all spoke virtual networks will be able to share the gateways deployed in Hub-VNet.

- Hub-VNet has an ExpressRoute gateway that is connected to the on-premises HQ building. The circuit can provide a low-latency direct connection to the on-premises. As the spoke networks are peered to the hub and gateway transit is enabled, all spoke virtual networks will be able to use the ExpressRoute connection to on-premises.

FIGURE 4.18 Enabling gateway transit

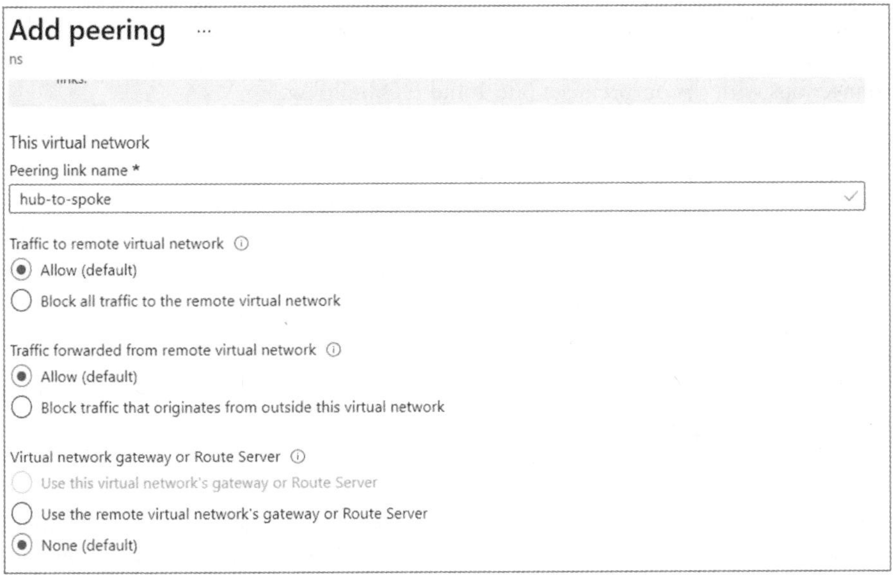

Add peering ...
ns
This virtual network
Peering link name *
hub-to-spoke
Traffic to remote virtual network
Allow (default)
Block all traffic to the remote virtual network
Traffic forwarded from remote virtual network
Allow (default)
Block traffic that originates from outside this virtual network
Virtual network gateway or Route Server
Use this virtual network's gateway or Route Server
Use the remote virtual network's gateway or Route Server
None (default)

FIGURE 4.19 Intersite connectivity architecture

Spoke-VNet-1
10.0.0.0/16
Peering
ExpressRoute Private Connectivity
ExpressRoute
Gateway
On-premises HQ building
10.100.0.0/16
Hub-VNet
192.168.0.0/16
Spoke-VNet-2
10.1.0.0/16
Peering
S2S VPN Tunnel
S2S VPN Tunnel
VPN Gateway
On-premises Site 1
10.30.0.0/16
Spoke-VNet-3
10.2.0.0/16
Peering
P2S VPN Tunnel

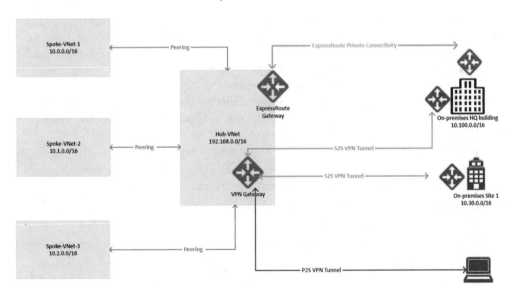

- We have a VPN gateway in the Hub-VNet that has established S2S connections with the HQ building and another site in on-premises. Though HQ already has ExpressRoute, you have added a VPN S2S connection as a backup option that also can be utilized by applications that don't require low latency. The low-latency ExpressRoute will be used by applications that require faster connection, and the rest of the connections will be established using the VPN S2S connection. Here also since the gateway transit is enabled, all the spoke virtual networks will be able to use a VPN gateway and establish connections with the on-premises Site 1 and HQ building.

▪ You have a client computer connected to the VPN gateway using a P2S connection.

The purpose of this architecture was to show the effective utilization of VPN gateways, peering, and ExpressRoute connections. By combining them, you will be able to implement highly available intersite architecture. This architecture can be further improvised by replacing the hub virtual network with the virtual WAN service. This service can help in setting up site connectivity to and through Azure. In the next section, we will cover an overview of the virtual WAN service.

Virtual WAN

Understanding virtual WANs is easy if you understood the reference architecture that you used in the previous section. In the last figure, we used a hub virtual network to connect the ExpressRoute, VPN, and virtual network peering connection. This hub virtual network can be replaced by a virtual WAN; there are features that a virtual WAN can offer rather than a virtual network. A virtual WAN is a network service offered by Microsoft, which you can establish connectivity to and through Azure to your branch offices. In a virtual WAN, Azure regions will act as a hub for connecting your branch offices. The Azure backbone network will be used to connect your branches. Every Azure region can have only one hub and can be peered with only the virtual networks from that region.

You can incorporate different connectivity methods such as S2S VPN, P2S VPN, and ExpressRoute into a centralized interface. Connectivity to Azure virtual networks can be established using virtual network peering. If you look at Figure 4.20, you can see that a virtual WAN is based on the hub-and-spoke architecture we discussed earlier.

The following are some of the features offered by a virtual WAN:

▪ **Integrated connectivity:** Connectivity between on-premises sites and the Azure hub and site-to-site configuration can be completely automated.

▪ **Seamless connectivity:** Azure workloads deployed to Azure virtual networks can be seamlessly connected to the hub.

▪ **Monitoring:** End-to-end flow can be monitored within Azure without the need to deploy any additional resources.

Two types of virtual WANs are offered by Azure: Basic and Standard (refer to Table 4.3).

FIGURE 4.20   Virtual WAN connectivity

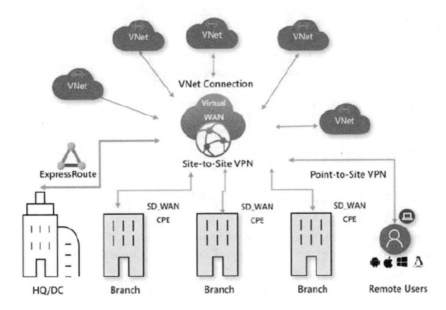

TABLE 4.3   Comparing Virtual WAN Types

Virtual WAN Type	Hub Type	Available Configurations
Basic	Basic	S2S VPN only
Standard	Standard	ExpressRoute, S2S, P2S, interhub, virtual network-to-virtual network through a hub

Summary

In this chapter, we mainly discussed intersite connectivity. We categorized intersite as Azure-to-Azure and Azure to on-premises to explain the connectivity methods. In Azure-to-Azure, we discussed two strategies to connect virtual networks to virtual networks. This includes virtual network peering and a VPN gateway virtual network to virtual network connection. The virtual network peering uses the Microsoft backbone network for communication, while the VPN gateway relies on the public Internet, however it's encrypted.

Later we discussed Azure to on-premises connectivity, which includes S2S connections, P2S connections, and ExpressRoute. You saw the implementation of S2S and P2S connections. Also, you studied concepts related to ExpressRoute.

You also saw how you can implement a hub-and-spoke architecture using the gateway transit feature. We concluded the chapter by discussing a virtual WAN, which can be used for connecting your branch offices to each other using the Azure global network. Now that you are familiar with the intersite connectivity methods, let's learn about network traffic management in Chapter 5, "Network Traffic Management."

Exam Essentials

Understand virtual network peering.   Understand how local and global peering is established between Azure virtual networks.

Understand virtual network to virtual network connectivity using a VPN gateway.   Learn to implement virtual network-to-virtual network connectivity using a VPN gateway.

Understand how to connect on-premises to Azure using a VPN gateway.   Understand the concept of S2S and P2S connections and their implementation.

Learn ExpressRoute.   Learn ExpressRoute, routing domains, and connectivity models.

Understand intersite connectivity.   Understand the concept of a gateway transit. Learn the reference architecture that shows co-existing VPN and ExpressRoute connections.

Learn Azure Virtual WAN.   Understand the basics of a virtual WAN and use-case scenarios.

Review Questions

1. Your organization is planning to connect virtual networks using virtual network peering. Which of the following statements about virtual network peering is not true?

   A. Peering can be easily configured.

   B. Peering can be made in virtual networks within the same region and to other Azure regions.

   C. Peering is transitive in nature.

   D. Gateway transit can be configured on the peering.

2. Which of the following Azure resources is created as a reference to the on-premises VPN device?

   A. Local network gateway

   B. P2S client certificate

   C. S2S connection

   D. NAT

3. Your company is preparing to implement a site-to-site VPN to Microsoft Azure. You are selected to plan and implement the VPN. Currently, you have an Azure subscription, an Azure virtual network, and an Azure gateway subnet. You need to prepare the on-premises environment and Microsoft Azure to meet the prerequisites of the site-to-site VPN. Later, you will create the VPN connection and test it. What should you do? Each answer presents part of the solution. (Select three.)

   A. Obtain a VPN device for the on-premises environment

   B. Obtain a VPN device for the Azure environment

   C. Create a virtual network gateway (VPN) and the local network gateway in Azure

   D. Create a virtual network gateway (ExpressRoute) in Azure

   E. Obtain a public IPv4 IP address without NAT for the VPN device

4. Your company is preparing to implement persistent connectivity to Microsoft Azure. The company has a single site, headquarters, which has an on-premises datacenter. The company establishes the following requirements for the connectivity:

   - Connectivity must be persistent.

   - Connectivity must provide for the entire on-premises site.

   You need to implement a connectivity solution to meet the requirements. What should you do?

   A. Implement a VPN gateway

   B. Implement an S2S VPN

   C. Implement a P2S VPN

   D. Implement a virtual network to virtual network VPN

5. You are configuring virtual network peering across two Azure two virtual networks, VNET1 and VNET2. You are configuring the VPN gateways. You want VNET2 to be able to use VNET1's gateway to get to resources outside the peering. What should you do?

   A. Select Allow Gateway Transit on VNET1 and use remote gateways on VNET2

   B. Select Allow Gateway Transit on VNET2 and use remote gateways on VNET1

   C. Select Allow Gateway Transit and use remote gateways on both VNET1 and VNET2

   D. Do not select Allow Gateway Transit or use remote gateways on either VNET1 or VNET2

6. You are configuring a site-to-site VPN connection between your on-premises network and your Azure network. The on-premises network uses a Cisco ASA VPN device. You have checked to ensure the device is on the validated list of VPN devices. Before you proceed to configure the device, what two pieces of information should you ensure you have? (Select two.)

   A. The shared access signature key from the recovery services vault

   B. The shared key you provided when you created your site-to-site VPN connection

   C. The gateway routing method provided when you created your site-to-site VPN connection

   D. The public IP address of your virtual network gateway

   E. The static IP address of your virtual network gateway

7. You manage a large datacenter that is running out of space. You propose extending the datacenter to Azure using a Multi-Protocol Label Switching virtual private network. Which connectivity option would you select?

   A. P2S

   B. S2S

   C. Multisite

   D. ExpressRoute

8. You are creating a connection between two virtual networks. Performance is a key concern. Which of the following will most influence performance?

   A. Ensuring you select a route-based VPN

   B. Ensuring you select a policy-based VPN

   C. Ensuring you specify a DNS server

   D. Ensuring you select an appropriate Gateway SKU

9. Which of the following statements about VPN gateway is not true?

   A. VPN gateways can be deployed and configured faster than virtual network peering.

   B. VPN gateway bandwidth is dependent on the SKU.

   C. VPN gateway can be deployed across availability zones.

   D. VPN gateways are charged per hour along with the data transfer charges.

10. Your organization wants to make use of a virtual WAN. Your manager has requested to keep the cost as low as possible and set up S2S connections to your branch offices. Which of the following solutions match your requirement?

    A. Basic virtual WAN

    B. Standard virtual WAN

    C. S2S virtual WAN

    D. S2S hub

11. You are already using VPN in Azure, and your organization has a new site on-premises that you need to connect to Azure. The current virtual network already has a VPN gateway. Which of the following actions need to be performed in Azure to connect the new site to Azure?

    A. Create a new VPN gateway in the virtual network and create S2S connection

    B. Create a new connection from the existing gateway

    C. Add a new VPN routing table for the new site

    D. Configure a P2S connection

12. Which of the following routing domains should be used to connect an Azure Storage service public endpoint to a new ExpressRoute circuit?

    A. Azure public peering

    B. Azure private peering

    C. Microsoft peering

    D. ExpressRoute Direct

13. Which of the following is not a supported authentication method for P2S VPN?

    A. Azure Active Directory

    B. Certificate

    C. RADIUS server

    D. TACACS

14. What is the name of the key that is shared with you, the service provider, and Microsoft while setting up ExpressRoute?

    A. Service key

    B. Secret key

    C. Circuit key

    D. Auth key

15. What is the maximum number of allowed peerings on a virtual network?

    A. 1

    B. 100

    C. 250

    D. 500

16. You are planning to implement ExpressRoute, and you need to make sure there won't be any additional costs for the bandwidth. How can you accomplish this?

    A. Unlimited tier of ExpressRoute

    B. Meter tier of ExpressRoute

    C. ExpressRoute Global Reach

    D. ExpressRoute Premium Add-on

17. Your organization is planning to connect your on-premises site to Azure DevOps using ExpressRoute. Which of the following routing methods should be used for this?

    A. Private peering to DevOps private endpoint

    B. Public peering

    C. Private peering to DevOps project

    D. Microsoft peering

18. You created a policy-based VPN gateway and per a request from your management you would like to switch to a route-based VPN gateway. Which is the correct method to migrate to a route-based VPN?

    A. Change the properties of the VPN gateway and switch to route-based.

    B. Route-based is supported by default; there's no need to change.

    C. Reconfigure the VPN profile.

    D. Delete and re-create the gateway as a route-based VPN gateway.

19. What is the smallest CIDR block you can use when you create the gateway subnet?

    A. /27

    B. /29

    C. /30

    D. /28

20. You created a virtual network peering connection and the status stays in Initiated state. What needs to be done to change the status to Connected? (Select two.)

    A. Create the reciprocal connection

    B. Enable allow traffic in the peering connection

    C. Delete and re-create the peering

    D. Wait for 5 to 10 minutes for the connection to sync

Chapter

5

Network Traffic Management

MICROSOFT EXAM OBJECTIVES COVERED IN THIS CHAPTER:

✓ **Configure load balancing**

- Configure Azure Application Gateway
- Configure an internal or public load balancer
- Troubleshooting load balancing

In the previous two chapters, we were talking about virtual networks and how you can establish connectivity to on-premises. It's also important to understand the implementation of load balancing in Azure. In this chapter, from an exam standpoint, you need to learn two services: Azure Load Balancer and Azure Application Gateway. However, there are two more services from a load-balancing standpoint. They are Azure Front Door and Azure Traffic Manager. Understanding these services will help you implement highly available load-balanced solutions in Azure.

Before getting start, let's understand what load balancing is. Load balancing is the mechanism of distributing the incoming requests to a set of servers deployed in the backend. The load-balancing solution will act as the front end and help in distributing the incoming requests to the backend. This implementation enhances the service availability and mitigates the risk of downtime. You already know that in the cloud you can easily scale out your resources. During a scale-out or autoscale event the number of servers will increase, and the load balancer plays the inevitable role of distributing the traffic across these servers (including the newly added ones).

We will kick off this chapter with Azure Load Balancer, and then we will move to Azure Application Gateway and wind up the chapter with a brief overview of Azure Front Door and Azure Traffic Manager. Each of the aforementioned solutions plays different roles when added to your architecture; later in the chapter you will be able to understand the differences among them. Before we start discussing Load Balancer, it's important to understand the concept of availability sets and availability zones. If you are already familiar with these concepts, you can skip to the Azure Load Balancer discussion.

Availability Options

When you deploy services in Azure, Azure offers different availability options depending on the service you are selecting. Most of the time, you will hear about availability sets and availability zones. Though these are common with the deployment of virtual machines, nowadays you will see zone-redundant and zonal-redundant architectures with other services as well. As you progress, you will see different availability options for different services. Nevertheless, understanding the concept of availability sets and availability zones is crucial to implementing highly available services in Azure. While explaining these concepts, we will be using virtual machines as the reference service.

By default, when you create a virtual machine, Azure automatically picks a server in the Azure datacenter to host the machine. Even if you deploy multiple instances to increase the availability, it's not necessary that high availability will be achieved. Using an availability set, you can make sure that the virtual machines are deployed to different hosts and thus ensure high availability.

Let's learn about availability sets.

Availability Sets

To achieve high availability, you need to deploy multiple instances of your application. Since we are using virtual machines as the reference service for explaining availability sets, you need to deploy multiple virtual machines each representing an instance of your application. In short, an *availability set* is a logical grouping of the VMs hosting our application. Since there are multiple instances, you are eliminating the single point of failure.

An availability set comprises update domains (UDs) and fault domains (FDs), and every virtual machine that you create will be associated with a UD and a FD. You can configure up to three FDs and twenty UDs. UDs represent a group of VMs and the underlying host that can be updated and rebooted at the same time. This will ensure that only one UD is rebooted at a time during planned maintenance events such as patching, firmware updates, etc. The default number of UDs is five, and if you are creating more than five VMs, the sixth VM will be placed on the first UD, the seventh will be on the second, and so forth depending upon the number of instances. While a UD is getting rebooted, it's given 30 minutes to recover before the maintenance task is started on a different domain.

Fault domains represent a set of virtual machines that share a common network switch, power, and air conditioning. FDs can be configured up to a maximum of 3, and this is the default value while setting up availability sets. Placing the instances to different fault domains will help protect the instances from hardware failures such as network outages, power failures, etc. Figure 5.1 shows how the update domains and fault domains are aligned in a datacenter. Along with the VMs, the disks are aligned with the fault domain.

FIGURE 5.1 Availability sets

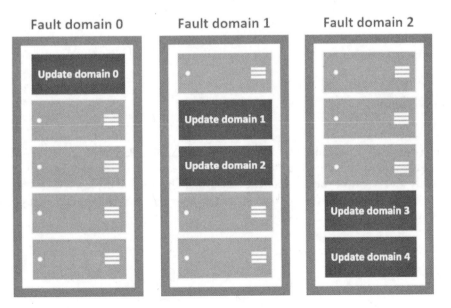

You can easily create availability sets from the Azure portal, Azure CLI, or Azure PowerShell. Search for *Availability Sets* in the Azure portal, and you can create the availability set by specifying the subscription, resource group, name, region, number of fault domains, number of update domains, and disk alignment, as shown in Figure 5.2

FIGURE 5.2   Creating availability sets

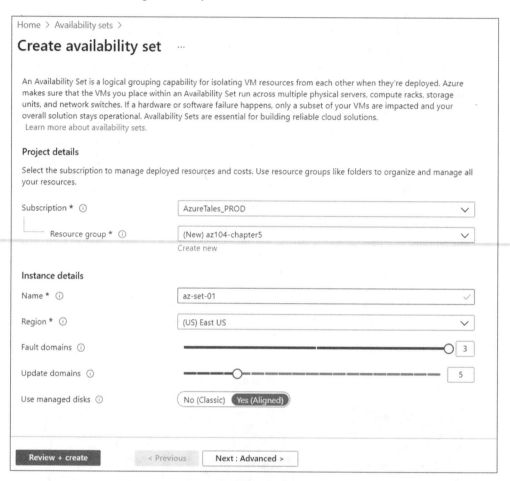

Along with the basic details, you can specify the proximity placement group that will allow us to group Azure resources physically closer together in the selected region. Once the availability set is created, you can reference the availability set and deploy VMs to the availability set. An availability set is free of cost, and you pay only for the instances that you are deploying.

An availability set avoids service downtime caused by hardware failure or planned maintenance. However, the protection offered is limited to the datacenter level. What if the entire datacenter is unavailable due to a power outage, natural disaster, or any other reasons? Since the datacenter is down, your workloads will not be available. Here comes the role of availability zones; let's understand the concept of availability zones.

Availability Zones

In Azure, every region comprises a set of datacenters that are interconnected with a regional low-latency network. Having more regions that any other cloud provider, Azure gives you the freedom to deploy across multiple regions and plan cross-region disaster recovery. In Chapter 2, you saw different terminologies related to regions and regional pairs. Within Azure regions, you have unique physical locations named zones. Each zone comprises one or more datacenters. Also, each zone has independent cooling, power, and networking. As these zones are physically isolated and located in different parts of the region, you can deploy our applications to availability zones to protect from datacenter failures.

When you are using availability zones, the instances can be spun across multiple zones within the region. If one of the zones goes down due to an outage, the instances deployed in the other zones will be able to serve your customers. Figure 5.3 gives the pictorial representation of Azure availability zones.

FIGURE 5.3   Availability zones

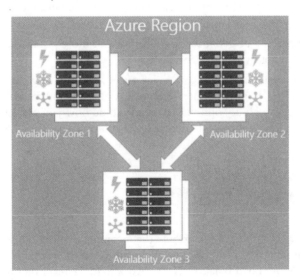

You can choose the zone to deploy to when you are creating a virtual machine and thus ensure that the VMs are deployed to different zones to protect from datacenter failures. Choosing availability zones and availability sets in your architecture can improve the overall SLA of the application compared to hosting the application in a single VM. In the next section, you will see how the SLA changes depending on the availability option you select.

Service Level Agreement

If you take the case of virtual machines, as per the SLA documentation available here:

`https://azure.microsoft.com/en-in/support/legal/sla/virtual-machines/v1_9`

the SLA of single VM varies with the type of disk you are choosing. The following are the SLAs offered for the single VM:

- At least 99.9 percent VM connectivity for any single instance of VM using Premium SSD or Ultra SSD for all OS disk and data disks
- At least 99.5 percent VM connectivity for any single instance of VM using Standard SSD disks for OS disk and data disks
- At least 95 percent VM connectivity for any single instance of VM using Standard HDD disks for OS disk and data disks

Depending upon the type of disk, the SLA offered varies. If you deploy two or more instances across availability zones or availability sets, then the SLA gets increased as follows:

- At least 99.95 percent VM connectivity when two or more instances are deployed in the same availability set
- At least 99.99 percent VM connectivity when two or more instances are deployed across two or more availability zones

Thus, you can conclude that adding more instances and spreading them across availability sets or availability zones will increase the SLA of your application. Now that you are familiar with the availability options, let's understand how you can leverage the load balancing solutions to distribute the load across the multiple instances. Let's start with Azure Load Balancer.

Azure Load Balancer

With Azure Load Balancer you can distribute the incoming requests across multiple instances of your application. The application can be deployed to virtual machines or virtual machine scale sets (VMSS). Azure Load Balancer is a network load balancer that operates at layer 4 of the OSI layer. As the requests are getting spread across the instances, you can ensure that high availability is achieved.

Both inbound and outbound traffic scenarios are supported by the Azure Load Balancer. The load balancer relies on the load balancing rules and health probes to distribute the traffic to the backend servers. The purpose of the load balancing rules is to determine how the traffic should be distributed across the backend servers. The health probes ensure that the backend server is healthy and is capable of handling the request. If the load balancer cannot determine the health of the backend server, the requests will no longer be distributed to the unhealthy server.

Figure 5.4 shows the high-level overview of the function of Azure Load Balancer.

FIGURE 5.4   Overview of Azure Load Balancer

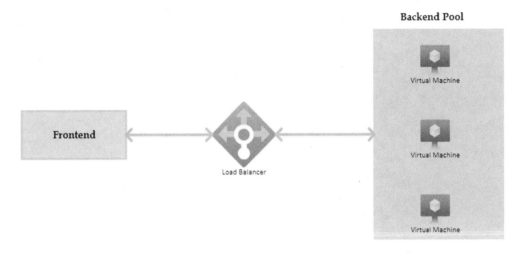

There are two types of load balancers: public and internal. Let's take a look at these types and understand the differences between them.

Types of Load Balancers

As you already know, the purpose of a load balancer is to distribute the traffic to the servers after verifying the health of the backend server. Depending upon the placement of the load balancer in the architecture, the load balancer can be categorized as a public load balancer and an internal load balancer.

Public Load Balancer

As the name suggests, a public load balancer will have a public IP address, and it will be Internet facing. In a public load balancer, the public IP address and a port number are mapped to the private IP address and port number of the VMs that are part of the backend pool. By using load balancing rules, you can configure the port numbers and handle different types of traffic. For example, if you want to distribute the incoming web requests across a set of web servers, you can deploy a public load balancer and spread the traffic. In short, an Internet endpoint is exposed in the case of a public load balancer.

Figure 5.5 shows how the incoming web requests from the Internet are distributed across the set of web servers added in the backend.

FIGURE 5.5   Public load balancer

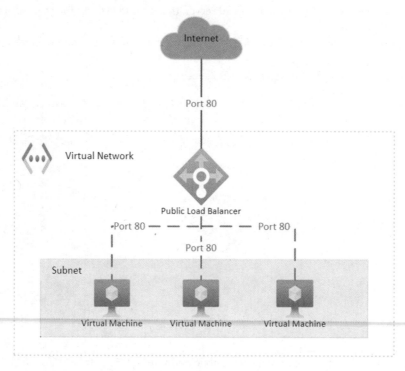

In Figure 5.5, you can see that all incoming requests to the front-end public IP address of the load balancer on port 80 are getting distributed to the backend web servers on port 80.

Internal Load Balancer

There will be scenarios where you want to load balance the requests between resources that are deployed inside a virtual network without exposing any Internet endpoint. For example, this could be a set of database servers that will distribute the database requests coming from the front-end servers. Since the backend database servers cannot be exposed to the Internet, you need to make sure that the load balancer has no public endpoint. Internal load balancers are deployed to distribute the traffic to your backend servers that cannot be exposed to the Internet. The internal load balancer will not have a public IP address and will be using the private IP address for all communication. This private IP address can be reached by the resources within the same virtual network, within peered networks, or from on-premises over VPN. This is ideal for deploying internal applications without exposing them to the Internet.

The internal load balancer can be easily demonstrated if you extend the architecture, as you saw in Figure 5.5. Let's assume that the VMs in Figure 5.5 are running an ASP.NET MVC application and you would like to send requests to the database for CRUD operations. Figure 5.6 shows the extension of architecture using an internal load balancer.

FIGURE 5.6 Internal load balancer

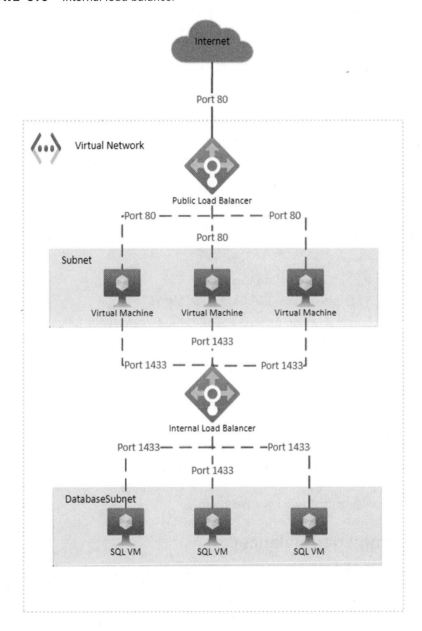

In Figure 5.6, you are using an internal load balancer to distribute the requests from our web servers to our backend database servers.

With that, you will now look into the load balancer SKUs that are available in Azure.

Load Balancer SKUs

While creating a load balancer in Azure, you can select the load balancer type (internal or public). In addition, you can select the SKU for the load balancer. The two SKUs you have in Azure are Basic and Standard. The Standard SKU is the newer version of the load balancer and offers more features and capabilities than the Basic SKU. All features of Basic SKU are already included in the Standard SKU along with additional features.

Basic SKU supports the following:

- Port forwarding
- Automatic reconfiguration
- Health probes (HTTP, TCP)
- SNAT
- Diagnostics for public-facing load balancers
- Support for VMs in a single availability set and VMSS

Standard SKU supports all the features of Basic SKU along with the following features:

- HTTPS health probes
- Support for availability zones
- Metrics and analytics using Azure Monitor
- HA ports
- Outbound rules
- SLA of 99.99 percent (for two or more VMs in the backend)
- Support for any VMs or VMSS in a virtual network

Depending upon the requirements, you can choose one of the SKUs. Now you will see how you can configure the Azure Load Balancer.

Configuring Load Balancer

While creating a load balancer, you need to configure several items such as the front-end and backend pools, load balancing rules, session persistence, and health probes. In Exercise 5.1, you will create an availability set and configure a load balancer; however, before that, let's learn the terminologies related to the Azure load balancer configuration. Let's start with backend pools.

Backend Pools

When you configure a load balancer, you need to specify the backend pool. The backend pool contains the IP address of the network interface cards that are attached to the set of virtual machines or virtual machine scale set. In Figure 5.4, you can see that the backend pool is represented using a set of VMs. Depending on the type of SKU you are choosing, the type of backend pool that can be associated will be different. The Standard SKU supports an availability set, a single virtual machine, or a virtual machine scale set.

In the Standard SKU, you can have up to 1,000 instances, and the Basic SKU can have up to 100 instances in the backend pool.

Health Probes

The purpose of a health probe is to let the load balancer know the status of the application. The health probe will be constantly checking the status of the application using an HTTP or TCP probe. If the application is not responding after a set of consecutive failures, the load balancer will mark the virtual machine as unhealthy. Incoming requests will not be routed to the unhealthy virtual machines. The load balancer will start routing the traffic once the health probe is able to identify that the application is working and is responding to the probe.

In the HTTP probe, the endpoint will be probed every 15 seconds (default value), and if the response is HTTP 200, then it means that the application is healthy. If the application is returning a non-2xx response within the timeout period, the virtual machine will be marked unhealthy. While configuring the HTTP probe, you can configure the port number, path to probe, interval, and timeout period.

Using the TCP probe will help you verify if the load balancer is able to establish a TCP connection on the specified port. If the connection is successful, then the endpoint is healthy. If the connection is refused, the probe fails, and the virtual machine will be marked as unhealthy. For the TCP probe, you configure the port, interval, and unhealthy threshold.

Load Balancer Rules

As mentioned earlier, load balancer rule decides how the traffic should be routed from the front-end pool to the backend pool. In other words, without the load balancer rules, the traffic that hits the front end will never reach the backend pool.

Front-end IP and port numbers are mapped to the backend IP addresses and ports using the load balancer rules. The backend pool, front-end IP address, and health probe are required before setting the load balancer rule. Load balancer rules can be also leveraged to facilitate remote access to the backend virtual machines. For example, you could map the front-end IP and a port number to the backend VM and RDP port for RDP access.

You will get to know more about the load balancing rule when you deploy the load balancer in Exercise 5.1.

Session Persistence

The load balancer will distribute the traffic equally among the backend servers, which is the default behavior. A five-tuple hash is used by the load balancer to spread the traffic to the available servers in the backend. The five tuple hash includes the source IP, source port, destination IP, destination port, and protocol. Session persistence specifies how the traffic from the client should be routed and which backend server will serve the request.

You have three distribution modes available in the load balancer to handle session persistence.

- **None/five tuple:** This is the default value, and any virtual machine can handle the incoming requests. Since the five tuples include the source port in the hash, clients may get redirected to different back-end servers for each session.

- **Client IP/source IP affinity/two-tuple hash:** Requests coming from the same source IP address will be handled by the same backend server. Here the hash between the source IP and the destination IP is used to map the backend servers.

- **Client IP and protocol/three-tuple hash:** Successive requests from the same client IP address and protocol will be handled by the same backend virtual machine. In a three-tuple hash, you are taking the hash of the source IP, destination IP, and protocol to map the servers.

The selection of the distribution mode is based on the application requirements. In some applications, you may require storing the logged-in user's profile. In this scenario, you need to use a client IP distribution mode. This will help the user to get redirected to the same server where they are logged in.

Now that you are familiar with the terminologies, it's time that you deploy a load balancer and distribute the traffic.

Implementing Azure Load Balancer

You will be creating an architecture similar to the one in Figure 5.7.

You can use the PowerShell script here:

```
https://github.com/rithinskaria/azure-infra/blob/main/loadbalancing.ps1
```

to create the virtual networks, subnet, availability set, jumpbox VM, and web servers. If needed, you can manually deploy each of the resources. Since the idea here is to deploy the load balancer, it would be better to write a script to deploy the rest of the resources. If you used the PowerShell script, the script would display the FQDN of the jumpbox VM and the private IP addresses of the web servers once the deployment is completed. Instead of jumpbox, you could also deploy a Bastion host.

See Exercise 5.1.

FIGURE 5.7   Configuring the load balancer, reference architecture

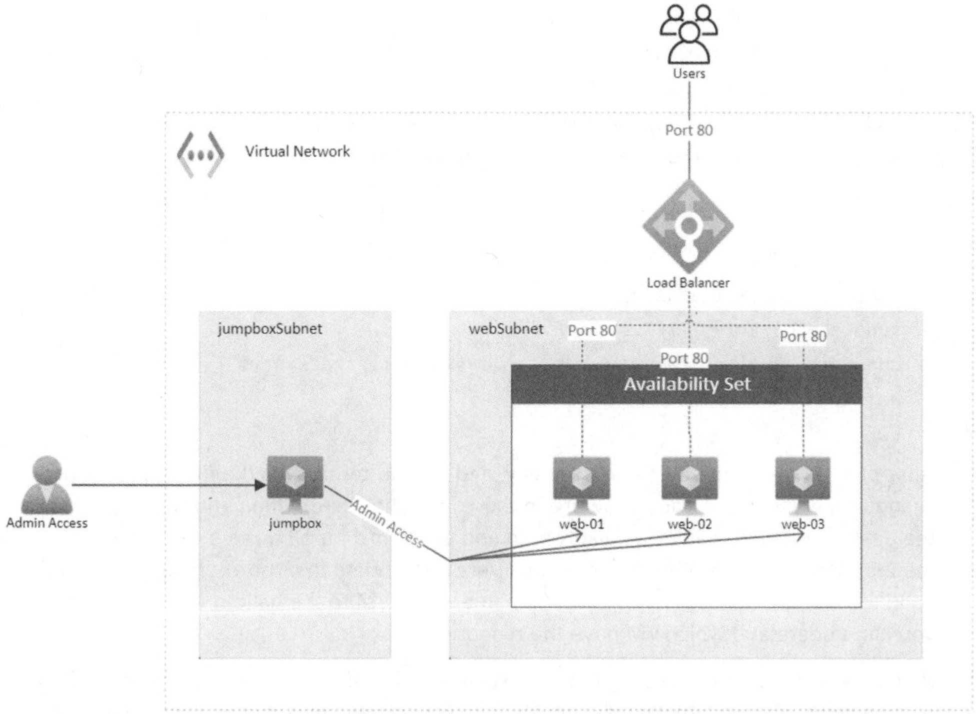

EXERCISE 5.1

Implementing Load Balancing in Azure

1. If you have successfully run the PowerShell script, all resources will be deployed. SSH to the jumpbox using the public IP address/FQDN of the VM.

2. Once you are in the jumpbox VM and run the command nano script.sh, this will open the nano text editor and you have to paste the following script:

```
#!/bin/bash
sudo apt update -y
sudo apt install sshpass -y
sshpass -p "VMP@55w0rd" ssh -o StrictHostKeyChecking=no
rithin@10.0.2.4 <<EOF
sudo apt install apache2 -y
sudo chmod -R -v 777 /var/www/
sudo echo "Hello from web-01" > /var/www/html/index.html
exit
```

```
EOF
sshpass -p "VMP@55w0rd" ssh -o StrictHostKeyChecking=no rithin@10.0.2.5 <<EOF
sudo apt install apache2 -y
sudo chmod -R -v 777 /var/www/
sudo echo "Hello from web-02" > /var/www/html/index.html
exit
EOF
sshpass -p "VMP@55w0rd" ssh -o StrictHostKeyChecking=no rithin@10.0.2.6 <<EOF
sudo apt install apache2 -y
sudo chmod -R -v 777 /var/www/
sudo echo "Hello from web-03" > /var/www/html/index.html
exit
EOF
```

3. After pasting the script, hit Ctrl+X, press y, and then Enter to save the file. If you have changed the username and password in the PowerShell script, then you have to update the Bash script with the correct username and password for all three sshpass commands. This script will SSH to our web servers and update the index.html file with a hello message. You will also append the name of the VM to the hello message so that you can understand which VM gave the response.

4. Run chmod +x script.sh to add the execute permission and then ./script.sh to run the script. Your environment is completely set up now, and you can deploy the load balancer. If you are not familiar with Bash scripts, then you can manually SSH to each machine and install the Apache Server.

5. Navigate to the Azure portal and search for *Load Balancer*. Click Create. In the initial screen, you will be asked to provide the following inputs:

   - **Subscription:** Select the subscription.

   - **Resource Group:** Select the resource group.

   - **Name:** Set the name of the load balancer.

   - **Region:** Choose a region for the load balancer. Make sure that you select the same region where your web servers are deployed.

   - **Type:** Internal or Public. Since you are load balancing the requests from the Internet, you need to select Public.

   - **SKU:** Standard or Basic. You will go with the default option Standard.

   - **Tier:** Regional or Global; go with the default option.

6. Once all details are filled in, click Next: Frontend IP Configuration to configure the front end.

7. On the Frontend IP Configuration tab, click Add A Frontend IP and create a public IP address. You also need to pass the name, IP version, and IP type. You can add multiple front-end IPs if required.

EXERCISE 5.1 *(continued)*

8. After saving the IP configuration, click Next: Backend Pools to configure the backend pool. In the backend pool, click Add A Backend Pool, which will take you to a window where you can add the backend pool details.

9. In the backend pool configuration, you need to input the following details:

   - **Name:** This is the name for the backend pool.

   - **Virtual Network:** Select the virtual network where your VMs are deployed.

   - **Backend Pool Configuration:** NIC or IP address. Select the default value.

   - **IP Version:** IPv4.

   - Under Virtual Machines, click Add, and select all web servers and then Add.

   - Finally, click Add at the bottom-left corner to save the backend pool configuration.

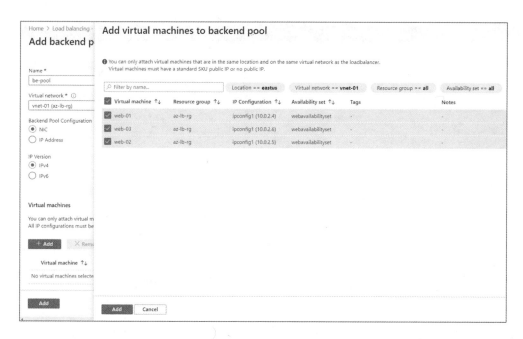

10. Once you save the configuration, you will be redirected to the load balancer create wizard, and your VMs are visible on the Backend Pools tab. Click Next: Inbound Rules to configure the inbound rules.

11. On the Inbound Rules tab, you are interested only with the load balancing rule, so click Add A Load Balancing Rule. On the right side, you will see a new pane to add the load balancing rule. You need to provide the following details:

   ▪ **Name:** This is the name for the load balancing rule. You can give any name.

   ▪ **IP Version:** IPv4.

   ▪ **Frontend IP address:** Select the frontend IP address you created earlier.

   ▪ **Protocol:** TCP, as you are planning to distribute web traffic.

   ▪ **Port:** 80 for web traffic.

   ▪ **Backend Port:** 80 as the Apache server is running on port 80 on the backend VMs.

   ▪ **Backend Pool:** Select the backend pool you added earlier.

   ▪ **Health Probe:** Since you haven't created the health probe yet, you can click Create New. As shown here, you can add the health probe details. The details include the name, protocol, port number, internal, and unhealthy threshold.

   ▪ **Session Persistence:** When set to None, this will perform five tuple hash.

EXERCISE 5.1 *(continued)*

12. Leave the rest of the options with the default value and click Add to add the load balancing rule. As you are not using any Outbound rules, you can skip that and click Review + Create. Once the validation is done, click Create to create the load balancer.

13. Once the load balancer is deployed, navigate to the Overview blade, and copy the public IP address. Try the IP address in your browser; you can see here that you are getting responses from different servers.

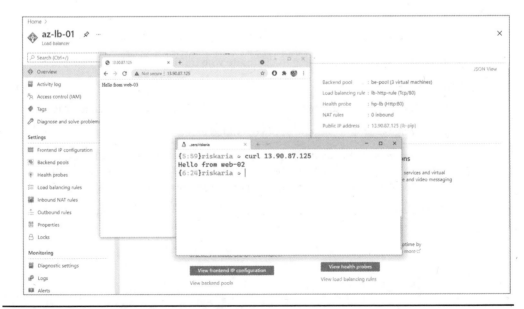

The responses in Exercise 5.1, step 13, have been taken from two different applications (one from the browser and the other from the terminal). Since you configured the load balancer session persistence as none, a five-tuple hash will take place. In a five-tuple hash, whenever one of the values changes, you will routed to another server. Here, the source port is different for these requests, and they have been routed to two different servers though they originated from the same source IP address.

On that note, you are concluding the Azure Load Balancer. In the next section, you will uncover Azure Application Gateway.

Azure Application Gateway

Azure Load Balancer could load balance any TCP/UDP traffic to the backend servers; however, Azure Application Gateway is designed to distribute the incoming web requests to a web application. Unlike Azure Load Balancer, which operates at layer 4, or the Transport layer, Application Gateway uses layer 7, or the Application layer, routing to route the traffic to the backend web applications. Since Application Gateway is operating at layer 7, the IP addresses of the backend servers are not considered; rather, hostnames and paths are used for routing. Application Gateway supports virtual machines, VMSS, Azure App Service, and even on-premises servers.

Requests are routed in a round-robin fashion to the backend servers. If you would like to implement session stickiness, Application Gateway supports that as well. Using session stickiness, you can override the default round-robin fashion, and client requests in the same session will be routed to the same backend server. Let's understand the features of Application Gateway:

- **Supported protocols:** It supports HTTP, HTTPS, HTTP/2, and WebSocket.
- **WAF support:** Web Application Firewall can be incorporated with Application Gateway to protect web applications.
- **Encryption:** It supports end-to-end request encryption.
- **Autoscaling:** You can dynamically scale Application Gateway to handle traffic spikes.
- **Redirection:** Traffic can be redirected to another site or from HTTP to HTTPS.
- **Rewrite HTTP headers:** It allows passing additional information with the request or response.
- **Custom error pages:** Instead of using the default error pages, you can use custom error pages.

Now you are familiar with the features of Application Gateway. Let's see how Application Gateway deals with client requests.

Request Handling Process

The architecture contains front-end, listener, backend, and WAF (optional). You have already seen how front-end and backend works in the case of a load balancer. In Figure 5.8 you can see how the traffic is getting routed from the front end to the backend.

FIGURE 5.8   Working of Application Gateway

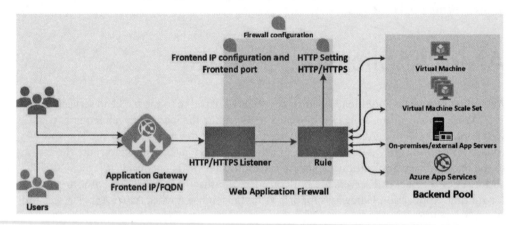

The following is the end-to-end process that happens when a request hits the Application Gateway:

- The users will be accessing the web application by sending the request to the front-end IP address of the Application Gateway. In real-world scenarios, you would be mapping the IP address of the Application Gateway to a DNS name, and the client reaches the Application Gateway by resolving that DNS name.

- Once the DNS returns the IP address of the Application Gateway, the request will be sent to the front-end IP address of the application.

- Application Gateway uses listeners to accept incoming traffic. As the name suggests, the listener listens or checks for connection requests. You can have multiple listeners configured with the front-end IP address, protocol, and port number.

- Optionally, you can add the web application firewall (WAF) to check the request headers of the body (if present) against the WAF rules. WAF can be used to determine if the incoming request is a legitimate one or a security threat.

- If the request is valid, based on the rules configured, the request will be routed to the backend pool.

Similar to an internal and public load balancer, you can use Application Gateway for internal applications and for Internet-facing applications. When you configure the Application Gateway as a public-facing one, you will have a public IP address mapped to the

Application Gateway. Throughout this section, we mentioned routing; however, we haven't covered the routing methods in Application Gateway. Let's take a look at the routing methods available in Application Gateway.

Routing Methods

In Azure Load Balancer, you saw that the load balancer relies on the source IP, source port, destination IP, destination port, and protocol for routing the traffic. Azure Load Balancer uses the five-tuple hash, three-tuple hash, or two-tuple hash for routing the traffic to the backend servers. Application Gateway is a layer 7 load balancer, so the routing mechanism is different from the one that you witnessed in the case of Azure Load Balancer.

The following are the routing methods available in Application Gateway.

Path-Based Routing

In path-based routing, Application Gateway inspects the URL paths and routes the traffic to the different backend pools. For example, you can direct the requests with the path /docs/* to the backend pool containing the documents. Similarly, all URLs containing the path /videos/* can be routed to the backend servers optimized for video streaming. In Figure 5.9, you can see how path-based routing is accomplished.

FIGURE 5.9   Path-based routing

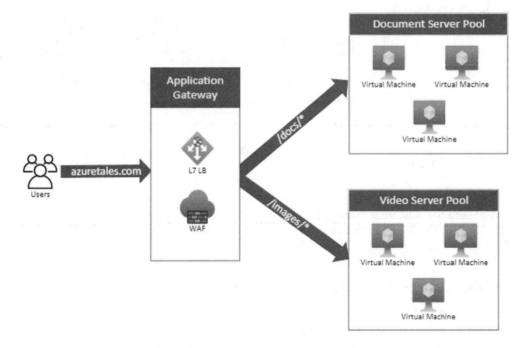

Multisite Routing

Multisite routing or multiple site routing lets you configure more than one web application behind the same Application Gateway. In this configuration, you need to map the front-end IP address of the Application Gateway to multiple CNAMEs. For example, say the front-end IP address of the Application Gateway is 13.67.11.172 and you have two web applications, such as `http://azuretales.com` and `http://azuretaleslabs.com`. You will map the front-end IP as a CNAME to both domains. When the requests hit the Application Gateway based on the URL, it will be routed to the appropriate web application. Figure 5.10 shows how the multisite routing is done.

FIGURE 5.10   Multisite-based routing

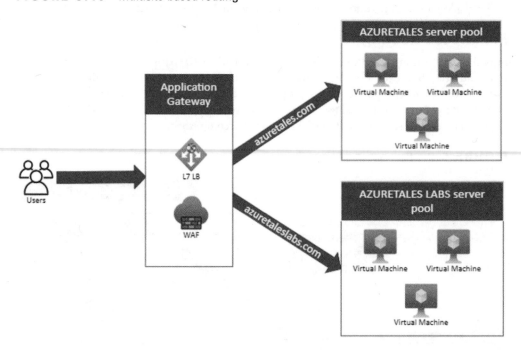

You need to configure separate listeners to wait for each site. Each listener is attached to a different rule, by which you can route the request to the backend pool for the respective site. Now, let's take a closer look at the configuration of Application Gateway.

Configuring Application Gateway

During the process of routing the requests from the front end to the backend, a series of components is involved. An understanding of these components is required for configuring Application Gateway. In Figure 5.11, you can see how the traffic routes from the front-end IP to the backend pool.

FIGURE 5.11   Routing of traffic from the front end to the backend

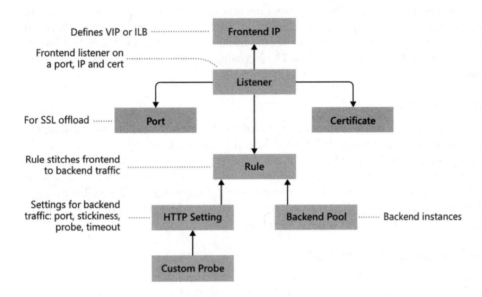

Now we will discuss each of these blocks.

Front-End IP Address

All the client requests will be hitting the front-end IP address of the Application Gateway. As discussed earlier, you can configure private IP address, public IP address, or both. You cannot have more than one public IP address and one private IP address.

Listeners

Listeners are responsible for accepting the incoming traffic based on the combination of protocol, port, host, and IP address. The listener listens for the selected traffic and routes the requests to the backend pool. You can configure basic or multisite listeners; we will cover this later in the chapter. You can also configure the certificates in the listener for HTTPS connections.

Routing Rules

Routing rules act like a bridge between the listener and the backend pools. Basically, the rule identifies how to interpret the hostname and path elements in the incoming URL request and direct the traffic to the backend pool. HTTP settings are also associated with the rule. HTTP settings imply whether the traffic is encrypted between the Application Gateway and the backend servers. HTTP settings also cover other configurations such as protocol, session stickiness, connection draining, request timeout period, and health probes.

Backend Pools

In Application Gateway, the backend pool refers to a set or collection of web servers. You need to provide the IP addresses of each web server that needs to be part of the backend pool. Application Gateway supports a set of virtual machines, VMSS, Azure App Service, or a collection of on-premises servers. The incoming requests are distributed across the backend pool.

Health Probes

As you saw in the case of Load Balancer, health probes are used to determine the health of the application and to decide whether the traffic should be routed to the server. If the response code is between 200 and 399, the server is considered as healthy. If the consecutive failures reach the threshold, the server will be marked as unhealthy. Application Gateway makes sure that the requests are not routed to the unhealthy servers. If you don't create a health probe, Application Gateway will create a default probe for checking the health of the server. The default threshold value is 30 seconds.

Web Application Firewall

Web Application Firewall (WAF) is an optional component that can be included in the Application Gateway. In Figure 5.11, you might not see the WAF component; however, it's visible in Figure 5.8. If you are using WAF, the incoming requests are scanned or validated before it reaches the listener. WAF relies on Open Web Application Security Project (OWASP) for checking the requests for threats. Identified threats include SQL injection, cross-site scripting, command injection, HTTP request smuggling, HTTP response splitting, remote file inclusion, bots, crawlers, scanners, and other HTTP protocol violations and anomalies. You can enable WAF on Application Gateway by selecting the WAF or WAFv2 SKU of Application Gateway.

Enough with the theory part, let's perform an exercise to implement Application Gateway and load balance the request between the web servers.

Implementing Application Gateway

For this exercise, you will be creating the architecture shown in Figure 5.12. Our goal is to implement path-based routing.

If the request goes to the `http://<frontendIP>/hello` path, then you should get a response from the helloPool, which contains three servers each running the Apache web server. To validate the load balancing is working, you will customize the response of each server. Similarly, any request to the `http://<frontendIP>/bye` path will be handled by the byePool. The byePool servers are also running Apache, and their landing pages will be customized using scripting. You also have a jumpbox to manage the web servers.

You can use the PowerShell script provided here:

```
https://github.com/rithinskaria/azure-infra/blob/main/appgw-infra.ps1
```

FIGURE 5.12   Application Gateway reference architecture

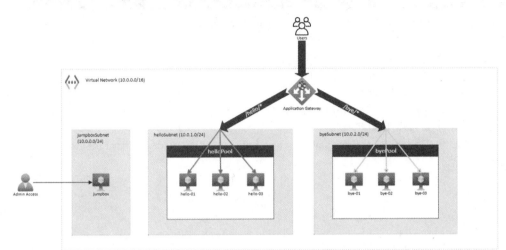

to deploy all the components except the Application Gateway. Make sure that you change the username and password for the VMs as per your requirements. The script will return the FQDN of the jumpbox and the private IP addresses of all the VM that you need to add behind the Application Gateway. See Exercise 5.2.

EXERCISE 5.2

Implementing Azure Application Gateway

1. If you have successfully run the PowerShell script, all resources will be deployed. SSH to the jumpbox using the public IP address/FQDN of the VM.

2. Once you are in the jumpbox VM and run the command `nano script.sh`, this will open the nano text editor, and you have to paste the following script. If the IP addresses of the VM don't match with the logic in the script, change that accordingly.

```bash
#!/bin/bash
sudo apt update -y
sudo apt install sshpass -y
echo "Setting up helloPool VMs"
for i in {1..3}
do
j=$(($i + 3))
ip="10.0.1.$j"
sshpass -p "VMP@55w0rd" \
```

```
   ssh -o StrictHostKeyChecking=no rithin@$ip bash -c  \
   "'export VAR=$i
   printenv | grep VAR
   echo "Setting up hello-0$i VM"
   sudo apt install apache2 -y
   sudo chmod -R -v 777 /var/www/
   mkdir /var/www/html/hello
   echo "HelloPool wants to say hi from hello-0$i" > /var/www/html/hello/
hello.html
   exit
   '"
   done

   echo "Setting up byePool VMs"
   for i in {1..3}
   do
   j=$(($i + 3))
   ip="10.0.2.$j"
   sshpass -p "VMP@55w0rd" \
   ssh -o StrictHostKeyChecking=no rithin@$ip bash -c  \
   "'export VAR=$i
   printenv | grep VAR
   echo "Setting up bye-0$i VM"
   sudo apt install apache2 -y
   sudo chmod -R -v 777 /var/www/
   mkdir /var/www/html/bye
   echo "ByePool wants to say bye from bye-0$i" > /var/www/html/bye/bye.html
   exit
   '"
   done
```

3. Hit Ctrl+X, press y, and then hit Enter to save the file. Once the file is saved, grant execute permissions by running chmod +x script.sh. Then you may run the script by entering ./script.sh.

4. The script may take some time to complete the execution. Once executed, you can send curl requests from the jumpbox to the individual web servers and verify the response.

```
rithin@jumpbox-vm:~$ curl 10.0.1.4/hello/hello.html
HelloPool wants to say hi from hello-01
rithin@jumpbox-vm:~$ curl 10.0.1.5/hello/hello.html
HelloPool wants to say hi from hello-02
rithin@jumpbox-vm:~$ curl 10.0.1.6/hello/hello.html
HelloPool wants to say hi from hello-03
rithin@jumpbox-vm:~$ curl 10.0.2.4/bye/bye.html
ByePool wants to say bye from bye-01
rithin@jumpbox-vm:~$ curl 10.0.2.5/bye/bye.html
ByePool wants to say bye from bye-02
rithin@jumpbox-vm:~$ curl 10.0.2.6/bye/bye.html
ByePool wants to say bye from bye-03
rithin@jumpbox-vm:~$ |
```

5. Now you need to create the Application Gateway, and for that you can navigate to the Azure portal and search for *Application Gateway*. Click Application Gateways from the search results.

6. From the Load Balancing - Help Me Choose (Preview) | Application Gateway window, click Create Application Gateway or simply Create in the toolbar.

7. In the wizard, you need to provide the following details in the Basics tab:

   - **Subscription:** Select the subscription.

   - **Resource Group:** Select the resource group. Create a new one if required.

   - **Application gateway name:** Give a name for the Application Gateway.

   - **Region:** Select East US as the PowerShell script created the resources in East US. If you have created the resources in another region, select the region accordingly.

   - **Tier:** Choose the default tier of Standard V2.

   - **Enable autoscaling:** Set this to Yes or No. If you select Yes, then you have to specify the min and max number of instances. If you disable autoscaling, you can specify the instance count.

   - **Availability zone:** Set to None.

   - **HTTP2:** Disabled.

   - **Virtual Network:** Select the virtual network where our web servers are deployed. The wizard will ask you to select the subnet. Application Gateway requires a dedicated subnet for the deployment; since you have created this infrastructure using the script, you haven't added the subnet. Nevertheless, you can click Manage Subnet Configuration and add a new subnet named ApplicationGateway. The CIDR block needs to be at least /26. Once the subnet is created, select the subnet.

EXERCISE 5.2 *(continued)*

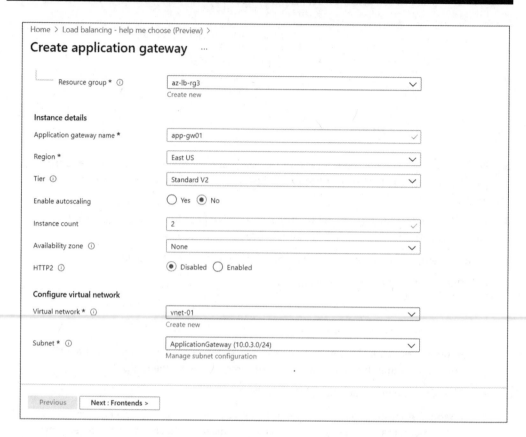

Home > Load balancing - help me choose (Preview) >
Create application gateway   ...

Resource group * ⓘ	az-lb-rg3 ⌄
	Create new

Instance details

Application gateway name *	app-gw01 ✓
Region *	East US ⌄
Tier ⓘ	Standard V2 ⌄
Enable autoscaling	◯ Yes ⦿ No
Instance count	2 ✓
Availability zone ⓘ	None ⌄
HTTP2 ⓘ	⦿ Disabled ◯ Enabled

Configure virtual network

Virtual network * ⓘ	vnet-01 ⌄
	Create new
Subnet * ⓘ	ApplicationGateway (10.0.3.0/24) ⌄
	Manage subnet configuration

Previous   Next : Frontends >

8. Click Next: Frontends to configure the front end. On the Frontend tab, select the front-end IP address type as Public and add a new public IP address.

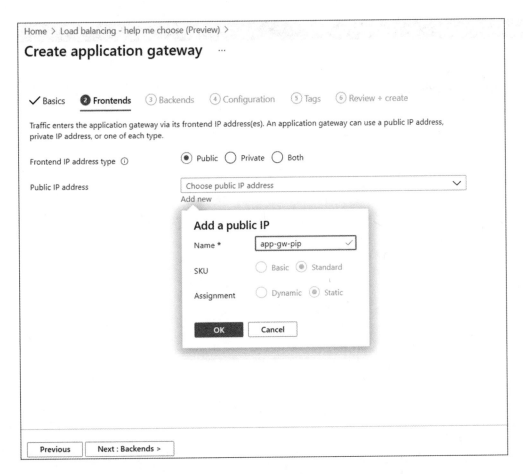

9. After completing the front-end configuration, you can move on to the backend configuration by clicking Next: Backends. Click Add A Backend Pool to add a backend pool.

10. Add the pool name as helloPool and set Add Backend Pool Without Targets as Yes. You will add the targets later. Once done, click Add.

11. Click Add A Backend Pool again to add the byePool. Here also you will create the backend without targets.

12. Once the backends are added, they will be displayed in the Backends tab.

EXERCISE 5.2 *(continued)*

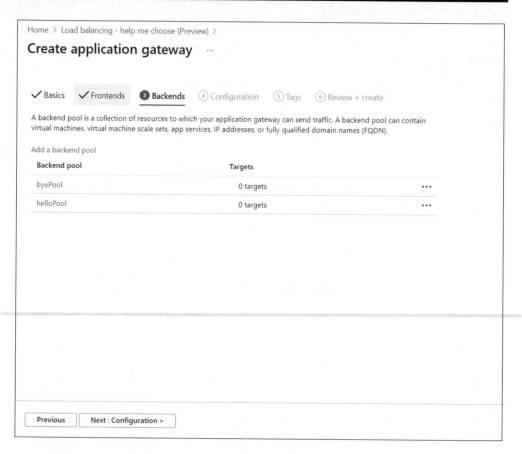

13. Proceed to the next step by clicking Next: Configuration. On the configuration tab, you will see the frontend and backend you created. The missing piece here is the routing rule, and you will add that now.

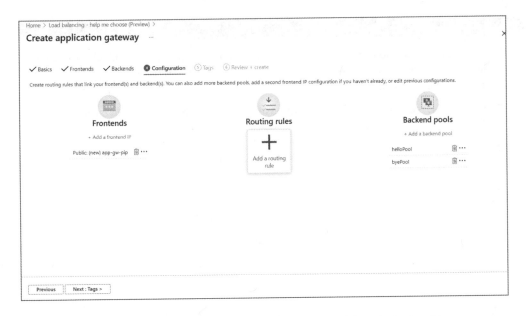

14. Click Add A Routing Rule in the Routing rules column to add a rule. In the side window that opens, specify the name for the rule and add the following details in the Listener tab:

   - **Listener name:** Provide the name of the listener.

   - **Frontend IP:** Select the public IP you created earlier.

   - **Protocol:** HTTP.

   - **Port:** 80.

15. Move on to the Backend tab in the same side window. Select the target type as Backend Pool and backend target as helloPool. This is going to be our default pool, which means any requests will be served by the helloPool servers. The HTTP settings are not created yet, so you will click Add New to add HTTP settings. Specify the following details in the HTTP settings:

   - **HTTP settings name:** Specify a name.

   - **Backend protocol:** HTTP.

   - **Backend port:** 80.

   - **Cookie-based affinity:** Disable.

   - **Connection Draining:** Disable.

   - **Request time out:** Default value, 20 seconds.

   - **Override backend path:** Not applicable.

16. The hostname section can be skipped. Click Add and the Azure portal will take you back to the Backend Targets tab, and you will be able to see that the HTTP setting you created has been selected.

17. Below HTTP settings, you will see path-based routing. Click Add Multiple Targets To Create A Path-Based Rule.

18. Configure the target as shown here.

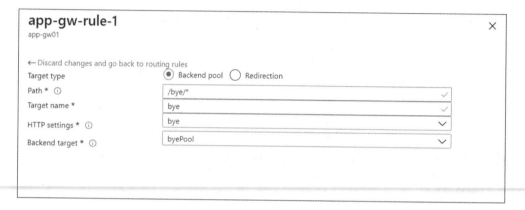

19. Save the rule and skip to the Application Gateway deployment. In our configuration the default pool is helloPool, and if the request has /bye/* in the URL, the response will be served by the byePool servers.

20. Open the Application Gateway and copy the public IP address from the Overview blade. Open the browser or any similar application and try navigating to http://<frontendIP>/hello/hello.html and http://<frontendIP>/bye/bye.html. In the following graphic, you are checking the response programmatically to verify the round-robin fashion. You could also check from browser, and during every refresh another server from backend would respond.

```
PS C:\Users\riskaria> for ($i=0; $i -lt 3; $i++){
(Invoke-WebRequest -Uri http://40.117.169.48/hello/hello.html).Content
}
HelloPool wants to say hi from hello-01

HelloPool wants to say hi from hello-03

HelloPool wants to say hi from hello-02


PS C:\Users\riskaria>
PS C:\Users\riskaria> for ($i=0; $i -lt 3; $i++){
(Invoke-WebRequest -Uri http://40.117.169.48/bye/bye.html).Content
}
ByePool wants to say bye from bye-01

ByePool wants to say bye from bye-02

ByePool wants to say bye from bye-03
```

With that we are concluding the Application Gateway section. As mentioned earlier, you have two more load balancers: Azure Front Door and Azure Traffic Manager. These are not part of the exam objective; however, understanding them will help you in your cloud journey.

Azure Front Door

You can implement instant global failover and high availability for our web applications by using Azure Front Door. Azure Front Door helps in multiregion load balancing for web traffic. Azure Front Door is very similar to Application Gateway; the only difference is Azure Front Door backend pools can be located in different regions, but Application Gateway is scoped to a single region.

Front Door uses the anycast protocol with split TCP and to improve the global connectivity, and Front Door relies on the Microsoft global network. Front Door is a layer 7 or HTTP/HTTPS load balancer, and you can include WAF if needed. Figure 5.13 shows a reference multi-architecture from the Microsoft documentation.

The following are the features offered by Azure Front Door:

- **Enhanced performance:** Users will be connected to the nearest point of presence (POP) using the split TCP anycast protocol.

- **Heath probes:** Using smart health probes in Azure Front Door you can monitor the latency and availability of the web application. Also, instance failover to another region can be triggered if the backend is found unhealthy.

- **URL based routing:** You can route based on the path in the URL.

- **Multiple-site routing:** This helps in hosting multiple sites behind the same Front Door.

- **Session affinity:** You can route the users to the same backend targets using the cookie-based session affinity feature.

- **TLS termination:** It supports TLS termination so that you can reduce the load on the backend servers.

- **Custom Domains and certificate management:** By default, Azure Front Door points to a record in the `azurefd.net` domain; however, you can add custom domains.

- **URL redirection:** You can redirect to another URL or from HTTP to HTTPS.

- **URL rewrite:** It helps in configuring additional headers in the request.

- **IPv6 and HTTP/2 support:** IPv6 and HTTP/2 are supported natively in Azure Front Door.

FIGURE 5.13   Azure Front Door

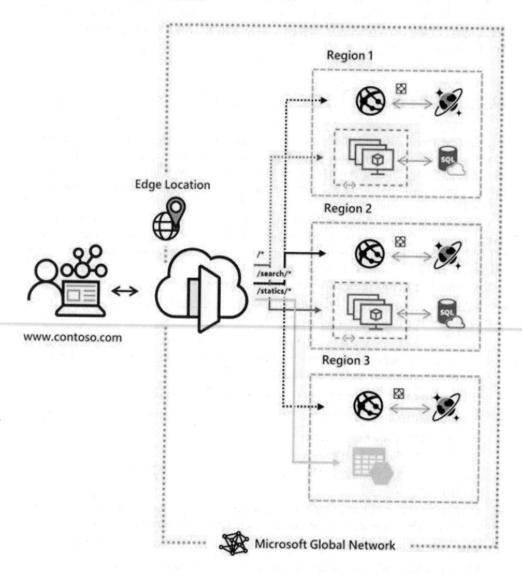

If you take a closer look at the aforementioned features, most of them align with the features of Application Gateway discussed earlier. As this is not part of the exam, you can refer to the exercise in the Microsoft documentation to implement Front Door.

https://docs.microsoft.com/en-us/azure/frontdoor/quickstart-create-front-door

On that note, you will move to the last load balancing solution in this chapter: Azure Traffic Manager.

Azure Traffic Manager

Azure Traffic Manager is a DNS load balancing or DNS resolver, which helps in distributing the traffic to different endpoints globally based on the routing method you configure. In all other load balancing solutions discussed so far, the request hits the front end and gets routed to the backend based on the rules you configure. However, in the case of Azure Traffic Manager, the requests hit the Azure Traffic Manager, and Azure Traffic Manager returns the endpoint address to the client as a DNS response. As the client is now aware of the endpoint, the client directly reaches out to the endpoint. In short, the traffic doesn't transit through the Azure Traffic Manager; instead, it returns the endpoint address to the client.

In Figure 5.14, taken from the Microsoft documentation, you can see how a request from the client is processed by Azure Traffic Manager.

The following is the complete workflow that has been illustrated in Figure 5.14:

FIGURE 5.14   Azure Traffic Manager

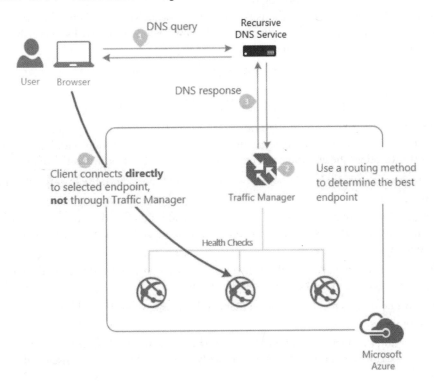

- The request from the client reaches the recursive DNS servers, and the request gets forwarded to the Azure Traffic Manager. For example, if you have a website www.azuretales.com, you will map the www record as a CNAME to the DNS name of the Azure Traffic Manager.

- A recursive DNS server will forward the request to the Azure Traffic Manager, and based on the routing method you have configured, Traffic Manager determines the best endpoint.

- Once the endpoint is determined, Traffic Manager will return the IP address of the back-end server as a DNS response to the client.

- Since the client knows the IP address to the endpoint, it will directly communicate with the endpoint returned by the Traffic Manager.

Traffic Manager also supports endpoint health checks and automatic endpoint failover. If one of the endpoints is not healthy, Traffic Manager will no longer return the endpoint to the client. Traffic Manager is ideal for creating highly available architecture that can withstand even the failure of an entire Azure region.

There are different routing methods supported by Traffic Manager. Since they are not part of the exam objective, you will not discuss deeply how each method works. Nevertheless, if you are curious to learn, then you can refer to this page:

https://docs.microsoft.com/en-us/azure/traffic-manager/traffic-manager-routing-methods

The following are the routing methods available for Traffic Manager:

- **Priority routing:** You can set the priority for each endpoint, and the requests will be served by the endpoint that has the highest priority. If the endpoint with high priority is not healthy, then the endpoint with the second highest priority serves the requests.

- **Performance routing:** Requests will be routed to endpoints with the lowest network latency.

- **Geographic routing:** Requests will be routed to endpoints based on the location of the client. This is ideal for serving websites in local language for customers accessing from a country.

- **Weighted routing:** This is ideal for distributing based on weight. If you set the weight equal for all endpoints, the traffic will be evenly distributed.

- **Multivalue:** This is ideal for profiles that can have only IPv4/IPv6 addresses as endpoints.

At this point, the question that will be popping up in your mind is, which one to use? Well, to clear that confusion, you will quickly compare the solutions discussed in this chapter.

Comparing the Load Balancing Solutions

Table 5.1 compares the technologies discussed in this chapter. These solutions can be deployed in a single load balancing solution or as a combination. In certain scenarios, you will have an Azure Traffic Manager pointing to two different Application Gateways, which further distributes the traffic to backend pools.

TABLE 5.1   Comparing Load Balancing Solutions

Service	Azure Load Balancer	Application Gateway	Azure Front Door	Azure Traffic Manager
Technology	Transport layer or L4	Application Layer or L7	L7 or HTTP/ HTTPS	DNS Resolver
Supported protocols	Any TCP or UDP protocol	HTTP, HTTPS, WebSocket, and HTTP/2	Split TCP-based anycast protocol	DNS resolution
Supported backends and end-points	Azure VMs and Azure VMSS	Azure VMs, Azure VMSS, Azure App Service, IP addresses, and host names	Internet-facing services hosted inside or outside Azure	Azure Cloud Services, Azure App Services, Azure App Service Slots, and Public IP addresses
Network connectivity	External and Internal	External and Internal	External and Internal	External

Summary

In this chapter we focused on network traffic management using the load-balancing solutions available in Azure. The services included in the scope of this chapter are Azure Load Balancer, Azure Application Gateway, Azure Front Door, and Azure Traffic Manager. We started the chapter with the availability options, which is required for building highly available architecture in Azure. The options we discussed included availability sets and availability zones. Availability sets can protect you from hardware failures and planned maintenance events within a datacenter. However, the catch is if the entire datacenter is down, your services will not be available. To overcome this crisis, we have availability zones in Azure; each zone is an isolated set of datacenters having separate power, cooling, and network lines. Deploying the services to availability zones mitigates the downtime caused by datacenter failure. Even if one zone goes down, your instance will be running in another datacenter serving your customers.

Then we discussed Azure Load Balancer, a layer 4 load balancer ideal for handling any TCP or UDP-based traffic. Load Balancer mainly focuses on the source IP, source port, destination IP, destination port, and protocol for routing the traffic to the backend pools. The supported services are limited to Azure VMs and Azure VMSS. After Azure Load Balancer, we covered Azure Application Gateway, which is ideal for implementing load balancing to web applications. As Application Gateway is a layer 7 load balancer, you have path-based routing and multiple-site routing unlike the Azure Load Balancer. There is an optional component called WAF—a web application firewall that can be incorporated into the Application Gateway for checking the request for any vulnerabilities before routing to the backend servers.

Additionally, we covered Azure Front Door and Azure Traffic Manager. Azure Front Door will help you build highly available architecture with global reach. The features are similar to Azure Application Gateway. The advantage is that Azure Front Door can work in a multi-region environment. On the other hand, Azure Traffic Manager is a DNS resolver that will return the DNS response to the client based on the routing method. Finally, we concluded the chapter with a comparison between the load-balancing solutions so that you can choose the right solution.

With this chapter, we are winding up the topic of Azure networking. In the past three chapters, we started from the basics of Azure networking, moved on to on-premises connectivity, and concluded with network management. In Chapter 6, "Azure Storage," we will be covering another core pillar of infrastructure: storage.

Exam Essentials

Understand availability options in Azure.   Learn about the concepts of availability sets and availability zones in Azure.

Understand Azure Load Balancer.   You should be able to deploy and configure Azure Load Balancer. Learn about the request workflow and routing methods.

Understand Azure Application Gateway.   Learn about Azure Application Gateway working, implementation, and configuration.

Review Questions

1. Your company provides customers with a virtual network in the cloud. You have dozens of Linux virtual machines in another virtual network. You need to install an Azure load balancer to direct traffic between the virtual networks. What should you do? Select one.

   A. Install a private load balancer

   B. Install a public load balancer

   C. Install an external load balancer

   D. Install an internal load balancer

2. Your organization has created seven NTP servers running in the Azure cloud. You were asked to create a load balancing solution that can handle the incoming requests from the client and can distribute to the backend servers. Which solution would you use?

   A. Azure Load Balancer

   B. Azure Application Gateway

   C. Azure Front Door

   D. Azure Traffic Manager

3. You are using an internal load balancer to distribute the requests from on-premises over VPN to a set of backend VMs. Which of the following facts about Azure Load Balancer is not true? (Select two.)

   A. Health probes can be configured in Load Balancer.

   B. Azure Load Balancer by default checks the endpoint every 20 seconds.

   C. A health probe threshold cannot be configured.

   D. An HTTP 200 response is considered as healthy.

4. Which criteria does Application Gateway use to route requests to a web server?

   A. The IP address of the web server that is the target of the request

   B. The region in which the servers hosting the web application are located

   C. The hostname, port, and path in the URL of the request

   D. The user's authentication information

5. Which load balancing strategy does the Application Gateway implement?

   A. Distributes requests to each available in a round-robin fashion

   B. Distributes requests to the server in the backend pool with the lightest load

   C. Polls each server in the backend pool in turn and sends the request to the first server that responds

   D. Uses one server in the backend pool until that server reaches 50 percent load and then moves to the next server.

6. Your company has a website that allows users to customize their experience by downloading an app. Demand for the app has increased, so you have added another virtual network with two virtual machines. These machines are dedicated to serving the app downloads. You need to ensure the additional download requests do not affect the website performance. Your solution must route all download requests to the two new servers you have installed. What action will you recommend?

    A. Add a user-defined route

    B. Create a local network gateway

    C. Add an Application Gateway

    D. Create an internal load balancer

7. You are deploying the Application Gateway and want to ensure incoming requests are checked for common security threats like cross-site scripting and crawlers. To address your concerns, what should you do?

    A. Install an external load balancer

    B. Install an internal load balancer

    C. Install WAF

    D. Install Azure Firewall

8. What is the default routing mechanism used by Azure Load Balancer?

    A. Round robin

    B. Five-tuple hash

    C. Two-tuple hash

    D. Three-tuple hash

9. Which one of the following is not considered for a three-tuple hash?

    A. Source port

    B. Source IP

    C. Destination IP

    D. Protocol

10. What is the SLA offered by the Basic SKU of Azure Load Balancer?

    A. 99.9 percent

    B. 99 percent

    C. 95 percent

    D. No SLA

11. Which SKU of the load balancer should be used to implement HTTPS health probe?

    A. Standard

    B. Basic

    C. Standard V2

    D. WAF

12. Which of the configurations in Azure Load Balancer lets the user connect to the same back-end server every time they log in?

   A. Cookie-based affinity

   B. Session persistence

   C. TLS termination

   D. Connection draining

13. Which of the following is not a supported endpoint for Azure Load Balancer?

   A. Azure VM

   B. Azure VMSS

   C. Availability set

   D. App service

14. Your organization wants to use Application Gateway for load balancing to a web application. Which of the following IP addresses is supported by Application Gateway?

   A. Private

   B. Public

   C. Private and public

   D. NAT

15. Out of all the load balancing solutions available in Azure, which one of these doesn't support internal network connectivity?

   A. Azure Traffic Manager

   B. Azure Load Balancer

   C. Azure Application Gateway

   D. Azure Front Door

16. Azure Front Door works in which layer of the OSI model?

   A. Layer 4

   B. Layer 7

   C. Layer 3

   D. Layer 2

17. WAF uses which rule set for threats?

   A. OWASP

   B. Metasploit

   C. Microsoft Threat Intelligence

   D. Defender Threat Feed

18. Health probes are receiving the following response codes from these servers:

Server A – 204

Server B – 300

Server C – 302

Server D – 403

Which of the following backend servers is unhealthy?

A. Server A

B. Server B

C. Server C

D. Server D

19. Which of the following distribution modes are not supported by Azure Load Balancer?

A. Five-tuple hash

B. Client IP affinity

C. Cookie-based session affinity

D. Client IP and protocol

20. Your organization wants to implement Azure Load Balancer. You will be adding and removing virtual machines manually to the virtual network. Which SKU should be selected to use any virtual machines or virtual machine scale sets in a single virtual network?

A. Basic

B. Standard

C. Standard V2

D. Premium

Chapter

6

Azure Storage

MICROSOFT EXAM OBJECTIVES COVERED IN THIS CHAPTER:

✓ **Secure storage**

- Configure network access to storage accounts
- Create and configure storage accounts
- Generate shared access signature (SAS) tokens
- Manage access keys
- Configure Azure AD authentication for a storage account
- Configure access to Azure Files

✓ **Manage storage**

- Export from Azure job
- Import into Azure job
- Install and use Azure Storage Explorer
- Copy data by using AzCopy
- Implement Azure Storage replication
- Configure blob object replication

✓ **Configure Azure files and Azure Blob Storage**

- Create an Azure file share
- Create and configure Azure File Sync service
- Configure Azure Blob Storage
- Configure storage tiers
- Configure blob lifecycle management

In this chapter, we are going to shift our focus from networking to storage. The Azure Storage service works as a data storage solution for Azure customers. In an enterprise environment, there will be different scenarios where you want to save data. For example, you can store images that need to be served by your website or store installation files. These are simple examples: Azure Storage can act as an object store for storing data objects, a file service, a messaging store, and a NoSQL storage.

We will start this chapter with an introduction of Azure Storage and its features. Then we will take a look at different tools that are available for managing the storage in Azure. Storing data in the cloud is easy; however, we need to make sure that the data is secure. Therefore, we will explore the methods available to secure our storage. Finally, we will end the chapter with two prominent storage options that are part of the Azure Storage: Azure Blob Storage and Azure File Storage.

Let's get started with Azure Storage.

Azure Storage Account

Microsoft offers a cloud storage solution that can be integrated with all modern data storage setups. In Azure, the storage components are aligned to the service called Azure Storage, which is top in its class in terms of the availability and scalability it offers. In order to use Azure Storage services, we need to create a storage account. Storage accounts can be used to segregate data objects such as blobs, file shares, tables, queues, and disks. Each storage account will have a unique name in Azure and will have endpoints. Using these endpoints, you can access the data objects from anywhere in the world over HTTP or HTTPS connections. The following are the features offered by Azure storage accounts:

Highly Available and Durable   Azure Storage offers multiple redundancy levels to ensure that your data is always highly available. You can replicate across data centers, zones, or even regions to protect the data from outage.

Secure   The storage service encrypts all the data written to the storage account. Using a firewall, RBAC, and shared access signatures, you can fine-tune the access to the storage.

Scalability   Azure Storage is a massively scalable service that can fulfill all modern data requirements.

Tools and Access   Over an HTTP or HTTPS connection, the data in the storage can be accessed from anywhere in the world. When it comes to tools, there are different tools like Storage Explorer and the Azure portal that offer a GUI, as well as Azure Power-Shell, the Azure CLI, AzCopy, and the REST API for scripting, to manage the data stored in the storage account. In addition, Azure Storage offers a rich SDK that supports languages such as .NET, Java, Node.js, Python, PHP, Ruby, and Go.

Before you learn about the types of storage account, tiers, and the storage services, let's take a look at the different types of data supported by Azure Storage. You can use Azure Storage as a datastore for our websites, desktop applications, and mobile applications deployed in Azure or any other platform. Further, you can integrate Azure Storage with Azure virtual machines and PaaS solutions like Azure App Services. We can broadly classify the data that can be stored into three categories.

Structured Data   Structured data can be stored in different Azure services such as Azure Cosmos DB, Azure SQL DB, and other relational databases. In the case of Azure Storage, you have a dedicated NoSQL store that can be used to store data.

Unstructured Data   Unstructured data are data objects that don't follow any structure. This category includes videos, images, text files, and binaries. In Azure Storage you can utilize the blob storage for storing unstructured data.

Virtual Machine Storage   Azure Files and Azure Disks can be used as storage for the virtual machines. Azure Disks represents persistent storage for Azure VMs, and Azure Files contains managed file shares offered by Azure.

We use Azure Storage mainly to store the aforementioned types of data. Now that you are familiar with the features and supported datasets, let's take a deep dive into Azure Storage. We will begin our saga with storage services.

Azure Storage Services

Five services are part of Azure Storage. Azure Storage facilitates unique namespace for each of these services with the help of a unique endpoint, namely, blobs, files, queues, tables, and disks. Let's take a close look at each of these.

Azure Blob Storage

In some documentation, you will see that Azure Blob Storage is referred to as Azure Containers or Azure Container Storage. The name *containers* is quite confusing in the Azure realm; you have containers in Azure Container Instances, Azure Container Registry, Azure App Services, and Azure Kubernetes Services, which all deal with the container images and containerization of applications. Then you have containers in Cosmos DB for storing data. Nevertheless, if you see the term *containers*, it refers to Azure Blob Storage. To avoid this confusion, let's stick to Azure Blob Storage.

Azure Blob Storage is the object storage service offered by Microsoft. This service is similar to the Amazon S3 service. You can leverage Azure Blob Storage to store unstructured data, such as videos, images, text, or binary data. The following are some of the scenarios where you can use Azure Blob Storage:

- Serving images or documents for a website
- Storing binaries or executables for download
- Streaming video and audio
- Data backup and restore
- Disaster recovery
- Data archiving
- Data store for on-premises data that can be used by analytics solutions in Azure

You will learn more about Azure Blob Storage later in this chapter. As the service is available via HTTP or HTTPS, you can access the data from anywhere in the world.

Azure Files

Network file shares can be created using the Azure Files service, which can be accessed via the SMB protocol. At the time of writing this book, Microsoft has launched NFS shares as well; however, this feature is still in preview. This file share can be mounted to multiple VMs or on-premises machines, which is ideal for sharing files across machines. The key difference between Azure Files and an on-premises file share is that you can access the Azure Files share over HTTP or HTPS, and it can be mounted to any server that is connected to the Internet or VPN. The access is enabled via the URL that is pointing to the file share via the shared access signature (SAS). Using the SAS, you can control access to the file share.

The following are some of the common scenarios where Azure Files can be utilized:

- In on-premises, you already have file shares; however, you need VPN or complex networking for the Azure VMs to access it. Using Azure Files, you can mount a common file share to both on-premises and Azure VMs.

- Migration from on-premises to Azure Files is easy. If you replace the existing on-premises file share, you can easily unmount the share and mount Azure file share with the same drive letter to minimize the downtime.

- Azure Files is ideal for storing common files and installation packages that can be accessed from both VMs and on-premises servers.

- Crash dumps, application logs, metrics, and diagnostic logs can be written to file share. If the application collapses, you can always mount the share to another server and analyze the logs to perform the root-cause analysis.

At the time of writing this book, Azure AD–based authentication and ACLs are not supported by Azure Files. However, you can use Azure Active Directory Domain Services and on-premises Active Directory Domain Services (AD DS) to provide identity-based authentication over SMB.

Azure Queues

Messages can be stored and retrieved using queues. These stored messages can be up to 64 KB in size and can be accessed from anywhere in the world over HTTP or HTTPS. Millions of messages can be handled in a queue, and the limit totally depends on the capacity of the storage account. Queues are appropriate for storing lists of messages that need to be asynchronously processed.

One of the examples that is cited in the Microsoft documentation is very apt for explaining the purpose of queue. An example is, assume you have an application to which customers can upload pictures. Either you can wait for all images to get uploaded and then create the thumbnail or you can create thumbnails while uploading the images. The latter one is user friendly, as the customer will be able to see the thumbnail as soon as they upload. This can be accomplished with the help of queues. When the customer finishes uploading an image, let the application write a message to the queue. An Azure Function App can be triggered that will retrieve the message from the queue and create the thumbnail. If you are not familiar with Azure Function Apps, then it's a service that can be triggered based on events. Functions are small chunks of code that can be executed to achieve certain tasks like the one you read about earlier. Azure Functions is an example of serverless technology.

Azure Tables

Tables is a NoSQL datastore that is now part of Azure Cosmos DB. Besides the Table Storage, Cosmos DB offers a new Table API with additional features such as turnkey failover, global distribution, automatic secondary indexes, and throughput optimized tables. Table Storage is suitable for storing nonrelational structured data.

Both tables and queues can be tested with application code only. As this book mainly focuses on the infrastructure part, we will not do a deep dive into these topics. Nevertheless, we will discuss blob storage and files in detail later in this chapter.

Azure Disks

Azure Disks provides persistent storage to Azure Virtual Machines, Azure Virtual Machine Scale Set, and the Azure VMware solution. The VMWare solution is under preview at the time of writing this book. With these four performance tiers, Azure Disks acts as a high-performance durable storage for our applications. The performance tiers are Standard HDD, Standard SSD, Premium SSD, and Ultra SSD. These tiers have different IOPS values.

There are two types of disks: unmanaged and managed. In managed disks, Azure takes care of the underlying storage account, and there will be one storage account per region that is used to store the virtual hard disk of our virtual machines. In unmanaged disks, you must create the storage account to hold the virtual machine hard disk. Microsoft recommends that you always use managed disks for better availability.

As mentioned in the introduction of this chapter, Azure Storage offers different redundancy levels based on your requirement. Now you will learn about the redundancy/replication methods available.

Storage Replication

The rationale behind storage replication is to ensure that high availability and durability are always there for the data you are storing in Azure Storage. Your data will be impacted due to planned and unplanned maintenance events such as hardware failures, network and power outages, natural disasters, and so on. Azure Storage replication will ensure that your data is copied and is protected from the aforementioned impacts. There are various types or levels of replication strategies offered by Azure. Starting from replication within the same datacenter, across availability zones, and even to cross-region replication, storage replication guarantees that the SLA for the storage service offered by Microsoft is met.

Before you start, the selection of replication strategy is a trade-off between the cost and durability. If you choose the cheapest replication strategy, then the durability will be also the least. Similarly, if you want a replication that offers the highest durability, the cost will also be on the higher side compared to other strategies. Also, the availability of these options may vary depending upon the type of storage account you are choosing. Nevertheless, we will cover the types and supported replication options later in this chapter. Let's now compare the different replication methods.

Locally Redundant Storage

Locally redundant storage (LRS) offers the least durability compared to other options you have. Since the durability is less, LRS offers the lowest cost. In LRS, you will have three copies of data within a single datacenter in different fault domains. The copies will always be up-to-date, and all changes are written to the storage account synchronously.

The downside here is that just like you saw in the case of availability sets for VMs, if the entire datacenter goes offline, your data will be inaccessible. This issue is addressed in the upcoming options. LRS offers a durability of 99.99999999999 percent (11 nines) over a given year. You shouldn't confuse this value with the SLA; durability is a commitment to ensure a level of data integrity.

Despite the limitations, there are certain scenarios where LRS can be the right candidate.

- If your data can be easily reconstructed in case of a data loss.
- Live feed, where the data constantly changes and there is no need to store data. All data written will be constantly changing.

Figure 6.1 shows how data is replicated in LRS.

FIGURE 6.1   Locally redundant storage

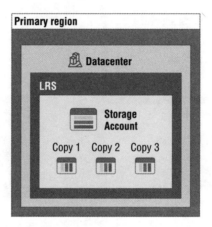

To overcome the drawbacks you saw in the case of LRS, you have another option called *zone redundant storage*.

Zone Redundant Storage

Remember that we discussed the concept of availability zones in Chapter 5, "Network Traffic Management"? In the case of zone redundant storage (ZRS), data is synchronously replicated across three storage clusters. These storage clusters are located in different availability zones. Depending upon the region, two or three availability zones will be hosting the storage clusters. The separation between these zones will overcome the datacenter failure issue that you saw in the case of LRS. Thus, enabling ZRS replication ensures that your data is accessible even if one zone is offline.

Now there are two downsides here. The first is that ZRS is not available in all regions; however, Microsoft is continually adding more regions to the list. Second, if an entire region comes down, ZRS cannot protect your data as all the zones hosting the storage cluster will be offline. Nonetheless, this is applicable only if all the zones are affected. Figure 6.2 is a pictorial representation of ZRS.

FIGURE 6.2 Zone redundant storage

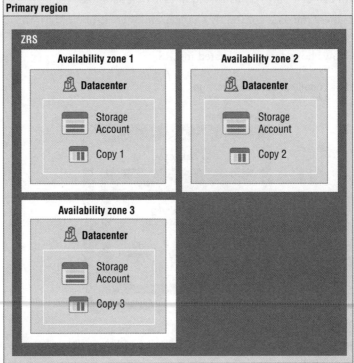

The durability offered by ZRS is higher than LRS, and the figure is 99.999999999999 percent (12 nines) over a given year.

Georedundant Storage

To overcome a regional wide outage, Microsoft offers GRS. In georedundant storage (GRS), your data is replicated to a secondary region. Ideally, the secondary region will be hundreds of miles away from the primary region. The secondary region is selected by Azure based on the regional pairs. This isolation ensures that if the primary is affected due to any calamity, it shouldn't affect the secondary. Cost-wise, GRS is more expensive than ZRS and LRS; with the increased cost comes more data durability. GRS offers a durability of 99.99999999999999999 percent (16 nine) over a given year.

GRS offers two variants.

GRS This method replicates the data to the secondary region; however, the data in the secondary is not readable. The data can be read only if a failover is initiated to the secondary region. The failover can be initiated by the customer manually or by Microsoft in the case of a regional outage.

Read-Access Geo Redundant Storage (RA-GRS) In RA-GRS, the replication works in the same way as GRS. The key difference here is that you have the provision to read from the secondary region regardless of whether a failover is initiated. The secondary region is always available for read requests.

If you have GRS or RA-GRS enabled, in the primary region you will have three copies. In the primary region, the replication is achieved using LRS, where the copies are within the same datacenter. Then this data is asynchronously replicated to the secondary region. In the secondary region also, you will have three copies of the data, replicated using LRS.

Figure 6.3 shows how the data is replicated in the primary and secondary using GRS/RA-GRS.

FIGURE 6.3 Georedundant storage

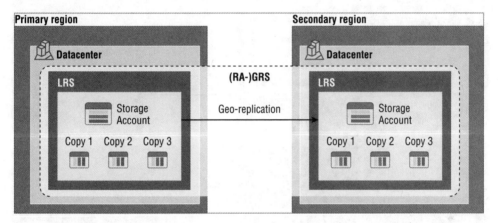

Since you are using LRS as the replication method, if both the datacenters in the primary and secondary region go offline, then your data will be inaccessible. This scenario is very unlikely; however, Azure an additional redundancy option called geo-zone-redundant storage.

Geo-zone-Redundant Storage

Like GRS, in geo-zone-redundant storage (GZRS) data is replicated to the secondary region for protection against regional outages. In GRS, you saw that the data is replicated using LRS in the primary region and is then replicated to the secondary region. In the secondary region also, you were relying on LRS for replication. With GZRS, your data will be replicated synchronously across three different storage clusters within the same region. This data is then replicated to the secondary region asynchronously and then further replicated across three different storage clusters. The storage clusters are physically separated from the others and reside in their own availability zone. Yes, you got it right; in GZRS you replicate the data synchronously in the primary region using ZRS, and then this data is replicated to the secondary region. In the secondary region, you will use LRS and maintain three copies of the data. GZRS also offers a durability of at least 99.9999999999999999 percent (16 nines) of objects over a given year.

As the data is distributed across the availability zones, GZRS offers the highest availability and protection from regional disasters. Applications that require maximum consistency, durability, availability, and performance should use GZRS.

Figure 6.4 shows how the replication happens in GZRS.

FIGURE 6.4 Geo-zone redundant storage

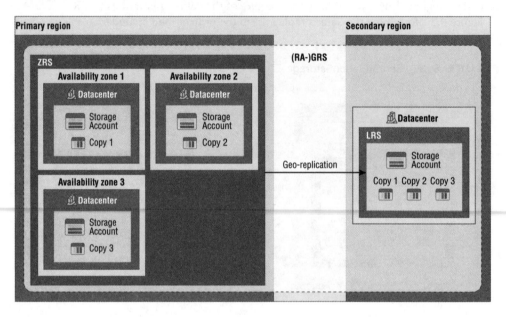

As you saw in the case of GRS, GZRS also has two variants: GZRS and RA-GZRS. If you understood the difference between GRS and RA-GRS, then the difference between GZRS and RA-GZRS is self-explanatory.

Table 6.1 gives a quick summary of the replication strategies we have discussed so far.

TABLE 6.1 Comparing Storage Replication Options

Particulars	LRS	ZRS	GRS/RA-GRS	GZRS/RA-GZRS
Node unavailable within a data center	✓	✓	✓	✓
Entire data center is unavailable	✕	✓	✓	✓
Region-wide outage	✕	✕	✓	✓
Read access to your data in the secondary region when primary is available	✕	✕	✓ (with RA-GRS)	✓ (with RA-GZRS)

The availability of the replication methods is totally dependent on the type of storage account that you are creating. Let's understand the different types of storage accounts you have in Azure.

Storage Account Types

Before we speak about the different types, it's good to understand the performance tiers offered by Azure Storage. The available tiers are Standard and Premium.

Standard Offers the lowest cost per gigabyte and is backed by magnetic drives (hard disk drives [HDDs]). Since you are using HDDs, the performance is lesser compared to Premium. Standard storage is ideal for storing data that is not frequently accessed.

Premium Offers low-latency performance and is backed by solid-state drives (SSD). It's best for I/O-intensive applications.

Now you will take a look at different storage account types. Each type supports different features, replication options, and performance tiers and has its own pricing model. Despite the differences, Microsoft ensures that account types are encrypted using the Storage Encryption Service (SSE). You can refer to Table 6.2 to compare the different types.

TABLE 6.2 Comparing Storage Account Types

Storage Account Type	Supported Services	Supported Performance Tiers	Replication Options
Blob Storage	Blob (block blobs and append blobs only)	Standard	LRS, GRS, RA-GRS
General Purpose v1 (GPv1)/ StorageV1	Blob, File, Queue, Table, and Disk	Standard, Premium	LRS, GRS, RA-GRS
General Purpose v2 (GPv2)/ StorageV2	Blob, File, Queue, Table, and Disk	Standard, Premium	LRS, ZRS, GRS, RA-GRS, GZRS, RA-GZRS
Block blob storage	Blob (block blobs and append blobs only)	Premium	LRS, ZRS (limited regions)
File Storage	Files	Premium	LRS, ZRS (limited regions)

Microsoft recommends that you use General Purpose v2 accounts when possible. General Purpose v1 (GPv1) is the legacy account for storing blobs, files, queues, tables, and disks. GPv2 offers more features and redundancy levels compared to GPv1.

Throughout the discussion, you read that storage accounts can be accessed from anywhere in the world over an HTTP or HTTPS connection. Next, we will cover storage endpoints.

Storage Account Endpoints

The name for the storage account is unique across Azure. Each object stored in the storage account is represented using a unique URL. During the creation of the storage account, you need to pass the name of the storage account to the Azure Resource Manager. Using this storage account name, endpoints are created.

Accessing Storage

As you know, there are different services offered by Azure Storage, namely, blobs, tables, files, and queues. The URL for each service is generated based on the storage account name and the service you want to access. For example, if the name of your storage account is systemstorage04, then the default endpoints will be as follows:

Blobs   `https://systemstorage04.blob.core.windows.net`

Tables   `https://systemstorage04.table.core.windows.net`

Files   `https://systemstorage04.file.core.windows.net`

Queues   `https://systemstorage04.queue.core.windows.net`

To access each object in a storage account, the path to the object is appended to the URL of the service. For instance, if you are using the blob service to store an image named `image.jpg` inside the container `images`, then the URL will be

`https://systemstorage04.queue.core.windows.net/images/image.jpg`

Accessing the service using the default domain may be hectic, and customers would like to use their own custom domains to represent their storage space. Let's see how you can map custom domains to our storage account for the ease of access.

Custom Domain Configuration

Custom domains can be configured on Azure Storage account. As mentioned earlier, the default endpoint for blob storage is `<storage-account-name>.blob.core.windows.net`. You could map this endpoint to your custom domain like `storage.azuretales`

.com. Whenever you need to connect to the blob endpoint, you can directly use the custom domain instead of using the default endpoint. There are two ways by which you can map our custom domain.

Direct CNAME Mapping   In direct CNAME mapping you will be creating a record in our custom domain that will point to the endpoint of the storage service. Table 6.3 shows how the mapping is done. This process will cause a minor downtime as the domain is getting updated.

TABLE 6.3   Direct CNAME Mapping

CNAME Record	Target
blobs.azuretales.com	\<storage-account-name\>.blob.core.windows.net

Intermediary Mapping with asverify   A minor downtime will be there when you update a domain that is already in use with Azure. You eliminate this downtime by using the asverify subdomain. Table 6.4 shows how the asverify intermediary mapping is done.

TABLE 6.4   Intermediary Mapping with asverify

CNAME Record	Target
asverify.blobs.azuretales.com	asverify.\<storage-account-name\>.blob.core.windows.net
blobs.azuretales.com	\<storage-account-name\>.blob.core.windows.net

Securing Storage Endpoints

By now, you know that the storage service can be accessed from anywhere in the world. This is actually a security concern when you are storing sensitive data in the cloud. The default option is to allow access from all networks; however, you can restrict the access from networks. Using the storage firewall, you can restrict the access to a list of allowed networks.

Once you create a storage account, in the Networking blade you will be able to control the access. As shown in Figure 6.5, you can restrict the access to a set of virtual networks and external CIDR ranges (on-premises or any other network outside Azure).

FIGURE 6.5 Securing storage endpoint

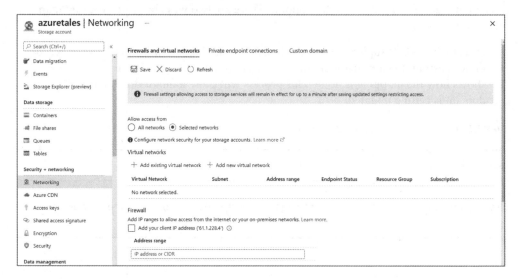

Here concepts like service endpoint and private endpoint will come into the picture. You have already seen these in the networking chapter. With that, we will move on to the next topic, Azure Blob Storage.

Azure Blob Storage

When we discussed Azure Storage services, you saw some of the use-case scenarios of Azure Blob Storage. As Azure Blob Storage is for unstructured data, you can store any type of text or binary data. Blob storage is also referred to as *object storage*.

Figure 6.6 shows a hierarchy of how objects are stored in Azure Blob Storage.

FIGURE 6.6 Blob Storage hierarchy

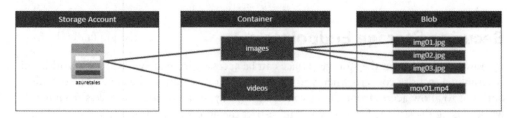

From the figure it's evident Blob Storage comprises three resources.

- The storage account
- The container in the storage account
- Blobs or objects stored in the container

We are already familiar with the concept of storage account, and blobs and objects are data stored in the storage account. The missing piece here is containers, so let's understand what a container in Blob Storage is.

Blob Containers

As you can see in Figure 6.6, the container provides a grouping of blobs. In the figure, we have grouped the blobs as videos and images. There is no limit to the number of containers you can have inside a storage account. Each container can accommodate an infinite number of blobs as well. When you perform Exercise 6.1, you will understand how you can create a container from the Azure portal.

When you create a container, you need to provide the public access level, which specifies whether you want to expose the data stored in the container publicly. By default, the contents are private. However, you have the following options to control the visibility:

- **Private:** This is the default option; no anonymous access is allowed to containers and blobs.
- **Blob:** This will grant anonymous public read access to the blobs alone.
- **Container:** This will grant anonymous public read and list access to the container and all the blobs stored inside the container.

It's important to understand these access levels to restrict the anonymous access to the sensitive data stored in the Blob Storage. You can also create containers from Azure Power-Shell and the Azure CLI.

Now you will explore a new concept called *blob access tiers*.

Blob Access Tiers

Based on the usage patterns, Azure provides different options for accessing the block blob data stored in Azure Blob Storage. The access tiers are defined based on the usage pattern or frequency of access. When you create a file, it will be accessed frequently; gradually the frequency of access will reduce, and eventually you will not be accessing the file. However, you would still like to keep the file because of the data retention policies and for auditing purposes. Choosing the right access tier will help you optimize the cost of data storage and data access. The following are the access tiers offered by blob storage:

Hot   Optimized for frequent access of objects. From a cost perspective, accessing data in the Hot tier is the least expensive compared to the other tiers; however, the data storage costs are higher. When you create a new storage account, this is the default tier.

Cool   Optimized for storing data that is not accessed very frequently and is stored for at least 30 days. Storing data in the Cool tier is cheaper than the Hot tier; however, accessing data in the Cool tier is more expensive than Hot tier.

Archive   Optimized for storing data that can tolerate hours of retrieval latency and will remain in the Archive tier for at least 180 days. When it comes to storing data, the Archive tier is the most cost-effective tier; however, accessing data is more expensive than accessing data from the Hot or Cool tier.

One thing to note here is if you are setting up the access tier from the storage account level, you will have only two choices: Hot and Cool. This access tier will be inherited by all objects stored in the storage account. The Archive tier can be set at the individual object level only. Based on the usage pattern, the access tier must be changed to use storage cost-effectively. Having said that, it's not practical to change the access tier of objects manually based on usage pattern, especially when you are storing a massive amount of data. You have a policy in Azure Storage by which you can automatically change the tier of the objects based on the frequency of access. Let's see how you can use this blob lifecycle management policy.

Blob Lifecycle Management

Each dataset has a unique lifecycle. People access data too often in the early stages of lifecycle, and this trend drops drastically. At a later point, the data will stay idle in the storage. Even though the data is idle, you will be charged for the amount of data stored. This data storage charge is totally dependent on the access tier. If you don't switch the access tier in an efficient and timely way, the data will stay in the wrong access tier and will incur charges.

As mentioned earlier, as your organization grows, the amount of data will also increase. It is not practical to manually change the access tier of the data to save costs. You can leverage Azure Blob lifecycle management policies to automatically change the access tier of the data based on the rules you configure. You can transition to any access tier, and after the retention period, you can automatically delete the data. Blob lifecycle management is available for GPv2, Premium Block Blobs, and Blob Storage accounts.

Using lifecycle management, you can do the following:

- The access tier of the blobs can be transitioned automatically (Hot to Cool, Hot to Archive, or Cool to Archive).

- You can optimize costs.

- You can delete blobs after the end of the lifecycle.

- You can configure rules to run once every day at the storage account level.

- You can filter and apply rules to selected containers and blobs.

In Figure 6.7, you can see that based on the last modified date, you can transition to another access tier or even delete the blob.

FIGURE 6.7 Blob lifecycle management

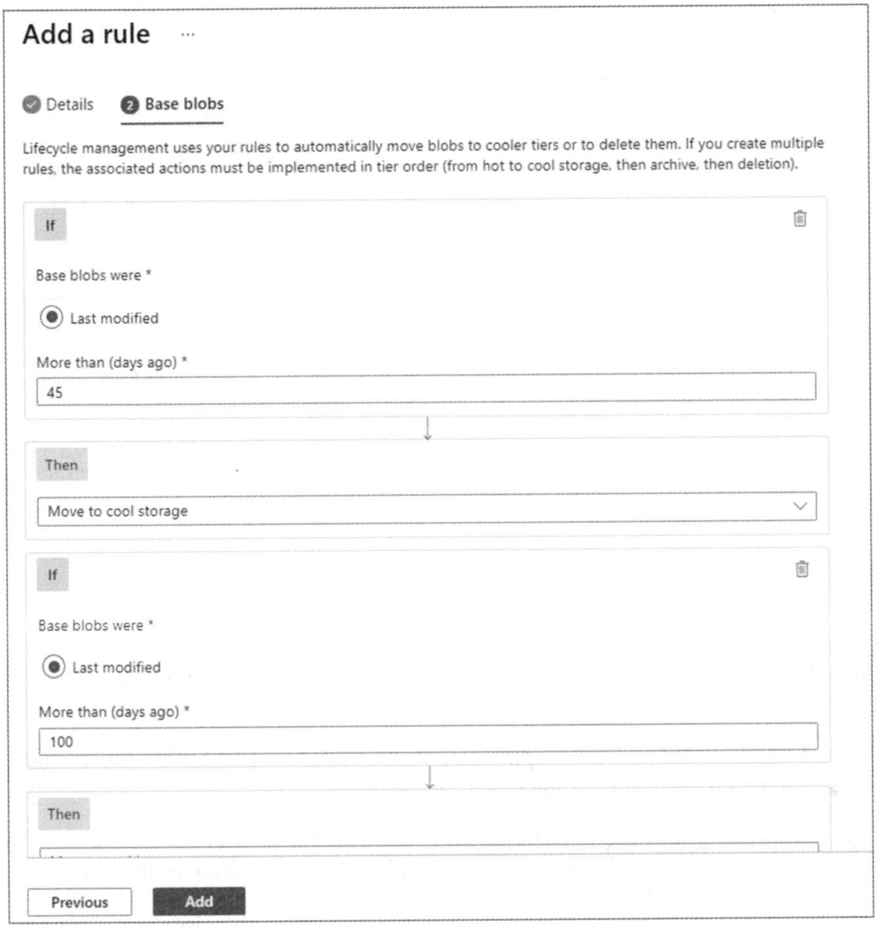

So far, you have seen different features and options available to manage the data. However, you haven't seen how the blobs can be uploaded or in fact how to get started with Azure storage accounts. Let's see how you can create a storage account and upload a blob.

Uploading Blobs

Blobs are unstructured data that can be of any type or size. Azure Storage supports uploading three types of blobs: block blobs, page blobs, and append blobs. During the upload, you can specify the type of the blob.

Figure 6.8 shows how the file can be uploaded to the container that is under the storage account.

FIGURE 6.8   Uploading blobs

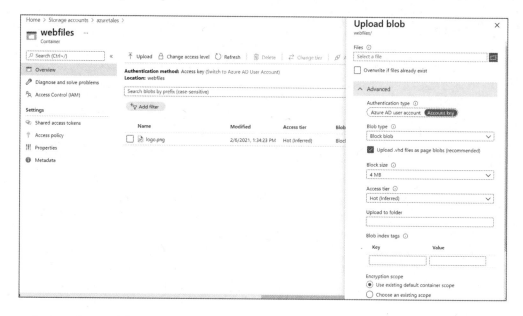

Let's understand these types of blobs:

Block Blobs (Default)   This is the default blob type. It is ideal for storing text and binary data such as images, videos, and files in Azure storage.

Append Blobs   Optimized for append operations, this is ideal for logging scenarios where the data is constantly appended to the storage.

Page Blobs   This is ideal for frequent read/write operations and can be up to 8 TB in size. Azure stores virtual machine OS disks and data disks in page blob format.

In Figure 6.8, you can see that you have an option to choose the blob type during the upload process. However, you cannot the change the type after the object is uploaded to the storage. Exercise 6.1 will teach you how to create the storage account and upload files to the storage.

EXERCISE 6.1

Uploading Blobs

1.   Sign in to the Azure portal and search for *Storage Accounts*.

2.   Click the Create button to take you through the creation process.

3.   In the Basics section, fill in these inputs:

- **Subscription**: Select your Azure subscription.

- **Resource Group**: Create a new resource group or select an existing resource group.

- **Storage account name**: Give a unique name to the storage account. If the name is already taken, Azure will warn you and will not let you create the storage account. You can use lowercase characters and numbers. The name must be between 3 and 24 characters.

- **Region**: Choose a region.

- **Performance**: Select Standard or Premium tier. The default selection is Standard.

- **Redundancy**: Choose the redundancy per your requirements. The default choice is RA-GRS. For testing, it's better to select LRS to reduce costs.

4. After completing the Basic tab, click Next: Advanced, and this will take us to the Advanced tab.

5. On the Advanced tab, none of the options needs to be changed, unless there is a need for that. One option to note here is Access Tier; you change this to Cool from Hot (default option) if needed.

6. Click Next: Networking. On the Networking blade, you can see the option to configure the connectivity method. By default, this will be set to Public Endpoint (All Networks); that means all connections from all networks are allowed. You have two more options: Private Endpoint and Public Endpoint (Selected Networks).

7. Click Next: Data Protection. On the Data Protection blade, you can control the soft delete configuration and the retention. No changes are required in this tab for this exercise.

8. Click Review + Create and wait for the validation to complete.

9. Once the resource is created, navigate to Storage Accounts, and click the storage account you created. Clicking the storage account will take you to the Overview blade.

10. Click Containers under Data Storage.

11. Inside the Containers blade, click + Container to add a new container. You need to give a name for the container and public access level. You will set the public access level to Blobs. Click to create the container.

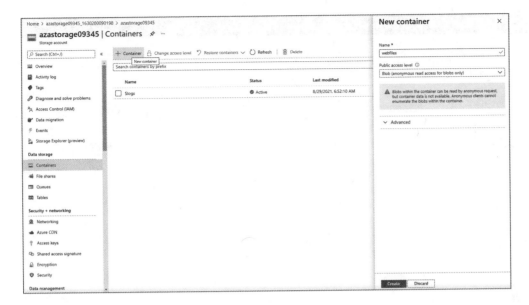

12. Once the container is created, click the container name, which will take you to the overview of the container. On the Overview blade, you will be able to see the Upload button.

13. Click the folder icon and upload an image from your local computer. Once you see the selected file name under Files, click the Upload button.

EXERCISE 6.1 *(continued)*

14. The uploaded blob will be visible in the container (refer to the first graphic shown here), and it will expose a link to you (refer to the second graphic shown here).

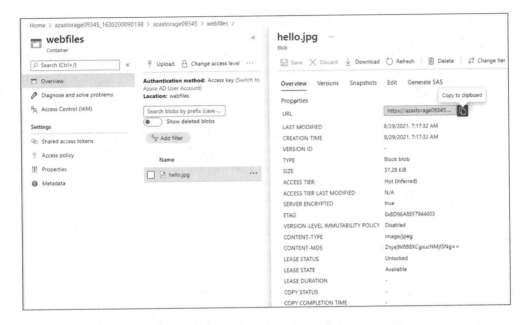

15. If you inspect the URL, it will contain the storage account name, container name, and blob name. In this case, the link is generated based on the inputs given, and in your environment the link will be based on the inputs you give. Paste the URL in a browser, and you will be able to see the image you uploaded.

You can keep the storage account from the previous exercise as you will need it in Exercise 6.2.

Additionally, you have other tools to upload files to the blob. These include AzCopy, Azure Storage Data Movement library, Azure Data Factory, Blobfuse, Azure Data Box Disk, Azure Storage Explorer, and the Azure Import/Export service. Out of these tools, we will cover Storage Explorer, AzCopy, and the Import/Export service in the "Managing Storage" section.

In the previous exercise, the blob is publicly available from any client anywhere in the world over HTTPS connection. This is possible because you have set the access policy as Blob, which means anonymous access to the object is allowed. In some cases, you might need to secure the data in your storage and grant access only to a set of users. Before we discuss Azure Files, let's take a step back and explore the storage security options.

Storage Security

Security is a major concern when storing data in a public cloud. Azure provides a set of comprehensive security capabilities to address these concerns. They can help developers to build secure applications in the cloud. In this section, we will mainly focus on the concept of Shared Access Signatures (SAS). You will also take a look at the Storage Service Encryption (SSE). The following are the security capabilities offered by Azure Storage:

Encryption   Azure encrypts all data written to Azure Storage automatically using the Storage Encryption Service. SSE is enabled on all new storage accounts and cannot be disabled.

Authentication   Azure Storage supports Azure AD–based authentication for Azure Blobs and Azure Queues. Using RBAC, you can control the access to the storage account.

Data in Transit   Client-side encryption, SMB, or HTTPS can be used to secure the data in transit.

Azure Disk Encryption   Using Azure Disk Encryption (ADE), you can encrypt OS disks and data disks of Windows and Linux virtual machines in Azure.

Shared Access Signatures (SAS)   You can control fine-grained access to data objects using SAS keys. Also, you can define time-bound access.

Now that you know the authentication methods, you will see how you can authorize these requests.

Authorization Options

You have read multiple times that storage accounts can be accessed from anywhere in the world, and all the requests coming to the storage services should be authenticated. In Exercise 6.1, you used anonymous access, which means you haven't used any usernames, passwords, or keys for accessing the object. The purpose of authorization is to make certain that the contents of the storage account are accessible only to the authorized people and only when you want them to be. The following are the authorization options available to Azure Storage:

Azure AD   Using Azure AD, you can authorize access to Azure Storage via role-based access control (RBAC). With RBAC, you can assign fine-grained access to users, groups, or applications.

Shared Key   Every storage account has two keys: primary and secondary. The access keys of the storage account will be used in the Authorization header of the API calls.

Shared Access Signatures   Using SAS, you can limit access to services with specified permissions and over a specified timeframe.

Anonymous Access to Containers and Blobs   If you set the access level to blob or container, you can have public access to the objects without the need to pass keys or grant authorization. In Exercise 6.1, you accessed the object using anonymous access.

Now you will take a deep dive to Shared Access Signatures.

Shared Access Signatures

Every storage account has two keys, called the *access keys*. You can share the access keys with the users, and they can use them in the Authorization header of their API calls. These access keys give complete access to the storage, and this exposes a vector of attack. If the key is compromised, then your sensitive data stored in the cloud is also compromised. Also, you cannot control the duration of access; if you have the key until the administrator revokes it, you will have complete access. This is not ideal when you are collaborating with partners for a limited duration. When the collaboration ends, you have to manually revoke the keys to stop further access. Another downside is that you cannot control access to services; one key is enough to access blobs, queues, tables, and files. If you want to give access to blobs only using access keys, that's not possible. Further, you cannot give read-only access; access keys will give read-write access to the people who possess them. All these concerns are addressed by SAS.

SAS is a URI that is composed of various parameters by which you can restrict access to Azure Storage. SAS is ideal for any scenarios where you don't want to expose or share your access keys. With the help of SAS keys, you can grant access to specific services for a specific period of time. SAS reduces the chances of compromising your account keys and adheres to the principle of least privileges.

SAS empowers you with the ability to grant granular access to the objects or services. Using SAS, you can configure the following parameters:

- Control access at the service level.
- Set a time frame during which the SAS is valid. You can specify the start and end time.
- Set permissions like read, write, delete, etc.

- Set IP ranges from which the SAS keys can be accepted.
- Set the protocol: HTTP or HTTPS.

By the way, there are three types of SAS: account level, service level, and user delegation SAS. Account-level SAS delegates have access to resources in one or more storage services like blob, table, queue, or file. Service-level SAS delegates access a resource in a single storage service. User delegation SAS is secured with Azure AD and can be used with Azure Blobs only.

Now that you are familiar with the parameters, let's learn to generate SAS keys.

Generating SAS

You can easily create the SAS URI from the Azure portal. First, you need to create a storage account; if you already have the storage account that you created in Exercise 6.1, you can reuse it. Under Security + Networking (refer to Figure 6.9), you will be able to see Shared Access Signature. Clicking this will take you to the blade to generate the SAS token.

FIGURE 6.9   Configuring SAS parameters

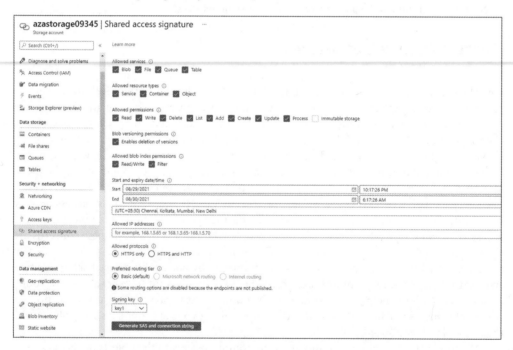

In Figure 6.9, you can see the following parameters are requested for the creation of SAS:

- **Allowed Services:** Choose the set of services you want to grant access to. Options include Blob, File, Queue, and Table.
- **Allowed Resource Types:** Select the resources you want to access with the SAS. You can select from Service, Container, and Object.

- **Allowed Permissions:** Select the set of permissions you want to grant. The choices are Read, Write, Delete, List, Add, Create, Update, and Process.

- **Blob Versioning Permissions:** If you would like to grant permission to delete blob versions, check this box.

- **Allowed Blob Index Permissions:** Permissions are for viewing, creating, or filtering blob indexes.

- **Start and Expiry Date/Time:** Specify the start time, end time, and time zone.

- **Allowed IP addresses:** Specify the IP range or IP address from which the SAS request will be accepted. If you leave this blank, requests from all IPs will be allowed.

- **Allowed Protocols:** Select HTTPS only or HTTPS and HTTP. The default option is HTTPS only.

- **Preferred Routing Tier:** Select basic routing.

- **Signing Key:** You can generate the SAS using key1 or key2. These are the access keys of the storage account. If you revoke the key used to sign the SAS, the SAS will also be revoked.

Select the options as shown in Figure 6.9 and click Generate SAS And Connection String. The connection string and the SAS URL will be generated as shown in Figure 6.10. You need to copy the SAS token and save it for later use. You will need this SAS token for Exercise 6.2. Otherwise, you can create an SAS token when you are performing Exercise 6.2.

FIGURE 6.10   Generating SAS URL/URI

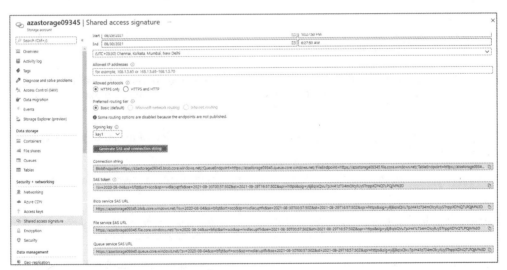

Since you have the SAS URI, let's see what changes these parameters will bring to the endpoint URL. Also, you will learn how to interpret the parameters when you see a URI.

URI and SAS Parameters

If you take the blob service, the default endpoint will be `https://<storage-account-name>.blob.core.windows.net`. For example, if the name of the storage account is mystorage01, the blob endpoint will be `https://mystorage01.blob.core.windows.net`. You can divide the URI into two parts: storage resource URI and the SAS token (see Figure 6.11).

FIGURE 6.11   Storage URI

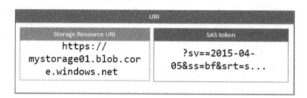

Let's take a sample URI to explain the parameters. The following is an example URI:

```
https://mystorage01.blob.core.windows.net/?restype=service&comp=properties
&sv=2015-04-05&ss=bf&srt=s&st=2015-04-29T22%3A18%3A26Z&se=2015-04-30T02%3A23%
3A26Z&sr=b&sp=rw&sip=168.1.5.60-168.1.5.70&spr=https&sig=F%6GRVAZ5Cdj2Pw4txx
xxx
```

Refer to Table 6.5 to understand each of the parameters.

TABLE 6.5   Understanding URI Parameters

Parameter	URI portion	Description
Resource URI	`https://mystorage01.blob.core.windows.net/?restype=service&comp=properties`	The blob endpoint; to get the service properties, you can make a GET call to this endpoint.
Storage services version	`sv=2015-04-05`	The version of the storage service.
Services	`ss=bf`	SAS applies to two services b=blob and f=file.
Resource types	`srt=s`	Access is granted for service-level operations, s=service.
Start time	`st=2015-04-29T22%3A18%3A26Z`	Start time of the SAS in UTC.
Expiry time	`se=2015-04-30T02%3A23%3A26Z`	Expiry time in UTC.

Parameter	URI portion	Description
Resource	`sr=b`	Selected resource is a blob.
Permissions	`sp=rw`	Permission to read and write.
IP range	`sip=168.1.5.60-168.1.5.70`	The IP address range.
Protocol	`spr=https`	Only HTTPS requests are permitted.
Signature	`sig=F%6GRVAZ5Cdj2Pw4txxxxx`	Signature that is used to authenticate access to the blob. The signature is an HMAC computed over a string-to-sign and key using the SHA256 algorithm and then encoded using Base64 encoding.

In the next exercise, you will use the SAS to access the blob you stored in Exercise 6.1. If you have deleted the storage account, you need to re-create a new storage account and a public container and upload an image to the container. Try copying the link of the image and check if you can access the image. If everything is configured correctly, you should be able to see the image in the browser. We will reuse the container and blob to demonstrate how the SAS keys work.

EXERCISE 6.2

Working with SAS Keys

1. Sign in to the Azure Portal and search for *Storage Accounts*.

2. Open the storage account you created in Exercise 6.1. If you don't have a storage account, create a new one using the steps outlined in Exercise 6.1.

3. Open the existing container and verify you can see the blob. If you are working with a new container, make sure you upload an image to the container for testing.

4. Click Change Access Level at the top and change it to Private. Changing it to Private will block all anonymous access to the container. Click OK to save the changes.

5. Click the stored blob and copy the link. Try accessing the link from the browser. You will get a `ResourceNotFound` error. This is because you have blocked all anonymous access to the container by setting the access level to Private.

6. Remember the SAS key that you copied earlier. If not, generate a new SAS key with all the permissions shown in Figure 6.9.

7. Append the SAS URL to the end of the link you pasted earlier and check if you are able to access the object stored in the storage account. As you can see, with SAS in the URL, you are able to see the image.

If you need, you can customize the parameters in the SAS key and generate a different URL based on your requirements. Next, we will cover Storage Service Encryption, which is responsible for protecting data at rest.

Storage Service Encryption

Storage Service Encryption is the encryption provided by the Azure platform to encrypt data at rest. Any data before persisting it to Azure Blob, Azure Queues, Tables, Azure Files, or managed disks will be automatically encrypted by the Storage Service Encryption service. This will help developers build secure applications in the cloud, without the need to develop encryption algorithms and solutions to encrypt the data.

Another key point here is that the SSE encryption, encryption at rest, decryption, and key management processes are totally transparent to the end users. Azure uses 256-bit AES encryption to encrypt the data before persisting to Azure Storage. This is one of the strongest block ciphers available.

Some organizations prefer to bring their own encryption keys and handle the encryption due to compliance requirements. SSE supports customer-managed keys as well. Having support for customer-managed keys offers flexibility and control over the keys. Since you are managing the keys, you have the option to create, disable, audit, rotate, and define access controls. The key will be stored in Azure Key Vault and will be utilized by the Azure Storage service whenever the key is required.

Figure 6.12 shows how you can add your own keys to handle encryption.

FIGURE 6.12 Setting up customer-managed keys

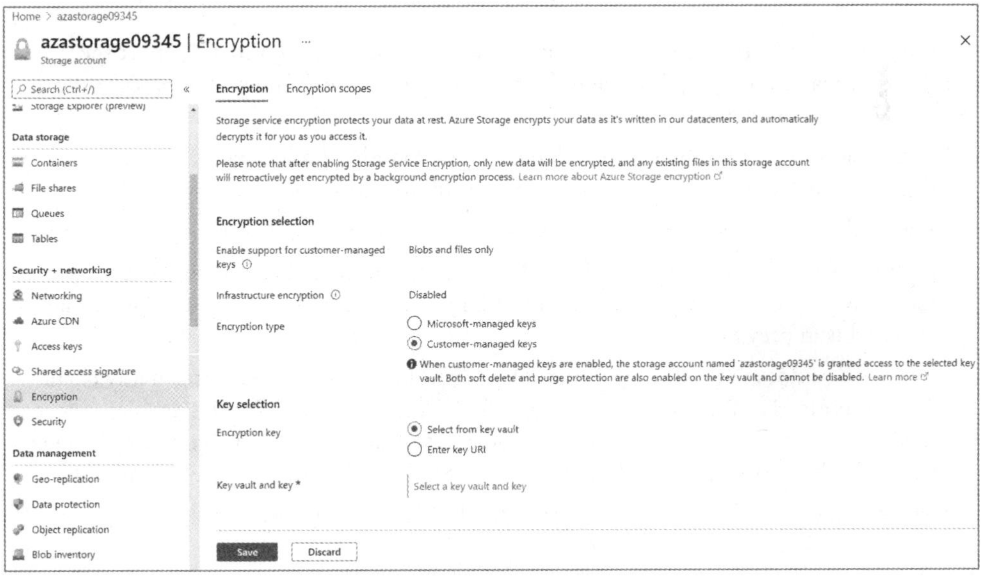

As shown in Figure 6.12, you need to select an existing key vault or create a new key vault and a key to save the configuration. With that, we will move on to the next topic of discussion, Azure Files and File Sync.

Azure Files and File Sync

When we were discussing the storage service, we went through a quick introduction to Azure Files. You know that Azure Blob can be used to store unstructured data like your videos, binaries, text files, etc. However, you can also save these kinds of files in Azure Files. Since both of them can store the file types, let's quickly compare the two options before we take a deep dive to Azure Files.

Azure Files vs. Azure Blobs

As both services support unstructured file storage, sometimes it's difficult to decide when to use Azure Blobs and when to use Azure Files. Let's take a minute to review the following points to understand the difference between Azure Files and Azure Blobs.

Azure Files   This is ideal for applications that are using system APIs to share data between servers. Second, you want to store debugging and crash dumps that need to be accessed from multiple virtual machines.

Azure Blobs   This is ideal for video streaming scenarios. It's a good choice for rendering images in static websites. You want to access the data from anywhere.

From the aforementioned points, you can understand that though they support the storage of similar data types, the scenarios they are used in are different. Other key differences include the following:

- Azure Blobs uses a flat namespace that includes containers and objects. Azure Files uses directory objects as you have seen with our traditional file shares.

- Azure Blobs is accessed via containers, and Azure Files is accessed through file shares.

- Azure Blobs is accessed via an HTTP/HTTPS connection, and Azure Files is accessed via the SMB protocol when mounted to a virtual machine. NFS for Azure Files is available also and is in preview.

- Azure Blobs doesn't need to be mounted and can be accessed directly from any client that supports HTTP calls. Azure Files needs to be mounted to virtual machines before working with the data. On a side note, you can still manage the files in Azure Files via tools like the Azure portal and Azure Storage Explorer without the need to mount it.

Well, it's time to see how you can manage the file shares in Azure.

Managing File Shares

To set up a file share, the first thing you need is a storage account. Once the storage account is created, all you need to do is provide the name and the tier of the file share. In Exercise 6.1, you already saw how you can create a storage account. If you haven't deleted the storage account that you created earlier, then you can reuse it. Otherwise, go ahead and create a new General Purpose v2 storage account.

Once you navigate to File Shares under Data Storage in the Storage Account, you will see File Share Settings (refer to Figure 6.13). The following are the preferences available:

Active Directory   For setting up authentication using on-premises AD or Active Directory Domain Services.

Soft Delete   Enables you to retain the deleted shares for a specified period of time. Once you click 7 days, as shown in Figure 6.13, you will get a slider to choose from 7 days to 365 days. Also, you can disable the soft delete option if you don't need it.

Maximum Capacity   The default value for this is 5 TB and can be increased to 100 TB.

FIGURE 6.13   Setting up a file share

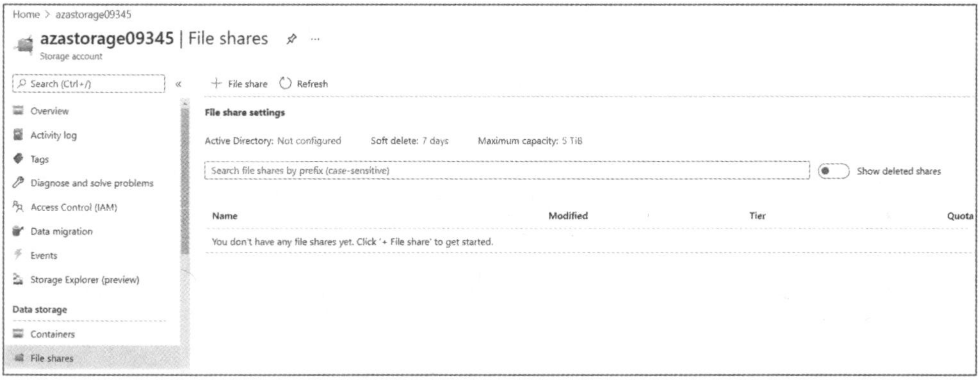

If you take a closer look at Figure 6.13, you can see at the top there is an option to add a new file share denoted by + File share. Upon clicking this option, you will be presented with an option to add the name and tier as shown in Figure 6.14. You can confirm the creation by clicking the Create button.

There are four tiers offered by file shares.

- **Transaction Optimized:** This is the default option. It's ideal for most scenarios where you need a file share as a data store.

- **Premium:** Premium file shares are backed up by SSDs, and this option will be available only if your storage account is a Premium storage account. For a Standard storage account, this option will be grayed out.

- **Hot:** This is optimized for general-purpose file shares such Azure File Sync and team shares.
- **Cool:** This is ideal for archiving scenarios.

You can always edit the quota of the file share once it's created. Since you created the file share with a 5 TB size, then the default quota value will be 5120 GB. The Edit Quota option will be available on the Overview blade of the file share (refer to Figure 6.14).

FIGURE 6.14   Creating a file share

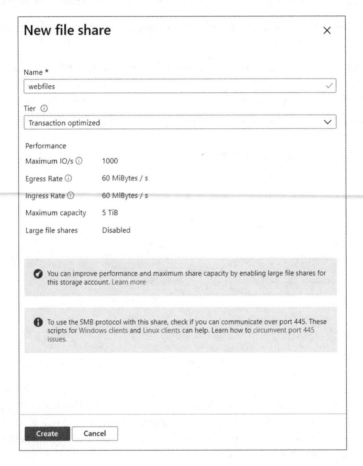

It's important to make sure that port 445 is open in Windows and Linux machines before you mount the file shares. If the file share is going to be consumed by Azure virtual machines, make sure you open TCP 445 in your NSG.

Mapping File Shares

Once you click the file share you create, at the top you'll see an option called Connect. Clicking Connect, Azure will display the scripts to mount or map the file share to Windows, Linux, and macOS computers, as shown in Figure 6.15:

FIGURE 6.15   Connecting to the file share

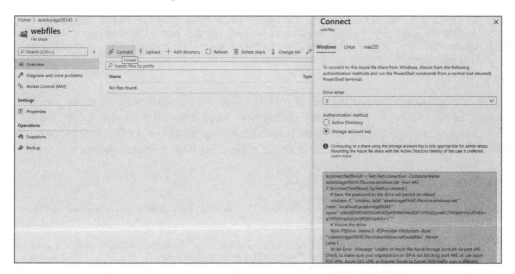

As of now, the authentication is happening using the Storage account key. If you have enabled Active Directory authentication, you can set up that as well. All you need to do is run the provided script in PowerShell, Shell, or Terminal for Windows, Linux, and macOS, respectively. To quickly demonstrate this, let's see how you can connect to Windows and Linux computers.

Windows

To mount the file share, copy the script that you see in Figure 6.15 and open PowerShell. You don't need to open an elevated terminal; a normal one will suffice. The following is a sample script:

```
$connectTestResult = Test-NetConnection -ComputerName azastorage09345.file
.core.windows.net -Port 445

if ($connectTestResult.TcpTestSucceeded)
{
    # Save the password so the drive will persist on reboot
    cmd.exe /C "cmdkey /add:`"azastorage09345.file.core.windows.net`"
/user:`"localhost\azastorage09345`" /pass:`"u0hG9DERY8K58QrBVKEjaYDt9bHSzsSEX1
UhSQQywa6/L7IhQxlt1OyLilTA5io+q1PKIlcHapEzQmWQ6OopNA==`""
```

```
    # Mount the drive
    New-PSDrive -Name Z -PSProvider FileSystem -Root "\\azastorage09345.file
.core.windows.net\webfiles" -Persist
}

else
{
    Write-Error -Message "Unable to reach the Azure storage account via port
445. Check to make sure your organization or ISP is not blocking port 445, or
use Azure P2S VPN, Azure S2S VPN, or Express Route to tunnel SMB traffic over
a different port."
}
```

The script will automatically check if port 445 is accessible. Currently, the script will mount the file to drive letter ZI. If you already have some other drive mounted to the same drive letter, consider changing the `Name` parameter in `New-PSDrive`. In Figure 6.16, you can see that the PowerShell terminal returns that the share has been mounted successfully.

FIGURE 6.16   Mounting the file share

```
PS C:\Users\riskaria> $connectTestResult = Test-NetConnection -ComputerName azastorage09345.file.core.windows.net -Port
445
PS C:\Users\riskaria> if ($connectTestResult.TcpTestSucceeded) {
>>     # Save the password so the drive will persist on reboot
>>     cmd.exe /C "cmdkey /add:`"azastorage09345.file.core.windows.net`" /user:`"localhost\azastorage09345`" /pass:`"u0l
G9DERY8K58QrBVKEjaYDt9bHSzsSEX1UhSQQywa6/L7IhQxlt1OyLilTA5io+q1PKIlcHapEzQmWQ6OopNA==`""
>>     # Mount the drive
>>     New-PSDrive -Name Z -PSProvider FileSystem -Root "\\azastorage09345.file.core.windows.net\webfiles" -Persist
>> } else {
>>     Write-Error -Message "Unable to reach the Azure storage account via port 445. Check to make sure your organizatio
n or ISP is not blocking port 445, or use Azure P2S VPN, Azure S2S VPN, or Express Route to tunnel SMB traffic over a di
fferent port."
>> }

CMDKEY: Credential added successfully.

Name       Used (GB)    Free (GB) Provider    Root                                       CurrentLocation
----       ---------    --------- --------    ----                                       ---------------
Z               0.00      5120.00 FileSystem  \\azastorage09345.file.core.wind...
```

You can verify if the file share is working by adding a file to the mounted file share and confirm if it's reflected in the Azure portal. In Figure 6.17, you can see that a file has been added to the drive.

Refreshing the file share will show the file you added from your local computer in the Azure portal (refer to Figure 6.18).

You can always dismount the file share from the Windows File Explorer or by using the `Remove-PSDrive` command from PowerShell. Now, you will mount the very same file share to a Linux machine and see if you can download the `hello.jpg` file.

FIGURE 6.17   Adding a file to the file share

FIGURE 6.18   Verifying files in a file share

Linux

In your Linux computer, you need to open a Terminal and run the script provided by Azure. The following is a sample script:

```
sudo mkdir /mnt/webfiles
if [ ! -d "/etc/smbcredentials" ]; then
sudo mkdir /etc/smbcredentials
fi
if [ ! -f "/etc/smbcredentials/azastorage09345.cred" ]; then
    sudo bash -c 'echo "username=azastorage09345" >>
/etc/smbcredentials/azastorage09345.cred'
    sudo bash -c 'echo
"password=u0hG9DERY8K58QrBVKEjaYDt9bHSzsSEX1UhSQQywa6/L7IhQxlt1OyLilTA5io+q1PKI
lcHapEzQmWQ6OopNA==" >> /etc/smbcredentials/azastorage09345.cred'
fi
sudo chmod 600 /etc/smbcredentials/azastorage09345.cred

sudo bash -c 'echo "//azastorage09345.file.core.windows.net/webfiles
/mnt/webfiles cifs
nofail,vers=3.0,credentials=/etc/smbcredentials/azastorage09345.cred,dir_
mode=0777,file_mode=0777,serverino" >> /etc/fstab'
sudo mount -t cifs //azastorage09345.file.core.windows.net/webfiles
/mnt/webfiles -o
vers=3.0,credentials=/etc/smbcredentials/azastorage09345.cred,dir_mode=0777,
file_mode=0777,serverino
```

The script will create a mount point in /mnt/webfiles, and it also updates the /etc/fstab file so that your share remains mounted even if you reboot the system. After running the script, you can see that the file share is mounted, and if you list the files in the share, hello.jpg is listed (refer to Figure 6.19). Similarly, you can mount the file share to macOS computers as well.

Since you are storing data in the file share, it's vital to think about the recovery options in case of an accidental deletion or unintended changes. You will see how you can leverage snapshots to overcome this situation.

File Share Snapshots

With file share snapshots, you can take a point-in-time, read-only copy of the contents of the file share. Though you can take a snapshot at the file share level, Azure provides retrieval at an individual file level. This is very helpful, as you don't need to restore the entire share for retrieving a single file. If you have taken snapshots of a file share, you cannot delete the file share until you delete the snapshots. You can easily add a snapshot from the Snapshots blade, as shown Figure 6.20.

FIGURE 6.19 Verifying files in the file share from a Linux machine

```
rithin@vm-01:~$ sudo mkdir /mnt/webfiles
etc/smbcredentials
fi
if [ ! -f "/etc/smbcredentials/azastorage09345.cred" ]; then
    sudo bash -c 'echo "username=azastorage09345" >> /etc/smbcredentials/azastorage09345.cred'
    sudo bash -c 'echo "password=u0hG9DERY8K58QrBVKEjaYDt9bHSzsSEX1UhSQQywa6/L7IhQxlt1OyLilTA5io+q1PKIlcHapEzQmWQ6OopNA==" >> /etc/smbcredentials
/azastorage09345.cred'
fi
sudo chmod 600 /etc/smbcredentials/azastorage09345.cred

sudo bash -c 'echo "//azastorage09345.file.core.windows.net/webfiles /mnt/webfiles cifs nofail,vers=3.0,credentials=/etc/smbcredentials/azastorag
e09345.cred,dir_mode=0777,file_mode=0777,serverino" >> /etc/fstab'
sudo mount -t cifs //azastorage09345.file.core.windows.net/webfiles /mnt/webfiles -o vers=3.0,credentials=/etc/smbcredentials/azastorage09345.cre
d,dir_mode=0777,file_mode=0777,serverinorithin@vm-01:~$ if [ ! -d "/etc/smbcredentials" ]; then
> sudo mkdir /etc/smbcredentials
> fi
rithin@vm-01:~$ if [ ! -f "/etc/smbcredentials/azastorage09345.cred" ]; then
>     sudo bash -c 'echo "username=azastorage09345" >> /etc/smbcredentials/azastorage09345.cred'
>     sudo bash -c 'echo "password=u0hG9DERY8K58QrBVKEjaYDt9bHSzsSEX1UhSQQywa6/L7IhQxlt1OyLilTA5io+q1PKIlcHapEzQmWQ6OopNA==" >> /etc/smbcredentia
ls/azastorage09345.cred'
> fi
rithin@vm-01:~$ sudo chmod 600 /etc/smbcredentials/azastorage09345.cred
rithin@vm-01:~$
rithin@vm-01:~$ sudo bash -c 'echo "//azastorage09345.file.core.windows.net/webfiles /mnt/webfiles cifs nofail,vers=3.0,credentials=/etc/smbcrede
ntials/azastorage09345.cred,dir_mode=0777,file_mode=0777,serverino" >> /etc/fstab'
rithin@vm-01:~$ sudo mount -t cifs //azastorage09345.file.core.windows.net/webfiles /mnt/webfiles -o vers=3.0,credentials=/etc/smbcredentials/aza
storage09345.cred,dir_mode=0777,file_mode=0777,serverino
rithin@vm-01:~$ cd /mnt/webfiles/
rithin@vm-01:/mnt/webfiles$ ll
total 42
drwxrwxrwx 2 root root    0 Sep  1 00:54 ./
drwxr-xr-x 4 root root 4096 Sep  1 01:16 ../
-rwxrwxrwx 1 root root 38176 Aug 29 01:37 hello.jpg*
rithin@vm-01:/mnt/webfiles$
```

FIGURE 6.20 File share snapshots

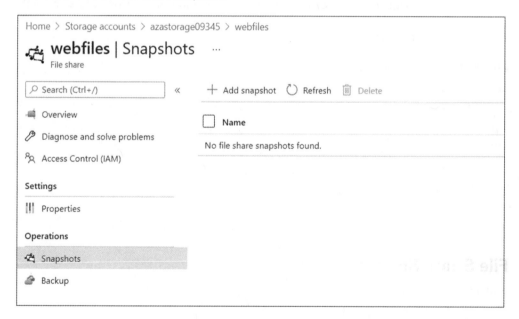

The snapshots are incremental, and the delta from the last snapshot is appended to the snapshot. Since it only saves the recent changes and doesn't take a complete snapshot every time you make a change, you can save money on storage. You can use snapshots in the following scenarios:

Protection Against Data Corruption and Application Errors   You can use file shares to store files, logs, and crash dumps. This means frequent read write operations will happen. If the application is misconfigured, this may lead to deletion of some data or even overwriting the data. As this is an irreversible change, there is no way you can restore the data. Using snapshots, you can restore to a point in time.

Accidental Deletions and Overwrite   In the last point, you saw application misconfiguration led to deletion and unintended changes. This may happen due to human errors, and accidental changes may happen. You can reverse these changes using snapshots.

Backup Purposes   You can rely on snapshots as a backup. Using a backup, you can maintain different versions of files taken from different timestamps.

For snapshots, you need to manually take them, and you cannot automate this based on a schedule. The workaround is to use the Azure REST API, Azure PowerShell, or Azure CLI for automating this action. Nevertheless, Azure offers an out-of-the-box solution called Azure File Share Backup. You can back up your data to a recovery service vault and attach a backup policy to run the backup automatically. In Figure 6.21, you can see that when you navigate to the Backup blade, you get the option to choose or create a recovery services vault and select the backup policy.

The next topic of discussion is Azure File Sync.

FIGURE 6.21   Azure File Share Backup

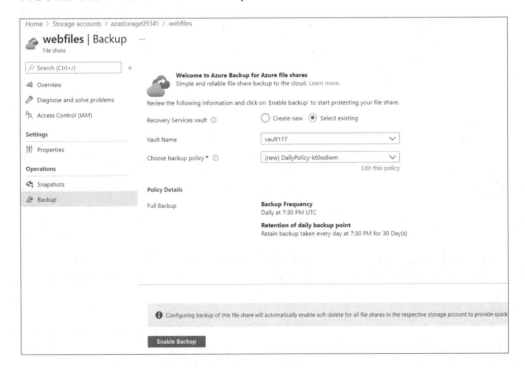

Azure File Sync

File shares are not something new; you still have on-premises file shares that serve your enterprise needs and requirements. Azure File Share is a cloud-based file share that enables you to access the file share from any computer anywhere in the world. With Azure File Sync, you will be using Azure Files as a centralized location for storing files without comprising the flexibility, performance, and compatibility that you had in your on-premises servers. In simple words, you can synchronize the files you have on-premises with Azure File Share. Our existing Windows Servers can be altered as cache for our Azure file share. The advantage is you can access the files locally using SMB, NFS, or even FTPS. If your organization has a global presence, then you can have multiple caches across the globe. The following are the advantages of File Sync:

Ease of Access   Using file sync, on-premises users doesn't need to make any changes to their existing shares. They can access them the same way they were accessed earlier.

No Need for Other Replication Methods   Since all your files are synchronized to the cloud, you don't need to use any other replication methods like DFS replication in your on-premises file servers.

Reduce On-Premises Footprint   Your on-premises servers will be acting as a cache only, and the data will be stored in the cloud. Without expanding the storage in your file servers, you can grow in the cloud.

Backup and DR   Azure Backup will make sure that your data is backed up. In the case of recovery, you can easily restore the files.

Archiving   Since the on-premises server is essentially a cache, only the recently accessed items are stored on-premises. Your data that is not frequently accessed will remain in the cloud using cloud tiering.

Easy to Add New Servers   If you have a new office and they need to back up or synchronize the data, then all they need to do is install the agent and connect to Azure storage.

Let's look at the components that are part of File Sync.

Components

It's important to understand the components of Azure File Sync before you work on it or implement it. Figure 6.22 shows the high-level components of File Sync.

Let's drill down and understand each component and its function.

Storage Sync Services   In File Sync, the Storage Sync service is the top-level resource you have in Azure. The Storage Sync service needs to be deployed in Azure as an independent resource and can be deployed to a resource group like a storage account. The Storage Sync Service will be connected with a storage account file share via sync groups. You can deploy multiple sync services in your subscription.

FIGURE 6.22   File Sync components

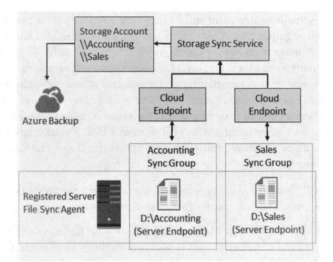

Sync Group   Each sync group represents a set of files that you want to synchronize with the file share. The synchronization is done via cloud endpoints, and each group requires its own cloud endpoint to connect with the storage sync service. The files that are part of the sync group are totally distinct, as you can see in Figure 6.22; one sync group is for Accounting, and the other one is for Sales.

Registered Server   This actually represents your on-premises file server. The reason why it's called registered is because it has a trust relationship established with the storage sync service. You cannot have more than one trust relationship at a time; in other words, your registered server can have a connection to a single storage sync service at a time. However, a single storage sync service can establish a relationship between multiple on-premises servers at a time.

Azure File Sync Agent   File Sync Agent will be installed on the on-premises servers that you want to transform to a cache for your Azure file share. The agent can be downloaded and installed on any Windows server. In File Sync Agent, you have three components:

- **FileSyncSvc.exe:** This background service is responsible for monitoring any changes happening on the server endpoints. If any changes are detected, sync sessions will be initiated.

- **StorageSync.sys:** This is responsible for tiering of files when cloud tiering is enabled. Cloud tiering is a process by which only recent files are cached in the on-premises servers. Unused files will be replaced by a pointer and are retrieved only when end users request it. The pointers point to a link for the Azure file share.

- **PowerShell cmdlets:** This is a set of PowerShell cmdlets that can be used to manage and interact with the Microsoft.StorageSync Azure resource provider.

Server Endpoint   Server endpoints are folders that are residing on the registered server. As long as the namespaces of the server endpoints do not overlap, multiple server endpoints can exist in the same volume such as `D:\locationA` and `D:\locationB`. You can have separate tiering policies for each endpoint.

Cloud Endpoint   A file share that is part of a sync group is called a cloud endpoint. An Azure file share can be a member of a single cloud endpoint only. In Figure 6.22, you can see that the `D:\Accounting` server endpoint is mapped to the `\\Accouting` file share, and `D:\Sales` is mapped to the `\\Sales` file share. So, in case you want two distinct sets of files to be synchronized, then you need two sync groups, in other words, two cloud endpoints pointing to two different files shares.

Deployment Steps

The deployment of File Sync comprises four main stages.

1. Create the Storage Sync service in Azure.

2. Prepare on-premises server(s).

3. Download and install the File Sync agent.

4. Register the Windows server(s).

The first thing you need to perform is to create a Storage Sync service in Azure. This is a stand-alone resource, and you can easily find it by searching the Azure Portal. As you can see in Figure 6.23, the creation requires only basic inputs from your end.

The next step in the process is to prepare our target servers. All servers that you plan to enroll with Azure File Sync should be prepared before you install the agent; this includes failover nodes in your failover cluster as well. You need to disable IE Enhanced Security and ensure that the latest PowerShell version is installed.

Once the prerequisites are met, then you can install the File Sync agent. At the time of writing this book, the executable is available to download from here:

`www.microsoft.com/en-us/download/details.aspx?id=57159`

You may refer to the Microsoft documentation if you are not able to download the file or if the link has changed. The installation is pretty quick, and Microsoft recommends using the default installation path for installing the agent. Also, make sure that you enabled Windows Update to get the latest updates for the agent.

The last and final stage in the process is to register the server where you prepared and installed the agent. The Server Registration window will automatically pop up when you complete the agent installation. The registration process will establish a trust relationship with the Storage Sync service you created earlier. Registration requires you to provide the Azure subscription ID, resource group name, and the Storage Sync server name. As explained earlier, you can register the server only with one Storage Sync service at a time. After registration, you need to configure the synchronization.

FIGURE 6.23   Creating Storage Sync services

Until now, you have uploaded the files to the storage account from the Azure Portal, and for Azure Files you tried uploading to the share. You have other tools available for importing or exporting data to or from the cloud. In the next section, we will cover some of the tools that will be helpful for you.

Managing Storage

When we say *manage*, we are actually looking for tools to manage the data that you store in the cloud. Management includes uploading files to the cloud, downloading files from the cloud, and doing other file operations. In the "Azure Blob Storage" section, we listed a set of tools that can be used to upload files to blob. Here, we are going cover three tools that can be used to manage the storage.

Azure Storage Explorer

Azure Storage Explorer is a desktop application that you can download to your Windows, Linux, and macOS computers to manage your Azure storage. This tool offers a rich GUI by which you can connect to multiple accounts, subscriptions, and storage accounts. The latest version of the Azure Storage Explorer can be downloaded from here:

`https://azure.microsoft.com/en-us/features/storage-explorer`

Using Azure Storage Explorer, you can easily manage, upload, and download blobs, queues, tables, and files. Azure Storage Explorer can work with Azure Data Lake Storage and Azure managed disks. You can control the permissions, access, and tiers from the tool. The installation of the tool is very straightforward. Once it's installed, you can connect your storage accounts.

Connection Options

There are multiple ways by which you can connect our Azure storage account with Azure Storage Explorer. Figure 6.24 shows the different methods available in the tool.

FIGURE 6.24 Connecting using Azure Storage Explorer

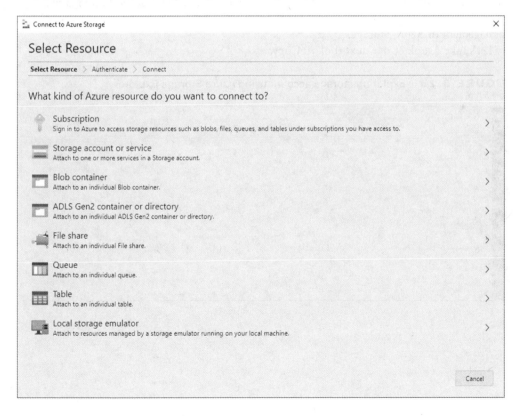

The following are the methods by which you can connect:

- *Subscription*: Sign in to Azure using your credentials to access the storage accounts to which you have access.

- *Storage account or service*: If you have the storage access key, shared access signature or connection string, you can directly connect to the storage account without the need to sign in to Azure subscription.

- *Blob container*: Connect to the blob container using Azure AD, SAS, or anonymously.

- *ADLS Gen2 container or directory*: Connect to Azure Data Lake Storage Gen2 using Azure AD, SAS, or anonymously.

- *File Share*: Connect to the file share.

- *Queue*: Connect to Azure Queue.

- *Table*: Attach to an individual table.

- *Local storage emulator*: You can attach to resources managed by a storage emulator running on your local machine.

- *Cosmos DB*: Connect to a Cosmos DB account using a connection string.

In Figure 6.25, you can see the storage account that was used in the previous demonstrations and the `hello.jpg` file. If you look at the toolbar, you can see several options such as Upload, Download, Open, New Folder, Select All, Copy, etc. The tool gives you complete management of Azure Storage.

Let's take a look at our next tool, AzCopy.

FIGURE 6.25   Exploring storage account using Azure Storage Explorer

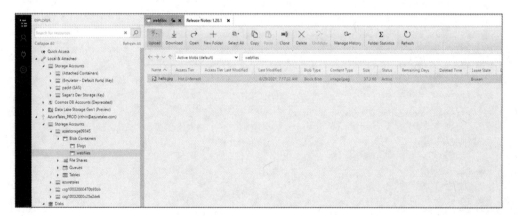

AzCopy

AzCopy is a next-generation command-line tool for copying data from or to Azure Blob and Azure Files. Behind the scenes, Azure Storage Explorer uses AzCopy to accomplish all the data transfer operations. The key difference is Azure Storage Explorer offers a rich, matured user interface, while AzCopy is a command-line tool. With AzCopy you can copy data in the following scenarios:

- Copy data from a local machine to Azure Blobs or Azure Files
- Copy data from Azure Blobs or Azure Files to a local machine
- Copy data between storage accounts

    AzCopy v10 is the latest version, and it can be downloaded from here:

    `https://docs.microsoft.com/en-us/azure/storage/common/storage-use-azcopy-v10#download-azcopy`

    The following are the new features offered by v10:

- You can synchronize a file system using AzCopy, which makes AzCopy ideal for incremental copying.
- It supports ADLS Gen2 APIs.
- It supports transferring all data from Azure Blob Storage to another one.
- There are no data transfer limits.
- Additionally, files can be listed or removed from a given path.
- It supports wildcard patterns.
- Copying is done as jobs, and for every job a related log file is created. This makes it easier to track jobs and restart them in case of any failure.
- It has improved performance.

Authentication

In the case of Azure Storage Explorer, you saw different options such as connecting using Azure AD, account keys, and SAS URL. AzCopy offers two methods by which you can authenticate yourself before working with the storage accounts. Let's take a look at the supported options. Before trying out the following commands, download AzCopy for your operating system from the aforementioned link. Also, you need to copy the executable file to your path variable. Take a look at the run instructions given by Microsoft here:

    `https://docs.microsoft.com/en-us/azure/storage/common/storage-use-azcopy-v10#run-azcopy`

Azure Active Directory

This method is applicable only for the Azure Blobs and ADLS Gen2 services. As Azure Files doesn't support Azure AD authentication, you cannot use this authentication type for managing Azure Files. The user who is going to authenticate using Azure AD should make sure that the Storage Blob Data Contributor role is assigned to perform write operations using Azure AD authentication.

You can run the following script by replacing the storage account name, resource group, and username in the cloud shell or any local PowerShell terminal that is connected to your Azure subscription, to assign the role to a user.

```
#Variables
$storageAccount = "azastorage09345" #Replace with storage account name
$rg = "storage-rg" # Replace with your resource group name
$user = "rithin@azuretales.com" # Replace with the username
$role = "Storage Blob Data Contributor" # Select role

#Get Id of the Storage Account
$id = (Get-AzStorageAccount `
    -StorageAccountName $storageAccount `
    -ResourceGroupName $rg).Id

#Assign role
New-AzRoleAssignment `
    -SignInName $user `
    -Scope $id `
    -RoleDefinitionName $role

#Verify role assignment
Get-AzRoleAssignment `
    -Scope $id `
    -RoleDefinitionName $role | Select SignInName
```

Once the role is assigned, you can connect AzCopy to Azure AD using the command azcopy login, and you will be asked to open the https://microsoft.com/devicelogin URL in your browser and input the code shown in the PowerShell terminal (refer to Figure 6.26).

FIGURE 6.26 AzCopy Azure AD login

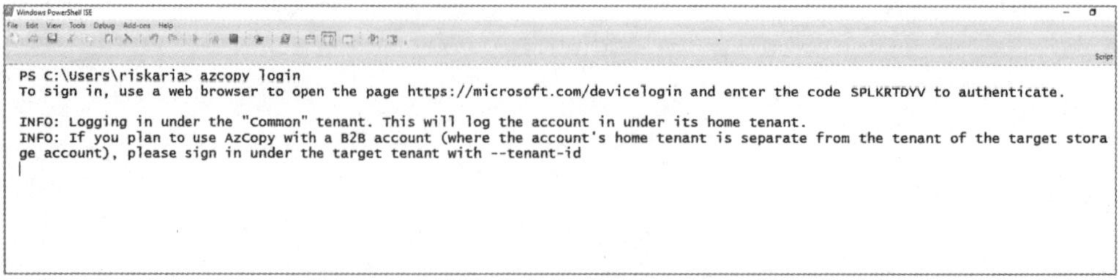

In the browser, you will be asked to sign in using your credentials. Make sure that you use the credentials that have the Storage Blob Data Contributor role assigned using the script. If the sign-in was successful, you will get a message that you signed in to the Azure Storage AzCopy application. You can close the browser and continue working from your command line.

SAS Token

Since both Azure Blobs and Azure Files support the use of SAS tokens, you can use SAS tokens for authentication and to manage the storage. You can create your SAS token from the Azure portal or by using the PowerShell command New-AzStorageAccountSASToken or the Azure CLI command az storage container generate-sas or az storage blob generate-sas.

You don't need to use the login command when you are authenticating with the SAS token; instead, you will append the token to the URL of the storage account for performing the operations.

Getting Started

AzCopy offers a lot of options when dealing with data. You can list all the options available in AzCopy using the command azcopy, and you will get a screen similar to Figure 6.27

FIGURE 6.27 Listing all commands

```
PS C:\Users\riskaria> azcopy
AzCopy 10.12.1
Project URL: github.com/Azure/azure-storage-azcopy

AzCopy is a command line tool that moves data into and out of Azure Storage.
To report issues or to learn more about the tool, go to github.com/Azure/azure-storage-azcopy

The general format of the commands is: 'azcopy [command] [arguments] --[flag-name]=[flag-value]'.

Usage:
  azcopy [command]

Available Commands:
  bench       Performs a performance benchmark
  completion  generate the autocompletion script for the specified shell
  copy        Copies source data to a destination location
  doc         Generates documentation for the tool in Markdown format
  env         Shows the environment variables that you can use to configure the behavior of AzCopy.
  help        Help about any command
  jobs        Sub-commands related to managing jobs
  list        List the entities in a given resource
  login       Log in to Azure Active Directory (AD) to access Azure Storage resources.
  logout      Log out to terminate access to Azure Storage resources.
  make        Create a container or file share.
  remove      Delete blobs or files from an Azure storage account
  sync        Replicate source to the destination location

Flags:
      --cap-mbps float                       Caps the transfer rate, in megabits per second. Moment-by-moment throughput might vary
slightly from the cap. If this option is set to zero, or it is omitted, the throughput isn't capped.
  -h, --help                                 help for azcopy
      --output-type string                   Format of the command's output. The choices include: text, json. The default value is '
text'. (default "text")
      --trusted-microsoft-suffixes string    Specifies additional domain suffixes where Azure Active Directory login tokens may be s
ent.  The default is '*.core.windows.net;*.core.chinacloudapi.cn;*.core.cloudapi.de;*.core.usgovcloudapi.net;*.storage.azure.net'.
Any listed here are added to the default. For security, you should only put Microsoft Azure domains here. Separate multiple entries
with semi-colons.
  -v, --version                              version for azcopy

Use "azcopy [command] --help" for more information about a command.
```

If you need help with a particular command, say copy, then you can get the help options by running azcopy copy --help. The syntax for getting help for any command under azcopy is as follows:

```
azcopy [command] --help
```

The syntax for working with copy is as follows:

```
azcopy copy [source] [destination] [flags]
```

The syntax is the same for all operating systems. The source will be the source of the data; it could be a local path in your system or URL to a container or file share in Azure. Similarly, the destination can also be a local path in your system when you are downloading data from the storage account, or it could be a URL pointing to a file share or blob.

In Exercise 6.3, you will use AzCopy to copy some files from your local computer to Azure Blob Storage and download some files from Azure Blob Storage to local storage. Let's get started.

EXERCISE 6.3

Working with AzCopy

1. You need some sample files to work with. You can create random files programmatically, and it's not necessary that you have the set of files shown here. For getting the most out of this demonstration, create some directories and files.

```
── exe
│   ├── binaries-1.bin
│   ├── binaries-10.bin
│   ├── binaries-2.bin
│   ├── binaries-3.bin
│   ├── binaries-4.bin
│   ├── binaries-5.bin
│   ├── binaries-6.bin
│   ├── binaries-7.bin
│   ├── binaries-8.bin
│   └── binaries-9.bin
── img
│   ├── image-1.jpg
│   ├── image-10.jpg
│   ├── image-2.jpg
│   ├── image-3.jpg
│   ├── image-4.jpg
│   ├── image-5.jpg
│   ├── image-6.jpg
│   ├── image-7.jpg
│   ├── image-8.jpg
│   └── image-9.jpg
── txt
    ├── text-1.txt
    ├── text-10.txt
    ├── text-2.txt
    ├── text-3.txt
    ├── text-4.txt
    ├── text-5.txt
    ├── text-6.txt
    ├── text-7.txt
    ├── text-8.txt
    └── text-9.txt

3 directories, 30 files
```

2. Run `azcopy login` and sign in using your Azure AD credentials. Make sure the user has the Storage Blob Data Contributor role assigned. How to sign in using Azure AD has been explained in the "Authentication" section.

3. Create a new container in your storage account from the Azure portal to which you will be uploading the files from your local directory. Let's call it `azcopyupload` and with the public access level as Public (container).

4. Copy `binaries-1.bin` file in the exe folder to Azure Blob Storage by running `azcopy copy .\exe\binaries-1.bin https://azastorage09345.blob .core.windows.net/azcopyupload`. You need to change the source and destination as per your setup before running this command.

```
PS C:\Users\riskaria\Documents\To Azure> azcopy copy .\exe\binaries-1.bin https://azastorage09345.blob.core.windows.net/azcopyupload
INFO: Scanning...
INFO: Authenticating to destination using Azure AD
INFO: Any empty folders will not be processed, because source and/or destination doesn't have full folder support

Job 3a469d7d-6e54-c746-6f5e-5d2d8e9cdebb has started
Log file is located at: C:\Users\riskaria\.azcopy\3a469d7d-6e54-c746-6f5e-5d2d8e9cdebb.log

0.0 %, 0 Done, 0 Failed, 1 Pending, 0 Skipped, 1 Total,
0.0 %, 0 Done, 0 Failed, 1 Pending, 0 Skipped, 1 Total, 2-sec Throughput (Mb/s): 4.9271

Job 3a469d7d-6e54-c746-6f5e-5d2d8e9cdebb summary
Elapsed Time (Minutes): 0.0671
Number of File Transfers: 1
Number of Folder Property Transfers: 0
Total Number of Transfers: 1
Number of Transfers Completed: 1
Number of Transfers Failed: 0
Number of Transfers Skipped: 0
TotalBytesTransferred: 1241088
Final Job Status: Completed
```

5. Looking at the portal, you can see that the file is present in the storage account.

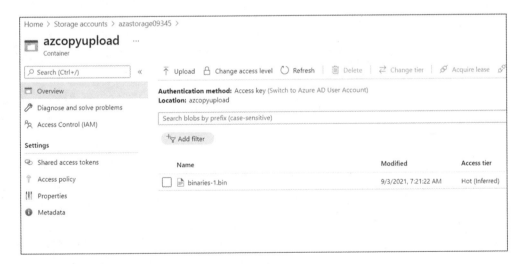

6. Now, you will see how you can upload an entire folder and its contents at once. For this you need to add the `--recursive` flag to the command. Let's copy all the contents of the `txt` folder. Run azcopy `copy .\txt\ https://azastorage09345` `.blob.core.windows.net/azcopyupload --recursive`. As you can see, the number of completed transfers is 10. You need to change the source and destination per your setup before running this command.

```
PS C:\Users\riskaria\Documents\To Azure> azcopy copy .\txt\ https://azastorage09345.blob.core.windows.net/azcopyupload  --recursive
INFO: Scanning...
INFO: Authenticating to destination using Azure AD
INFO: Any empty folders will not be processed, because source and/or destination doesn't have full folder support

Job 0d450bd2-7e46-b84d-75d9-aa359e192f31 has started
Log file is located at: C:\Users\riskaria\.azcopy\0d450bd2-7e46-b84d-75d9-aa359e192f31.log

0.0 %, 0 Done, 0 Failed, 10 Pending, 0 Skipped, 10 Total,
0.0 %, 0 Done, 0 Failed, 10 Pending, 0 Skipped, 10 Total, 2-sec Throughput (Mb/s): 8.6815

Job 0d450bd2-7e46-b84d-75d9-aa359e192f31 summary
Elapsed Time (Minutes): 0.0669
Number of File Transfers: 10
Number of Folder Property Transfers: 0
Total Number of Transfers: 10
Number of Transfers Completed: 10
Number of Transfers Failed: 0
Number of Transfers Skipped: 0
TotalBytesTransferred: 2170880
Final Job Status: Completed
```

7. If you check the portal, you can see that the entire `txt` folder was copied to Blob Storage.

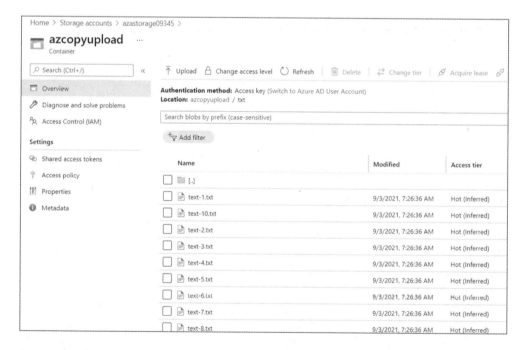

8. Similarly, you can download items from Blob Storage by switching the source and destination.

Tools like AzCopy and Storage Explorer are ideal only for uploading or downloading a few terabytes of data, and you should have higher bandwidth if the size of the data is huge. In certain scenarios, you will have many terabytes of data and you don't have the bandwidth to migrate them to the cloud or from the cloud. Luckily, Azure has a solution for you, the Import/Export service. Let's understand how it works.

Import/Export Service

To upload a large amount of data from an environment where you have bandwidth constraints, you can use the Import/Export service. The Import/Export service doesn't require bandwidth because you are shipping the disks to the Azure datacenter. You can use this service to upload data from the on-premises datacenter to Azure Blob Storage or move data from Azure Blob Storage to the on-premises datacenter. In both scenarios, it is the responsibility of the customer to supply the disks.

The following are some usage cases of the Import/Export service:

- **Data migration to cloud:** Data can be moved to Azure in a cost-effective and quick manner.

- **Content sharing:** Share data with customers quickly.

- **Backup:** Take a backup of your on-premises data and store it in Azure Blob Storage for recovery services.

- **Recovery:** Data stored in Azure Blob Storage can be moved to on-premises to recover the data.

To send data from on-premises to Azure, you need to create an import job. Similarly, to move data from Azure Blob Storage to on-premises, you need to create an export job. Let's understand the steps involved in import and export jobs.

Import Jobs

By shipping drives to the Azure data center, you can securely transfer large amounts of data to Azure Blob Storage. You will be shipping hard drives containing the data to an Azure datacenter. Figure 6.28 shows the end-to-end process involved in an import job.

FIGURE 6.28   Import job workflow

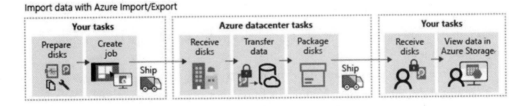

The following are the steps required to move data from on-premises to Azure using an import job:

1. Create a storage account in Azure.

2. Depending upon the amount of data, you need to identify the number of disks required to copy the data.

3. Find a computer to prepare the disks using the WAImportExport tool.

4. Using the WAImportExport tool, prepare the disk, encrypt the drive with BitLocker, and generate journal files.

5. Create an import job in Azure referencing the destination storage account. Also, provide the location of the destination, and Azure will share the shipping address with you.

6. Ship the disks containing the data to the Azure datacenter.

7. Update the import job with the tracking number of the shipment.

8. Once the disks arrive at the Azure datacenter, Microsoft authorized personnel will copy the data to the storage account and ship the disks back to you.

The data will be visible in the Azure storage account. The next scenario is that you want to download the data from Azure Blob Storage and bring it to your on-premises data center.

Export Jobs

Data from Azure Blob Storage can be transferred to an on-premises datacenter using an export job. You need to ship the disks to the Azure datacenter, and once the data is transferred, the Azure datacenter staff will ship the disks back to you. Figure 6.29 shows the end-to-end process involved in an export job.

FIGURE 6.29   Export job workflow

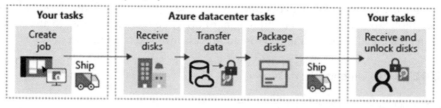

The following are the steps required to move data from Azure storage to on-premises using an export job:

1. Identify the storage account and data you need to export.

2. Compute the number of disks required to accommodate the data you want to transfer.

3. Referencing the storage account, create an export job from the Azure portal.

4. Specify the blobs that are part of the transfer process, return address, and your carrier account number. This will help Microsoft to ship the disks back to you once the transfer is complete.

5. Ship the disks to the Azure datacenter where your storage account is residing. Also, update the export job with the tracking number of the shipment.

6. Azure datacenter staff will transfer the data from the storage account to disks as soon as they receive the shipment.

7. After copying the data, the drive will be encrypted using BitLocker and be shipped back to you.

8. Once you receive the shipment, you can decrypt the disks using the BitLocker recovery keys available in the Azure portal.

For both import and export jobs, you need to use the Import/Export tool, which is also known as the WAImportExport tool. Next, we will quickly cover the tool.

WAImportExport Tool

The Azure Import/Export tool is also known as the WAImportExport tool and is what you use to prepare the drives and to repair the drives that you use with the Azure Import/Export service. The following are the functions of the tool:

- Copy data to hard drives that will be shipped to the Azure datacenter
- Repair data that is imported to Azure Blob Storage
- Repair files on the drives when you receive the disks with data from an export job

The requirements for WAImportExport tool are as follows:

- 64-bit Windows client or server
- Internal SATA II/III HDDs or SSDs

Data copy, volume encryption, and the creation of journal files are all handled by the WAImportExport tool to ensure the integrity of the data. Journal files are essential for both import and export jobs.

Summary

This chapter focused on Azure Storage; we started the chapter with Azure Storage accounts and the storage services. We have five main services that are offered by Azure Storage for blobs, queues, tables, files, and disks. You explored the different use-case scenarios of these services.

One of the main features of Azure Storage is the replication methods and the durability it offers. So, we couldn't continue the chapter without discussing these methods. All replication methods and the number of copies stored in each method were explained. Azure Storage can be accessed from anywhere in the world over an HTTP/HTTPs connection. Understanding the endpoints and securing them is important for administrators. We covered the ways to secure our endpoints and to associate custom domains.

In the second half of the chapter, we shifted our focus to two of the storage services: Azure Blob Storage and Azure File Storage. In Azure Blob Storage, you learned the hierarchy of the blob storage, access tiers for storage cost optimization, lifecycle management for automated transition of access tiers based on the modified data, and how to upload files to Blob Storage. In the first exercise, you uploaded a file, and it was available on the public endpoint. It was very important to understand the storage security and how to access the files privately. We covered Storage Service Encryption, which is an encryption provided by Azure, and then we covered storage access signatures for controlling access to our storage services.

After Blob Storage, you studied Azure File Storage. We discussed how to create a file share and mount the file share to a Windows/Linux computer. The next topic of interest was File Sync; you had a chance to understand File Sync, the components of File Sync, and how to work with File Sync. Microsoft is recommending Azure Files as an enterprise-grade file share, so it's necessary to understand the recovery options like snapshots and backup for Azure Files.

The last section of the chapter was all about getting familiar with the toolsets available for managing Azure Storage. We discussed Azure Storage Explorer, a tool with a graphical interface that can be used to move files from and to Azure Storage. Second, we covered AzCopy, a command-line tool, which is ideal for scripting and automating the data movement to and from Azure Storage. The first two tools require an Internet connection, and you cannot use them for moving larger terabytes of data. To move a large amount of data without worrying about bandwidth, you have the Import/Export service. Based on the direction of data flow, the import or export job needs to be created in the Azure portal.

From the previous chapters, you learned Azure networking and Azure storage; now it's time to explore the third pillar of Azure infrastructure, i.e., Azure compute. In the next two chapters, you will be working with Azure VMs and how you can automate the deployment of the resources using ARM templates. Though you deployed VMs throughout our exercises, you didn't get a chance to learn about virtual machines. Now the time has arrived; in the next chapter you will explore Azure virtual machines.

Exam Essentials

Understand Azure Storage services.   Learn the purpose and use-case scenarios related to storage services such as for blobs, files, tables, queues, and disks.

Learn replication methods.   Learn replication methods like LRS, ZRS, GRS, RA-GRS, GZRS, and RA GZRS and how they work.

Understand storage endpoints.   Understand the endpoints of each storage service and how to secure them using firewall rules and networking options.

Learn about Azure Blob Storage.   Understand the hierarchy of Blob Storage, as well as accessing Blob Storage, access tiers, lifecycle management policies for automated access tier transition, and managing blobs from the Azure portal.

Learn about Azure Files.   Understand how Azure Files works, including the creation and mounting of file shares in Windows, Linux, and macOS computers.

Understand Azure File Sync.   Understand the need for synchronization of on-premises files shares with Azure. Learn the components and workings of File Sync.

Familiarize yourself with the tools.   Get familiarized with the tools used for managing storage like Azure Storage Explorer and AzCopy. Understand how to Import/Export service works.

Review Questions

1. You work for an open source development company. You use Microsoft Azure for a variety of storage needs. Up to now, all the storage was used for internal purposes only. It is organized in block blobs. Each block blob is in its own container. Each container is set to the default settings. In total, you have 50 block blobs. The company has decided to provide read access to the data in the block blobs as part of releasing more information about their open source development efforts. You need to reconfigure the storage to meet the following requirement:

    ▪ *All block blobs must be readable by anonymous Internet users.*

    A. Create a new container, move all the blobs to the new container, and then set the public access level to Blob

    B. Set the public access level to Blob on all the existing containers

    C. Create a new shared access signature for the storage account, and then set the allowed permissions to Read, set the allowed resource types to Object, and set the allowed services to Blob

    D. Create a new access key for the storage account and then provide the connection string in the storage connectivity information to the public

2. Your company is planning to store log data, crash dump files, and other diagnostic data for Azure VMs in Azure. The company has issued the following requirements for the storage. You need to choose the storage type to meet the requirements.

    ▪ *Administrators must be able to browse to the data in File Explorer.*

    ▪ *Access over SMB 3.0 must be supported.*

    ▪ *The storage must support quotas.*

    Which storage type should you use?

    A. Azure Files

    B. Table Storage

    C. Blob Storage

    D. Queue Storage

3. Your company provides cloud software to audit administrative access in Microsoft Azure resources. The software logs all administrative actions (including all clicks and text input) to log files. The software is about to be released from beta, and the company is concerned about storage performance. You need to deploy a storage solution for the log files to maximize performance. What should you do?

    A. Deploy Azure Files using SMB 3.0

    B. Deploy Azure Table Storage

    C. Deploy Azure Queues Storage

    D. Deploy Blob Storage using append blobs

4. Your company is building an app in Azure. The app needs to store images and videos that need to be rendered in your website. Which of the following storage services should be used?

   A. Azure Data Lake store

   B. Azure Table Storage

   C. Azure Blob Storage

   D. Azure File Storage

5. You need to provide a contingent staff employee with temporary read-only access to the contents of an Azure storage account container named *media*. It is important that you grant access while adhering to the security principle of least privilege. What should you do?

   A. Set the public access level to Container

   B. Generate a shared access signature (SAS) token for the container

   C. Share the container entity tag (Etag) with the contingent staff member

   D. Configure a cross-origin resource sharing (CORS) rule for the storage account

6. You are using blob storage. Which of the following is true?

   A. The Cool access tier is for frequent access of objects in the storage account.

   B. The Hot access tier is for storing large amounts of data that is infrequently accessed.

   C. The performance tier you select does not affect pricing.

   D. You can switch between the Hot and Cool performance tiers at any time.

7. You are planning a delegation model for your Azure storage. The company has issued the following requirements for Azure storage access:

   - *Development environments should have limited access to the storage account and should be automatically revoked after the development deadline.*

   - *Production applications should have complete access to storage accounts in an unrestricted manner.*

   What should you do? (Select two.)

   A. Use shared access signatures for the nonproduction apps

   B. Use shared access signatures for the production apps

   C. Use access keys for the nonproduction apps

   D. Use access keys for the production apps

   E. Use stored access policies for the production apps

   F. Use cross-origin resource sharing for the nonproduction apps

8. Your company has a file server named FS01. The server has a single shared folder that users can access to get to shared files. The company wants to make the same files available from Microsoft Azure. The company has the following requirements:

   - *Microsoft Azure should maintain the same data as the shared folder on FS01.*

   - *Files deleted on either side (on-premises or cloud) shall be subsequently and automatically deleted from the other side (on-premises or cloud).*

You need to implement a solution to meet the requirements. What should you do?

A. Deploy DFS namespaces

B. Install and use AzCopy

C. Deploy Azure File Sync

D. Install and use Azure Storage Explorer

E. Deploy storage tiering

9. Which of the following replicates your data to a secondary region, maintains six copies of your data, and is the default replication option?

A. LRS

B. GRS

C. RA-GRS

D. ZRS

10. You have an existing storage account in Microsoft Azure. It stores unstructured data. You create a new storage account. You need to move half of the data from the existing storage account to the new storage account. What tool should you use?

A. Use the Azure portal

B. Use File Server Resource Manager

C. Use the Robocopy command-line tool

D. Use the AzCopy command-line tool

11. Which of the following replication method doesn't make use of availability zones during the replication?

A. RA-GRS

B. ZRS

C. GZRS

D. RA-GZRS

12. Your organization created a storage account named diagstorage01 for storing diagnostics logs in blob storage. Which of the following is the endpoint to connect to the blob storage?

A. `https://diagstorage01.core.windows.net`

B. `https://diagstorage01.blobs.core.windows.net`

C. `https://diagstorage01.blob.core.windows.net`

D. `https://diagstorage01.blobs.core.azure.net`

13. Your organization doesn't have a tiering mechanism implemented. The files that you use in your environment are needed only for 30 days; after that they don't need to be stored. To be on the safer side, your organization wants to autodelete blobs that are not modified for more than 60 days. What solution should you use?

    A. Storage access tier policy

    B. Blob scavenging

    C. Blob lifecycle management

    D. Shared access signature

14. You are using Azure Files and would like to implement a recovery solution for the file shares. The solution should automatically take a snapshot of the file shares. What solution would you recommend?

    A. Azure File Snapshots

    B. Azure File Backup

    C. Azure File PITR Recovery

    D. DFS Backup

15. Which of the following replication options are supported by Azure Files premium tier? (Select all that apply.)

    A. LRS

    B. ZRS

    C. GRS

    D. GZRS

16. Which of the following methods should be used to disable Storage Service Encryption?

    A. Disable from Storage Account ➤ Encryption blade.

    B. Disable from the key vault where the key is stored.

    C. Delete the certificates used for encryption.

    D. SSE cannot be disabled.

17. Which of the following is not a tier offered by Azure Disks?

    A. Standard SSD

    B. Premium SSD

    C. Super SSD

    D. Ultra SSD

18. Your organization is using Azure Blob Storage, and you would like to change the default endpoint domain to a custom domain. What should be done to map the domain with zero downtime?

   A. Direct CNAME mapping

   B. Intermediary mapping with asverify

   C. Direct A record mapping

   D. Intermediary A record mapping with asverify

19. Which of the following storage account should be used to store blob data in GZRS replication?

   A. StorageV2

   B. StorageV1

   C. Premium BlobStorage

   D. Standard BlobStorage

20. Which of the following is not a connection method in Azure Storage Explorer?

   A. Connection string

   B. SAS URL

   C. Bearer token

   D. Azure AD

Chapter

7

Azure Virtual Machines

MICROSOFT EXAM OBJECTIVES COVERED IN THIS CHAPTER:

✓ **Configure VMs**

- ▪ Configure Azure Disk Encryption
- ▪ Move VMs from one resource group to another
- ▪ Manage VM sizes
- ▪ Add data disks
- ▪ Configure networking
- ▪ Redeploy VMs
- ▪ Configure high availability
- ▪ Deploy and configure scale sets

From the beginning of this book, you started deploying virtual machines for several exercises; however, you never got a chance to take a deep dive into Azure Virtual Machines. In this chapter, you will learn about Azure Virtual Machines and several concepts related to virtual machines (VMs).

Azure Virtual Machines is an infrastructure-as-a-service (IaaS) offering. This means you will choose virtual machines if you need complete control over the computing environment, compared to platform-as-a-service (PaaS) solutions such as App Services. Virtual machines come with an operating system, storage, and networking components, and you will have the capability to administer each of these components. These computing components can be easily scaled up and down per your requirements, and you pay only for your usage.

In an enterprise environment, you use virtual machines for a variety of purposes, starting from development and testing all the way to big data analysis. Let's understand the use-case scenarios of Azure Virtual Machines.

Development and testing: VMs can be used to set up development and testing environments easily, and they can be deprovisioned as required. The whole process is simple and quick. Developers can set up massive development and test environments for application testing and can fully utilize the scaling capacities of the cloud.

Website hosting: You have used virtual machines in several exercises to host websites. Yes, VMs can be used to host web servers, and the expenses will be less than the traditional hosting methods.

Backup and recovery: Backup and recovery systems can be easily set up on virtual machines and can act as a recovery strategy.

High-performance computing (HPC): HPC clusters can be hosted using virtual machines; these clusters are packed with a lot of computing power that can be used for compute-intensive tasks such as solving complex equations and problems involving billions of calculations.

Big data analysis: VMs can be used to host big data analysis solutions for ETL and other data warehousing purposes.

Extend your on-premises datacenter: If your on-premises physical servers are exhausted, you can extend your datacenter to the cloud and start deploying VMs in Azure.

Before you start deploying VMs in Azure, let's understand how you can plan the deployment of a virtual machine. You will see a list of parameters or options that should be considered in the planning activity.

Virtual Machine Planning

The following decisions or aspects of the VM should be evaluated during the virtual machine planning:

- Virtual network
- Name
- Location and pricing
- Size
- Storage
- Operating system

Let's take a deep dive into each of the aforementioned factors and understand their relevance in the planning.

Virtual Network

As you read in Chapter 3, "Virtual Networking," before deploying a virtual machine, you should plan a virtual network from which the VM gets the private IP address. In other words, a virtual network facilitates private connectivity between your virtual machines and other Azure services.

You should be planning the virtual network and subnets based on the number of hosts required. Changing the virtual network configuration at a later point is a management overhead. Therefore, always plan your virtual networks and subnets before deploying the virtual machine.

Name

Some organizations don't pay much attention when it comes to the naming of the VM, or in fact any resource in Azure. The VM name will be used as the computer name or host name for the VM you are creating. For a Windows VM, it can be up to 15 characters, and Linux VMs can support up to 64 characters.

The reason you need to pay attention to the naming is because this can't be changed once the VM is deployed. A workaround is to redeploy the VM with the desired name. To avoid the redeployment, you will define the name of the VM wisely. It's a good convention to add the following details to your VM name:

- **Environment:** This is used to identify the environment the resource belongs to. Examples are dev, qa, uat, prod, etc.

- **Location:** Including the location in the name helps you understand the VM location by looking at the name. For example, eus is for East US, wus is for West US, ci is for Central India, etc.

- **Role:** You can add the role of the VM. For example, use db, web, messaging, etc.

- **Application:** If you have an application name, add the name of the application. Examples include payroll, website, registration, etc.

- **Instance:** If you have multiple instances created to improve the high availability, then start numbering them as 01, 02, etc.

Combining these details, if you use the VM name `payroll-prod-eus-db-01`, you can clearly understand that the VM is running the database for the payroll application that is deployed in the East US production environment, and this is instance 1. Also, when you are exporting the usage details of your subscription, you will be easily able to identify the cost by using the VM names.

Location and Pricing

Azure has more regions than any cloud providers, and this means you can deploy your services all over the world. Each region comprises multiple availability zones (for a maximum of three), and each zone consists of multiple datacenters. You can use this to create a highly available architecture. In Azure, the regions are grouped together to create geographies.

When you create a VM in Azure, you can choose to which region you need to deploy this VM. This helps in keeping the VMs closer to your customer base. While planning the location, you need to take into account the following considerations:

Availability of Services   Not all services are supported in all regions. You need to check the following and verify if the region supports the service:

`https://azure.microsoft.com/en-in/global-infrastructure/services`

Pricing   The price of Azure services varies by region. If you are flexible with the location and the performance metrics, then feel free to deploy the resource in a cheaper region.

Compliance   Verify if your organization has any location restrictions or policies that limit the deployment to a certain region. For example, due to GDPR, organizations cannot store data of European customers outside the European Union.

When it comes to pricing, the following are the costs associated with a VM:

Compute Costs   This is the cost for the compute resources (CPU and memory), and this is billed on an hourly basis. If you run your VM for 120 minutes, you pay for two hours of usage. Once you deallocate the VM and release the hardware allocated, you are no longer charged for the compute. One thing to keep in mind here is if you shut down the VM from the operating system—for example, by clicking the Windows button and select Shutdown—then you will be charged for the VM as the hardware allocated is not released.

License Cost   When you are choosing an operating system that requires a license (Windows Server, RHEL, SUSE), then you will see the license cost for your VM. You can use your existing licenses purchased from Software Assurance to cut down this cost. This reduction method is called Azure Hybrid Benefit (AHUB). AHUB can be used for Windows, Linux (RHEL and SUSE), and SQL virtual machine licenses. There are several operating systems that don't require a license such as Ubuntu and CentOS; for these VMs you will not see the license cost.

Storage Cost   This is the cost for the storage that your VM consumes. When we discuss the storage options later in this chapter, we will cover the different storage tiers. The cost of the storage has no relation to the status of the VM; this means you will still be charged for the storage even if the VM is in a deallocated state.

Network Cost   This includes the cost for the public IP address if your VM is using a public IP address. In Azure Cost Management, you will see that the cost of the public IP address is mapped to the public IP resource. Nevertheless, since you are using it for the VM, you can consider it an expense for the VM.

Two payment methods are available when it comes to purchasing virtual machines.

Consumption-Based   In a consumption-based model, you pay for what you use; this is called the *pay-as-you-go* model. This is ideal for virtual machines that you deploy for a short term or for testing purposes.

Reserved Instances   This is ideal for production workloads meant to run for a longer period, at least for a year. Using reserved instances (RIs), you can pay the cost of the compute in an upfront or monthly manner. Since you are making this commitment, you will see up to a 72 percent discount in the cost compared to the consumption-based model.

Size

Once you have the network, location, name, and purchase model decided, it's time to decide the size of the VM. In Azure, VMs come in different sizes with a predefined set of CPU, memory, and storage capacities.

The OS disk capacity and the temp disk capacity will be decided by the size. You don't have to define these values independently; rather, choose the appropriate size. These sizes have been categorized into different VM families based on the underlying hardware used. The key factor behind choosing the size is the type of workload you are running on the VM. Table 7.1 lists the available VM sizes at the time of writing this book. Please note that Microsoft is constantly adding new VM sequences to the list, and it is always recommended that you refer to the Microsoft documentation for size planning and newer sizes.

TABLE 7.1   VM Types and Sizes

Type	Sizes	Description
General purpose	B, Dsv3, Dv3, Dasv4, Dav4, DSv2, Dv2, Av2, DC, DCv2, Dv4, Dsv4, Ddv4, Ddsv4	Balanced CPU to memory ratio. Used for testing, development, small to medium databases, and low to medium traffic web servers.
Compute optimized	FSv2	High CPU to memory ratio as this is compute optimized. Ideal for medium traffic web servers, network appliances, parallel processing, and application servers.
Memory optimized	Esv3, Ev3, Easv4, Eav4, Ev4, Esv4, Edv4, Edsv4, Mv2, M, DSv2, Dv2	High memory to CPU ratio as this is memory optimized. Great choice for medium to large cache and databases.
Storage optimized	Lsv2	Offers high disk throughput and I/O, making it ideal for big data, SQL, NoSQL, and data warehousing.
GPU	NC, NCv2, NCv3, ND, NDv2, NV, NVv3, NVv4	Offers single and multiple GPUs. Ideal for graphic-intensive workloads such as video rendering and model training.
HPC	HB, HBv2, HC, H	High-performance computing offers powerful and fastest CPU with optional high throughput network interfaces.
Confidential compute	DCsv2	Supports a larger range of deployment capabilities, has 2x the Enclave Page Cache (EPC), and has a larger selection of sizes compared to the DC-Series VMs.

Azure also allows you to change the size of the virtual machines per your business requirements. This process is called *VM resizing*, and you can resize to any supported size. During the resize, the VM will reboot. Hence, it is recommended that you schedule a maintenance window while resizing critical workloads.

Storage

Your Azure virtual machine requires storage to install the operating system files. We call this storage *disks* in Azure. This is like the hard disk you have in your computer, however, in a virtual form. All virtual machines have at least two disks: an OS disk and a temporary disk. You can have additional disks added to the virtual machines to store data; these additional disks are called *data disks*. All the disks use Azure Storage for storing the virtual hard disk (VHD) files. Figure 7.1 shows a graphical representation of the disks in an Azure VM.

FIGURE 7.1   Disks in Azure VM

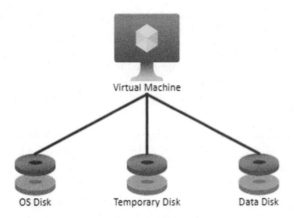

Disks can be classified based on the type of data stored on them, the performance tiers, and how the disk is managed. Let's see how you can categorize based on the type of data stored.

Type of Data

Disks can be classified based on data stored on them. For example, if the disk is containing OS files, then it's an *OS disk*. The following are the disk classifications in Azure:

Operating System Disks (OS Disks)   Every virtual machine requires an operating system to run. Every virtual machine will have one disk that is labeled as an OS disk from which the VM boots. This will be the C: drive in Windows and /dev/sda (root is mounted to the sda1 partition) in Linux VMs.

Temporary Disks   These disks are used to store pages or swap files and are not intended to be a persistent storage for your critical files. The reason is that during a planned maintenance event, redeployment, or host change, the data stored in the temporary disk will be erased. Data will be available during normal reboots, though. Therefore, any data on the drive should not be critical to you as it is prone to loss. In Windows, the temporary disk will be labeled as the D: drive, and in Linux, the disk will be labeled as /dev/sdb.

Data Disks   Data disks are used to store application data or any other data that you don't want to keep in the OS disk. These disks can be labeled with any letter in Windows, and in Linux data disks are labeled from /dev/sdc onward. The maximum supported size is 4 TB. The size of the virtual machine is what determines how many data disks can be attached to a VM.

Performance

Azure Disks offers different performance tiers to match your application needs. High-performance, low-latency disks can be attached to Azure VMs for your I/O-intensive workloads. The following are the performance tiers in Azure Disks:

- *Standard HDD*: Offers the lowest cost and is backed by the HDD drives. This is ideal for disks that require fewer I/O operations such as backup storage. The maximum IOPS is 2,000, and the maximum throughput is 500 MB per second.

- *Standard SSD*: Offers lower latency compared to Standard HDD as these drives are using SSDs under the hood. This is ideal for web servers and medium I/O-intensive workloads. The maximum IOPS is 6,000, and the maximum throughput is 750 MB per second.

- *Premium SSD*: Excellent choice for production and I/O-intensive workloads. As the name suggests, these disks are also using SSDs; however, they are faster than Standard SSD. The maximum IOPS is 20,000, and the maximum throughput is 900 MB per second.

- *Ultra disk*: Perfect for transaction-heavy workloads such as SAP HANA, SQL, Oracle, etc. This offers massive IOPS up to 160,000 and a maximum throughput of 2,000 MB per second.

All tiers except Ultra disk offer a maximum disk size of 32,767 GB; on the other hand, Ultra disk can support up to a maximum value of 65,536 GB. The availability of Ultra disk is limited to certain regions and VM sizes. Some of the supported sizes include ESv3, Easv4, Edsv4, Esv4, DSv3, Dasv4, Ddsv4, Dsv4, FSv2, LSv2, M, Mv2, HBv2, HB, HC, NDv2, ND, NC_T4_v3, NCv2, NCv3, NVv3, and NVv4. Also, Ultra disks are available only as data disks, not as OS disks. The limitation of Ultra disk is covered here:

```
https://docs.microsoft.com/en-us/azure/virtual-machines/disks-
types#ga-scope-and-limitations
```

Refer to this document before you plan to use Ultra disk. Now you will learn about how the disks are classified based on management.

Management

Based on the level of management, disks can be categorized as managed disks and unmanaged disks. Behind the scenes, when you create a disk, it gets stored inside an Azure Storage account. The classification you are about to learn is solely dependent on who manages this underlying storage account. Let's understand the differences between these two.

Managed Disks   As the name suggests, the disks are managed by Microsoft, and you don't have to create any storage accounts to work with managed disks. The encryption, recovery plan, and control of the storage account are controlled by Microsoft, and you will not have any control over these factors. Microsoft recommends going with managed disks in all possible scenarios. Since you don't manage the storage account, the storage account limits don't apply, and you can have up to 20,000 disks per region.

Unmanaged Disks   In unmanaged disks, you need to create the storage account that will be used to store the disk. Since you created this storage account, you will have complete control over the storage account and all the contents of the storage account. Here, you need to take care of the encryption, data recovery, etc.

Operating System

Azure supports various OS images that can be installed into the virtual machine. The list includes several versions of Windows and popular distros of Linux. You need to select the OS wisely as it will directly impact your billing. The reason for this is if you are selecting a Windows-based OS, then you will be charged for the license as well. So, it's better to look at different options before you commit to the purchase.

In addition to the popular Windows and Microsoft-endorsed Linux distros, you have customized images available in Azure Marketplace. For example, if you would like to set up a WordPress site, then you need to deploy a Linux VM and install all the dependencies such as Apache, PHP, and MySQL. However, if you check Azure Marketplace, there are preconfigured images available for WordPress that you can directly use and avoid the hassle of configuration.

Nevertheless, if you can't find the operating system that you are looking for, then you can bring your own virtual image to Azure that can be used to deploy virtual machines. If you are planning to bring your own image, note that Azure supports only 64-bit operating systems.

Now that you are familiar with the factors that need to be considered for the virtual machine planning, let's go ahead and deploy some virtual machines.

Deploying Virtual Machines

You can create a virtual machine from the Azure portal, Azure PowerShell, Azure CLI, Azure SDK, and the REST API. You have already seen how the VMs are created using Azure PowerShell and Azure CLI from our previous exercises. Now, we will focus on the creation of virtual machines from the Azure portal.

Since you have a variety of options available for the operating system, you need to decide which image you need to use. In the next exercises, you will deploy a Windows VM. In this section, you will only create the VM; after that, we will discuss different methods to connect to the VM. See Exercise 7.1.

EXERCISE 7.1

Creating a Windows Virtual Machine

1. Sign in to the Azure portal and search for *virtual*. Click Virtual Machines in the search results.

2. Click Create and then click Virtual Machine.

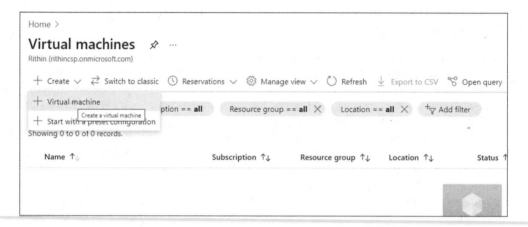

3. Most of the configuration parameters are familiar to you. On the Basic blade, you will select the subscription, resource group, region, image (you will choose Windows Server 2019 Datacenter - Gen 1 as you are creating a Windows VM), size of the VM, administrator credentials, and inbound rules. As this is a guided wizard, you will be able to see the explanation of each field in the Azure portal.

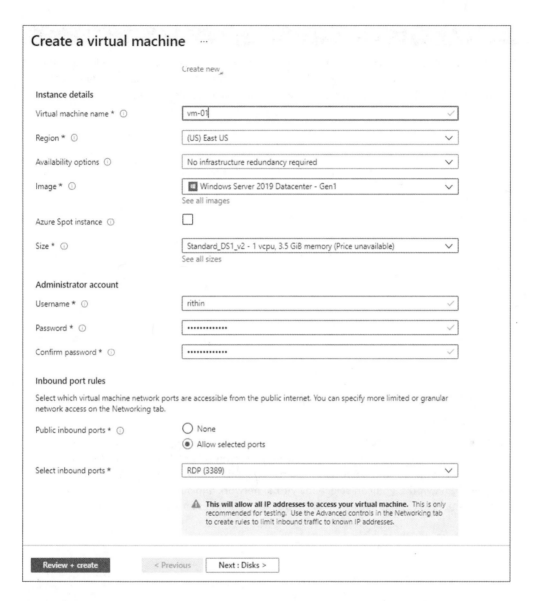

4. Technically, this is enough to create a VM unless you want to customize the rest of the parameters such as disk type and virtual network configuration. If you would like to create a VM and skip the remaining steps, feel free to click Review + Create to start the validation and then click Create.

5. If you would like to customize the rest of the sections, click Next : Disks > to jump to the next section. Here you will choose the disk type such as Premium SSD, Standard SSD, or Standard HDD. In addition, you can add additional data disks if required.

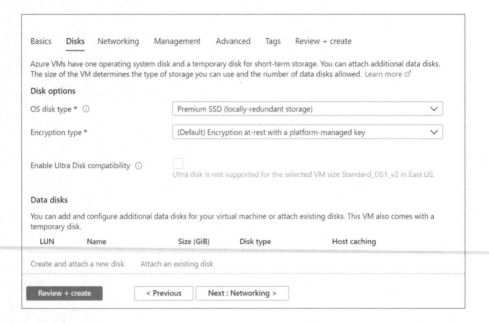

6. After completing the disk configuration, click Next: Networking > to configure networking. If there are no virtual networks in the region selected, then Azure will automatically come up with a new virtual network configuration for your VM. If there are existing networks, you can select any virtual network and subnet as required. Also, you will be able to configure the public IP, NIC NSG, and load balancing (if required).

Network interface

When creating a virtual machine, a network interface will be created for you.

Virtual network * ⓘ	vm-01_group-vnet ⌄
	Create new
Subnet * ⓘ	default (10.0.0.0/24) ⌄
	Manage subnet configuration
Public IP ⓘ	(new) vm01ip615 ⌄
	Create new
NIC network security group ⓘ	◯ None ◉ Basic ◯ Advanced
Public inbound ports * ⓘ	◯ None ◉ Allow selected ports
Select inbound ports *	RDP (3389) ⌄

[Review + create]   [< Previous] [Next : Management >]

7. If you move on to the next section, Management, you will see a set of management options such as Backup, Login With Azure AD, Auto Shutdown, Guest OS Update Configuration, Boot Diagnostics, etc. If needed, you can customize these options; otherwise, go with the default configuration. Click Next: Advanced > to see the advanced configuration.

8. Advanced configuration can be used to perform additional configurations such as agents, extensions, and scripts that can be executed during the VM creation. In our scenario, these are not required. The next blade is Tags, and you don't want to add any resource tags.

9. Skip to the last section to review the deployment by clicking Review + Create. The validation phase will start; if the validation was successful, then you will see the Create button. Click the Create button to deploy the VM.

10. The deployment may take a couple of minutes; the Azure portal will automatically redirect to the deployment status page where you can track the progress of the deployment.

Now that you have created a Windows machine, you can easily create a Linux Ubuntu VM. Instead of choosing the Windows image, here you will choose Ubuntu image, as shown in Figure 7.2.

FIGURE 7.2 Choosing a Linux distro

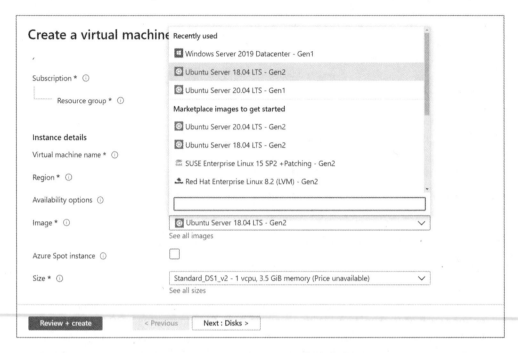

The process is similar to a Linux VM except for the authentication part. Unlike Windows machines, Linux machines can be authenticated using the username and password or using the SSH key pair. If you are confident with the VM creation process, let's see how you can connect to the machines you created.

Connecting to Virtual Machines

As an administrator, you need to connect to the virtual machines to change the virtual machine configuration you created or install some roles such as database, web, or messaging. Though there is no drastic change in how to deploy a Windows versus Linux VM, the way you connect to them is different. For Windows and Linux machines, there are a different set of connectivity options. In both scenarios, you are connecting to the public IP address of the virtual machine. Let's explore the options.

Windows Connections

You can connect to Windows machines using two options, namely, Remote Desktop Protocol (RDP) and Windows Remote Management (WinRM).

Remote Desktop Protocol

You can connect to the graphical user interface (GUI) of the Windows VM using RDP. RDP uses TCP port 3389, and you need to make sure that you have opened this port in your NSG to establish connectivity. If you navigate to the Azure portal, go to Virtual Machines, and open the Windows VM you created in Exercise 7.1. You will see the Connect button on the Overview blade (refer to Figure 7.3). Clicking this button will show you the RDP option to download the RDP file.

FIGURE 7.3   Downloading the RDP file

Let's see how you can connect to the Windows VM using RDP; see Exercise 7.2.

EXERCISE 7.2

Connecting to a Windows VM Using RDP

1. Sign in to the Azure portal and search for *virtual*. Click Virtual Machines in the search results.

2. Select the Windows VM from the list of VMs and click Connect from the Overview blade (refer to Figure 7.3).

3. Click Download RDP File on the next screen.

EXERCISE 7.2 *(continued)*

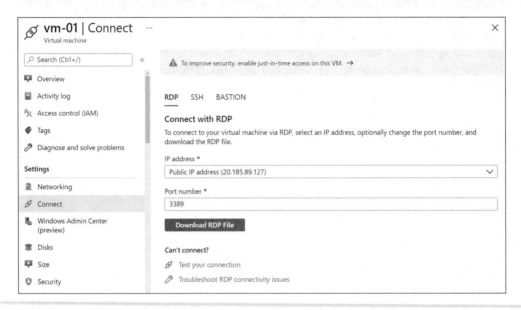

4. A file with an .rdp extension will be downloaded to your computer, and you need to open it. If you are using a Windows computer, then you will have a built-in RDP client provided by Microsoft. If you are performing this lab from a Linux or macOS computer, then you may need to download the RDP client to connect via RDP.

5. Opening the file will give you a warning that the publisher is not identified. You can ignore this warning, as you know that the IP address corresponds to the VM you created. Click the Connect button.

6. You will be asked to enter the credentials for the VM. You can use the username and password entered during the VM creation. If you are using a domain-joined computer, you may see that the system is trying to connect using your domain credentials. You can click More Choices and select Use A Different Account to get the screen shown here.

7. After entering your credentials, you can connect to the VM. You will see a certificate warning; you can ignore this as you trust the remote computer. Click Yes to proceed with the connection.

8. Soon, you will be connected to the Windows GUI, and you can work with the Windows VM over RDP.

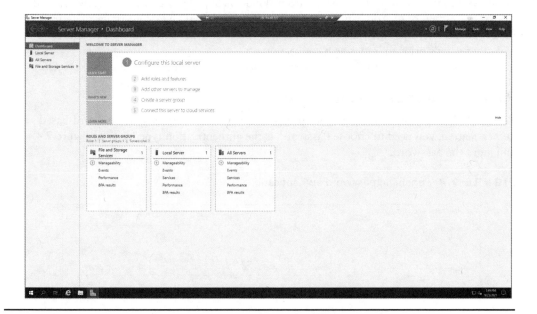

You can work with the Windows VM as you normally work with a Windows machine. Further, you can install the IIS role on the VM and run a web server. To verify the working of web server, you need to make sure that you allowed HTTP traffic on your NSG. Now let's review the second method to connect to Windows VMs.

Windows Remote Management

You used RDP to establish connectivity to the graphical interface; however, if you would like to establish connectivity to the command-line session, then you can use WinRM. This session will be helpful to run PowerShell scripts that require no user intervention. Additionally, you can configure certificates to improve the security of the session. If you are planning to use certificates, then you should add the certificate to Azure Key Vault prior to establishing the connection. Once the certificate is uploaded, you can reference the certificate URL from the key vault in the VM configuration.

The communication is facilitated over TCP port 5986, so you need to ensure that this port is opened for communication in your NSG. Nevertheless, this port is user configurable, and you can always change the port.

Linux Connections

In Linux, you use SSH to establish connectivity to your VMs. The classification here is based on whether you are using SSH key pair authentication or password-based authentication. Let's see how this can be leveraged to connect to our Linux VMs. There are different tools available called SSH clients that can be used to establish SSH connections. Linux and macOS can use the Terminal. If you are using the latest version of Windows 10, then you can use Windows Terminal (can be downloaded from Windows Store) or Putty (can be downloaded from www.putty.org). You can use either. Windows Terminal gives you connectivity from the command line, and Putty has a user interface where you can enter the host IP address and other details prior to initiating a connection.

We will stick to Windows Terminal as the cmdlets will be similar for Linux and macOS.

Password-Based Authentication

You can SSH to our VMs using password-based authentication. To enable password-based authentication, you need to choose Password as the authentication type (refer to Figure 7.4) and input the password.

FIGURE 7.4   Enabling password authentication

Administrator account	
Authentication type ⓘ	○ SSH public key ◉ Password
Username * ⓘ	rithin ✓
Password * ⓘ	············· ✓
Confirm password * ⓘ	············· ✓
Inbound port rules	

If you recall, in all our exercises from previous chapters you entered the password for the SSH connection to establish a connection to the Linux VM. Now let's create a Linux VM using the Azure CLI and see how you can connect to it using password-based authentication; see Exercise 7.3.

EXERCISE 7.3

Connecting to a Linux VM Using a Password

1. You can use the cloud shell or a local shell to perform this exercise. If you are using the local shell, make sure you install Azure CLI on your computer. In the local shell, you can log in using the az login command.

2. Create a new resource group using the command az group create -n <name> -l <location>; change the name and location per your requirements.

3. Create a VM using the command az vm create -n <name> -g <resource-group> --image UbuntuLTS --admin-username <username> --admin-password "<password>". You are passing the name of the VM, name of the resource group, admin username, password, and image as parameters to the command. You can use your own values to customize the deployment. This command may take a couple of minutes to complete. Once completed, you will be presented with the public IP address of the VM.

```
PS C:\Users\riskaria> az vm create -n vm-02 -g az-linux-vm --image UbuntuLTS --admin-username rithin
--admin-password "P@55w0rd@123"
It is recommended to use parameter "--public-ip-sku Standard" to create new VM with Standard public I
P. Please note that the default public IP used for VM creation will be changed from Basic to Standard
 in the future.
{
  "fqdns": "",
  "id": "/subscriptions/9698ce5f-1999-4bed-9b70-768dd3cdba77/resourceGroups/az-linux-vm/providers/Mic
rosoft.Compute/virtualMachines/vm-02",
  "location": "eastus",
  "macAddress": "00-0D-3A-1C-82-64",
  "powerState": "VM running",
  "privateIpAddress": "10.0.0.4",
  "publicIpAddress": "138.91.117.183",
  "resourceGroup": "az-linux-vm",
  "zones": ""
}
```

4. Now you can connect to the VM using SSH from the cloud shell or local shell using the format ssh username@publicIP. The public IP address can be obtained from the output of the az vm create command. You might need to input yes to save the signature of the host.

```
PS C:\Users\riskaria> ssh rithin@138.91.117.183
The authenticity of host '138.91.117.183 (138.91.117.183)' can't be established.
ECDSA key fingerprint is SHA256:buqzpXLlnOj7JPa8/btGW/ejnsPLEYN9ESQy/vuaMiA.
Are you sure you want to continue connecting (yes/no/[fingerprint])? yes
Warning: Permanently added '138.91.117.183' (ECDSA) to the list of known hosts.
rithin@138.91.117.183's password:
Welcome to Ubuntu 18.04.6 LTS (GNU/Linux 5.4.0-1056-azure x86_64)

 * Documentation:  https://help.ubuntu.com
 * Management:     https://landscape.canonical.com
 * Support:        https://ubuntu.com/advantage

  System information as of Thu Sep 23 15:53:04 UTC 2021

  System load:  0.08              Processes:             108
  Usage of /:   4.6% of 28.90GB   Users logged in:       0
  Memory usage: 5%                IP address for eth0: 10.0.0.4
  Swap usage:   0%

0 updates can be applied immediately.


The programs included with the Ubuntu system are free software;
the exact distribution terms for each program are described in the
individual files in /usr/share/doc/*/copyright.

Ubuntu comes with ABSOLUTELY NO WARRANTY, to the extent permitted by
applicable law.

To run a command as administrator (user "root"), use "sudo <command>".
See "man sudo_root" for details.

rithin@vm-02:~$
```

5. Now you are connected to VM, and you can work with the Linux VM over SSH.

SSH Key Pair

Though SSH operates via an encrypted connection, using password-based authentication is not considered a safe method. Passwords are prone to brute-force attacks, and you need to come up with a complicated password to avoid the risk of password guessing. The most preferred and secured method of connecting to a Linux VM is using an SSH key pair. The key pair comprises a public key and private key; these are also known as SSH keys.

The public key will be placed on the VM, and the private key is stored in the clients from which you want to connect. You need to make sure that this file is protected and is not shared. The SSH key pair authentication works with a key challenge; the remote VM will check if the client has access to the private key. If the client possesses the key, then access is granted; otherwise access is denied. You can also have a single key pair to connect to all the VMs or you can have a separate key for individual VMs. The public key can be shared with anyone; however, the private key should be possessed by the clients that need to connect to the VM.

In Azure, the key can be generated in multiple ways. First, you need to make sure that the authentication type is set to the SSH public key while creating a VM. You can generate a new key pair, use an existing key stored in Azure, or use an existing public key from your infrastructure (refer to Figure 7.5). If you want to bring your own key, you can generate keys using the ssh-keygen command. Currently, Azure uses a 2048-bit key length and SSH-RSA format for public and private keys.

FIGURE 7.5   Enabling SSH key authentication

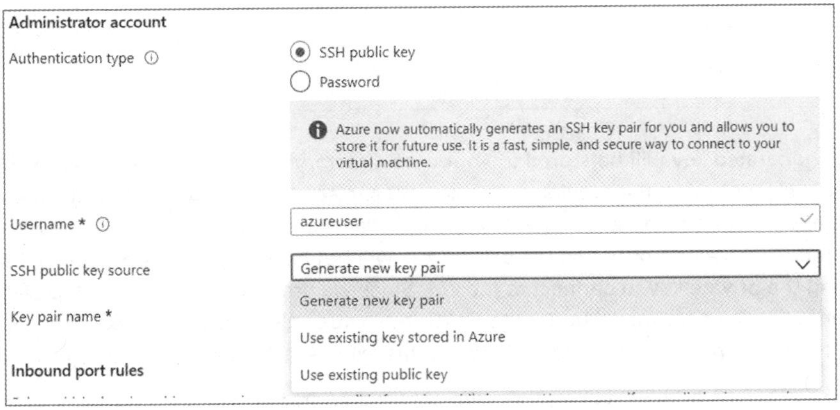

Now that you have an idea about the SSH keys, let's create a VM from Azure CLI and generate the key on the fly; see Exercise 7.4. Later, you will use this key to connect to the VM.

EXERCISE 7.4

Connecting to Linux VM Using SSH Keys

1. You can use the cloud shell or local shell to perform this exercise. If you are using local shell, make sure you install Azure CLI on your computer. In the local shell, you can log in using the az login command.

2. Create a new resource group using the command az group create -n <name> -l <location>; change the name and location per your requirements. If not required, you can reuse the resource group from the last exercise.

3. Create a VM using the command az vm create -n <name> -g <resource-group> --image UbuntuLTS --admin-username <username> --generate-ssh-keys. You are passing the name of the VM, name of the resource group, admin username, and image as parameters to the command. In the previous exercise, you used the parameter --admin-password to input the password; since you need the keys to be generated, you will replace this parameter with --generate-ssh-keys. You can use your own values to customize the deployment. This command may take a couple of minutes to complete.

EXERCISE 7.4 *(continued)*

```
PS C:\Users\riskaria> az vm create -n vm-03 -g az-linux-vm --image UbuntuLTS --admin-username rithin --generate-ssh-keys
SSH key files 'C:\Users\riskaria\.ssh\id_rsa' and 'C:\Users\riskaria\.ssh\id_rsa.pub' have been generated under ~/.ssh to allow SSH access to the
 VM. If using machines without permanent storage, back up your keys to a safe location.
It is recommended to use parameter "--public-ip-sku Standard" to create new VM with Standard public IP. Please note that the default public IP us
ed for VM creation will be changed from Basic to Standard in the future.
{
  "fqdns": "",
  "id": "/subscriptions/9698ce5f-1999-4bed-9b70-768dd3cdba77/resourceGroups/az-linux-vm/providers/Microsoft.Compute/virtualMachines/vm-03",
  "location": "eastus",
  "macAddress": "00-0D-3A-57-26-18",
  "powerState": "VM running",
  "privateIpAddress": "10.0.0.5",
  "publicIpAddress": "52.255.134.16",
  "resourceGroup": "az-linux-vm",
  "zones": ""
}
```

4. The generated key will be stored to your user directory under the `.ssh` directory. If you take a closer look at the previous graphic, you can see that the Azure CLI will tell you the exact location where the private and public keys are stored. The public key will end with the extension `.pub`, and the private key will not have any extension. You will be using the private key to connect to the VM. Since we are using a Windows client for the demo, the key gets stored under the `C:\Users\<User>\.ssh\` directory. Depending on the OS from which you are performing this exercise, the directory will change.

5. In the previous graphic, you can see the public IP address of the VM and the directory where the private key is stored. You can connect to the VM by specifying the key in the SSH command using the `-i` parameter. For example, use `ssh -i <path-to-private-key> username@publicIP`. Like password authentication, you will be prompted to save the fingerprint of the remote machine; proceed by typing `yes`, and you will be connected to the VM.

```
PS C:\Users\riskaria> ssh -i .\.ssh\id_rsa rithin@52.255.134.16
The authenticity of host '52.255.134.16 (52.255.134.16)' can't be established.
ECDSA key fingerprint is SHA256:z0iFbP1negbrUVAuxW1CZJZdisYjFyGIwL7j51KIo6Q.
Are you sure you want to continue connecting (yes/no/[fingerprint])? yes
Warning: Permanently added '52.255.134.16' (ECDSA) to the list of known hosts.
Welcome to Ubuntu 18.04.6 LTS (GNU/Linux 5.4.0-1056-azure x86_64)

 * Documentation:  https://help.ubuntu.com
 * Management:     https://landscape.canonical.com
 * Support:        https://ubuntu.com/advantage

  System information as of Fri Sep 24 04:21:45 UTC 2021

  System load:  0.0               Processes:            108
  Usage of /:   4.6% of 28.90GB   Users logged in:      0
  Memory usage: 5%                IP address for eth0:  10.0.0.5
  Swap usage:   0%

0 updates can be applied immediately.


The programs included with the Ubuntu system are free software;
the exact distribution terms for each program are described in the
individual files in /usr/share/doc/*/copyright.

Ubuntu comes with ABSOLUTELY NO WARRANTY, to the extent permitted by
applicable law.

To run a command as administrator (user "root"), use "sudo <command>".
See "man sudo_root" for details.

rithin@vm-03:~$
```

In the case of both Windows and Linux VMs, you connected to a VM via the public IP address. This is not a commonly used method as you need to open the RDP/SSH ports to the Internet. If you remember the exercise from previous chapters, you used a jumpbox VM to connect to VMs that don't have a public IP address associated to them. To an extent, this will help you avoid using a public IP address for all the VMs. However, the jumpbox VM is also a virtual machine with the IP public address exposed to the Internet; you need to harden this machine as much as possible because if this VM is compromised, the entire infrastructure is compromised. Hardening the jumpbox VM and keeping it away from vulnerabilities are always tedious tasks for the administrator. Azure offers a life-saver service called Azure Bastion to solve this problem. Let's see how Azure Bastion is different from the jumpbox VM you are used to.

Azure Bastion

With Azure Bastion, you can connect to Azure virtual machines without the need to have public IP addresses. The catch here is Azure Bastion, which is a platform-as-a-service (PaaS) solution; this means you don't have to worry about hardening the infrastructure, as this will be handled by Microsoft Azure.

When you were using the jumpbox VM, you had to use RDP/SSH clients to connect to other machines; in the case of Azure Bastion, the connection is directly established from the Azure portal over SSL. To work with Azure Bastion, you need to deploy the Bastion host to the virtual network where your VM is deployed. Azure Bastion requires a dedicated subnet of size (minimum /27) called AzureBastionSubnet. During the initial days of Azure Bastion, you were required to deploy Bastion hosts on every virtual network where you had your virtual machines; however, with the recent update, you can use a single Bastion host to access all virtual machines that are part of peered networks. This means you could deploy this to your hub virtual network and access virtual machines on all spoke virtual networks. Using Azure Bastion, without the need of any client or public IP address, you can seamlessly establish RDP/SSH connections directly from browser.

In Exercise 7.5, you will deploy a VM without a public IP address and use the Azure Bastion service to verify the connectivity.

EXERCISE 7.5

Connecting to Linux VM Using SSH Keys

1. Navigate to the Azure portal and create a new Linux virtual machine with password authentication. On the Networking tab, make sure Public IP is set to None.

Create a virtual machine ···

Basics   Disks   **Networking**   Management   Advanced   Tags   Review + create

Define network connectivity for your virtual machine by configuring network interface card (NIC) settings. You can control ports, inbound and outbound connectivity with security group rules, or place behind an existing load balancing solution. Learn more ☐

Network interface

When creating a virtual machine, a network interface will be created for you.

Virtual network * ⓘ	(new) azure-bastion-rg-vnet ⌄
	Create new
Subnet * ⓘ	(new) default (10.1.0.0/24) ⌄
Public IP ⓘ	None ⌄
	Create new
NIC network security group ⓘ	○ None
	◉ Basic
	○ Advanced

---

2. Since you have set the public IP address to None, no public IP address will be assigned to the VM. You can complete the deployment by clicking Review + Create. Once the validation is done, click Create to create the VM.

3. While the VM is getting created, in the Azure portal search for *Bastion*, and you will see Bastions in the search result. Click Bastions, and this will redirect to the Bastions blade.

4. Once you are in the Bastions blade, click Create to create a Bastion host.

5. Creation of Bastion host requires the following input from your end:

   - **Subscription:** Select the Azure subscription.

   - **Resource Group:** Select the resource group to deploy the Bastion host.

   - **Name:** Give a name for the host.

   - **Region:** Choose a region for the Bastion host. The region should be the same as the region of the virtual network where you want to deploy the host.

   - **Tier:** Basic or Standard. We will go with Basic. At the time of writing this book, Standard is in preview. You can see the comparison between the SKUs here:

     ```
     https://docs.microsoft.com/en-us/azure/bastion/
     configuration-settings#skus
     ```

- **Instance count:** You can specify the number of instances. The value can be from 2 to 50. Here we will go with the default value of 2.

- **Virtual Network:** Select the virtual network to which you have deployed the VM. Once you select the virtual network, you might see an error message stating that Azure is not able to find any subnet with the name AzureBastionSubnet. As mentioned earlier, you require a dedicated subnet to host Bastion. You can ignore this warning, and you will configure the subnet as the next option.

- **Subnet:** As of now, there are no subnets with the name AzureBastionSubnet. You can click Manage Subnet Configuration, which will redirect you to the Subnet blade of the virtual network. You can add a new subnet with the name AzureBastionSubnet and a subnet prefix of /27. Once you are done, click Create A Bastion, which will take you back to the Bastion creation wizard. Alternatively, you could create the subnet beforehand to avoid the hassle of going back and forth. The creation wizard will automatically pick up the subnet you created, and you will no longer see the warning.

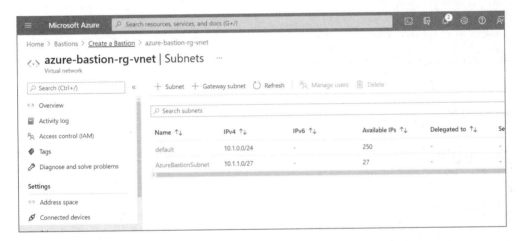

- **Public IP address:** Create a new public IP address or associate an existing one. Since you don't have any free public IPs, you can create a new one. If you have an existing public IP address, you can check this option and select the public IP address.

- **Public IP address name:** This is shown only if you are creating a new public IP. Give a name for the public IP address.

6. Click Review + Create to start the validation. Once the validation is done, click Create to create the Bastion host. The creation may take longer, and you can resume once the host is created.

EXERCISE 7.5 *(continued)*

7. After deploying the Bastion host, navigate to the Virtual Machines blade and click the virtual machine you created in steps 1 and 2. You clearly don't have a public IP address for this VM.

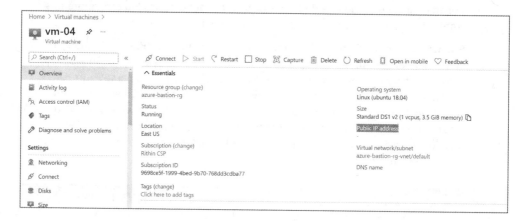

8. Click Connect at the top and select Bastion.

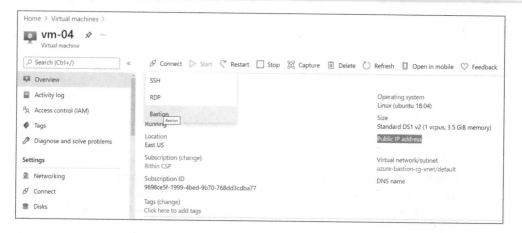

9. Selecting Bastion will take you to the Bastion tab under the Connect blade. Click Use Bastion to use the Bastion service.

10. In the new window, you will be asked to enter the username and choose the authentication type. Since you used password authentication, select Password (default option). Input your password, and you are good to connect to the VM using Bastion. You can check the Open In New Window to open the session in a new browser tab. If you are checking this option, you need to ensure that the browser is not blocking the pop-up.

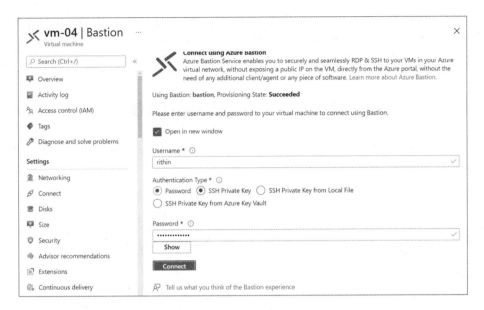

11. **Click Connect, and you will be connected to the VM.**

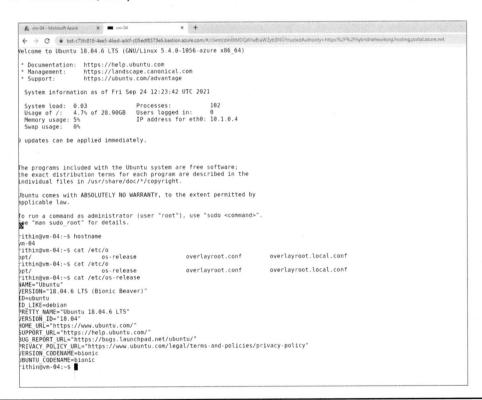

By using Bastion, you eliminated the need for public IP, and you connected to the VM over a secure channel. Using Bastion eliminates brute-force attacks and zero-day exploits against your critical VM workloads.

Availability of Virtual Machines

In Chapter 5, "Network Traffic Management," you saw the purpose of availability sets and availability zones. Using availability sets and availability zones, you can improve the high availability of the VM.

You can create availability zones while creating the VM, or you can create them beforehand. During the VM creation, if you select the Availability option as the availability set, as shown in Figure 7.6, you can select an existing availability set (if you have one) or create a new one by specifying the number of fault domains and update domains.

FIGURE 7.6   Using an availability set

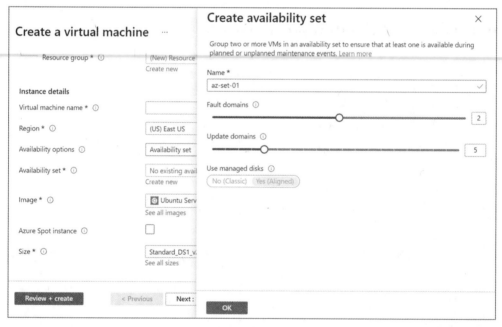

Similarly, while deploying a VM, you can choose to which availability zone you want to deploy the VM. You can configure this by selecting the Availability option for Availability Zone during deployment. The Azure portal will ask you to choose the zone for deployment, as shown in Figure 7.7. You can span your VMs across multiple availability zones to increase the high availability.

FIGURE 7.7   Using availability zones

Region * ⓘ	(US) East US	⌄
Availability options ⓘ	Availability zone	⌄
Availability zone * ⓘ		⌄
	1	
Image * ⓘ	2	
	3	
Azure Spot instance ⓘ	☐	
Size * ⓘ	Standard_DS1_v2 - 1 vcpu, 3.5 GiB memory (Price unavailable)	⌄
	See all sizes	

If you are not able to understand the concept of availability set and zone, it's recommended that you go through these concepts from Chapter 5 again.

Now you will explore the scaling options available for virtual machines.

Scaling Concepts

Scaling is one of the features of cloud. You can use the scalability of the cloud to control the infrastructure. When it comes scaling, you have two types of scaling: vertical scaling and horizontal scaling. Let's understand the difference between these scaling concepts.

Vertical Scaling

In vertical scaling, you increase or decrease the size of the virtual machine. This process is also known as *scale up and scale down*. Using size, you are making the virtual machine more powerful (*scale up*) or less powerful (*scale down*). Figure 7.8 shows the graphical representation of vertical scaling.

FIGURE 7.8   Vertical scaling

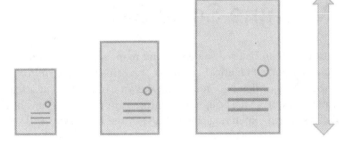

The following are the use-case scenarios of vertical scaling:

- Changing the size of the virtual machine to a larger size to accommodate larger demand
- Reducing the size of underutilized virtual machines

Now let's talk about horizontal scaling.

Horizontal Scaling

Horizontal scaling is also known as *scale out and scale in*, where the number of instances is increased or decreased based on the demand. The increasing process is called *scale out*, and the decreasing process is called *scale in*. When it comes to vertical scaling, sometimes the size of the VM will hit the upper limit or there is no capacity in the region to further increase the size of the VM; in these scenarios, you can rely on horizontal scaling to automatically increase or decrease the instances. Also, during vertical scaling, the VM needs to be stopped and restarted. But during horizontal scaling, existing workloads are not disturbed. Figure 7.9 shows the graphical representation of horizontal scaling.

FIGURE 7.9   Horizontal scaling

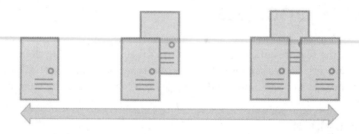

Horizontal scaling is ideal in scenarios where you have unexpected load and the infrastructure needs to be scaled based on the load. In Azure, you can use virtual machine scale sets (VMSS) to increase or decrease the number of VM instances based on the load. Let's understand more about VMSS.

Virtual Machine Scale Sets

Virtual machine scale sets can be used to deploy and manage a group of identical VMs. Earlier, virtual machines supported identical instances only; this is called *uniform orchestration*. Now with the introduction of flexible orchestration, you can implement a scale set with identical or multiple types of VM. Though this feature is in public preview at the time of writing this book, it is worth explaining this because in the future you will see this option.

For VMSS, no pre-provisioning of the VM is required. VMSS targets major workloads such as parallel processing, big data, and containerized workloads. VMSS is being used as nodes for the Azure Kubernetes Service because of the scalability. In short, as demand grows, more instances will be added based on the rules or a schedule. You can accomplish the scaling manually or using automation.

The following are the benefits offered by VMSS:

- Under uniform orchestration, all VMs that are part of the scale set are created using the VM configuration and OS image. This makes the configuration and network management much easier.

- All VMs in a scale set will have only private IP addresses, and the scale set can be placed as a backend pool for Azure Load Balancer or Azure Application Gateway.

- Since there are multiple instances of your application, if there is an issue with one instance, customers can be redirected to another instance with minimal interruption.

- Based on the demand, the number of instances can be increased or decreased. VMSS is ideal for all kinds of unexpected demand.

- VMSS supports up to 1,000 VMs in a scale set. If you are using custom images, you can have up to 600 VMs.

Implementing a Scale Set

You can implement a scale set from the Azure portal, Azure PowerShell, the Azure CLI, and the REST API. The process is very similar to creating a virtual machine. In the Azure portal, you can search for VMSS, and you will see *Virtual Machine Scale Set* in the search results. Once you click it, you will be redirected to the Virtual Machine Scale Set blade; then click Create.

The Basic tab consists of basic details such as subscription, resource group, virtual machine scale set name, region, and availability zone. Using the availability zones, you can span your scale set across zones. Further, you can select the orchestration mode: Uniform or Flexible. To select Flexible mode, you need to register your subscription as this feature is in preview. Also, you will be able to configure the instance details including the image, size, authentication type, username, etc., as shown in Figure 7.10.

As you move to the next tab, Disks, you will be able to configure the disk type and encryption of the disk. This tab is the same as that of a virtual machine. Clicking Next will take you to the Networking tab, where you need to specify the virtual network, subnet, and load balancer (if you have one). The next tab is Scaling (refer to Figure 7.11), which is not something you have seen in virtual machines. On this tab, you will be able to define the scaling rules. You can describe the initial instance count, the scaling policy, and the scale-in policy. As of now, you will set the scaling policy to Manual, and you will learn about custom scaling policies in the next section.

FIGURE 7.10 Creating a scale set, Basics tab

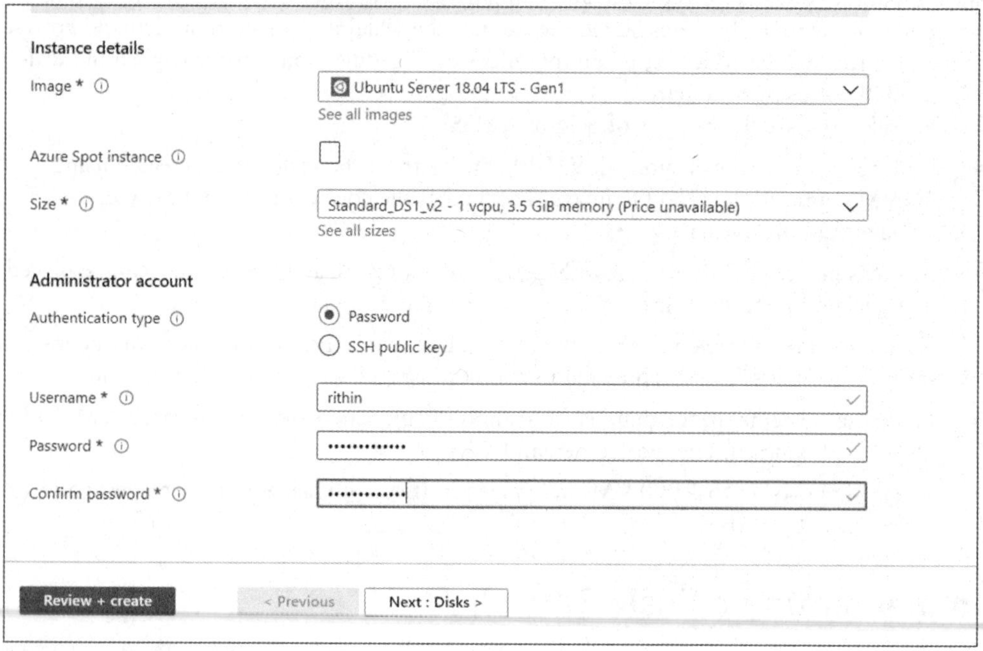

Instance details

Image * ⓘ

Ubuntu Server 18.04 LTS - Gen1

See all images

Azure Spot instance ⓘ

Size * ⓘ

Standard_DS1_v2 - 1 vcpu, 3.5 GiB memory (Price unavailable)

See all sizes

Administrator account

Authentication type ⓘ

◉ Password
○ SSH public key

Username * ⓘ

rithin

Password * ⓘ

••••••••••••

Confirm password * ⓘ

••••••••••••

Review + create   < Previous   Next : Disks >

FIGURE 7.11 Creating a scale set, Scaling tab

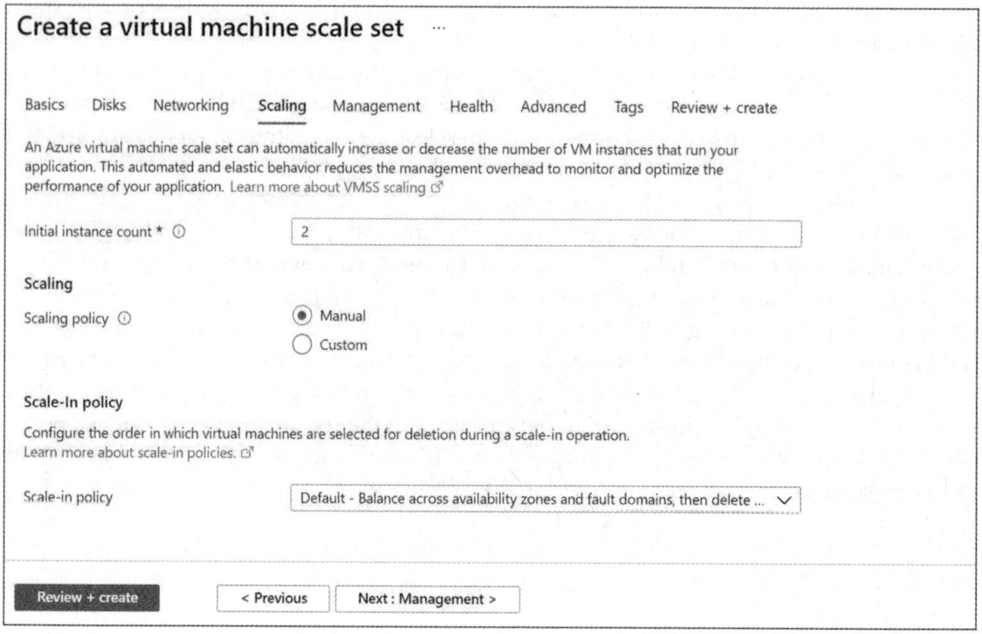

Create a virtual machine scale set ⋯

Basics   Disks   Networking   **Scaling**   Management   Health   Advanced   Tags   Review + create

An Azure virtual machine scale set can automatically increase or decrease the number of VM instances that run your application. This automated and elastic behavior reduces the management overhead to monitor and optimize the performance of your application. Learn more about VMSS scaling ☐

Initial instance count * ⓘ

2

Scaling

Scaling policy ⓘ

◉ Manual
○ Custom

Scale-In policy

Configure the order in which virtual machines are selected for deletion during a scale-in operation.
Learn more about scale-in policies. ☐

Scale-in policy

Default - Balance across availability zones and fault domains, then delete ... ∨

Review + create   < Previous   Next : Management >

The next tab is Management; the options are like that of virtual machines. Going forward, you will see the Health tab where you can configure application health monitoring. Here you will be able to set up a health probe on a TCP port and check if the application is responding. The health of the instances is decided based on the response code from the instances. This process is similar to load balancing health probes.

As you move on, the next tab is Advanced (refer to Figure 7.12). Here you will have advanced configuration such as enabling scaling beyond 100 instances, spreading algorithm, and fault domain count. If you check the Enable Scaling Beyond 100 Instances option, then only the scale set will scale beyond 100 instances. The spreading algorithm decides how the instances are spread across fault domains.

FIGURE 7.12   Creating a scale set, Advanced tab

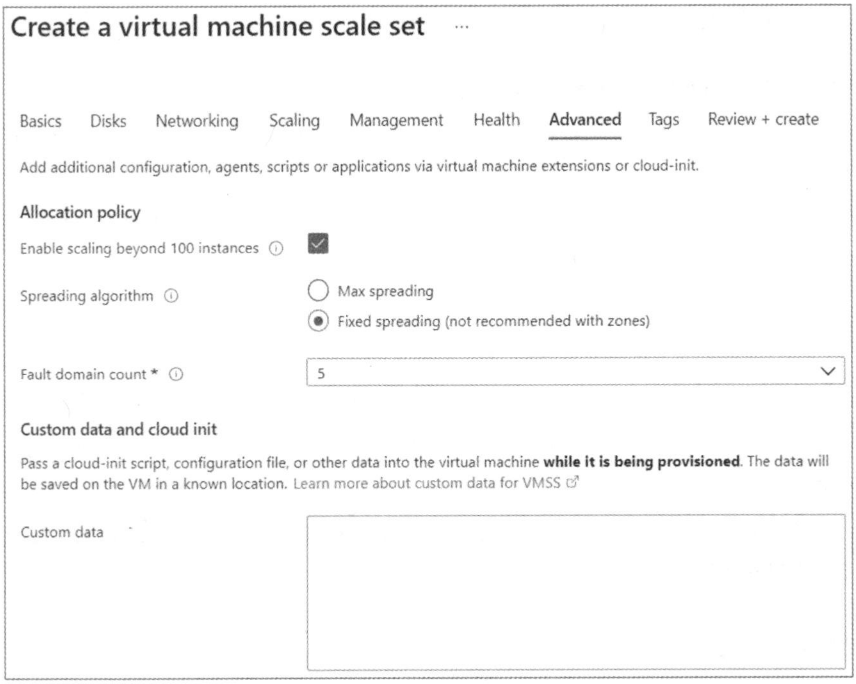

You can create the virtual machine scale set after the validation. Though we have talked about all the options, let's quickly run through the main options or parameters that are important in the creation of VMSS:

- **Initial instance count:** When the VMSS is created, this will be the initial instance count in the scale set. The value can be 0 to 1000.

- **Instance size:** Define the size of the instance in the scale set.

- **Azure Spot instance:** These are low-priority VMs that are allocated from Azure's excess capacity in the region. Using spot instances can reduce the cost of instances rather than running them as regular instances.

- **Enable scaling beyond 100 instances:** As mentioned earlier, this acts as a billing barrier to stop the scaling at 100 instances. If enabled, the scaling can go all the way up to 1,000 instances and 600 instances for custom images.

- **Scaling policy:** This can be Manual or Custom. Custom is used to set up autoscaling.

- **Spreading algorithm:** This determines how the instances should be spread across fault domains. Microsoft recommends using max spreading to spread the instances across all fault domains.

Once the scale set is created, you will be able to see the instances on the Instances blade (refer to Figure 7.13). Since you created the initial instance count with two, you have two instances in the scale set. This is the default value.

FIGURE 7.13   Instances in scale set

Now that you know how to create a scale set, let's see how you can set up autoscaling to deal with the unexpected load.

Autoscaling

By enabling autoscaling, you can automatically increase or decrease the number of application instances. In other words, you don't have to worry about the unexpected demand. When there is demand, more instances are created automatically, and when there is no demand, the instances will be automatically deleted.

The advantages of using scale set include automatic capacity adjustment, less overhead, and scale based on schedule. Let's learn how you can implement autoscaling in a scale set. During the creation process itself, you can enable autoscaling by setting the scaling policy to Custom in the Scaling tab. Nevertheless, you can always navigate back to the scale set and enable it as required.

As you change the scaling policy to Custom, you will see the following options (refer to Figure 7.14):

- **Minimum number of VMs:** Minimum value for autoscale
- **Maximum number of VMs:** Maximum value for autoscale
- **Scale out CPU threshold:** The value at which autoscaling will be triggered
- **Number of VMs to increase by:** The increment value whenever the scale-out rule is triggered
- **Duration in minutes:** How long the threshold value should be retained to trigger the rule
- **Scale in CPU threshold:** The value at which the scale-in rule will be triggered
- **Number of VMs to decrease by:** The decrement value whenever the scale-in rule is triggered

FIGURE 7.14   Enabling autoscaling

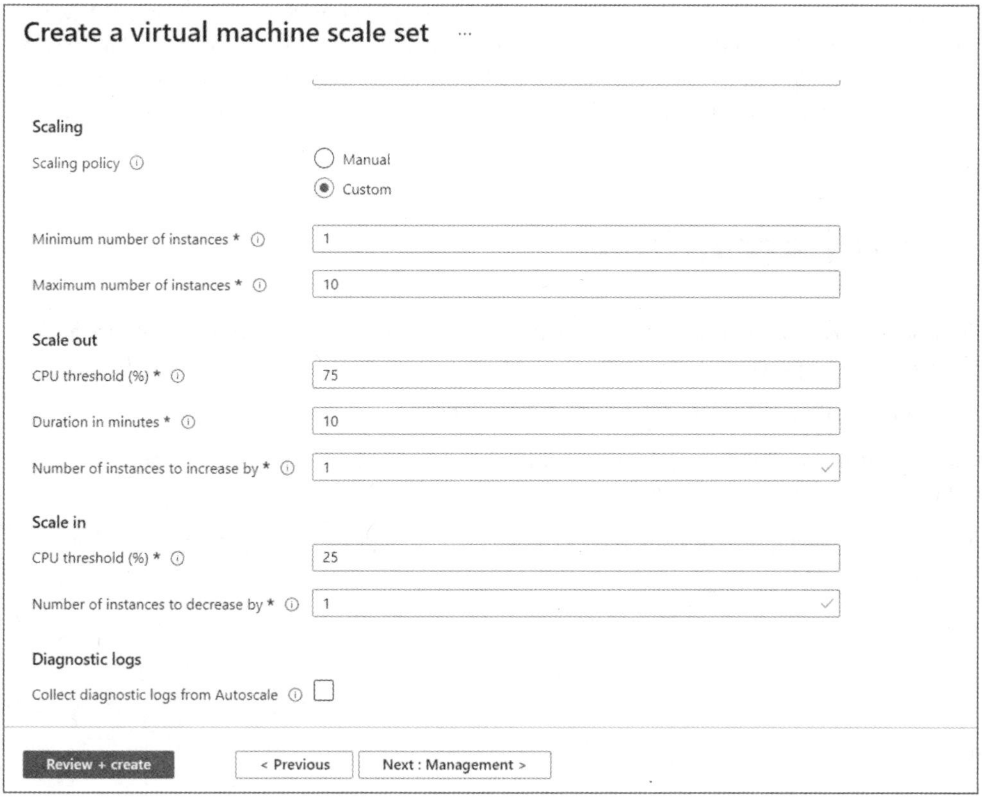

Create a virtual machine scale set   ⋯

Scaling

| Scaling policy ⓘ | ◯ Manual |
| | ⦿ Custom |

| Minimum number of instances * ⓘ | 1 |
| Maximum number of instances * ⓘ | 10 |

Scale out

CPU threshold (%) * ⓘ	75
Duration in minutes * ⓘ	10
Number of instances to increase by * ⓘ	1 ✓

Scale in

| CPU threshold (%) * ⓘ | 25 |
| Number of instances to decrease by * ⓘ | 1 ✓ |

Diagnostic logs

Collect diagnostic logs from Autoscale ⓘ ☐

| Review + create | < Previous | Next : Management > |

Summary

Though you worked with virtual machines in most of the previous chapters, in this chapter you got full coverage of virtual machines. We started the chapter with virtual machine planning, where you saw some of the vital decisions that you need to plan prior to deploying a VM. After that, you learned how to create Windows and Linux machines from the Azure portal.

After creating a VM, we discussed different methods by which you can connect to Linux and Windows VMs. We covered RDP, WinRM, and SSH. Also, we discussed the Azure Bastion service. This service is useful in establishing SSH/RDP connections from the Azure portal without the need to use public IP addresses. After covering virtual machines, we reviewed the availability options discussed in Chapter 5. You also explored the scaling concepts: vertical scaling and horizontal scaling.

Finally, we covered scale sets. This is an ideal solution for customers who want to increase or decrease the number of instances based on the demand. You also saw how you can implement the autoscaling rule to automatically scale in and scale out. So far, you created VMs from the Azure portal and using images that are available in Azure. Assume that you have a custom image and need to bring that image to Azure. In the next chapter, you will see how you can automate the deployment of resources using Azure Resource Manager templates, and you will also see how you can create custom images in Azure.

Exam Essentials

Understand Azure virtual machines.   Learn how to create virtual machines in Azure and how to connect to them.

Understand scaling concepts.   Understand the types of scaling.

Learn about the availability options.   Understand the purpose of availability sets and availability zones and how they work.

Understand virtual machine scale sets.   Learn how to deploy VMSS and set up the autoscale rule.

Review Questions

1. You host a service with two Azure virtual machines. You discover that occasional outages cause your service to fail. What two actions can you do to minimize the impact of the outages? (Select two.)

   A. Add a load balancer

   B. Put the virtual machines in an availability set

   C. Put the virtual machines in a scale set

   D. Add a third instance of the virtual machine

2. You are researching Microsoft Azure for your company. The company is considering deploying Windows-based VMs in Azure. However, before moving forward, the management team has asked you to research the costs associated with Azure VMs. You need to document the configuration options that are likely to save the company money on their Azure VMs. Which options should you document? Each answer presents part of the solution. (Select four.)

   A. Use HDD instead of SSD for VM storage

   B. Use unmanaged premium storage instead of managed standard storage

   C. Bring your own Windows custom images

   D. Use different Azure regions

   E. Use the least powerful VMs that meet your requirements

   F. Place all VMs in the same resource group

   G. Bring your own Windows license for each VM

3. You are planning to deploy several Linux VMs in Azure. The security team issues a policy that Linux VMs must use an authentication system other than passwords. You need to deploy an authentication method for the Linux VMs to meet the requirement. Which authentication method should you use?

   A. SSH key pair

   B. Azure MFA

   C. Access keys

   D. Certificate

4. Another IT administrator creates an Azure virtual machine scale set with five VMs. Later, you notice that the VMs are all running at max capacity with the CPU being fully consumed. However, additional VMs are not deploying in the scale set. You need to ensure that additional VMs are deployed when the CPU is 75 percent consumed. What should you do?

   A. Increase the instance count

   B. Add a scale set to Azure Automation

   C. Enable the autoscale option

   D. Use PowerShell DSC

5. Your company is preparing to deploy an application to Microsoft Azure. The app is a self-contained unit that runs independently on several servers. The company is moving the app to the cloud to provide better performance. To get better performance, the team has the following requirements:

   - *Should be able to increase or decrease number of instances based on business requirement*

   - *Should be able to deploy more than 100 instances*

   You need to deploy a solution to meet the requirements while minimizing the administrative overhead to implement and manage the solution. What should you do?

   A. Deploy an ARM template

   B. Deploy the app in a VMSS

   C. Deploy the app in an availability set

   D. Deploy the app using Terraform

6. Your company is deploying a critical business application to Microsoft Azure. The uptime of the application is of utmost importance. The application has a web tier, an app tier, and a database tier. You need to ensure that each tier should be protected from hardware failures, and they shouldn't go down together.

   A. Deploy one VM from each tier into one availability set and the remaining VMs into a separate availability set.

   B. Deploy the VMs from each tier into a dedicated availability set for the tier.

   C. Deploy the application and database VMs in one availability set and the web VMs into a separate availability set.

   D. Deploy a load balancer for the web VMs and an availability set to hold the application and database VMs.

7. Your organization has a security policy that prohibits exposing SSH ports to the outside world. You need to connect to an Azure Linux virtual machine to install software. What should you do?

   A. Use the Bastion service

   B. Configure guest configuration for Azure VM

   C. Use a custom script

   D. Enable port forwarding

8. Which of the following protocols can be used to interact with Azure Linux VM by default?

   A. SSH

   B. RDP

   C. WinRM

   D. LinuxRM

9. Which of the following disk types can be used to achieve optimal IOPS for mission-critical virtual machines in Azure?

   A. Standard HDD

   B. Standard Blobs

   C. Premium SSD

   D. Standard SSD

10. In SSH key pair authentication, if the user needs to enable password authentication, which of the following methods can be used? The solution should not cause any downtime and doesn't require redeployment. (Select two.)

    A. Use the Reset Password option in the Azure portal and create a new user with a password.

    B. Log in using an SSH key pair and enable password authentication in the SSH configuration.

    C. Password authentication cannot be enabled while the key pair is in use.

    D. Use an ARM template to deploy a replica of the VM.

11. Which of the following facts about Azure Bastion is not true?

    A. Azure Bastion can be used to connect to virtual machines without the use of public IP addresses.

    B. We can establish RDP/SSH connections from the Azure portal using Azure Bastion.

    C. It's the responsibility of the customer to make sure that the Bastion host is updated with the latest OS updates.

    D. Azure Bastion is a platform-as-a-service solution.

12. How can you enable autoscaling for a single VM?

    A. Enable auto scaling from the Scaling blade of the VM.

    B. Enable metrics to trigger autoscaling.

    C. Enable diagnostics logs to start autoscaling.

    D. Single VMs don't support autoscaling.

13. Which of the following facts about vertical scaling is not true?

    A. Using vertical scaling, you can add more hardware capabilities to the existing VMs.

    B. The scaling events are called scale up and scale down based on the action.

    C. Vertical scaling doesn't involve any downtime.

    D. Using vertical scaling, you can reduce the billing by reducing the size of the development or test VM during nonproduction hours.

14. In the case of managed disks, how can you control the access to the storage account in which the disk is stored?

   A. Granting RBAC to the storage account.

   B. Using access keys.

   C. Using SAS keys.

   D. Managed disk storage accounts are managed by Microsoft; therefore, no access can be granted.

15. What is the maximum number of instances supported by virtual machines scale set for an image customized by you?

   A. 1,000.

   B. 600.

   C. 100.

   D. User-customized images cannot be used in a scale set.

16. Your organization is planning to use SSH key pairs to connect to Linux machines. As this is a key pair, which key(s) should be protected and should not be shared to avoid unauthorized access to the VM?

   A. Both keys.

   B. Public.

   C. Private.

   D. Both keys are encrypted and cannot be read without decryption keys.

17. You are planning to limit access to Windows machines over the command-line interface only. After research, you found that WinRM can be used to connect to Windows VMs to have a command-line session. Which port needs to be opened on the NSG to allow this communication?

   A. WinRM uses the same port as RDP: 3389.

   B. WinRM doesn't require any ports to be open.

   C. WinRM uses HTTP: 443 for secure communication.

   D. WinRM uses TCP: 5986.

18. Your organization requires high CPU to memory ratio VMs for running a firewall solution. Which VM family should you suggest for this?

   A. General purpose

   B. Memory optimized

   C. High-performance computing

   D. Compute optimized

19. Which of the following scaling options are supported by scale set? (Select all that apply.)

   A. Scale based on schedule

   B. Scale based on metric

   C. Manual scaling

   D. Scale across regions

20. You have implemented a scale set, and you need to load balance the incoming requests. Which solutions can be considered? (Select all that apply.)

   A. Azure Load Balancer

   B. Azure Firewall

   C. Azure Application Gateway

   D. Azure Front Door

Chapter

8

Automation, Deployment, and Configuration of Resources

MICROSOFT EXAM OBJECTIVES COVERED IN THIS CHAPTER:

✓ **Automate deployment of virtual machines (VMs) by using Azure Resource Manager templates**

- Modify an Azure Resource Manager template
- Configure a virtual hard disk (VHD) template
- Deploy from a template
- Save a deployment as an Azure Resource Manager template
- Deploy virtual machine extensions

In this chapter, you will see how you can automate the deployment and configuration of Azure resources using Azure Resource Manager (ARM) templates. So far, you have deployed several types of resources using the Azure portal, Azure PowerShell, and the Azure CLI. You deployed all these resources by interacting with a layer called Azure Resource Manager. First, you will understand the role of Azure Resource Manager and then the automation using ARM templates.

Further, you will see how you can create custom VHD templates in Azure. This will be useful in bringing custom images to Azure without the need to perform further configuration management. Also, you see the function of extensions that can be installed on your virtual machines. There are numerous extensions available for Azure Virtual Machines based on the OS you are selecting. These extensions can be quite useful in performing multiple actions inside the VM, including configuration management, security, protection, backup, and so on. In this chapter, you are interested in the configuration management extensions; however, it's important to understand that there are other extensions for various purposes. For example, the Anti Malware extension can be used for endpoint protection of your virtual machines.

Let's get started with Azure Resource Manager.

Azure Resource Manager

If you look at the deployment of a virtual machine, there are multiple dependencies that are created along with the virtual machines. These include the virtual hard disk, network interfaces, network security groups, etc. Azure Resource Manager helps in interacting with the underlying resource providers and creates these resources. For example, if you are creating a virtual machine, you will send our inputs to the Azure Resource Manager, and Azure Resource Manager will forward the request to Compute resource provider (Microsoft.Compute) after validation. The resource provider will deploy the resource and update you with the status via ARM. Similarly, when you create a networking resource like a virtual network, the resource provisioning is done by the Microsoft.Network resource provider.

ARM is not only responsible for the deployment of the resources, but also responsible for the management of resources. Resource groups are a feature of ARM. With them, ARM lets you manage the resources together as a group. Using ARM, you can create, update, or delete a single resource or several resources. In addition to the resource groups, ARM offers several other features such as enhanced security, tagging, resource locks, etc. Prior to ARM, you had Azure Service Manager (ASM), which lacked these capabilities. The resources created using

ASM are called Classic resources. You might still see the option of Classic resources in the Azure portal; nevertheless, Microsoft recommends using ARM resources and migrating Classic resources to ARM if you have any. The Classic deployment model is retiring on August 31, 2024; if you have any existing Classic resources, you need to upgrade them to ARM before this date.

Any request from the user will be taken care of by this consistent layer, as represented in Figure 8.1.

FIGURE 8.1   Azure Resource Management

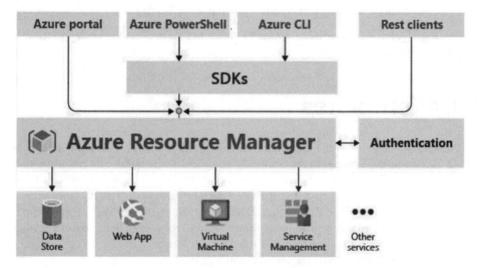

The following are the benefits offered by Azure Resource Manager:

- Instead of handling resources individually, you can manage and deploy them as a group.
- ARM helps you build a consistent infrastructure by leveraging reusable templates.
- Deployment is powered by declarative automation rather than scripting.
- ARM supports RBAC and the inheritance of RBAC from a higher level.
- It supports resource tags for logical organization and chargeback.

Also, learning the following terminology will help you get the most from this chapter:

Resource   Any item that is created and is managed in Azure is termed a *resource*. Examples of resources include virtual machines, virtual networks, SQL databases, and many more.

Resource Group   This is a container used to logically group resources together so that the access, policy, and lifecycle of the grouped resources can be managed together.

Resource Provider   Whenever you supply inputs to the ARM to create a resource, ARM will share this information with the resource provider. The resource providers are responsible for provisioning requests related to the ARM resources. For example, a compute resource is provided by the resource provider Microsoft.Compute. Similarly, networking resources are provided by the Microsoft.Network resource provider.

ARM Template   An ARM template is a JSON file that can be used for the deployment of one or more resources to a resource group.

Declarative Syntax   ARM templates follow a declarative syntax. In declarative syntax, you just have to let ARM know what resources you intend to create; ARM will take care of the deployment. In this way, you don't have to worry about how these resources are deployed, as it is the responsibility of the Resource Manager.

Now that you have an idea about Azure Resource Manager, let's explore Azure Resource Manager templates.

ARM Templates

ARM templates comprise all the resources that you intend to deploy. This template will be injected as a single deployment to the resource, regardless of the number of resources that you have mentioned inside the template. As mentioned in the terminologies earlier, an ARM template is a JSON document that is written in a declarative syntax. This declarative syntax is what powers the declarative automation. *Declarative automation* refers to the automated deployment of resources that you define without the need to worry about how they will be deployed. The "how" part is the liability of the Azure Resource Manager, and it will make sure that whatever resources you requested are indeed deployed.

Before you start writing a template, it's good that you take a look at the template design approaches. The following are some approaches that are commonly taken by administrators to design templates. Nevertheless, you always have the liberty to design in your own style and define your resources as required.

Template Design

For explaining the template design, let's take a three-tier application that consists of an Azure virtual machine that serves a front end, Azure App Service that acts as a business logic, and finally a SQL database that will be the datastore for the whole solution. The end user will be interacting with the front end, and input from the user will be evaluated by the business logic, which will be written to the database.

The first approach here is to include all the resources that you need in a single template, as shown in Figure 8.2, and deploy to the resource group as a single operation. In the template itself, you can give the reference of the SQL database to the Azure App Service for them to communicate with each other.

FIGURE 8.2   Single template approach

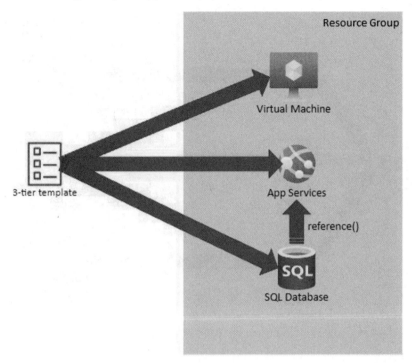

The second approach is that you don't have to define the entire infrastructure in a single template file. If you have multiple resources, it makes total sense to break down your template into different templates targeting individual resources. Remember how we used to write programs? We used to define classes in different files and then call them in the main file as required. You will take a similar approach here. There will be a parent template or a master template that links to the individual templates. Figure 8.3 shows how the master template and individual templates are deployed to the resource group.

Let's say you have different lifecycles for your application tiers; then you may need to associate them to different resource groups. In the last two approaches, you were deploying the resources to a single resource group. However, in this approach, you will be writing a separate template for individual tiers targeting different resource groups. As you already know, a resource group is a logical group and will not hinder the communication between the tiers. These tiers can still interact with each other, though they are deployed to different resource groups. Figure 8.4 shows the pictorial representation of this approach.

As mentioned in the opening, the aforementioned are some of the common approaches. Nevertheless, an alternate approach can be taken per your requirements. Now, you will learn the structure of the ARM template and the relevance of each section.

FIGURE 8.3   Nested template approach

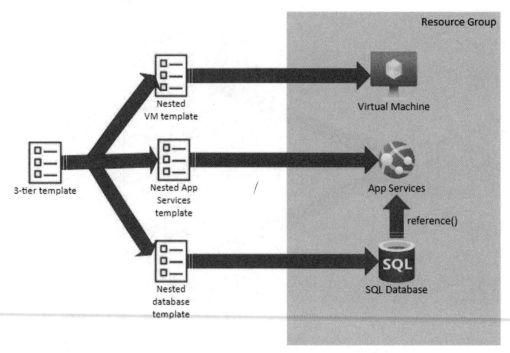

Template Modes

ARM template can be deployed in two modes as follows:

Incremental Mode   This is the default mode of deployment for ARM template deployment unless you override the mode. In incremental mode, Azure Resource Manager will not alter any resources that are already present in the target resource group. The resources that are declared in the template will be added to the existing resources in the resource group.

Complete Mode   In complete mode, ARM compares the list of resources declared in the template and the list of resources already existing in the resource group. Any resource that is not part of the template that is already present in the resource group will be deleted. It's recommended that you always make use of the "what-if" operation before deploying the template if you are using the complete mode. By doing so, you will be able to see the resources that are going to get created, deleted, or updated as part of the deployment. This will lead to the accidental deletion of resources.

FIGURE 8.4   Individual template approach

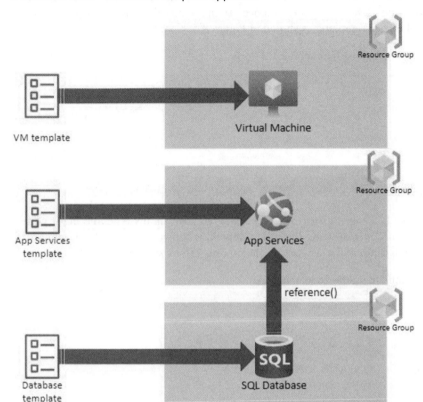

In Azure PowerShell, you can use the -Mode parameter in the New-AzResourceGroupDeployment command to change the deployment mode. If you don't specify this parameter, then ARM will proceed with the incremental mode. Similarly, in Azure CLI, you have the --mode parameter in az group deployment create to control the deployment mode.

Template Sections

Writing ARM templates is easy if you use Visual Studio code and an Azure Resource Manager extension. This is more of a personal choice; you can choose any text editor that you prefer to write a template. Visual Studio Code offers better IntelliSense with the help of an extension, and there is a set of shorthand commands that can be used to invoke the ARM template snippets. The extension can be downloaded from here:

https://marketplace.visualstudio.com/items?itemName=msazurermtools
.azurerm-vscode-tools

If you are using Visual Studio Code, you will be able to generate the skeleton of the ARM template by typing arm in the code pane. You need to make sure that the language is set to Azure Resource Manager Template, as shown in Figure 8.5.

FIGURE 8.5   Selecting the language in VS Code

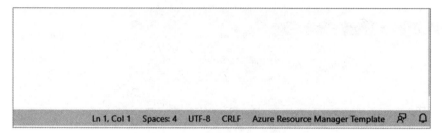

After selecting the language as shown in Figure 8.5, you can simply type arm in the code pane, and VS Code will start showing the code snippets, as shown in Figure 8.6. If you are not able to see it, you can hit Ctrl+Space and the pop-up will be shown.

FIGURE 8.6   Generating the code snippet

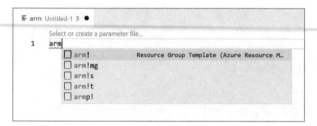

Selecting the first one in the list will generate a resource group deployment skeleton for you. This is a blank deployment without any resources. You will be using this skeleton to explain the sections of the ARM template. If you selected correctly, you will be able to see code similar to the following:

```
{
    "$schema": "https://schema.management.azure.com/schemas/2019-04-01/
deploymentTemplate.json#",
    "contentVersion": "1.0.0.0",
    "parameters": {},
    "functions": [],
    "variables": {},
    "resources": [],
    "outputs": {}
}
```

Now you will learn the role of each of the sections in the aforementioned code; these are the mandatory fields in every ARM template you create.

Schema (schema)

This URL points to the location of the JSON schema file that explains the version of the template language. The version number will vary according to the scope of the deployment and text editor you are using. If you are using Visual Studio Code with the Azure Resource Manager extension, then the schema will be as follows:

```
https://schema.management.azure.com/schemas/2019-04-01/
deploymentTemplate.json#
```

If you are not using the extension, other text editors including Visual Studio Code will not be able to process this schema. Microsoft recommends using the following for text editors without the Azure Resource Manager extension:

```
https://schema.management.azure.com/schemas/2015-01-01/
deploymentTemplate.json#
```

If you deploy to another scope, like the subscription scope, management scope, or tenant scope, the schema will vary. Luckily, using the ARM extension on VS Code, you will be able to change the schema using code snippets without the need to memorize them. Figure 8.6 shows other code snippets like arm!mg, arm!s, and arm!t. These represent the management group, subscription, and tenant-level code snippets, respectively.

Content Version (contentVersion)

This is used by the end user to identify the version of the ARM template they are using. For example, you can give a value like 1.0.0 to represent that this is the version and then later if you need to make any changes to the template, you can modify the version to say 1.1.0. The content version will help the user to ensure that they are deploying the right version of the template that they authored. If you are saving the template to source control or any repository, the content version will help you find the latest version of your ARM template. It's not mandatory that you need to update the version numbers unless you are using source control; you can reuse the same version number for multiple deployments.

Parameters (parameters)

Parameters are used to specify the values that are configurable when you execute the template. The following is an example that shows how parameters are mentioned in the parameters section:

```
"parameters": {
    "resourceLocation": {
        "type": "string",
        "metadata": {
            "description": "Location of resource"
            }
        }
    },
```

In this example, you are specifying a parameter called `resourceLocation`. Along with that you are adding the type of data that you expect from the user and description for a second person to understand the purpose of the parameter when they read the ARM template. When you run the template from Azure PowerShell, the Azure CLI, or the Azure portal, ARM will be expecting the user to input the values for these two parameters. If the user is not providing any parameter, then the deployment will fail.

There are more options available for each parameter like `minLength` and `maxLength` to specify the minimum and maximum length of the parameter if the parameter is a string. Then, `maxValue` and `minValue` specify the minimum and maximum values of the parameter in the case of integers. Then you have `defaultValue`, which will be considered as the value of the parameter if the user is not providing any value for the parameter when the template runs. Also, you can specify the list of allowed values via `allowedValues`. In VS Code, it's not hard to understand this, thanks to the Azure Resource Manager extension and IntelliSense.

Functions (functions)

All object-oriented programming languages have functions. Functions are used to define a set of procedures that you don't want to repeat in your template. For example, if you want to write a program to find the factorial of a number and if there are multiple instances throughout the program where you need to find the factorial, instead of writing the code multiple times, you can write a function to find the factorial. Whenever you need to find the factorial of a number, the factorial function will be called, and the number will be passed to the function. With the help of code defined inside the function, it will be able to return the factorial of the number. In the ARM template, functions serve the same purpose.

The following is an example of a function created in an ARM template that can be used to generate unique names for resources that required a unique naming convention. The function will accept a parameter that will be provided by the user and then concatenate that with a string that you defined inside the function. The output of the function will be a unique name that can be used for our resource.

```
"functions": [
    {
      "namespace": "azuretales",
      "members": {
        "nameGenerator": {
          "parameters": [
            {
              "name": "userInput",
              "type": "string"
            }
          ],
          "output": {
            "value": "[concat(toLower(parameters('userInput')),'ax04b-m4')]",
            "type": "string"
```

```
            }
        }
    }
}
],
```

Here the value from the end user is passed to the function via the `userInput` parameter, and that is converted to a lowercase and then concatenated with the string `ax04b-m4` to generate a unique name. Here you use `namespace` to distinguish this function from other functions in the template.

Variables (variables)

This is yet another concept that you see in all programming and scripting languages. Variables are used to hard-code certain values to keywords so that they can be reused throughout the template. Later, if you need to change the value of an item, you don't have to change all occurrences; instead, you can update the variable. Once you update the variables, all references will be updated with the new value.

The following is an example of a few variables that are used to describe the name of the virtual network and subnet:

```
"variables": {
    "vnet": "vnet-01",
    "vnet-address": "10.0.0.0/16",
    "subnet-1": "workload",
    "subnet-1-cidr": "10.0.0.0/24"
},
```

As you can see, you are storing certain values that will be used in our template using variables. When you explain the resources section, you will understand how these variables are referenced.

Resources (resources)

In the `resources` section, you will be defining the Azure resources that you want to create. The set of resources referenced in this section make up your deployment. The following is an example used for creating a virtual network, and you can see how you are referencing the parameters and variables that you declared earlier.

It's easy to generate code snippets for resources. For example, if you need to create a virtual network, then you can start typing **vnet** in the `resources` section, and Visual Studio Code will start showing the suggestions (refer to Figure 8.7).

FIGURE 8.7 Resource code snippets

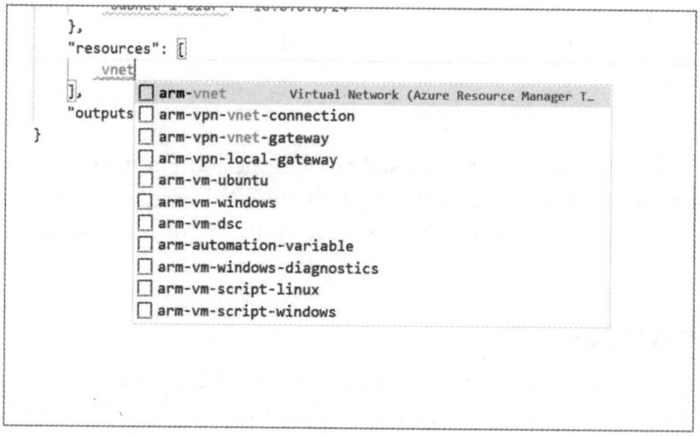

Selecting the first one in Figure 8.7 generates the ARM code for the virtual network with all the required fields. Now you can tweak this per your requirements. In the following example, you can see how we are referencing parameters and variables:

```
"resources": [
    {
        "name": "virtualNetwork1",
      "type": "Microsoft.Network/virtualNetworks",
      "apiVersion": "2020-11-01",
      "location": "[parameters('resourceLocation')]",
      "properties": {
         "addressSpace": {
            "addressPrefixes": [
                "[variables('vnet-address')]"
                    ]
                },
         "subnets": [
             {
                "name": "[variables('subnet-1')]",
                "properties": {
                   "addressPrefix": "[variables('subnet-1-cidr')]"
                        }
                    }
                ]
            }
        }
    ]
```

If the code block is hard to interpret, refer to Figure 8.8.

FIGURE 8.8   Resource code for virtual network

```
"resources": [
    {
            1 child: ${subnet-1} (subnets)
        "name": "[variables('vnet')]",
        "type": "Microsoft.Network/virtualNetworks",
        "apiVersion": "2020-11-01",
        "location": "[parameters('resourceLocation')]",
        "properties": {
            "addressSpace": {
                "addressPrefixes": [
                    "[variables('vnet-address')]"
                ]
            },
            "subnets": [
                {
                    Parent: ${vnet} (virtualNetworks)
                    "name": "[variables('subnet-1')]",
                    "properties": {
                        "addressPrefix": "[variables('subnet-1-cidr')]"
                    }
                }
            ]
        }
    }
],
```

Outputs (outputs)

Finally, you have the outputs section. This section can be used to output any information to the end user when they run the template. Let's say you are deploying a virtual machine, and when the template runs, you want to output the DNS label of the VM so that the user can connect to the VM immediately without the need to check the IP address or label. This is not mandatory; you can still complete the deployments without outputs.

An example has been added for your reference:

```
"outputs": {
 "hostname": {
 "type": "string",
 "value": "[reference(variables('publicIPAddressName')).dnsSettings.fqdn]"
 }
}
```

Now that you know different sections of the ARM template, let's compose an ARM template and see how you can deploy that to a resource group.

Composing Templates

You can compose templates in any text editor you like. However, Visual Studio Code offers the best IntelliSense and code snippets. Once the template is composed, you will be deploying that to a resource group using the Azure portal, Azure PowerShell, or the Azure CLI. In Azure PowerShell, you will be using the New-AzResourceGroupDeployment command by specifying the ARM template using the TemplateUri or TemplateFile parameter. You can use TemplateUri if you have the template file stored in some shared location or source control, and you can use TemplateFile if you composed the file locally. Similarly, in the Azure CLI, you will be using az group deployment create and specify the template location using --template-file or --template-uri. In both Azure PowerShell and the Azure CLI, you need to give a name for the deployment to track it and the targeted resource group name.

Let's write our first ARM template and deploy it to our Azure subscription in Exercise 8.1.

EXERCISE 8.1

Composing an ARM Template

1. In Visual Studio Code, open a new file by pressing Ctrl+N or selecting File ➢ New File.

2. Select Azure Resource Manager Template as the language, as you saw in Figure 8.5.

3. Type **arm**, and the code snippets will start showing up; if not, after typing hit Ctrl+spacebar. From the suggestions, select arm!, which is the code snippet for a resource group deployment.

4. The skeleton code with all the sections will be populated on your screen. Now without making any changes, let's deploy this as a template.

5. From the Visual Studio Code toolbar, select Terminal ➢ New Terminal. This will open a new PowerShell terminal toward the bottom of the screen.

6. Here you need to make sure that the Azure PowerShell module is installed on the computer you are trying this on. You can download the Azure PowerShell module from here:

   https://docs.microsoft.com/en-us/powershell/azure/
   install-az-ps?view=azps-6.5.0

7. Log in to your Azure account using the Login-AzAccount command. A sign-in window will pop up, and you can complete the sign-in.

8. Once you are signed in, create a new resource group using the New-AzResourceGroup command, for example, New-AzResourceGroup -Name <name of the resource group> -Location <location>.

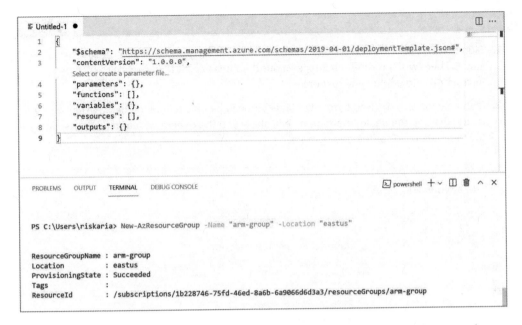

9. Save the file in JSON format by hitting Ctrl+S, and now that you have the target resource group, let's push the template to the resource group using the `New-AzResourceGroupDeployment` command. The mandatory parameters include the name of the deployment, resource group, and path to the template file, for example: `New-AzResourceGroupDeployment -Name "deployment-1" -ResourceGroupName "arm-group" -TemplateFile .\Documents\template-1.json`.

10. If the deployment is successful, you will see a succeeded message in the terminal.

```
DeploymentName          : deployment-1
ResourceGroupName       : arm-group
ProvisioningState       : Succeeded
Timestamp               : 19-10-2021 07:56:21
Mode                    : Incremental
TemplateLink            :
Parameters              :
Outputs                 :
DeploymentDebugLogLevel :


                    >
PS C:\Users\riskaria>
PS C:\Users\riskaria> █
```

EXERCISE 8.1 *(continued)*

11. Sign in to the Azure portal and navigate to the resource group that you created in step 8. There won't be any resources as our resources section was empty and didn't instruct ARM to deploy any resources.

12. If you navigate to the Deployments blade, you will be able to see the deployment-1 you made. Clicking the deployment name will show you the overview, inputs, outputs, and the template used for the deployment.

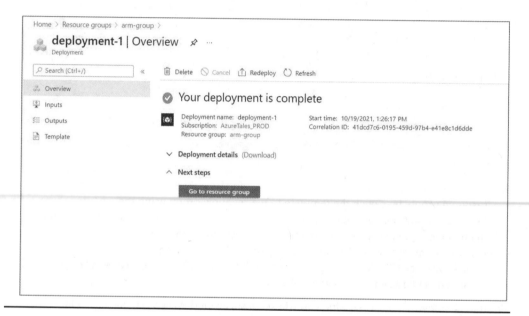

In Exercise 8.1, you saw how to deploy using the ARM templates. Now you will start writing a template that is a bit more advanced. Though this is not marked as an exercise, you can consider this an exercise and build this template by following the instructions. Let's start by creating the code snippet of the resource group deployment from Visual Studio Code. Once you have the skeleton, you will skip the schema and content version and start defining the parameters first.

In this example, you will be creating a storage account. Let's assume that your organization creates storage accounts in a frequent manner for your application needs. You need a template where the user will input a keyword and a storage account is created based on the following requirements:

- The template should take a parameter called namePparam that should be of minimum length 3 and maximum length 10.

- The template should take a parameter called location. The default value for this should be the location of the resource group.

- You need a variable called `storageAccountName` that is constructed by appending the name parameter to the string datastore.

- You need a parameter called `accountType`. The default value is `Standard_LRS`. Other supported values include `Standard_GRS` and `Standard_ZRS`.

- After deployment, the storage endpoints should be shown to the end user.

Let's see how you can build a template based on the requirements.

Defining Parameters

You will start by defining the parameters as this is the first section in our template. If needed, you can define the parameters in a separate file that can be referenced when you run the template. In this case, you will be writing the parameters in your template file itself.

If you navigate to the `parameters` section and press N in Visual Studio Code, you will see the code snippet to add a new parameter, as shown in Figure 8.9.

FIGURE 8.9 Adding a new parameter

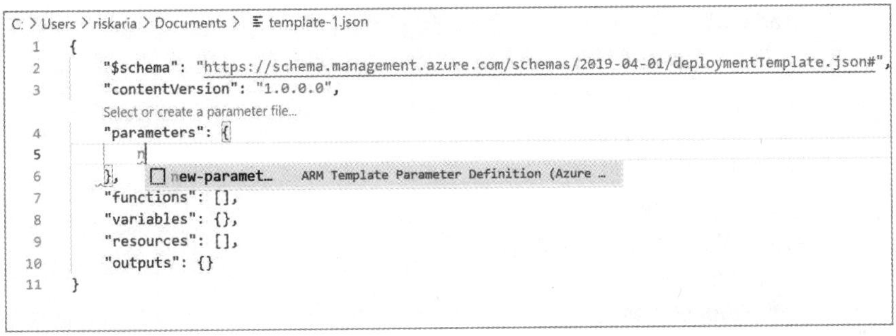

You can select the code snippet and Visual Studio will immediately generate the code snippet for a new parameter as shown in Figure 8.10.

FIGURE 8.10 New parameter code block

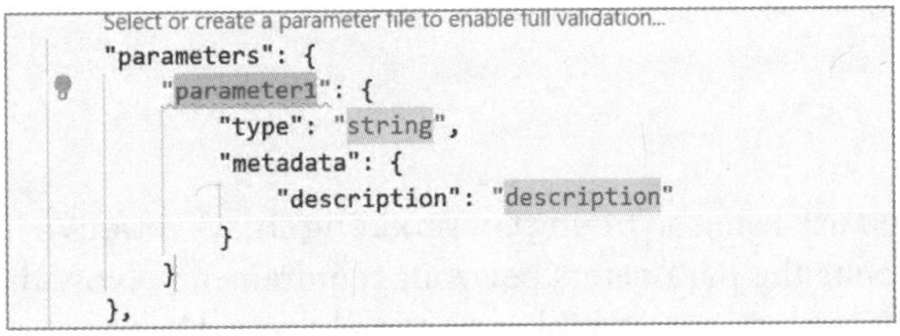

Per the requirements, you need the following parameters:

- **nameParam:** This has a minimum length of 3 and maximum length of 10.
- **location:** The default value is the location of the resource group. This can be pulled using `[resourceGroup().location]`.

■   **accountType:** The default value is `Standard_LRS`. Allowed values include `Standard_GRS` and `Standard_ZRS`.

The following is the parameter list with the requirements incorporated:

```
"parameters": {
    "nameParam": {
        "type": "string",
        "minLength": 3,
        "maxLength": 10,
        "metadata": {
            "description": "User input - name"
        }
    },
    "location": {
        "type": "string",
        "defaultValue": "[resourceGroup().location]",
        "metadata": {
            "description": "Location of the resource"
        }
    },
    "accountType": {
        "type": "string",
        "defaultValue" : "Standard_LRS",
        "allowedValues" : [
            "Standard_LRS",
            "Standard_GRS",
            "Standard_ZRS"
        ],
        "metadata": {
            "description": "Account type"
        }
    }
},
```

As you can see, you are using `minLength`, `maxLength`, `allowedValues`, and `defaultValue` to define the parameters per your requirements. Now that you have your parameters ready, let's declare our variable `storageAccountName`.

Defining Variables

You will be using the `variables` section in your template to define your variables. Per the requirements, you need to append the `nameParam` parameter and a string datastore to declare a variable called `storageAccountName`. You will be using the `concat()` option to concatenate the name parameter and the string. Here you can also leverage the code snippets in Visual Studio Code. In the following code, you can see that we are appending `nameParam` and a string and then storing the value to the variable:

```
"variables": {
    "storageAccountName": "[concat(parameters('nameParam'),'datastore')]"
    },
```

Since you declared your variable, let's go ahead and see how you can create your resource referencing the parameters and variables.

Defining Resources

The `resources` section is an array; you can add multiple resources that need to be deployed in this section. In this case, you only need a storage account, and you will make use of the code snippet to generate the code block. In the `resources` section, you can start typing `storage`, and you will see `azure-storage`, as shown in Figure 8.11.

FIGURE 8.11   Adding resource

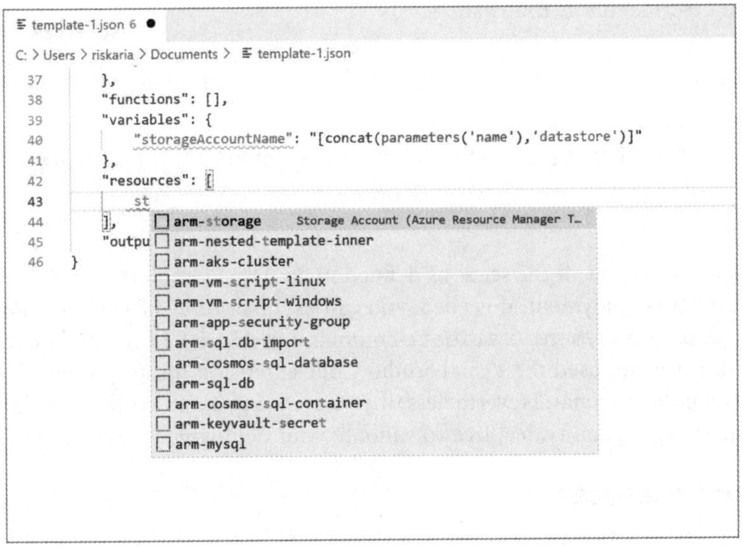

Now you can remove the default values and give references to your parameters and variables. The final code will look similar to the following:

```
"resources": [
    {
        "name": "[variables('storageAccountName')]",
        "type": "Microsoft.Storage/storageAccounts",
        "apiVersion": "2021-04-01",
```

```
        "location": "[parameters('location')]"
        "kind": "StorageV2",
        "sku": {
            "name": "[parameters('accountType')]",
            "tier": "Standard"
        }
    }
]
```

You can remove tags and other options that are not mandatory. The only thing remaining is to display the storage endpoints once the deployment is done. Let's define that under outputs.

Defining Outputs

As explained earlier, you can use the outputs section to display any properties once the template is executed. In this case, you need to display the endpoints of the storage account that you are creating. This can be retrieved from the primaryEndpoints object. In our template, we can describe this as follows:

```
"outputs": {
    "endpoints": {
        "type": "object",
        "value": "[reference(variables('storageAccountName')).primaryEndpoints]"
        }
    }
```

Now you will combine all the sections defined in an ARM template and proceed with the deployment. Before deployment, if needed, you can use the what-if switch in PowerShell or the az group deployment validate command in Azure CLI to validate the template you authored. Since you used the Visual Studio Code extension for authoring, chances of syntax errors will be minimal. Nevertheless, if you are using a text editor that doesn't have the syntax checking capability, feel free to validate your deployment prior to deployment.

Deploying Resources

You can use the New-AzResourceGroupDeployment command that you used earlier to deploy this template. Unlike the last time, you will be passing the value for the nameParam parameter. You can pass any string with a minimum length of 3 and a maximum length of 10. Make sure that you save and run the template, as shown in Figure 8.12.

As you can see in Figure 8.12, you are providing values to the parameter you defined. If you don't provide this value, you will not be able to deploy the ARM template. Once the deployment is completed, you will be able to see the storage endpoints, which you added to your outputs section, as shown Figure 8.13.

FIGURE 8.12 Deploying an ARM template

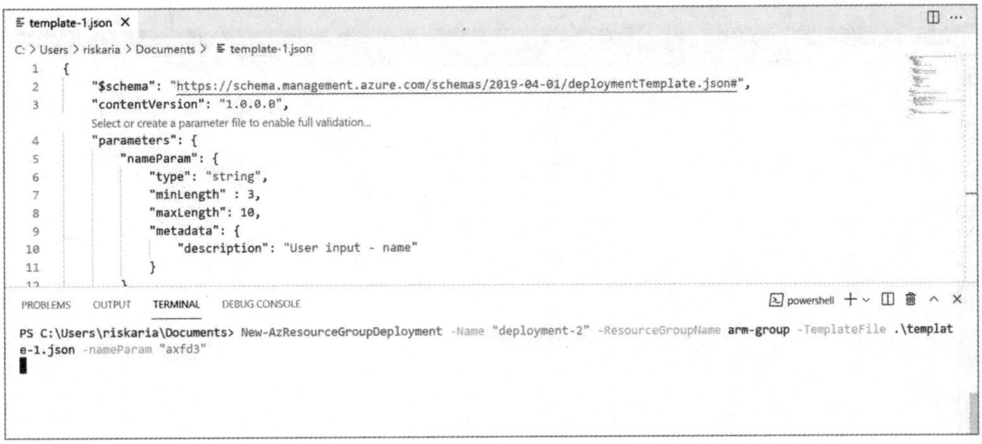

FIGURE 8.13 Reviewing output

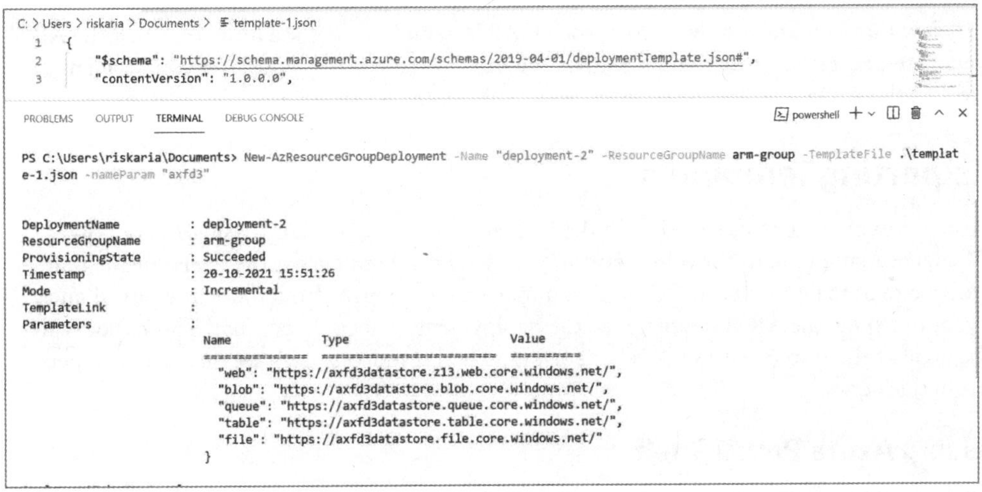

If you are not interested in composing ARM templates, Microsoft offers Azure QuickStart templates. These templates are contributed by Azure enthusiasts across the globe and are maintained by Microsoft. You can access the QuickStart templates from here:

```
https://azure.microsoft.com/en-in/resources/templates
```

Also, there is a visualization tool by which you can upload your ARM template and visualize the resources that are going to get deployed as part of the operation, as shown in Figure 8.14. The tool name is ARMVIZ and is available at `http://armviz.io`.

FIGURE 8.14 ARMVIZ tool

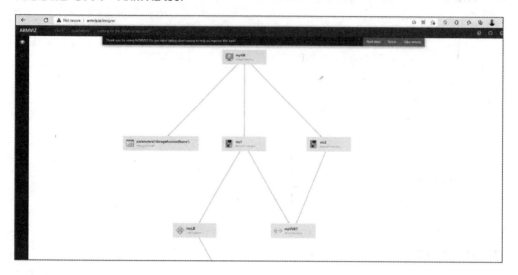

Now that you know how to compose an ARM template, let's see how to export the ARM template of a resource that you already deployed in Azure. This is useful if you accidentally deleted the ARM template or want to recover the ARM template used for deployment.

Exporting Templates

You can export the template file of a deployment you made in Azure. Using Azure Power-Shell, the Azure CLI, or the Azure portal, you will be able to export the deployments that you make in the Azure portal. Even if you make a deployment from the Azure portal and want to export the ARM template for the deployment, you could get that. This export can be done at the resource group level or for individual resources. Let's see how you can perform this action.

Using Azure PowerShell

In Azure PowerShell, you can use the `Export-AzResourceGroup` command to download or export the template of a resource group or resource. You need to specify the resource group using the `-ResourceGroupName` parameter to download the template for all resources in a resource group. Further, you can use the `-Resource` parameter to download a template of a single resource instead of exporting the entire resource group. For this command to work, you need to pass a local directory to the `-Path` parameter. The files will be downloaded to the directory you specify in the `-Path` parameter.

To download resource group template, use this:

```
Export-AzResourceGroup -ResourceGroupName <Name> -Path <path>
```

Similarly, to download for a single resource, use this:

```
$resource = Get-AzResource -ResourceGroupName <Name> -ResourceName <Name of resource>
Export-AzResourceGroup -ResourceGroupName <Name> -Resource $resource.Id -Path <path>
```

Figure 8.15 shows an example.

FIGURE 8.15 Exporting templates using Azure PowerShell

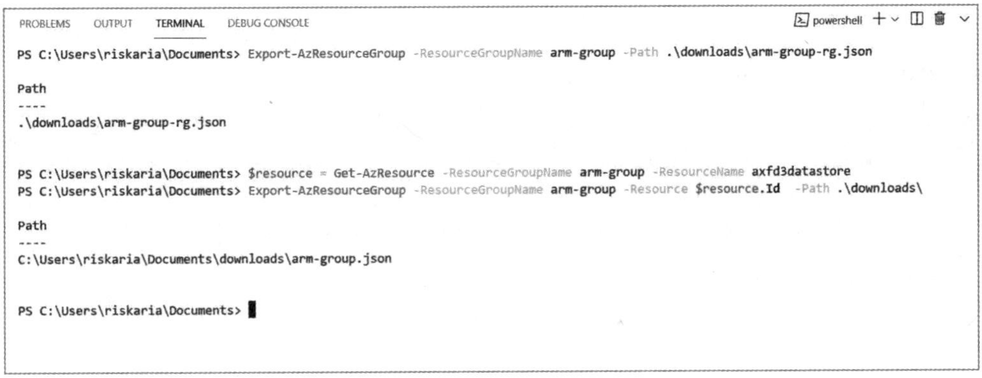

Now you will see how you can accomplish the same thing using the Azure CLI.

Using the Azure CLI

In the Azure CLI, you can use the `az group export` command to export the template. The command accepts two parameters; one is the name of the resource group, and if required, you can pass the resource ID of a resource to be specific.

You will take a similar approach that you have seen in the case of Azure PowerShell. To export all resources in a resource group, use this:

```
az group export -g {name of the resource group} --verbose > /path/to/file
```

Instead of exporting all resources in the resource group, you can select which resources to export. To export one resource, you need to find the resource ID of the resource and pass that to the command using the `--resource-ids` parameter. You can also pass multiple IDs to export multiple resources.

```
$resourceId=$(az resource show -n <name of resource> -g <resource-group> --resource-type <resource type> --query id)
az group export -g <resource group> --resource-ids $resourceId
```

The variable declaration method will vary depending upon the terminal and OS you are using. If you are using the Azure CLI on a Windows computer from a PowerShell terminal, then variables are declared as $variable. The Azure CLI on Linux or macOS from Terminal uses a variable name without the $ symbol for declaration.

As you can see in Figure 8.16, the template can be saved to a location file using the redirection method. If you don't specify any redirection, the template will be shown to you in the terminal itself. This is useful if you don't want to export and still need to take a peek at the template.

FIGURE 8.16   Exporting using the Azure CLI

```
PS C:\Users\riskaria\Documents> az group export -n arm-group --verbose > group.json
INFO: Command ran in 3.837 seconds (init: 0.368, invoke: 3.469)
PS C:\Users\riskaria\Documents> $resourceId=$(az resource show -n axfd3datastore -g arm-group --resource-type Microsoft.Storage/storage
Accounts --query id)
PS C:\Users\riskaria\Documents> az group export -g arm-group --resource-ids $resourceId
{
    "$schema": "https://schema.management.azure.com/schemas/2019-04-01/deploymentTemplate.json#",
    "contentVersion": "1.0.0.0",
    "parameters": {
      "storageAccounts_axfd3datastore_name": {
        "type": "String"
      }
    },
    "resources": [
      {
        "apiVersion": "2021-06-01",
        "kind": "StorageV2",
        "location": "eastus",
        "name": "[parameters('storageAccounts_axfd3datastore_name')]",
        "properties": {
          "accessTier": "Hot",
          "allowBlobPublicAccess": true,
          "encryption": {
            "keySource": "Microsoft.Storage",
            "services": {
              "blob": {
                "enabled": true,
                "keyType": "Account"
```

You can also export the templates from the Azure portal; let's see how that is done.

Using the Azure Portal

For downloading the template from the Azure portal, you need to navigate to the resource group where you have deployed the resource. You can follow these steps:

1. Log in to the Azure portal and navigate to the resource group.

2. Open the Deployments blade, and you will be able to see all the deployments made in the selected resource group (refer to Figure 8.17).

3. Select the deployment that you need to view the template for and click View Template.

4. The template will be shown to you, and you can click Download to download the template (refer to Figure 8.18).

FIGURE 8.17 Listing resource group deployments

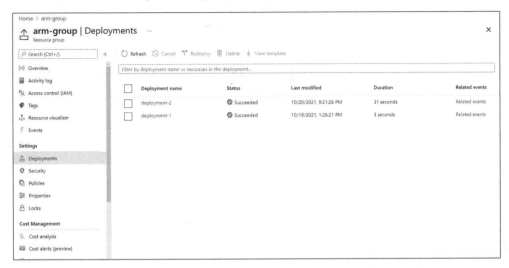

FIGURE 8.18 Downloading template

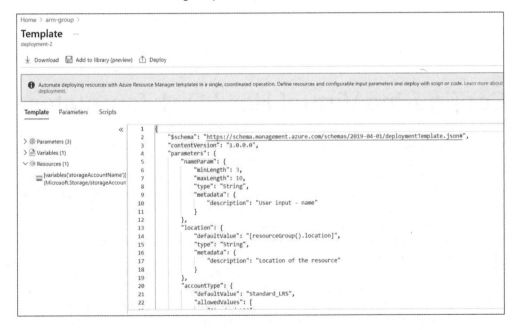

Let's say you are not able to find the right deployment as you don't remember the name of the deployment. You can always export by navigating the resource and use the Export Template options, as shown in Figure 8.19.

FIGURE 8.19   Export Template option

You have seen how you can export the template of a resource group or resource using Azure PowerShell, the Azure CLI, and the Azure portal. Next, you will see how you can create a virtual hard disk template to bring custom VM images to Azure.

Configuring Virtual Hard Disk Templates

In on-premises, whenever you create VMs, we used to follow the regular OS installation process. But in the cloud, you simply provide the username and password during the deployment; once the VM is deployed, you can use it with the username and password you provided during the deployment. If you have noticed, whenever you create a virtual machine in Azure, instead of the OS, you select the option image to select what OS you need. The image comprises the operating system (OS) and other preconfigured software.

Azure will be using this image to create the virtual hard disk. When you start our VM, the VM boots from this virtual hard disk. Further, you can install additional software on this VM per your requirements. When it comes to images, there are Microsoft-endorsed images, and there is a plethora of images available in Azure Marketplace.

In Azure Marketplace, different publishers publish their customized images so that you can directly use them without the need for further configuration. For example, if you need to host a WordPress site, then you need to create a Linux machine and install the Word-Press package, MySQL, Apache, and PHP. Instead of going through this hassle of installation and configuration, you can directly use any WordPress images available in the Azure Marketplace.

Let's say you are not able to find an image that matches your requirements or organization's standards in Azure Marketplace; then you can bring your own image into Azure and create VMs. Every image in Azure is a preconfigured version of a particular operating system. Before we discuss the deployment of VM from VHD, you need to understand the difference between a generalized image and a specialized image.

- **Generalized image:** You can create custom images by generalizing a virtual machine. You can build an image either using Hyper-V or using an Azure VM. Once the VM is ready, you will install the required software. After configuring the VM, you can create a generalized image of the VM. During this process, user accounts, passwords, and the hostname will be erased from the VM. However, the packages that are installed will be retained.

- **Specialized virtual image:** This is a copy of a live virtual machine. Usually, these images are created when you reach a specific state and are used as a recovery point. During the process, the user account, passwords, hostname, and configuration will be retained in the final image produced.

Now we will discuss how you can create an image of a VM in Azure using the Azure portal.

Create a VM from a VHD

You can create generalized or specialized virtual images from the Azure portal, Azure PowerShell, or the Azure CLI. To create an image from the Azure portal, you can navigate to the virtual machine and click the Capture option, as shown in Figure 8.20.

FIGURE 8.20 Capture a VM from the Azure portal

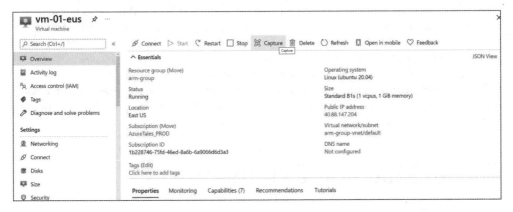

This will take you through the process for creating an image. Here you have to specify the image gallery, version, and other details of the image that you are planning to create. You can version the image inside an image gallery, and this can be used for future deployments. There is an option that is called Operating System State, and you will have two options: Generalized and Specialized (refer to Figure 8.21).

FIGURE 8.21   Creating an image of a VM

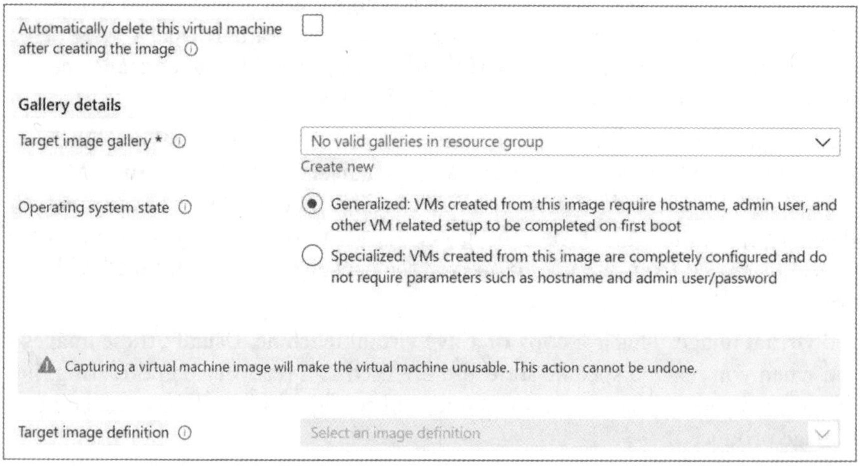

The portal gives a clear explanation of generalized and specialized. One thing you have to keep in mind is if you create a generalized image, the virtual machine will become unusable. This action cannot be reversed. Usually, you create a VM with the desired OS, install all the packages you need, and then create the generalized image. The portal shows a warning on the screen whenever you select the generalized option (refer to Figure 8.21). During the generalized image creation process, the VM will be deallocated, and a new image is created without any username, password, hostname, and other related setup. All this needs to be configured during the first boot. If you are selecting the specialized image, this won't affect the current state of the existing VM, and you can have a copy of the VM. This will be useful if you want to roll back to a certain stage in the configuration if something goes wrong.

Based on the requirements, you will be able to create a generalized or specialized image of our virtual machine. This image can be used for future deployments. In Figure 8.22, you can see a sample image created in the Azure portal.

You can use this image to create VMs or VMSS per your requirements. In certain scenarios, you might not need to create a custom image and may prefer to configure our VMs post-deployment. There are a set of tools that can be leveraged for this post-deployment configuration; let's understand more about this.

Virtual Machine Extensions

By now, you know how to create a VM and gain access to the VM. Let's say you want to create hundreds of VMs and want to configure them with a software or application. Creating and managing these VMs manually is a time-consuming and repetitive task. When you perform these actions repetitively, chances of mistakes are likely. You need to figure out a way by which you will be able to automate this whole thing and make your life easier.

FIGURE 8.22   Images in the Azure portal

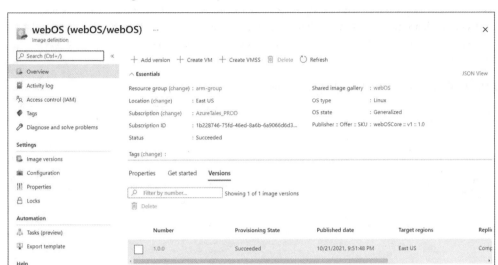

Honestly, manual configuration requires a lot of time, and it is quite boring. For each virtual machine, you need to create the VM, install the software, configure the software, perform security hardening (if required), and apply updates. There will be cases where you need to redeploy the architecture for testing or recovery. Software development teams use virtual machines for testing, and they need a new set of VMs with preconfigured software during every test cycle. It is not easy to deploy and configure machines manually for each test cycle. Also, if there is a regional failure, you should be able to deploy the architecture in another region. While trying to recover from the failure, you will not have the time to manually configure every virtual machine.

The solution for this is to use some automation tool. You can reduce the complexity of the architecture and pass the configuration as a script or configuration file to these automation tools. These tools will help with the configuration of the VM without any manual intervention. Since there is no manual work involved, the chances of mistakes are minimal. By leveraging these tools, your organization can become more cost effective and productive. In this section, we will introduce the concept of virtual machine extensions.

The post-deployment configuration and automation tasks on Azure VMs can be accomplished using small applications that are called *virtual machine extensions*. Azure VM extensions can be managed from Azure CLI, Azure PowerShell, the Azure portal, or Azure Resource Manager templates. The extensions can be bundled with the VM deployments or can be provisioned on any existing VMs.

You will be focusing on two main extensions: Custom Script for Linux Extension and the Desired State Configuration extension. These extensions are not the only ones available in Azure; there are also other extensions that we can use for monitoring, security, backup, and other virtual machine configurations. The extensions are offered by Microsoft for both Windows and Linux virtual machines, there are extensions provided by third parties as well.

If you navigate to the extension blade of an existing VM, you will be able to see the list of available extensions (refer to Figure 8.23). The list of supported extensions may vary depending upon the operating system of the virtual machine.

FIGURE 8.23 Virtual machine extensions

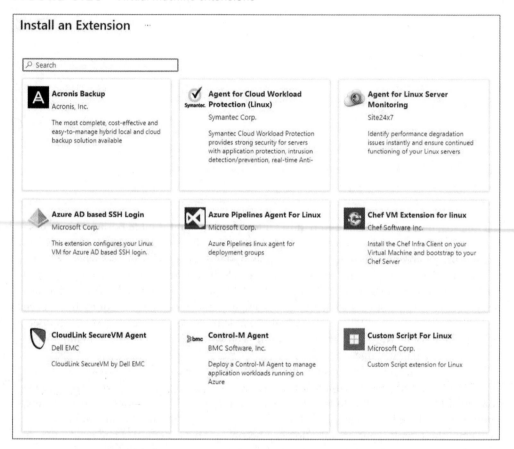

In Figure 8.23, you can see you can see the Custom Script for Linux extension in the search results. So, let's understand more about this extension and its purpose.

Custom Script Extension

As the name suggests, you can use the Custom Script for Linux Extension (CSE) to automatically invoke scripts and run them on virtual machines post-deployment. The script may include commands for configuration, and these commands will be executed on the VM once it is deployed.

You can install this extension from the Azure portal, as you saw in Figure 8.23. From an automated perspective, you can include this extension in your ARM template and have the script executed once the deployment is completed. The following is an excerpt from the ARM template showing the provisioning of CSE:

```
"properties": {
    "publisher": "Microsoft.Azure.Extensions",
    "type": "CustomScript",
    "typeHandlerVersion": "2.1",
    "autoUpgradeMinorVersion": true,
    "settings": {
      "fileUris": [
        "https://github.com/rithinskaria/customConfig/customScript.sh"
          ],
              "commandToExecute": "sh customScript.sh"
          },

    }
```

Here you can see that we are passing in the URL to the script using the `fileUris` property and then executing the script using the `commandToExecute` option. CSEs have 90 minutes to execute the script, so you need to make sure that the actions you specify in the script can be completed in 90 minutes. If the script takes longer than 90 minutes, it is marked as timed out. Also, your VM should be running to execute the script. One downside is if your VM requires a reboot, then CSE cannot continue the execution of the script as the execution process will be terminated during the reboot.

To make sure our VMs can overcome the reboot and execute the script, you have another extension called the Desired State Configuration (DSC) extension.

Desired State Configuration

In the case of CSE, you cannot deal with complex installation procedures such as reboots. Desired State Configuration helps you overcome this crisis and define a state for your virtual machines instead of writing scripts. Desired state configuration files are easy to interpret and implement.

You can define the state of a machine and enforce the state using the DSC extension handler. You could store these configuration files in Azure Storage, in internal storage, or even in source control. The handler is responsible for pulling the configuration and implementing the desired state on the virtual machine. Even if there are installations that require reboots, DSC will continue the execution of the remaining scripts after reboot.

Similar to the CSE implementation, you can add the DSC handler extension to the virtual machine from the Azure portal. You could also incorporate the extension in an ARM template and make sure the target machine achieves the desired state post-deployment. The following is an excerpt from the ARM template showing how to use the DSC extension:

```
"properties": {
        "publisher": "Microsoft.Powershell",
        "type": "DSC",
        "typeHandlerVersion": "2.9",
        "autoUpgradeMinorVersion": true,
        "settings": {
          "modulesUrl": "https://rithin.blob.core.windows.net/DSCModules/dsc.zip'",
          "sasToken": "artifactsLocationSasToken",
          "configurationFunction": "Configure"
            },
        "protectedSettings": {}
        }
```

In this template, you are storing the configuration in Azure Blob Storage and injecting that to the target virtual machine for the desired state configuration.

Summary

In this chapter, you studied Azure Resource Manager and Azure Resource Manager templates. As you know, ARM acts like a consistent management layer for resource management, and the ARM template is the declarative automation method for creating resources in Azure. You studied the template design, template modes, and template sections. Then you focused on different sections of an ARM template. Later, you started composing ARM templates using Visual Studio Code. The ARM extension in Visual Studio Code is a boon, and you can create code snippets easily using this extension. Also, you saw how you can export the template of a resource that is already deployed using the Azure portal, Azure PowerShell, and the Azure CLI.

Further, you studied how to create generalized and specialized virtual images in Azure. Using these images, you can create more virtual machines in Azure without the need to configure the VMs. Also, you explored Azure virtual machine extensions. Using extensions, you will be able to perform post-deployment configurations in an automated fashion. Mainly you studied two extensions: Custom Script for Linux Extension and Desired State Configuration extension. The advantage DSC has over CSE is it can be used for a configuration that requires complex procedures such as reboots. Both scripts can be incorporated into ARM templates, and the scripts can be pulled into the target VM for configuration after the deployment is completed.

When you are modernizing applications, it's recommended that you always take a PaaS-first approach. PaaS solutions offer more productivity, features, and better pricing than IaaS machines. From a shared responsibility model, PaaS requires less effort as most of the underlying infrastructure and runtime management tasks are done by Microsoft. In Chapter 9, "PaaS Compute Options," you will start exploring some PaaS solutions.

Exam Essentials

Learn about ARM and ARM templates.   Learn the function of ARM in resource management and resource automation using ARM templates.

Understand how to export templates.   Understand the process of exporting templates of resource groups and resources that are already deployed.

Learn how to create custom images.   Understand the concept of generalized and specialized virtual images. Also, understand how they can be created.

Understand VM extensions.   Learn the purpose of common VM extensions used for post-deployment configuration.

Review Questions

1. Which of the following is the correct format for ARM templates?
    A. MD document
    B. TXT document
    C. JSON document
    D. XML document

2. You are planning to create a resource group for testing using an ARM template. Which values are mandatory for the successful creation of the resource group? (Select two.)
    A. Location
    B. Size
    C. Subscription
    D. Tags
    E. Name
    F. Region

3. Which of the following is not a supported template scope? (Select all that apply.)
    A. Resource group
    B. Subscription
    C. Management groups
    D. Resource

4. You are using complete mode for deployment using an ARM template. Which of the following facts are true? (Select all that apply.)
    A. Existing resources are not affected.
    B. Existing resources will be autorenamed to accommodate the new.
    C. Existing resources will be destroyed, and resources described in the ARM template are deployed.
    D. The ARM template will stop deployment as it is not a supported mode.

5. Which command can be used to test the template before deployment?
    A. What-if operation
    B. New-AzResourceGroupDeploymentValidate
    C. New-AzTemplateValidation
    D. Verbose

6. You are designing an ARM template for the deployment of 10 VMs. You would like to pass the hostname, username, and password dynamically during the template run. Which of the following should be used to perform this action?

A. Use parameters.

B. Use functions and create a function to supply the hostname, username, and password.

C. Use variables.

D. This scenario is not possible using ARM templates.

7. You want to export the template of a resource using Azure PowerShell. The resource name is web-vm-01, and the resource group name is web-eus-dev-rg. For some reason when you use `Export-AzResourceGroup -ResourceGroupName web-eus-dev-rg -Resource web-vm-01 -Path /path/file.json`, the command fails. What could be the reason? You have Contributor role at the subscription scope.

A. You need to pass the resource ID, not the resource name.

B. You need to have the Owner role to export the resource.

C. You cannot use the local path; you need to provide a storage account name.

D. You need to use the Azure CLI for exporting resources.

8. You would like to install the Active Directory Domain Services role on a Windows Server. Once the role installation is completed, you would like to promote the server as a domain controller. After promotion, you would like to add a set of users and DNS records to servers. You need to repeat the same steps for five servers; they will represent five different domains. Which tool is best for this?

A. PowerShell ISE

B. Custom Script extension

C. Desired State Configuration extension

D. Bash

9. Your team manages parameters in a different file called `parameters.json`. How can you use this file when you run the template in PowerShell?

A. Use the `-TemplateFile` parameter

B. Use the `-TemplateParameterFile` parameter

C. Use the `-ParameterFile` parameter

D. Not possible; declare parameters in the template file itself

10. You are trying to declare the following `location` parameter and the template fails during the execution. What could be the problem?

```
"parameters": {
  "location": {
    "type": "string",
    "defaultValue": "eastus",
    "allowedValues": [
```

```
        "westus",
      "centralus",
      "northcentralus"
        ],
    "metadata": {
      "description": "Location of the resource"
        }
      }
    }
```

A. type needs to be changed to `location`.

B. The default value `"eastus"` is not part of the allowed list.

C. The North Central US region is unavailable.

D. You cannot use `allowedValues` and `defaultValue` at the same time.

11. Your manager asked you to design an ARM template for creating Cosmos DB accounts. As part of the requirements, there should be a parameter called `cosmosDbName`. The parameter needs to have a minimum of 5 characters and maximum of 11. You have written the following code; however, there is an error in the template. What could be the reason? (Select all that apply.)

```
"parameters": {
    "cosmosDbName": {
        "type": "string",
        "minValue" :5,
        "maxValue": 11,
        "metadata": {
        "description": "Name of the DB account"
            }
          }
      },
```

A. `defaultValue` is missing.

B. `minValue` and `maxValue` cannot be used with strings.

C. Replace `minValue` and `maxValue` with `minLength` and `maxLength`.

D. Use quotes for 5 and 11.

12. You are creating an Azure Key Vault using an ARM template. You need to make sure the Key Vault endpoint is displayed after deployment. How can you accomplish this?

A. Write a function to display the endpoint.

B. Store the value in a variable and use the `print()` function.

C. Use the `output` option to display an endpoint.

D. Run an API call and return JSON output.

13. You want to create a virtual machine. However, before creating the VM, you need to ensure that the NIC, NSG, virtual network, and public IP address are already created. How can you accomplish this using ARM templates? (Select all that apply.)

   A. Use the `dependsOn` option

   B. Deploy the resources one by one

   C. Write the template in the order you prefer

   D. Use the `orderBy` option

14. Which of the following syntax options is used by Azure Resource Manager?

   A. Imperative syntax

   B. Declarative syntax

   C. Correlation syntax

   D. Transformative syntax

15. What options do you have to deploy a template? (Select all that apply.)

   A. Azure portal

   B. REST API

   C. Azure CLI

   D. Azure cloud shell

16. You are planning to use custom images in virtual machine scale set stateless workloads. You need to create an image with the Apache web server installed on it and all the web files. Since you don't have any on-premises deployments, you plan to create this image in Azure. Which of the following is the right approach with minimal manual work?

   A. Create a snapshot of the VM

   B. Create a specialized image of the VM

   C. Create a generalized image of the VM

   D. Use the Azure portal

17. Which of the following extensions can be used to run a shell script on a Linux machine post-deployment?

   A. Desired State Configuration Extension

   B. Custom Script Extension

   C. Remote Console Extension

   D. Azure waagent Extension

18. Which of the following elements are mandatory for every ARM template? (Select all that apply.)

   A. `$schema`

   B. `contentVersion`

   C. `apiProfile`

   D. `variables`

    E. `parameters`

    F. `functions`

    G. `resources`

    H. `outputs`

19. How do you reference a `variable` called `storageAccount` in the name section for the storage account? The missing part is highlighted.

```
"resources": [
  {
    "name": "",
    "type": "Microsoft.Storage/storageAccounts",
    "apiVersion": "2021-04-01",
    "location": "eastus"
    "kind": "StorageV2",
    "sku": {
        "name": "Premium_LRS",
        "tier": "Premium"
          }
      }
    ],
```

    A. `"name": "variables('storageAccountName')"`

    B. `"name": "[variables['storageAccountName']]"`

    C. `"name": "(variables('storageAccountName'))"`

    D. `"name": "[variables('storageAccountName')]"`

20. You are designing an ARM template, and you need to make sure that instead of specifying the location for the resource, you need to deploy the resource directly to the location where the resource group is created. How can you reference resource group location in your ARM template?

    A. `"[resourceGroup.location]"`

    B. `"(resourceGroup().location)"`

    C. `"[resourceGroup[].location]"`

    D. `"[resourceGroup().location]"`

Chapter

9

PaaS Compute Options

MICROSOFT EXAM OBJECTIVES COVERED IN THIS CHAPTER:

✓ **Create and configure Azure App Service**

- Create an App Service plan
- Configure scaling settings in an App Service plan
- Create an App Service
- Secure an App Service
- Configure custom domain names
- Configure backup for an App Service
- Configure networking settings

✓ **Configure deployment settings**

✓ **Create and configure containers**

- Configure sizing and scaling for Azure Container Instances
- Configure container groups for Azure Container Instances
- Configure storage for Azure Kubernetes Service (AKS)
- Configure scaling for AKS
- Configure network connections for AKS
- Upgrade an AKS cluster

We started exploring the compute options available in Azure starting in Chapter 7. In the Chapter 8, we discussed the tools that can be used to automate the deployment of Azure resources. Virtual machines and virtual machine scale sets are classic examples of infrastructure-as-a-service (IaaS) solutions. As the name of the chapter suggests, we will explore the platform-as-a-service (PaaS) options available in Azure. According to the shared responsibility model, IaaS offers more control over the operating system; in fact, you can control every aspect of the operating system. However, in the case of PaaS, it offers a hosting environment for you to deploy your application without worrying about the underlying operating system and compute elements. The advantage is that the end customer can focus on more productive tasks than building the hosting environment. The hosting environment will be provisioned and managed by Microsoft Azure.

Let's take a deep dive and understand the common PaaS compute options. You will start with App Service plans.

Azure App Service Plans

Every App Service you create in Azure runs inside an App Service plan. If you are not aware of App Service, you can consider it as an instance of your application for the time being. In other words, every application you create runs inside an App Service plan. The plan is responsible for providing the compute resources for the application to run. The compute resources are similar to the server farms in conventional web hosting.

App Service plans are created at a regional scope. For example, if you create an App Service plan in East US, then a set of compute resources will be provisioned in East US for you. The compute resources will be used as a hosting environment to deploy your web apps. The pricing of every application is done at the App Service plan level, which means even if you don't deploy any applications to the plan, you will be still charged for the plan as the compute resources are provisioned. As long as there is enough room, you can deploy more applications to a single App Service plan.

From a cost optimization standpoint, it's better to use a single App Service plan for hosting multiple applications. As long as there are enough resources to handle the workload, you can keep adding applications to the same plan. It's important that you determine the number of resources required for the app to run before pushing it to the plan. An application with high resource utilization may collapse other co-existing applications in the plan if there is no room. This kind of overloading may lead to potential downtime of all applications deployed in your plan. You can think of creating a new App Service Plan when:

- You are deploying a resource-intensive application.
- You require independent scaling from other apps.
- Your app needs to be deployed to a different Azure region.
- You require a different operating system for your application stack.

The aforementioned criteria can be kept as a baseline for creating additional App Service plans. The App Service plan comes in different pricing tiers packed with different features and capabilities. Let's take a glimpse at the pricing tiers available for App Service plans.

Pricing Tiers

In the case of VMs, there were different VM families targeting a different set of workloads. Each of these VM families comes with different hardware combinations and capabilities. Likewise, in Azure App Service plans you use the pricing tier to determine the features that you get as part of the plan and also how much you pay for the plan. The following are the available pricing tiers:

- **Free and Shared:** This provides a shared environment for deploying applications. As this is a shared environment, your applications will be deployed to the same underlying VMs alongside other customer deployments. This tier is not recommended for production purposes and has time constraints. You can use this tier for development and testing purposes only, and these tiers are not backed up by any sort of SLA.

- **Basic:** This is ideal for applications with low traffic requirements, and at the same time, you don't need autoscaling or advanced features. This tier offers a dedicated environment unlike the Free and Shared. Also, it has a built-in load balancer for load balancing between instances.

- **Standard:** This is ideal for running production applications. It offers autoscaling and other advanced capabilities. Like Basic, you have a built-in load balancing for balancing traffic across the instances.

- **Premium:** This offers better performance for production apps. The key difference from Standard is that Premium offers SSD storage, faster processors, and double the memory-to-core ratio.

- **Isolated:** This provides a native virtual network integration and targets mission-critical workloads. This helps customers to run apps in a private, dedicated, and isolated environment.

Table 9.1 shows a quick comparison between these tiers and the set of supported features.

TABLE 9.1   App Service Plan: Pricing Tiers

	Free	Shared	Basic	Standard	Premium	Isolated
Target	Free environment	Shared environment for testing	Dedicated environment for dev/test	Run production workloads	Enhanced performance for production workloads	High-performance, security, and isolation
Web, mobile, or API apps	10	100	Unlimited	Unlimited	Unlimited	Unlimited
Disk space	1 GB	1 GB	10 GB	50 GB	250 GB	1 TB
Max: instances	X	X	Up to 3	Up to 10	Up to 30	Up to 100
Custom domain	X	✓	✓	✓	✓	✓
Autoscale	X	X	X	X	✓	✓
Hybrid connectivity	X	X	✓	✓	✓	✓
Virtual network connectivity	X	X	X	✓	✓	✓
Private endpoints	X	X	X	X	✓	✓
Compute type	Shared	Shared	Dedicated	Dedicated	Dedicated	Isolated

For Premium and Isolated plans, the maximum number of instances will vary based on the selected region. You can reach out to Microsoft Support and see if the limit can be increased.

In Table 9.1, you can see that autoscaling is supported from Standard tier onward. Let's understand how scaling is done in an Azure App Service plan.

Scaling

As you have seen in the case of virtual machine scale sets, you have two scaling methods available for App Service plans: scale out and scale up. From the Standard tier onward, you can enable autoscaling for your plan. The Basic tier supports manual scaling, while Free and Shared don't support any sort of manual or autoscaling features. The two workflows available for scaling are here:

Scale Up/Down   In the case of VMs, you scale up and down to increase or decrease the hardware specifications. Also, this process is practiced for resizing under-utilized resources. You can move from one tier to another using the scale-up/down option. For example, you started with Basic tier, and due to business requirements, you need more resources and capabilities like autoscaling. The solution here is to move to the Standard tier. Likewise, in the future if needed, you can scale to Premium as well. Conversely, you could come back to Basic if there are no business requirements. This will help you save costs. In short, the transition between tiers to increase or decrease the CPU, memory, and features is what is called *scale up/down*. If you are increasing, it is called *scale up*, and if you are downsizing, it's called *scale down*.

Scale In/Out   Increasing or decreasing the number of instances based on business requirements is termed as *scale in/out*. This process can be triggered manually, based on metric or schedule. In Table 9.1, you can see the maximum number of instances supported by each tier. For example, if you enable autoscaling for the Standard tier, you can have up to 10 instances. On the other hand, Isolated can scale out up to 100 instances, and where there is no business demand, it can scale in to the minimum number of instances you defined.

Let's create an App Service plan and explore these scaling options. Note that it's not necessary to create an App Service plan beforehand to create an App Service. You could create the App Service plan on the fly when you create the App Service. You will create a Free Tier and upgrade that to Standard and then explore the autoscaling options.

EXERCISE 9.1

Creating an App Service Plan

1. Sign in to the Azure portal and search for App Service plans. Click App Service Plans, which will take you to the App Service Plans blade.

2. Click Create to create the plan. Under the project details, you need to fill in the following details:

   - **Subscription**: Select a subscription.

   - **Resource group**: Select a resource group.

   - **Name**: Provide a name for the App Service plan.

   - **Operating system**: Select Linux or Windows. In this demonstration, you will be creating a Windows plan.

   - **Region**: Select an Azure region.

   - **Pricing Tier**: This is where you choose the pricing tiers that were discussed in Table 9.1. You will select Free Tier (F1) from the Dev/Test tab. Free Tier offers only 60 minutes/day for running your application.

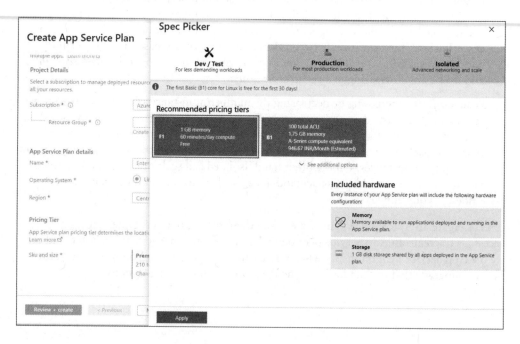

3. Once you have filled in all the details, you can click Review + Create.

4. After completing the validation, click Create, and the plan will be created. You need to wait for the plan to get provisioned.

5. Once the plan is provisioned, if you go back to the App Service Plan blade, you will be able to see that the plan is ready for consumption. Opening the plan will take you to the Overview, and you can see the basic details and metrics of the plan.

EXERCISE 9.1 *(continued)*

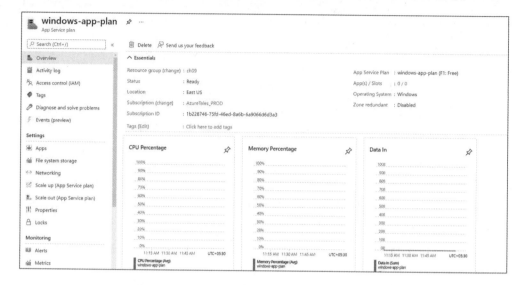

6. On the left menu, you will be able to see the Scale Up (App Service Plan) and Scale Out (App Service Plan) options. You will not be able to enable the scale-out options because manual scaling and autoscaling are not supported in the Free tier. Clicking Scale Out will throw an error message.

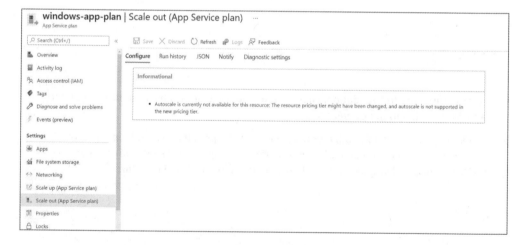

7. To configure the scale-out options, you need to upgrade the pricing tier. For this, you can click the Scale Up option. You will be presented with the set of available tiers. Let's upgrade to the Standard: S1 tier by going to the Production tab and then selecting S1.

S1 stands for Standard 1; there are others like S2 and S3 that offer more memory and disk space. Once you select S1, click Apply to save the configuration.

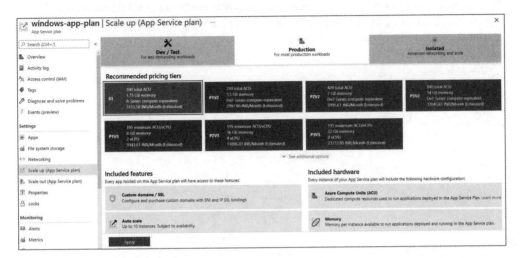

8. Now that you have upgraded to the Standard tier, let's see if you can configure the scale-out options. On the Scale Out blade, you will be presented with the Manual Scale and Custom Autoscale options.

9. Manual Scale can be used to specify the number of instances manually, and the plan will maintain that particular instance count. The slider can be used to control the number of instances.

10. Choosing Custom Autoscale will show the options to configure autoscaling. As you can see, the scaling can be executed based on a metric or a schedule. You saw a similar configuration with virtual machine scale sets.

11. As of now, you haven't deployed any apps to the plan. You simply created the compute resources. In the next section, we will talk about App Services, and then you will start deploying apps to this plan.

Azure App Services

Azure App Services refers to the applications, websites, mobile backends, or REST APIs that you deploy to the App Service plans. Earlier, App Services were known as web apps. In some documentation, you might still find this reference. So, if you see this term, that's an App Service. The following are some of the benefits offered by App Services:

- **Multiple frameworks and languages:** App Services support ASP.NET, Java, PHP, Node.js, Ruby, and Python. In addition, you can execute PowerShell and other scripts as background services.

- **DevOps integration:** Continuous integration can be set up with Azure DevOps, GitHub, and BitBucket.

- **Container support:** You can use images from Docker Hub or Azure Container Registry to run containerized applications. Continuous integration can be set up for these applications as well.

- **High availability:** From the Basic tier onward, you have support for a built-in load balancer. Autoscaling is available from the Standard tier onward.

- **Compliance:** ISO, PCI, and SOC compliance is available for App Services. You can easily integrate authentication providers such as Azure AD and other social logins (Google, Facebook, Twitter, and Microsoft) for authenticating users.

- **Marketplace templates:** Popular applications like WordPress, Joomla, and Drupal can be deployed to App Services from Azure Marketplace.

- **Visual Studio integration:** Publishing apps is seamless in the Visual Studio IDE. There are dedicated tools available for publishing and managing apps.

- **API and mobile features:** Extended features like CORS support, offline data sync, and push notifications are available for App Services.

- **Serverless code:** You can run functions or scripts on demand.

To explain the features of App Services, it's better to create an App Service and explain the features on the fly. In Exercise 9.2, you will be adding an App Service to the App Service plan that you created in Exercise 9.1.

EXERCISE 9.2

Creating an App Service Plan

1. Sign in to the Azure portal and search for *App Service*. Click App Service, and this will take you to the App Service blade.

2. Click Create to start creating an App Service. You need to fill in the basic details such as the subscription and resource group. In our demonstration, we are planning to use the App Service plan you created in Exercise 9.1, so you need to select the resource group to which the plan is created. Along with that, you need to add instance details.

3. In the instance details, you need to provide the following details:

   - **Name:** This is the name of the App Service, and it needs to be unique across Azure as the app will be created under the `azurewebsites.net` domain. For example, if the name of your app is ax0f45, then the URL will be `ax0f45.azurewebsites.net`.

   - **Publish:** You can choose either Code or Docker Container. If you choose Code, you need to select the runtime stack of our code, and if you are selecting Docker Container, you need to specify the image repository and image name.

   - **Runtime stack:** This is shown only if the publish is set to Code. You can select a runtime stack that includes various versions of .NET, Java, Node, PHP, Python, and Ruby. For this demo, you will select ASP.NET V4.8.

- **Operating system**: In our case, we selected ASP.NET V4.8, which is supported only on Windows. So, we will not be able to change the operating system. However, if you are choosing a cross-platform language like Python or .NET Core, then you will be able to switch between Linux and Windows.

- **Region**: Select an Azure region. This is important because if you are planning to associate an existing App Service plan, then you need to choose the same region as the plan.

4. If you have selected the resource group and region that contains an existing App Service plan that matches the selected operating system, then that plan will be autoselected. Otherwise, Azure will prompt you to create a new plan and select the pricing tier. It's easy to understand this by looking at the plan name. If the plan name is prefixed with "(new)," that means a new plan will be created. As you can see, we are using an existing plan; hence, the (new) prefix is missing. Again, if you need a new one to be created, you can choose the Create New option.

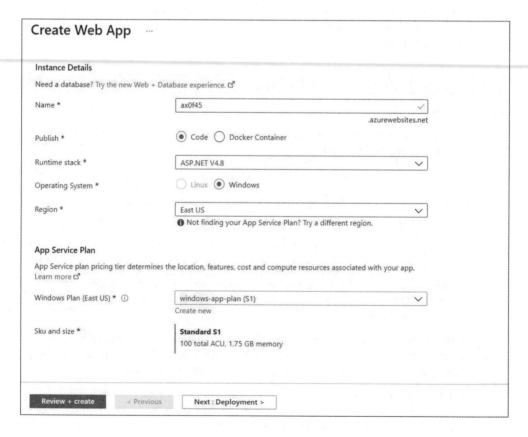

5. Clicking Next will be take you to the Deployment blade. Here you can set up continuous deployment. We will talk about the deployment options later in this chapter. As of now, we will go with the default value: Disable.

6. The next blade is Monitoring. This option will be enabled, and you will be asked to create an Application Insights instance. In our case, we are not planning to implement monitoring as of now, so you can change this to No.

7. Click Review + Create, and you will be taken to the validation phase. Once the validation is done, click Create to create the App Service, and wait for the service to get provisioned.

8. Once provisioned, navigate back to the App Services screen, and look for the new web app you created. Open the web app by clicking the name, and this will take you to the Overview blade.

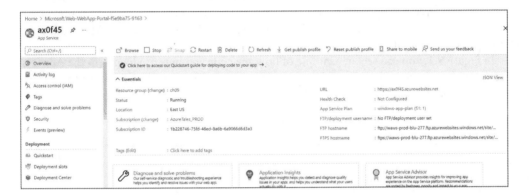

9. Click URL shown in the Overview blade, and this will take you to a landing page similar to the one shown here.

You have successfully created the App Service, and you are able to access it. Now the question is how to bring your code to Azure. There are multiple ways to bring code to Azure starting from FTP all the way to DevOps strategies. Next, you will see the continuous deployment options available for deploying the code to an Azure App Service.

Continuous Deployment

Azure App Services have out-of-the-box support for continuous integration and deployment from a variety of providers. You can continue using your favorite source control program, be it Azure DevOps, GitHub, BitBucket, or any local Git; you can seamlessly integrate this with Azure App Services. No complex configuration is required; all you need do is connect the repository to the Azure App Service. Whenever there is a code change, the Azure App Service will automatically sync all changes from the code repository. Furthermore, if you are already using Azure DevOps, you can create your build and release process, run the tests, build the release, and automatically deploy the code to the App Service every time your developers commit the code. The best part is all this happens seamlessly and implicitly without any sort of manual intervention.

In Figure 9.1, you can see an example of how the code commits are logged in the App Service and deployment is done. This example uses Azure Repos as the source control for storing the code.

FIGURE 9.1   Continuous deployment from Azure Repos

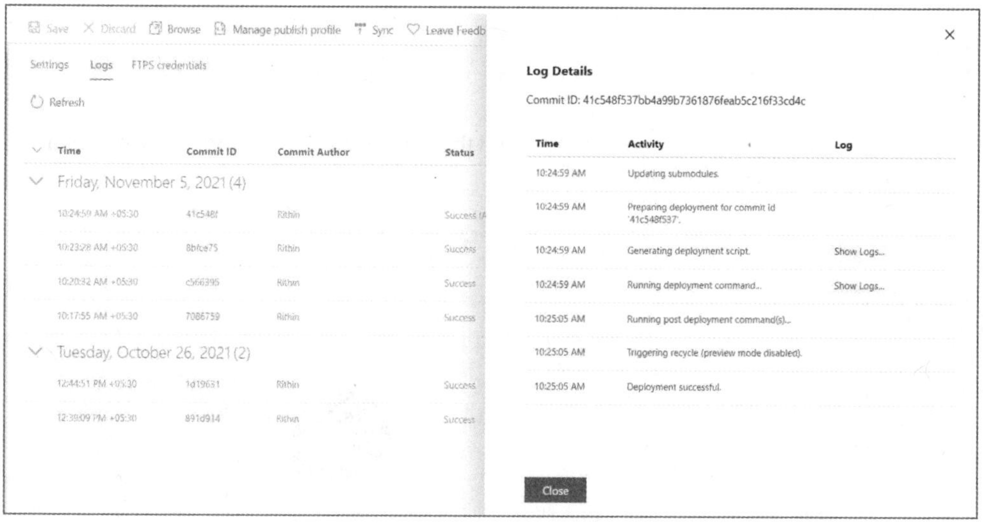

The deployment options can be classified into automated deployment and manual deployment. Let's see the set of tools or options available under each of these deployment options.

Automated Deployment

Automated deployment is also called *continuous integration*. In this process, the code will be updated with new code changes as soon as the developers commit. This process is ideal for pushing for new features and bug fixes in a repetitive and fast manner. During the process, the impact will be minimal on the end users. The following options are supported:

- **Azure DevOps:** You can push your code to Azure DevOps, and you can create our build and release process, run the tests, build the release, and automatically deploy the code to the App Service every time the developers commit the code.

- **GitHub:** Being one of the popular source control programs, Azure App Service supports continuous integration from GitHub directly. Any changes pushed to the main branch will be automatically deployed.

- **BitBucket:** This is another remote repository like GitHub. Based on the commits made in the repository, changes will be automatically pushed to the App Service.

- **Local Git:** If you are maintaining a local Git repository, you can connect that to Azure App Service. All committed changes will be reflected automatically.

Manual Deployment

You can manually push code to Azure via the following options. These options require you to manually push the code every time when you update the code.

- **FTP/S:** You can push code using FTP or FTPS; this is a traditional way of pushing code. Any FTP client can be used to push the code.

- **Visual Studio:** The Visual Studio IDE has tools that can be used to deploy the code, map dependencies, and configure monitoring for the App Service.

- **ZIP Deploy:** You can use any HTTP utility or command-line tool like curl to deploy the code to the App Service as a ZIP file.

- **Azure CLI:** Using the az webapp up command, you can package the code and deploy it. You can create a new App Service using the same command if you haven't created one.

- **External Git:** You can push code from an external Git to an Azure App Service.

- **OneDrive/Dropbox:** The code can be stored in OneDrive or Dropbox. You need to provide authorization to connect to OneDrive or Dropbox.

If you navigate to the Deployment Center blade of our App Service, you will be able to choose the source of the code (refer to Figure 9.2).

In Figure 9.2, you can see that there is a tab for FTPS credentials. Navigating to this tab will show the credentials for deploying the code via FTP/S. Now that you are familiar with the continuous deployment options, let's talk about the deployment slots.

FIGURE 9.2   Deployment Center blade

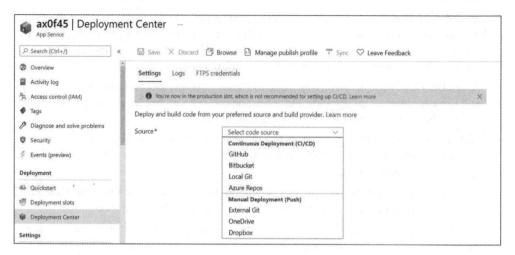

Deployment Slots

In the Standard, Premium, and Isolated App Service plan pricing tiers, you can use the deployment slots feature. You can use one slot for deploying your production code, and additional slots can be added to run your staging environments. Each slot will have its own unique URL, and you can easily swap the code and configuration between these slots. The following are the advantages of using separate staging and production slots:

- Code changes and configuration changes can be reviewed before swapping the staging slot to the production slots. This will help in avoiding code issues and bugs.

- This eliminates the downtime by ensuring that all instances of the slot are pushed to the production slot during the swap.

- During the swap, the previous code in the production slot moves to the staging slot, and code in the staging slot moves to the production slot. Since the last known good configuration is preserved, it will be easy for you to roll back.

- Offers DevOps capabilities, where you can swap slots automatically whenever a new code is committed to the slot.

Creating Deployment Slots

You can create new deployment slots with an empty or cloned configuration. There are certain properties that can be swapped, and some of them cannot be swapped during the swap process. The following list gives you an idea about which settings can and cannot be swapped:

These are settings that are swapped:

- General settings including the framework version

- App settings

- Connection strings
- Handler mappings
- Public certificates
- WebJobs content
- Hybrid connections
- Service endpoints
- Azure CDN

These are settings that are not swapped:

- Publishing endpoints
- Custom domain names
- Nonpublic certificates
- Scale settings
- IP restrictions
- Diagnostic settings
- Always-on configuration
- CORS
- Virtual network integration
- Managed identities

Microsoft is planning to remove some entries from the settings that are swapped, so it's a best practice to review the following document to get the updated list of settings:

`https://docs.microsoft.com/en-us/azure/app-service/`
`deploy-staging-slots`

Deployment slots can be created by navigating to the Deployment Slots blade of your App Service. As shown in Figure 9.3, you will be able to create a new slot by clicking the Add Slot button. You can give a name for the slot; for example, if you name the slot ax0f45-dev, then this slot name will be appended to the App Service name in the `azurewebsites.net` domain. In our case, it will be `ax0f45-ax0f45-dev.azurewebsites.net`, where `ax0f45` is the name of the App Service and `ax0f45-dev` is the name of the slot.

In Figure 9.3, you can see that you have an option to clone the settings or start from scratch. Once you click Add, the slot will be created. This slot can be treated as an individual app and will be consuming resources from our App Service plan. If you are planning to add more slots, make sure that you have enough resources in the plan to accommodate these slots. Otherwise, due to a lack of resources, your production slot will be affected. Let's see how you can swap the slots in the App Service.

FIGURE 9.3   Adding a deployment slot

Swapping Deployment Slots

After creating the slot, if you navigate back to the Deployment Slots blade, you will be able to see the production slot and the staging slot. If you notice in Figure 9.4, you can also control the amount of traffic that can be sent to each slot. In this case, you have set the traffic 50 percent; that means 50 percent of the users will hit the production slot, and the remaining 50 percent will be going to the staging slot. This is ideal if you would like to send a portion of your customers to the new app to evaluate the new features and share feedback. All the load balancing will be handled by the App Service, and you don't have to create any additional load balancers. If you don't want your users to access the staging slot, you can route 100 percent of the traffic to the production slot.

FIGURE 9.4   Identifying deployment slots

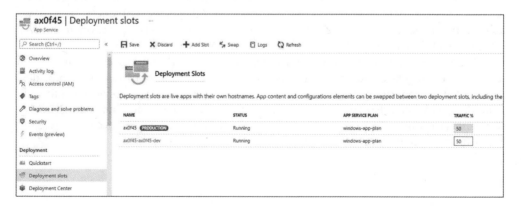

In Figure 9.4, you can see that there is an option to swap the slots. Clicking the Swap button will take you to the swap pane. As you can see in Figure 9.5, you will be asked to provide the source and destination slots. The portal is intuitive and will show us the configuration changes that will happen during the swap process. Clicking Swap will swap the slots.

FIGURE 9.5   Swapping deployment slots

Once the swap is completed, the code that was in the staging slot will be moved to the production slot. Any user accessing the web app using the URL will be using the new code. The previous production code will be moved to the staging slot, and you can still access this code by going to the URL of the slot. In this case, you have not made any code changes to your application, so the swap will make no difference to your application. However, in real-world scenarios, the deployment slot can be used to push the code in the staging environment to the production environment without any downtime.

Now that you know how to handle code in the slots, let's see how you can secure your application by integrating with an authentication provider.

Securing App Service

If you are deploying your application to a virtual machine, you need to write code to integrate with an authentication provider. For example, let's say you want your end users to sign in using Facebook and Google. This requires you to write code for integrating this authentication provider by exporting the necessary libraries and plugins. In the case of an App Service, it has a built-in authentication and authorization support. You can integrate supported authentication providers without adding any code to your application. The following are the options supported in Azure App Service:

- **Allow anonymous requests:** This is the default action, and users will be able to access your application without supplying any credentials. For accessing the APIs, you don't need to provide any information in the HTTP headers as the app supports anonymous access.
- **Allow only authenticated requests:** This option is used when you are adding an identity provider to your application. All users need to complete the authentication to access the app.

Adding Identity Provider

As mentioned, if you would like to enable authentication support for your application, then you need to add an identity provider. This can be achieved by navigating to the Authentication blade of your App Service (refer to Figure 9.6). Supported providers include Microsoft, Facebook, Google, OpenID Connect, and Twitter.

FIGURE 9.6   Adding an identity provider

Clicking Add Identity Provider will let you choose from the supported providers. Choosing Microsoft requires you to create a service principal in Azure AD; this will be used for authentication purposes. For other platforms, you need to create service accounts in the respective developer portal and update the App Service with the client ID and client secret.

For easier demonstration, you can choose Microsoft and integrate Azure AD sign-in to your application. Selecting Microsoft will take you to the app registration poral where you need to specify the account types and name of the app registration that will be created in Azure AD (refer to Figure 9.7).

FIGURE 9.7 Adding Azure AD authentication

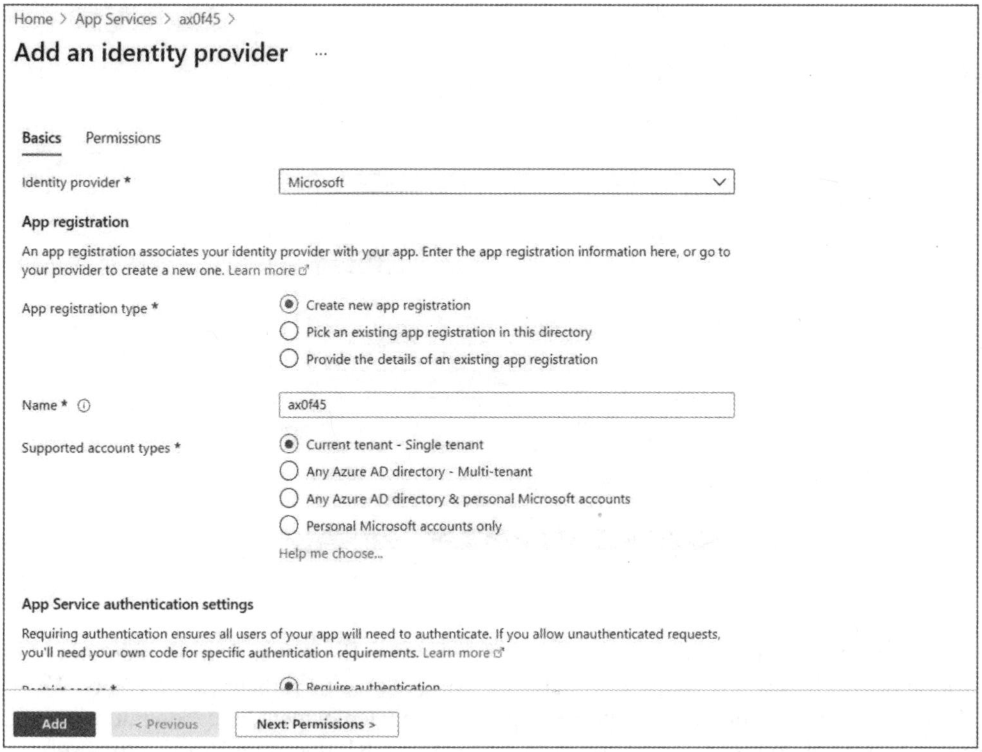

You can go with the default configuration and add the identity provider. Now, if you navigate to the browser and try to access your application, it will request you to sign in using your Azure AD credentials, as shown in Figure 9.8.

Since you have selected a single tenant as the account type, only the users from this tenant will be able to access the application. In this scenario, you restricted the access to the entire application, which might not be the case for all applications. There will be cases where you need to show the home page and then authenticate access to certain paths. This can also be accomplished.

The authentication and authorization module in App Service is responsible for the following actions:

- Authenticates users with the selected identity providers
- Validates, stores, and refreshes the tokens
- Manages the authenticated session
- Injects identity information to all HTTP request headers

FIGURE 9.8   Verifying Azure AD authentication

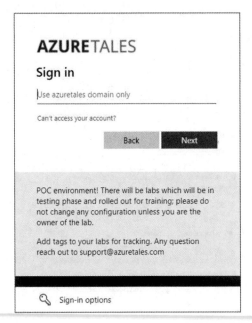

You can enable application logging and get insights into the authentication and authorization traces. This will be helpful in analyzing issues related to authentication errors. We talk more about monitoring in Chapter 8, "Automation, Deployment, and Configuration of Resources." As of now, our application is created with a URL that is under the azurewebsites.net domain; to add the branding, you need to use your own domain. Let's see how you can add custom domains to your application.

Custom Domains

Adding custom domain names to your application offers several advantages such as they are easy to remember, they offer branding, and they enable easier integration with other services. As you already know, if you create an app with the name myapp01, then your URL will become myapp01.azurewebsites.net. For production apps, most of the customers prefer to use a custom domain name rather than the default one.

When it comes to the configuration, the following are the steps you need to follow:

- **Register your domain:** If you haven't already reserved your domain, the easiest way to get one is from the Azure portal. You must pay a fee for this purchase, though. In Figure 9.9, you can see that there is an option to buy App Service domains. Let's say you already own a domain that you purchased from another domain registrar like Go Daddy; you can use that as well. The advantage of using App Service domains is that the DNS zones will be created in the Azure portal, and it will be easy for you to manage the records without the need to go to any third-party websites.

- **Create DNS records:** You can use an A or CNAME record to map the App Service to your domain. You can choose one of the available options and create a record. If you are choosing an A record, Azure will show you the IP address that needs to be mapped to the A record. In the case of CNAME, you can add a CNAME for the App Service URL (`azurewebsites.net`).

- **Validation:** Once the record is created, you need to run the validation to make sure that the record is in place. Be sure to test it.

Figure 9.9 shows how a custom domain is mapped to the Azure App Service. Depending on the hostname type that you are selecting, the portal will show you the records that need to be added to your DNS domain.

FIGURE 9.9   Mapping a custom domain to the app

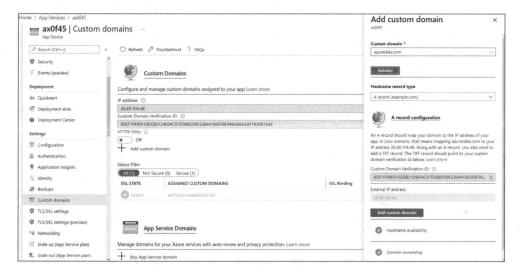

Please note that the custom domain mapping is available only in paid tiers of App Service plans. If you are not able to add a custom domain to your app, it's time to upgrade to one of the paid tiers.

So far, you have seen different features associated with App Services such as deployment slots, securing, and custom domains. Let's cover one more feature, i.e., backup.

Backup

Since you are hosting mission-critical applications in Azure App Services, it's important to know about the options available for backup and restore. As the name suggests, the Backup and Restore feature can be used to create a backup manually or on a schedule and restore them in the case of a catastrophic failure. Like a virtual machine backup, you can define a policy for your backup, which includes the schedule and retention period. Using the restore option, you can roll back the app to a previous state by overwriting the existing application data. Also, you can restore to a different app if needed.

Backup operations can back up the following data:

- Configuration of the app
- Content of files
- Database connected to the app, supporting SQL Database, Azure Database for MySQL, Azure Database for PostgreSQL, and MySQL in-app

The following are considerations while using the backup and restore functionality:

- The feature requires having the Standard or Premium tier of Azure App Service plan to utilize the backup and restore feature.
- The backup is taken to a storage account; hence, you need to have a storage account and container in the same subscription you want to back up. Every backup you take comprises a `.zip` file and an `.xml` file. The `.zip` file contains the backup data, and the `.xml` file acts like a manifest for the contents of the `.zip` file. You can unzip the `.zip` file and browse the files or push to another App Service without performing the restore operation.
- The default backup is a full backup. During the restore process, all the content in the App Service is replaced by the backed-up content. Files that are not part of the backup will be deleted.
- Partial backup is also supported. You can specify which files need to be backed up in the case of a partial backup. During the restore of a partial backup, any content in the excluded directories remains untouched; only content that is part of the backup gets overwritten.
- The feature supports the exclusion list to exclude files and directories from backup.
- The backup size can be up to 10 GB of app and database content.
- Backing up to storage accounts behind a firewall is not supported as of now.
- TLS-enabled databases are not supported, and storage accounts using a private endpoint are not supported as of now.

You can configure the Backup and Restore options from the Azure portal by navigating to the Backup blade of the App Service (refer to Figure 9.10).

As you can see in Figure 9.10, you need to configure a storage account for setting up the backup. Also, the option to enable a scheduled backup and database backup is visible.

In this section, you saw how you can create an App Service and configure various features such as deployment slots, custom domains, authentication, continuous integration, and backup. With that, you are moving on to the next service: container instances.

FIGURE 9.10   Backing up an App Service

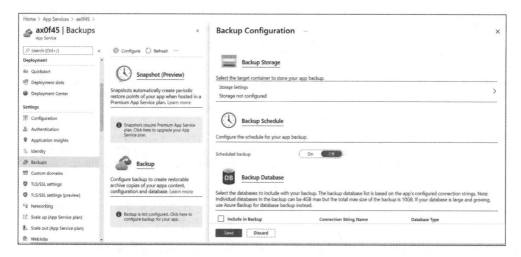

Container Instances

Containers took virtualization of computing resources to the next level. Virtual machines run on specialized software called *hypervisors*. In traditional virtualization, you used to create separate virtual machines for isolating environments. For example, if you needed to run a web server, you needed to create a Linux or Windows VM and then install Apache or IIS on top of that. If you needed multiple environments for testing purposes, you needed to create multiple virtual machines. The drawback with this approach is that the resource utilization will be high as the footprint of the VM is large. To understand the concept clearly, let's take look at the comparison between container and virtual machines (refer to Table 9.2).

TABLE 9.2   Comparison Between Virtual Machines and Containers

Feature	Virtual Machines	Containers
Isolation	Strong isolation is offered between different virtual machines and the host operating system.	Lightweight isolation from other containers and host. Not offering a strong isolation as compared to VM.
Operating system	Runs a full-fledged operating system including kernel and all binaries.	Customized with required services and runs only the user mode portion of an operating system.
Footprint	Requires more resources as you are running a full-fledged operating system.	Lightweight as you are only running the required binaries.

TABLE 9.2 Comparison Between Virtual Machines and Containers *(continued)*

Feature	Virtual Machines	Containers
Deployment	Using the hypervisor console. For example, Hyper-V Manager, VMware vCenter, etc.	Deployed using a container runtime. For example, Docker. Further you can use orchestrators like Kubernetes.
Persistent storage	Uses a VHD for storing the OS files and data. File shares can be also mounted, which can be consumed by multiple VMs.	Container storage is ephemeral. In Azure, you can use Azure Disks and Files to create persistent storage.
Fault tolerance	VMs can fail over to another server in a cluster.	Containers can be quickly re-created using orchestrators in case of a failure.
Deployment time	Takes two to three minutes on an average.	Quick (mostly less than a minute).
Image size	Most operating systems are in gigabyte size.	Mostly in megabtye size.
Image source	Official websites. In Azure you can use Microsoft-endorsed images, Marketplace images, and custom VM images.	Images can be stored in Docker Hub, Azure Container Registry, and private repositories.

In Figure 9.11, you can see how virtual machines are different from containers from an architectural perspective.

Containers serve the same purpose of VMs, which is packaging your application along with all the required dependencies. The advantage is they are lightweight in size and can be used to test multiple applications quickly without the need to deploy multiple virtual machines. In the case of VMs, they are virtualized on top of a hypervisor running on the host operating system. However, in the case of containers, they are using a container runtime to run the containers. The container runtime is software that is running on the host machine like the hypervisor. Now that you are aware of the differences, let's learn more about one of the popular container runtimes, Docker.

Docker

In Figure 9.11, you saw that containers are deployed with the help of a container runtime that is hosted on the host OS. Docker is an example of a container runtime that empowers developers to containerize their application. Every container is a package that comprises application code, runtime, system tools, and configuration.

FIGURE 9.11 Architectural comparison between virtual machines and containers

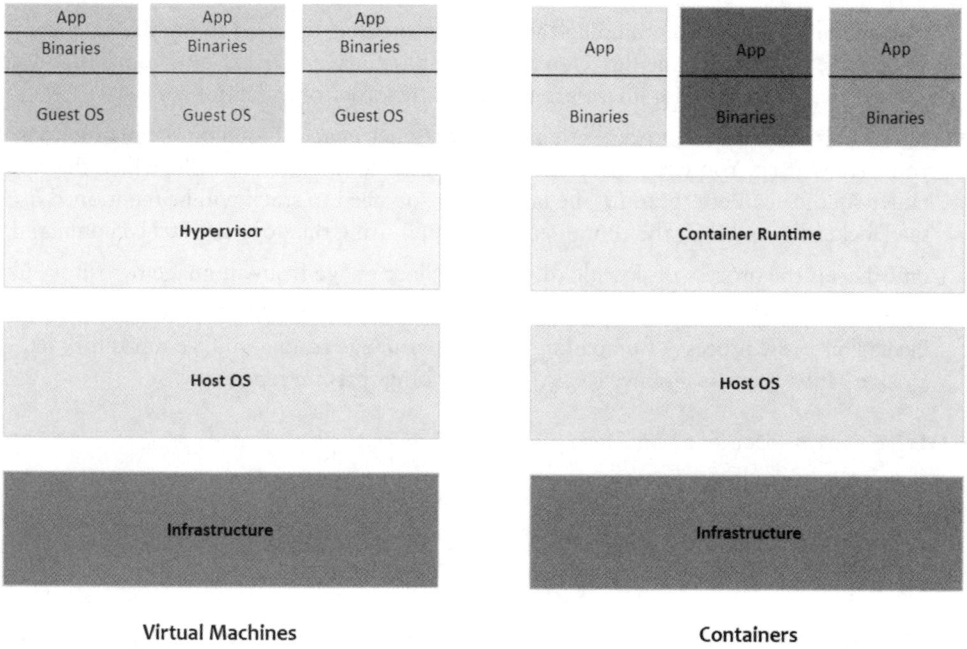

Virtual Machines   Containers

Figure 9.12 shows the Docker architecture. In this architecture, the host machine that is considered the Docker host is responsible for hosting the Docker engine. Users or developers will be interacting with the Docker engine via the Docker client. The Docker client translates the requests and sends this to the Docker engine via the REST API. Docker Engine oversees the local images, downloads images from Docker Hub, and deploys containers based on requests from the end users. Docker Hub is an online image repository where thousands of images are uploaded by different publishers. Once the image is downloaded, Docker Engine maintains a local copy of it so that the next time it can deploy the container without downloading the image.

The Docker platform is available for both the Linux and Windows operating systems; also, it can be hosted on Azure. In Azure, you can leverage Azure container instances to run a Docker container without the need to manage the infrastructure. The underlying infrastructure will be managed by Azure, and you can run your containerized applications easily.

When you work with Docker, there are certain terminologies that you need to be familiar with. The following are the key terminologies:

- **Container:** This refers to an instance of a Docker image. Every container can be used to represent the execution of a single application, process, task, or service.

- **Container image:** This is the package from which the container is created. The package includes a manifest of the dependencies and configuration. Usually, the container image is derived from a base image by stacking different configurations on top of another. Once the image is created, it's immutable.

- **Dockerfile:** This is a file containing the set of instructions required to build a Docker image. The first line will be the reference to the base image. Further operations that need to be executed on the base image are written in the order of execution.

- **Build:** This refers to the process of building container images based on the instructions you have written. You write these instructions to a file called Dockerfile, which the container runtime can interpret. All the layers that you need to stack will be mentioned in the Dockerfile, and then the container can be built using the `docker build` command.

- **Pull:** This is the process of downloading a container image from an image repository like Docker Hub, Azure Container Registry, or any other private repository.

- **Push:** This is the process of uploading a container image from an image repository like Docker Hub, Azure Container Registry, or any other private repository.

FIGURE 9.12   Docker architecture

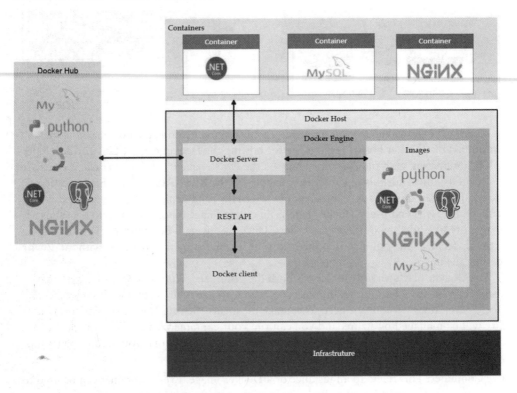

I hope that this will give you some basic understanding of containers and why they are popular nowadays. Now, you will see how you can deploy containers in Azure.

Azure Container Instances

As you have seen in the Docker architecture, you can deploy containers to a virtual machine running on Azure. Since virtual machines are an infrastructure-as-a-service solution, more administration and intervention from the user side is required. On top of that, along with virtual machine updates, you need to manage the container runtime updates. When you modernize applications, Microsoft recommends that you always follow a PaaS-first strategy instead of relying on IaaS. Azure container instances offer the easiest way to run containers in Azure without the need to manage any VMs or infrastructure.

Containers are widely adopted to package, deploy, and manage cloud applications. Being a platform-as-a-service solution, Azure container instances offer the simplest way to run containers in Azure. You don't have to create virtual machines or install a container runtime; all you need to do is specify the location of your container image, and Azure will create the instance for you. Figure 9.13 shows the architecture of an Azure container instance. In the architecture, the image is pulled from the Azure container registry, and you can also open access to the Internet, for example, accessing a web server over port 80.

FIGURE 9.13 Azure container instance architecture

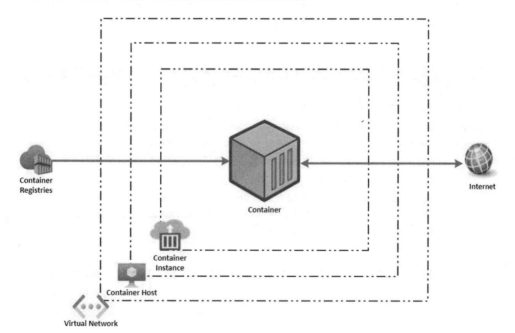

The following are the features of an Azure container instance:

- **Faster start-up:** Containers are lightweight, and they can start in seconds without the need to create virtual machines.

- **Public IP connectivity:** Containers can be used to deploy Internet-facing workloads.

- **DNS labels:** It supports creation of DNS labels, ideal for Internet-facing workloads.

- **Scaling:** Based on the resource demands, container nodes can be scaled dynamically.

- **Persistent storage:** This supports mounting Azure Files instances as persistent storage.

- **Linux and Windows containers:** The scheduling of Linux and Windows containers is supported.

- **Container groups:** Multiple containers can be hosted together in a group so that you can manage the lifecycle and share resources easily.

- **Virtual network support:** Container instances can be deployed to Azure virtual networks.

In Exercise 9.3, you will build a container image from Dockerfile and push it to Azure Container Registry, and you will create a container instance using the image. For this exercise, you will be using the Azure CLI for building the container and pushing it to Azure Container Registry. The plan is to build a container image with nginx as the base image and update the default landing page with a custom HTML page.

EXERCISE 9.3

Building and Running Containers in Azure

1. If you have the Azure CLI installed locally, you can use that to build the container image. Otherwise, you can go with the Azure cloud shell. In this demonstration, you will be using the cloud shell as it is easier. Open the Azure portal and start the cloud shell.

2. The cloud shell has a built-in code editor that you can use for writing your Dockerfile. For this, in the shell, type code Dockerfile. Here, Dockerfile is the name of the file you are going to create. You will get a code pane as shown here.

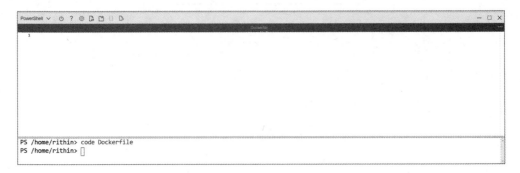

3. You need to add the following lines to the file:

```
FROM nginx:latest
COPY ./index.html /usr/share/nginx/html/index.html
```

4. The code means you are pulling the latest version of nginx as the base image and then you are copying a local file to a location inside the container. The /usr/share/ nginx/html/ location is where nginx stores the default landing page.

5. Save the file using Ctrl+S and quit the editor by tapping Ctrl+Q.

6. In the code, we mentioned that there is an index.html file. However, you haven't created that yet. In the home directory, create the index.html file using code index.html.

7. An editor window similar to the previous screen will open, and you need to input the following HTML code:

```
<html>
    <body>
        Hello all
    </body>
</html>
```

8. You can add any HTML code you prefer; this is just an example. Save the file by hitting Ctrl+S and quit the editor using Ctrl+Q.

9. If you are following along, then you should have the Dockerfile and index.html file in your home directory.

```
PowerShell ∨   ⊙  ?  ⊛  ⤓  ⤒  {}  ⤒
PS /home/rithin> ls -lh
total 8.0K
lrwxrwxrwx 1 rithin rithin 22 Nov  9 09:25 clouddrive -> /usr/csuser/clouddrive
-rw-r--r-- 1 rithin rithin 69 Nov  9 07:53 Dockerfile
-rw-r--r-- 1 rithin rithin 55 Nov  9 09:38 index.html
PS /home/rithin>
```

10. Before building the container image, you need to create a container registry to save the image. You will create a resource group and a container registry using the following commands. You can change the name of the resource group, container registry, and location accordingly. Please make sure you use a unique name for the container registry as the name is unique across Azure.

Syntax:

```
az group create -n <name of rg> -l <location>
az acr create -g <rg name> -n <ACR name> --sku <sku> --admin-enabled true
```

Example:

```
az group create -n containers -l eastus
az acr create -g containers -n acrch09ex3 --sku Basic --admin-enabled true
```

11. The cloud shell will show you a lengthy JSON response if the creation was successful. Now you will build the container image and push it to the container registry. You can use the command az acr build.

Syntax:

```
az acr build -t <image:tag> -r <name of ACR>  -f <file> <path>
```

Example:

```
az acr build -t website:v1 -r acrch09ex3  -f Dockerfile .
```

12. In the previous command, you need to specify the image name in the format image:tag. You can use a tag to label the images. Here we mention the name of the image as website and the tag value as v1, which means that this is version 1 of the website image. You can use any tag you prefer to label the images. Since you are executing this command from the home directory, the path to the Dockerfile can be referenced using a period (.). The period means the current directory from which you are executing the command. If you are executing this command from some other directory, then you need to specify the path to the Dockerfile. If the build was successful, you will see a message similar to the following one.

```
PowerShell ∨   ⏻ ? ⚙ ⎙ 🗗 {} ⎙
2021/11/09 09:50:55 Successfully populated digests for step ID: build
2021/11/09 09:50:55 Step ID: push marked as successful (elapsed time in seconds: 7.119417)
2021/11/09 09:50:55 The following dependencies were found:
2021/11/09 09:50:55
- image:
    registry: acrch09ex3.azurecr.io
    repository: website
    tag: v1
    digest: sha256:faf35b124d07cb4b4782ab9712258e87141c3c95668a53a4b5260a064c25ac34
  runtime-dependency:
    registry: registry.hub.docker.com
    repository: library/nginx
    tag: latest
    digest: sha256:644a70516a26004c97d0d85c7fe1d0c3a67ea8ab7ddf4aff193d9f301670cf36
  git: {}

Run ID: ca1 was successful after 17s
```

13. Now that the image is built and pushed to the container registry, you will create a container instance from the Azure portal with this image. Sign in to the Azure portal and search for *container instances*. Click Create, and the portal will take you to the creation wizard.

14. You need to provide the following details:

   ▪ **Subscription**: Select a subscription.

- **Resource group**: Select a resource group.

- **Container name**: Provide a name for the container instance.

- **Region**: Choose East US or any region you prefer.

- **Image source**: You have three options: Quickstart Images, Azure Container Registry, or Docker Hub or other registry. Since our image is in Azure Container Registry, you will select that.

- **Registry**: Select the registry you created in step 10.

- **Image**: The image will be selected automatically. If not, select the image you created from the Dockerfile.

- **Image tag**: This will be selected automatically. If not, select the tag of the image you created.

- **OS type**: This is not editable; it is populated based on the image you select.

- **Size**: You can choose the number of vCPUs, memory, and GPU. You can go with the default values.

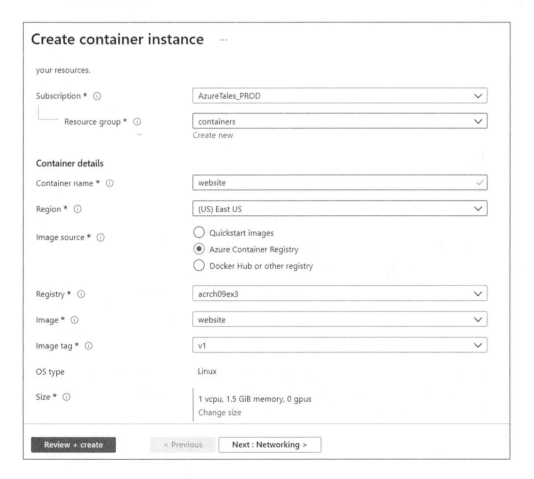

15. Clicking Next will take you to the Networking tab. You can set the Networking type to Public as you need to access this container from the Internet. For now, you will leave the DNS label as blank. If you fill in the DNS label, you will get a DNS record for the instance under the `<region>.azurecontainer.io` domain. Also, make sure that port 80 is added to the Ports section.

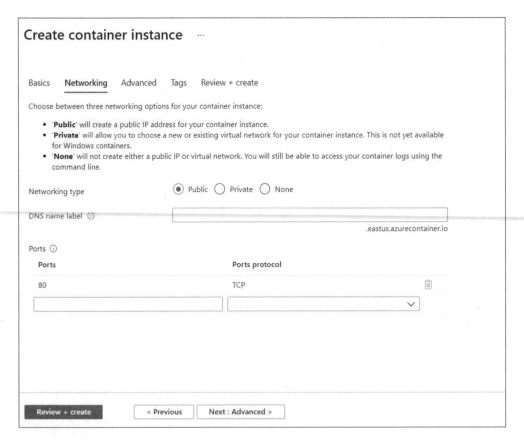

16. Next is the Advanced tab, but you don't need to make any configuration changes here. Click Review + Create to trigger the validation. Once the validation is completed, proceed with the creation of the container instance. One thing you will notice here is that the deployment time is much less compared to that of a virtual machine. You will wait for the instance to get created.

17. Once the instance is created, navigate back to the Container Instances blade, and you can see the new instance you created. Click the instance name, and it will take you to the Overview blade. Copy the Public IP address and try it in your browser.

18. You will be able to see the rendered HTML code that you added to the `index.html` file during the image build process.

With that, you have successfully created a container image, pushed it to Azure Container Registry, and pulled it to create your container instance. Now, you will learn about container groups.

Container Groups

A *container group* is a collection of containers that are scheduled on the same host machine. Since they are scheduled to the same host machine, you can share lifecycles, resources, local networks, and persistent storage volumes. In the next section, we will talk about pods in Kubernetes; container groups are a similar concept. If you look in the Azure portal, you won't find an option to create container groups; they can be deployed only via a YAML file or ARM templates. An ARM template is the recommended method if you are planning to use services like Azure Files, as the integration is easier in ARM. On the other hand, YAML requires more steps for integration. Nonetheless, it's recommended if you are deploying container instances only without any service dependencies. Figure 9.14 is a pictorial representation of container groups.

From the diagram it's evident that a container group has the following attributes:

- Scheduled on the same host machine
- Has a DNS label assigned
- Public IP exposed on a port
- Multicontainer; one is exposed on port 80 to the Internet and the other one listens on port 1433.
- Two File shares that will act as the persistent storage

The following are some scenarios where you can leverage container groups and multi-containers:

- One container runs the web server application, and the other container pulls the latest code from the source control.

- One container runs the application, and the other container is responsible for pulling logs and metrics from the application container.

- One container is running the web server application, and the other one is running a database container.

Azure Kubernetes Service

Kubernetes is a platform that is very popular and is used for managing containers at scale. Along with container orchestration, it helps in managing associated dependencies such as networking and storage components. In Kubernetes, you follow declarative deployments like ARM templates.

Using Kubernetes, you can orchestrate and manage the availability of applications. Both stateful and stateless applications can be orchestrated using Kubernetes. With the wide adoption of microservices architecture, Kubernetes is gaining more popularity. Since Kubernetes is an open source platform, you can build your applications using your preferred language, operating system, frameworks, and libraries. Existing CI/CD pipelines can be integrated with Kubernetes easily.

You can download the Kubernetes binaries and create a cluster using Azure VMs; we call this type of cluster *unmanaged clusters*. AKS, on the other hand, is a managed cluster. Since it's managed, most of the cluster and core management tasks will be taken care of by the Azure platform. Using managed clusters offers a lot of freedom from complex configurations and tasks. The master node that controls the cluster will be managed by Azure, and you pay for only the number of nodes you add to the cluster. These nodes are responsible for hosting your applications. An open source container engine called Azure Container Service Engine (acs-engine) is used to build AKS.

AKS is a completely platform-managed cluster, and you can easily create Kubernetes clusters in Azure and deploy your applications. AKS offloads the complex management and configuration tasks to Azure so that developers and administrators can focus on the application deployment. As mentioned earlier, the Kubernetes service is totally free, and you pay only for the number of nodes in the cluster. The following are the features of Azure Kubernetes Service:

Numerous Deployment Options   AKS offers multiple deployment options such as portal, command line, ARM templates, and pipelines. Further, you can use infrastructure-as-a-code solutions such as Terraform for deploying AKS clusters. During the cluster creation, the nodes are autoconfigured. You can also add extra add-ons such as Azure AD integration, container monitoring, and advanced networking if needed during the deployment process.

Identity and Access Control   RBAC is supported by AKS clusters. You can integrate the cluster with Azure AD, making it possible to configure access using Azure AD identities.

Logging and Monitoring   There are lot of third-party tools and solutions available for Kubernetes. AKS offers a built-in add-on called *container monitoring* to monitor the health of containers, nodes, and cluster. Using this add-on, you can retrieve rich performance metrics. This data will be stored in a Log Analytics workspace, which you can analyze using the Kusto Query Language.

Scaling   Based on the demand, the number of nodes can be increased or decreased; also you can configure the minimum number of nodes that the cluster will always be running.

Upgrades   Kubernetes also requires upgrades, and AKS offers several Kubernetes versions during the deployment. As a new version is released, you can plan your upgrade from the Azure portal or the CLI. During the upgrade process, the nodes are cordoned and drained. By this process, the running applications will be moved to another node during the upgrade process to avoid downtime.

HTTP Application Routing   By enabling HTTP application routing solutions, you can configure the ingress controller on your AKS cluster.

GPU Support   For solutions that run compute-intensive, graphics-intensive, and visualization workloads, AKS offers support for GPU-enabled nodes. You can select single or multi-GPU models for running these workloads.

Tooling   Being an open source solution, Kubernetes has a plethora of development and management solutions offered by different vendors. AKS supports all these tools natively without any additional configuration. Examples include Helm, Visual Studio Code extension for Kubernetes, etc. You can also leverage Azure Dev Spaces to run debug containers for testing purposes.

Virtual Network Integration   AKS clusters can be integrated to virtual networks by directly deploying to them. By doing so, every pod gets an IP address from the virtual network address space enabling the pods to communicate with other resources in the virtual network, resources across peered virtual networks, and resources in on-premises via ExpressRoute or VPN connections.

Image Repository   AKS supports Docker Hub, Azure Container Registry, or any other image repository that you maintain.

Terminology

There are different terminologies that are associated with Kubernetes. In the previous section, you might have noticed the keyword *pod*; that is Kubernetes terminology. Figure 9.15 explains the terminology.

FIGURE 9.14 Azure container groups

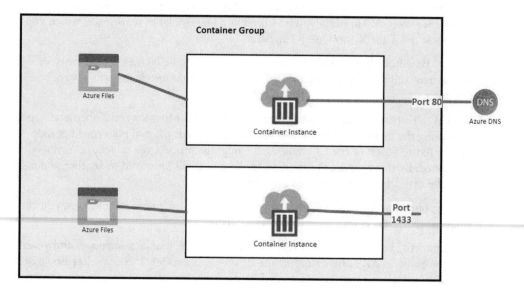

Pools refers to a group of virtual machines (nodes) having identical configurations. For example, you could create a pool with Windows VMs for running Windows containers and a pool with Linux VM for running Linux containers. Pools are also called *node pools*.

Nodes are the virtual machines in which the containerized applications are running. These nodes are grouped using pools. Earlier nodes used to be known as *minions*. The cluster schedules the containerized applications to these virtual machines based on resource availability.

Pods represent the smallest execution unit in Kubernetes. A pod encapsulates one or more applications, in other words, one or more containers.

A *container* represents the executable image that is composed of all binaries, libraries, and software required to run your application. These containers are encapsulated inside the pod. The container is created using container images that are stored in repositories like Docker Hub, Azure Container Registry, etc.

Deployment is another Kubernetes primitive used to run one or more identical pods. During the creation of the deployment, you can specify the number of pods required, and Kubernetes will make sure that it maintains this number no matter what happens. Even if you delete one pod that is part of a deployment, Kubernetes will immediately spin up another pod to match the number of replicas.

A *manifest* is the YAML or JSON file used for the creation of Kubernetes primitives like pods, deployment, etc. Every item in Kubernetes is created using a YAML/JSON file. This is similar to an Ansible playbook or Chef recipe.

As this book is not about the workings of these primitives, you will be focusing on the configuration of Kubernetes on Azure using AKS. If you are interested in learning more about these terminologies, please visit `https://kubernetes.io`.

Now you will learn about cluster components in AKS.

Cluster Components

An Azure Kubernetes Service cluster can be divided into two components.

- Azure-managed nodes
- Customer-managed nodes

Azure-managed nodes are the masters of the cluster, and they're responsible for managing the cluster. When you create an AKS cluster, this node is automatically provisioned and configured with all the management-layer components. As this layer is managed by Azure, customers will not be able to access or make configuration changes to this one. Also, you are not paying for this node.

Customer-managed nodes are the virtual machines on which containerized applications are running. You can have one or more nodes in a cluster. As shown in Figure 9.16, a Kubernetes customer-managed node runs the following components:

- Kubelet is responsible for processing the requests that are coming from the Azure-managed node or the master node. Also, kubelet processes the scheduling requests sent by the scheduler to run the containers.

- Kube-proxy is managing the virtual networking on each node. The proxy handles network routes and IP addressing for services and pods.

- The container runtime is something you learned about in the "Container Instances" section. This component is responsible for running the container and setting up interactions with network and storage. The AKS cluster running Kubernetes version 1.19 or higher uses container as the runtime, and versions prior to 1.19 use Moby as the container runtime.

Customer-managed nodes can be grouped together into node pools based on the configuration. During the creation of the cluster, you can specify the initial number of nodes and the size of the node. These nodes will be added to the default node pool.

Let's see how networking is implemented in AKS.

FIGURE 9.15 AKS terminology

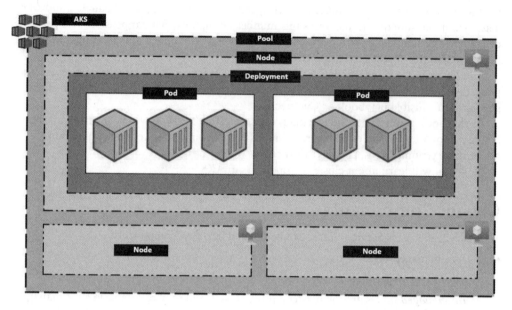
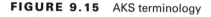

Networking

Networking is crucial in AKS because without networking you will not be able to establish communication between the components. As you saw in Figure 9.16, the Kube-proxy service running on each node is responsible for providing inbound and outbound connectivity for pods.

In Kubernetes, a *service* is responsible for providing different connectivity and load balancing options for the pods. Complex networking configuration can be applied using ingress controllers. Traffic filtering and security can be controlled using network policies. Services in Kubernetes group pods together and provide them with connectivity; there are different types of services available in Kubernetes.

- `ClusterIP`: Creates internal IP addresses for communication within the AKS cluster. This is ideal for internal communication between components. This is the default service type (refer to Figure 9.17).

- `NodePort`: Creates a port mapping from a port in the node to port in the container (refer to Figure 9.18). Users can access the component by navigating to <Node IP>:<NodePort>.

- `LoadBalancer`: Creates an internal/external Azure Load Balancer and adds the pods to the backend pool. External traffic is routed to the pods based on the load balancing rules (refer to Figure 9.19).

- `ExternalName`: Maps the service to a DNS name.

FIGURE 9.16   Components of a customer-managed node

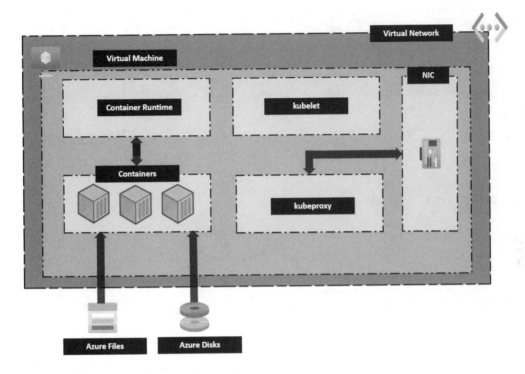

FIGURE 9.17   Cluster IP

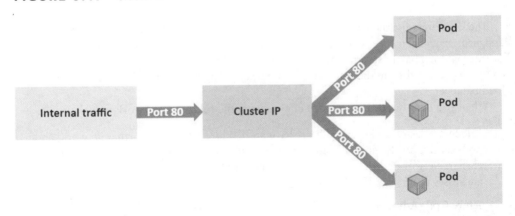

FIGURE 9.18   Node port

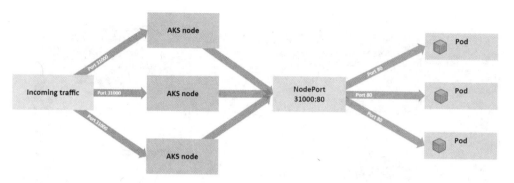

FIGURE 9.19   Load Balancer

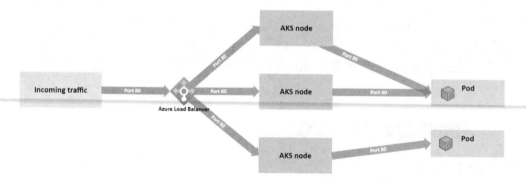

The IP address for the load balancer is provided by Azure and can be dynamically assigned, or you can specify one of the existing static IP addresses. You can create an internal or external load balancer. Internal load balancers will have only a private IP address and cannot be accessed from the Internet. Any Internet-facing workloads should use an external load balancer.

When you deploy clusters, you can choose from the following network models:

Kubenet   Using Kubenet, nodes receive an IP address from the virtual network, and pods receive an IP address from a different address space that is managed within the cluster. Network address translation is configured to translate virtual network IP addresses to internal IP addresses.

Azure CNI (Advanced Networking)   With Azure CNI, pods and nodes receive an IP address from the Azure virtual network. Because of this, the pods can be accessed directly. Since every pod gets an IP address from the virtual network, chances of IP address exhaustion are high. Hence, you need to plan your virtual network address space carefully. The IP addresses for the nodes will be reserved up front to avoid issues during scaling.

Now you will learn how storage is configured in the AKS cluster.

Storage

When you run applications, you need to store and retrieve data. For certain applications, you don't need the data to be persistent. However, in some other cases, you need to persist data and make sure that they are not deleted, even if the container is deleted. Storage is also needed to inject environmental variables and secrets into your pods. Figure 9.20 shows the high-level components that are part of AKS storage.

FIGURE 9.20 Storage components

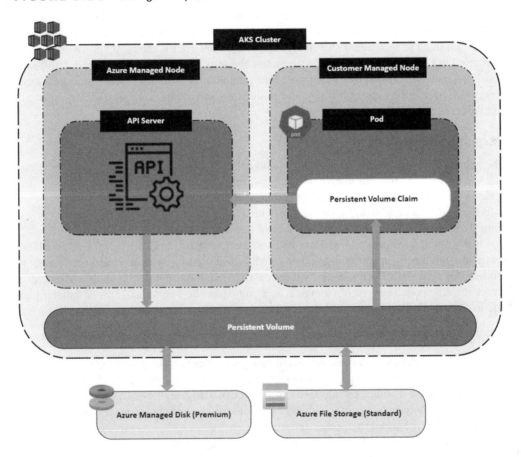

Let's take a deep dive into each of these concepts and understand it. The concepts are implemented in Kubernetes by declaring these in YAML files. Since writing YAML files is out of scope for this book, you will learn the concepts only.

Volumes

As mentioned earlier, applications need storage to store and retrieve data. Pods are ephemeral in nature, which means the data stored will be deleted when the pod is deleted. Volume refers to a method by which you can store, retrieve, and persist data across pods and application lifecycles. The storage for the pods can be manually assigned to the pods, or you can let Kubernetes automatically create them. In AKS, data volumes can be created using Azure Files or Azure Disks.

Azure Disks can be referenced in the YAML file as a `DataDisk` resource. Both Azure Standard storage (HDD) and Premium storage (SSD) is supported. Since there is premium storage with high-performance SSD, this is ideal for production workloads that demand high IOPS. Azure Disk is mounted as `ReadWriteOnce`, so it will be available to a single node. If you are planning to implement shared storage, then Azure Files is the right choice.

Azure Files uses SMB 3.0 and lets you mount the same storage to multiple nodes and pods. In Azure Files also you have support for Standard storage and Premium storage. These files can be accessed by multiple nodes and pods at the same time, making it ideal for shared storage scenarios.

Persistent Volumes

The volumes that are created as part of the pod are ephemeral, and storage follows the same lifecycle as the pod. You can use a persistent volume (PV) to store that data beyond the lifecycle of the pod. PVs are managed and created by the Kubernetes API.

Both Azure Files and Azure Disks can provide PVs. The choice depends on whether you want the storage to be shared or to be attached to a single node.

Cluster administrators can provision PVs statically, and you can let the Kubernetes APIs create it dynamically on demand. In other words, when a pod is scheduled and the storage requested is unavailable, Kubernetes will create a PV using Azure Files or Azure Disks and attach it to the pod. The type of storage is determined by the `StorageClass` parameter you add in the YAML file.

Storage Classes

As mentioned earlier, you can use Standard or Premium tiers of both Azure Files and Azure Storage while creating persistent volumes in Azure. The type of storage is determined using `StorageClasses`. Inside `StorageClasses`, you can also define `reclaimPolicy`. Using `reclaimPolicy`, you can control whether the underlying storage resources should be deleted or persisted when the pod is deleted.

The following are the different types of storage classes supported by AKS:

- `default`: This is the default `StorageClass` when no `StorageClass` is specified for a PV. Here, the default is to use Azure Standard SSD to create managed disks.
- `managed-premium`: Azure Premium storage is used to create a managed disk.
- `azurefile`: Standard storage is used to create an Azure File Share instance.
- `azurefile-premium`: Azure File Share is created using Azure Premium storage.

In all the scenarios, `reclaimPolicy` is used to determine whether you want to retain or delete the volume when you delete the pod.

Persistent Volume Claims

A persistent volume claim (PVC) requests storage by specifying the access mode and size. In AKS, PVC requests disk or file storage of a `StorageClass`. If there are no existing resources to fulfil the claim, the Kubernetes API will dynamically provision storage in Azure based on the `StorageClass`. Persistent volumes are mapped to claims one to one. You can specify the claims in your pod definition while creating the pod.

If you are interested to see how a PVC is created and is attached to a pod in a YAML manifest, refer to the following:

`https://github.com/rithinskaria/azure-infra/blob/main/azure-pv-pvc-sample.yaml`

Also, you can always refer to the official Kubernetes documentation to gain more insights.

Cluster Upgrade

You need to upgrade your Kubernetes version to address the security vulnerabilities and to use the latest features. When you create a cluster in Azure, you can select the Kubernetes version. In Figure 9.21, you can see the version available in Azure at the time of writing this book.

FIGURE 9.21   Kubernetes versions in AKS

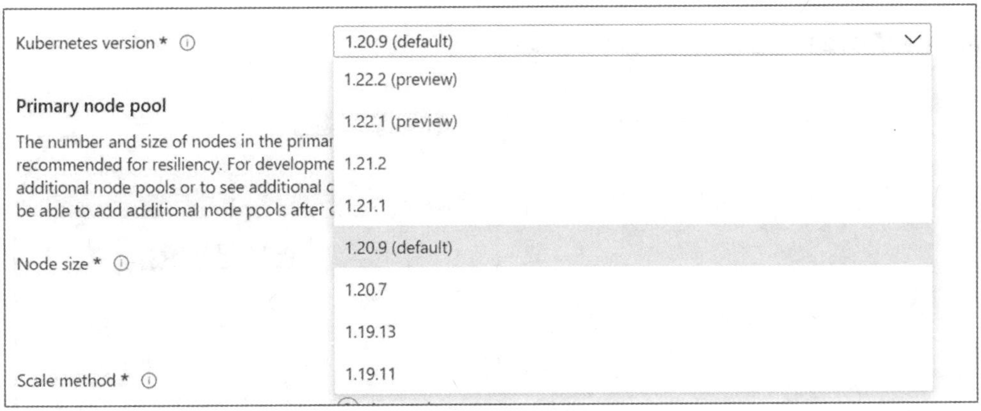

However, you have the option to choose from multiple versions; you also need to upgrade these clusters at some point. The good thing is, Azure provides tools to orchestrate the upgrade of the AKS cluster. The orchestration includes an upgrade of both Azure-provided nodes and customer-managed nodes. As you saw in Figure 9.21, for upgrades also, you will see the list of available versions. Once you select the version, Azure will orchestrate the process of cordoning and draining on each AKS node. During the draining process, all the pods will be evicted from the node and moved to another node. To eliminate the downtime, the upgrade will be performed as a rolling upgrade. In other words, only one node gets upgraded at a time so that other nodes can run the application.

During the upgrade process, AKS nodes are cordoned individually from the cluster. Cordoning ensures that no new pods are scheduled on the node. Once cordoned, the draining process will start. In draining, Kubernetes will drain all the pods in the current node to a different node. The following steps happen during a cluster upgrade:

1. Pods are terminated and scheduled on the remaining nodes.

2. The node undergoes the upgrade and reboot. Once the upgrade is completed, the node joins back to the AKS cluster.

3. The node is uncordoned, which means pods can be scheduled on the node again. However, the drained nodes are not rescheduled back to this node.

4. The next node gets cordoned and drained. The process continues until all the nodes are upgraded.

Scaling

When you run applications in AKS, you may need to increase or decrease the number of computer instances based on the demand. AKS offers several scaling mechanisms to accommodate the rapidly changing demands. AKS supports both manual and autoscaling options. Let's understand the different scaling options available in AKS.

Figure 9.22 shows the autoscaling components of AKS.

FIGURE 9.22 Kubernetes scaling options

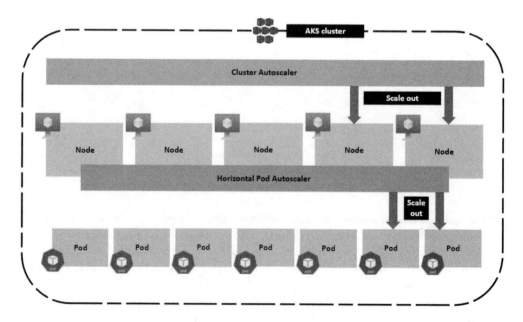

Manually Scale Pods or Nodes

As the name suggests, you can manually increase the number of replicas of the pod. Also, if the pods need more compute resources, you can increase the size and number of nodes. This is ideal if you want to run your application with a defined set of resources. Since you control the scaling manually, you will be aware of the cost incurred. To manually increase the number of replicas, you can update the manifest file, and the Kubernetes API will increase the number of replicas.

Horizontal Pod Autoscaler

In Kubernetes, you have the horizontal pod autoscaler (HPA) to increase the number of replicas based on metrics. By default, every 30 seconds, HPA will check the Metrics API to determine if there is any need to change the replica count. Based on the output from the Metrics API, the demand is estimated, and the number of replicas is increased or decreased accordingly. AKS clusters with Metrics Server for Kubernetes 1.8+ supports HPA.

When you configure the HPA, you can decide on the minimum number of instances, the maximum number of instances, and the metrics that need to be monitored. For example, you can choose the Percentage CPU metric to trigger the HPA and increase or decrease the replicas according to the threshold.

As the HPA polls the Metrics API every 30 seconds, there is a chance for a race condition. Since 30 seconds is a small window, the previous scale events may not have successfully completed before another check is made. Therefore, the HPA may change the number of replicas before the previous scale event is completed. To minimize this race condition, you can configure the cooldown or delay values. The delay value will make the HPA wait after a scale event before another scale event can be triggered. You can configure separate delay values for scale-up and scale-down events. The default value for a scale-up event is 3 minutes, and a scale-down event is 5 minutes. If your application is not getting the adequate number of replicas quickly, you can fine-tune these values.

Cluster Autoscaler

Using HPA, you will be able to increase the number of replicas of a pod. However, what if you need more computing resources for the pods to run? In other words, what if the capacity of the nodes is not enough to meet the demand? Well, you have cluster autoscaler to adjust the number of nodes based on the requests. Like HPA, the cluster autoscaler checks the API server for any requirement changes every 10 seconds. If there is a requirement change, then the number of nodes is increased or decreased accordingly. AKS clusters with RBAC enabled and running Kubernetes 1.10.x and higher support the cluster autoscaler.

HPA and cluster autoscalers are used to provide optimal scaling. When combined, HPA increases or decreases the number of pods per application demand, and the cluster autoscale will adjust the number of nodes accordingly to run the pods.

Bursting from AKS with ACI

When you are using HPA for accommodating sudden application demand, HPA will increase the replica count. If the number of nodes is not enough to schedule these new pods, the cluster autoscaler will add more nodes. However, it may take a few minutes to bring the new nodes online and schedule the pending pods. Because of the faster startup time offered by Azure Container Instances (ACI), you can create a virtual node quickly. The virtual Kubelet component installed in the AKS cluster can abstract ACI as the node to the cluster. Kubernetes can then schedule pods that run as ACI instances through virtual nodes, not as pods on VM nodes directly in your AKS cluster.

Figure 9.23 shows how ACI acts as an extension to the AKS cluster to run pods.

FIGURE 9.23 Bursting from AKS with ACI

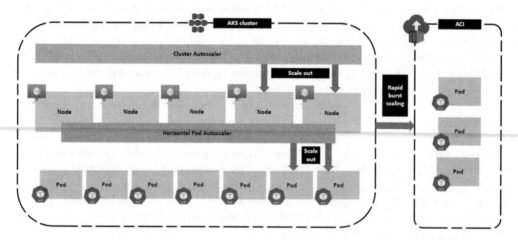

To use the virtual node, your application requires no code change or architectural change. Virtual nodes are deployed to a different subnet in the virtual network in which the AKS cluster is deployed. As they are part of the same virtual network, the communication between AKS and ACI is secured. Also, like AKS cluster, ACI offers a secure and isolated compute resource.

In the next exercise, you will deploy an AKS cluster. You will be using one of the manifest files available in the Azure documentation to create your application in the cluster. Also, you will be using kubectl to interact with the cluster. As this is pre-installed in the cloud shell, you will be using the cloud shell to deploy our application. You can install the kubectl binaries to your local computer by executing `az aks install-cli`.

EXERCISE 9.4

Running Applications in an AKS Cluster

1. Open the Azure portal and search for *AKS*; you will see Kubernetes Services in the search results. Click it to open it.

2. Click Create and select Create Kubernetes Cluster to create the cluster. You will be taken to the Basics tab of the cluster creation page.

3. On the Basics tab, you need to provide the following details.

Project Details

- **Subscription**: Select an Azure subscription.

- **Resource Group**: Select or create a resource group to hold the AKS cluster.

Cluster Details

- **Preset configuration**: The default option is Standard. Preset helps us to select the configuration per our requirements. Other options include dev/test, cost-optimized, batch processing, and hardened access. There are price differences and feature-wise differences between these presets. In our case, we will choose the default one.

- **Kubernetes cluster name**: Provide a name for the cluster.

- **Region**: Select the Azure region.

- **Availability zones**: By default, all three zones will be selected, helping us to deploy our nodes across availability zones. If needed, you can limit the deployment to certain zones.

- **Kubernetes version**: As you saw earlier, there are multiple versions available. At the time of writing this book, the default value is 1.20.9, and we will proceed with that.

Primary Node Pool

- **Node size**: This is the size of the node; the default choice is Standard DS2_v2. If you want, you can select any available VM sizes.

- **Scale method**: Here the options are Manual and Autoscaling. The default option is Autoscale, and you will see the node code range to specify the minimum and maximum number of nodes. However, we will go with the Manual scaling option.

- **Node count**: Since you selected Manual, you get to choose the node count. The default value is 3.

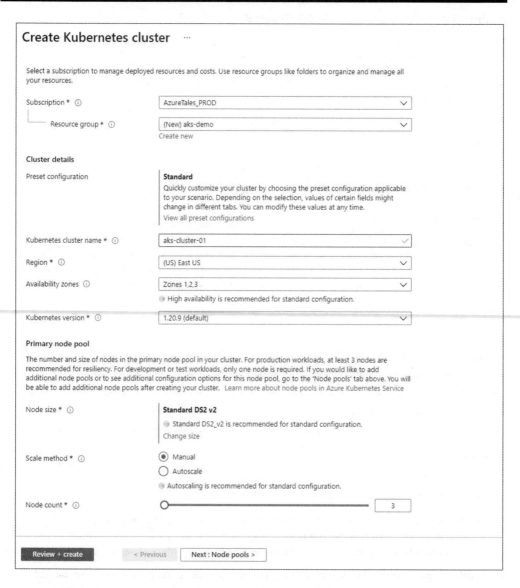

4. You don't need to make any configuration changes on the remaining tabs. You can click Review + Create to start the validation. Once the validation is done, click Create to create the cluster. The process may take some time to deploy, so you can sit back and relax.

5. Once the cluster is created, launch a cloud shell console, and let's connect to the cluster using the command az aks get-credentials --resource-group <resource-group-name> --name <cluster-name>. Here's an example: az aks get-credentials --resource-group aks-demo --name aks-cluster-01. This command will download the context and save it in your home directory.

6. Check the number of nodes using the command kubectl get nodes. Since you created a three-node cluster, you should be able to see three nodes.

```
PowerShell ∨   ⏻  ?  ⊗  ⎘  ⎙  { }  ⎗
PS /home/rithin> az aks get-credentials --resource-group aks-demo --name aks-cluster-01
Merged "aks-cluster-01" as current context in /home/rithin/.kube/config
PS /home/rithin> kubectl get nodes
NAME                                 STATUS   ROLES   AGE   VERSION
aks-agentpool-47695231-vmss000000    Ready    agent   62m   v1.20.9
aks-agentpool-47695231-vmss000001    Ready    agent   62m   v1.20.9
aks-agentpool-47695231-vmss000002    Ready    agent   62m   v1.20.9
```

7. You need to download the YAML file from the GitHub repository. For that, run curl -o file.yml https://raw.githubusercontent.com/rithinskaria/azure-infra/main/aks-demo.yml; this command will download the YAML file from the GitHub and save it as file.yml.

8. Use the file.yml file to deploy the components. If you inspect the file, you can see that it contains two Deployment components, ClusterIP, and a LoadBalancer. Deploy the application using kubectl apply -f file.yml.

9. In the terminal, you will see the list of components deployed.

```
PowerShell ∨   ⏻  ?  ⊗  ⎘  ⎙  { }  ⎗
PS /home/rithin> curl -o file.yml https://raw.githubusercontent.com/rithinskaria
  % Total    % Received % Xferd  Average Speed   Time    Time     Time  Current
                                 Dload  Upload   Total   Spent    Left  Speed
100  1632  100  1632    0     0   8727      0 --:--:-- --:--:-- --:--:--  8680
PS /home/rithin> kubectl apply -f file.yml
deployment.apps/azure-vote-back created
service/azure-vote-back created
deployment.apps/azure-vote-front created
service/azure-vote-front created
```

10. Now you need to find the IP address of the load balancer using the command kubectl get service azure-vote-front --watch. The --watch parameter will keep the command running, and you can stop it by pressing Ctrl+C once you see the external IP address. Copy the external IP address.

```
PS /home/rithin> kubectl get service azure-vote-front --watch
NAME               TYPE           CLUSTER-IP      EXTERNAL-IP     PORT(S)        AGE
azure-vote-front   LoadBalancer   10.0.188.112    20.85.158.122   80:32673/TCP   104s
^C
```

11. Open a browser and paste the external IP address of the load balancer. You will be able to see the application running. You can start voting and reset the value if needed.

Now our application is containerized and is running in an AKS cluster. You are accessing the application externally using the IP address of Azure Load Balancer.

Summary

This chapter explored different PaaS compute options available to you. You started the chapter with Azure App Services, which is a solution that offers a hosting environment for deploying web applications, mobile backends, and restful APIs. There are multiple tiers available for Azure App Service plans based on the requirements and type of workload you are running. Also, we covered the scaling options available for App Service plans. Later, you saw how you can deploy Azure App Services to these plans and leverage features such as continuous deployment, deployment slots, authentication, custom domains, and backup.

After completing App Services, we covered container instances. Azure Container Instances offers the easiest way to deploy containerized applications in Azure. In the exercise, you created a customized nginx image from scratch, pushed it to Azure Container Registry, and deployed the image to Azure Container Instances. Since ACI offers public IP connectivity, you verified the connectivity to your nginx container from the browser.

When you are handling containers at scale, Azure Container Instances might not be the right solution, and you need container orchestrators. Azure offers the Azure Kubernetes Service, which provides a managed platform for container orchestration. As this is a managed cluster, all cluster management and control plane maintenance and configuration are managed by Azure. Though the intention of this book is not to teach Kubernetes, still we covered core concepts related to AKS such as cluster components, networking, storage, upgrades, and scaling.

In Chapter 10, "Data Protection," we will cover backup and recovery. The goal of the next chapter is to familiarize yourself with the Azure Backup solution and Azure Site Recovery, which is a disaster recovery solution.

Exam Essentials

Learn about Azure App Service plans and Azure App Service.   Learn the pricing tiers and scaling of Azure App Service plans. Along with that, learn how apps can be deployed to an Azure App Service plan.

Learn the configuration of features in the Azure App Service.   Understand features such as continuous deployment, deployment slots, authentication, custom domains, and backup.

Understand the basics of containers.   Understand the difference between containers and virtual machines. Also, learn how Docker containers are hosted.

Learn about Azure container instances.   Learn the architecture and deployment of ACI. Additionally, learn how to build container images and push them to ACR.

Learn about the Azure Kubernetes Service.   Understand the Kubernetes terminology and architecture of AKS.

Learn the Azure Kubernetes Service core topics.   Learn the core topics of AKS including storage, network, and scaling.

Review Questions

1. Your organization has asked you to enable manual scaling on the App Service plan called ASP-09ax4. However, when you navigate to the scaling option, you are not able to see the manual scaling option. What should be done to enable manual scaling, and which solution is the cheapest?

   A. Upgrade the tier to Basic

   B. Upgrade the tier to Standard or Premium

   C. Downgrade to Basic

   D. Downgrade to Shared

2. You are planning to test an application in Azure App Service. The testing duration is 120 minutes per day. Which should be the cheapest tier for this purpose?

   A. Free

   B. Standard

   C. Basic

   D. Shared

3. You are planning to use autoscaling for your application. Per the calculation using the current usage pattern, the application needs to scale to 25 instances to support the demand during peak hours. Which tier is right for this? Select the cheapest solution.

   A. Basic

   B. Standard

   C. Premium

   D. Isolated

4. Which of the following tiers is recommended for running production workloads?

   A. Free

   B. Shared

   C. Basic

   D. Standard

5. Your organization is using Azure DevOps and OneDrive to store the code. Currently, the App Service is configured to pull the code from OneDrive. However, when the developers update the code, that is not reflected on the application hosted in Azure. What needs to be done to reflect the changes as soon as the developers commit the code? (Select all that apply.)

   A. Enable continuous deployment for OneDrive

   B. Store the code as a ZIP in OneDrive

   C. Start using Azure DevOps as the code source for CI/CD

   D. Use a source control program

6. Which of the following configurations is not swapped during a deployment slot swap? (Select all that apply.)

   A. Connection strings

   B. Connection strings

   C. Handler mappings

   D. Virtual network integration

7. Which are the types of records that can be used to enable custom domains in Azure App Service? (Select all that apply.)

   A. A

   B. MX

   C. SRV

   D. CNAME

8. Which of the following authentication methods is not available out of the box for Azure App Service? (Select all that apply.)

   A. LinkedIn

   B. Twitter

   C. Facebook

   D. Google

9. How many deployment slots are available for the Basic tier?

   A. 1

   B. 3

   C. 0

   D. 5

10. Enabling Azure AD authentication creates which of the following entities in Azure?

    A. Azure Key Vault for storing keys

    B. Service principal

    C. Azure AD User

    D. Azure AD Group

11. You are backing up your App Service. Which of the following is included in the backup? (Select two.)

    A. App configuration

    B. Azure Database for MySQL

    C. Firewall-enabled storage account

    D. SSL-enabled Azure Database for MySQL

12. Which of the following is not true about container groups?

    A. Are scheduled on multiple host machines

    B. Expose a single public IP address, with one exposed port

    C. Consist of two containers

    D. Include two Azure file shares as volume mounts

13. You decide to move all your services to the Azure Kubernetes Service. Which of the following components will contribute to your monthly Azure charge?

    A. Azure-managed node

    B. Pods

    C. Customer-managed nodes

    D. Applications

14. You can have multiple apps running in a single App Service plan. True or False?

    A. True

    B. False

15. Which of the following is the Kubernetes agent that processes the orchestration requests and schedules running the requested containers?

    A. Controller

    B. Container runtime

    C. kube-proxy

    D. kubelet

16. You are configuring networking for the Azure Kubernetes Service. Which of the following maps incoming direct traffic to the pods?

    A. AKS node

    B. NodePort

    C. LoadBalancer

    D. ClusterIP

17. You are deploying applications to AKS, and you need to make sure that the number of pods are increased or decreased automatically based on the demand. Which solution should you choose?

    A. HPA

    B. Cluster autoscaler

    C. Bursting with ACI

    D. Virtual Kubelet

18. Which of the following should be created first to use Premium Azure Files with a pod in AKS?

   A. PVC

   B. PV

   C. Mount point

   D. Pod

19. Which of the following features of Kubernetes let us use ACI as a node during the bursting?

   A. Storage classes

   B. Cluster autoscaler

   C. Virtual Kubelet

   D. HPA

20. Your organization wants to provide IP addresses for pods directly from the virtual network. Which of the following should be used to implement this?

   A. Load Balancer

   B. Azure CNI

   C. Kubenet

   D. Calico

Chapter

10

Data Protection

You have seen the implementation of several services, and in all these services you store data; in other words, you depend on these services to store or retrieve your data. Since you are handling sensitive business-critical data, it's crucial to be aware of solutions for data protection. Data protection strategies include backup, restore, disaster recovery, and business continuity. Backup and restore deals with files and folder backups. Azure Site Recovery helps in implementing a disaster recovery or regional failover in case an entire Azure region goes down.

File and Folder Backups

In this section, you will see how you can back up files and folders using Azure Backup. This solution can be used to back up both cloud and on-premises data. Let's start with Azure Backup.

Azure Backup

Azure Backup is a cloud-based backup solution that replaces existing on-premises backup solutions because of its reliability, security, and competitive cost. This service can be used to back up or protect and restore data in the Microsoft cloud.

A traditional backup solution requires infrastructure to be deployed to host backup services; however, with the help of a lightweight agent, you will be able to back up your servers securely to the cloud. Regardless of whether the server is in Azure, on-premises, or in any other cloud provider, you can back up and save the data in Azure Recovery Services Vault. The following are the benefits offered by Azure Backup:

Replaces On-Premises Backup Solution It replaces traditional backup solutions with a simple interface and configuration. The backup can be audited, tracked, and monitored from the Azure portal.

Disaster Recovery Since the backup is stored in the cloud, Azure Backup provides reliability in the case of an on-premises datacenter failure.

Unlimited Data Transfer There is no restriction on the amount of inbound or outbound data transfer. This is ideal if you want to back up servers storing terabytes of data.

Secure Storage   You can encrypt the backup before transferring it to the cloud. The passphrase for decryption can be retained on-premises, which makes it more secure.

App-Consistent Recovery Points   Application consistent backup can back up both in memory as well as in pending operations. With the help of these restore points, you can quickly return to the running state of the application during the restore process.

Long-Term and Short-Term Retention   Azure Backup supports long-term and short-term retention. You can keep the backups as long as you want, and Azure Backup has a limit of 9,999 recovery points per instance.

Automatic Storage Management   For backups, storage is provisioned and allocated automatically based on the backup size. This way, you don't have to pre-provision storage or pay for large disks; you need to pay only for the data you store. Heterogenous storage is required in most hybrid scenarios, as in some parts on-premises and some in the cloud. For these scenarios, as the on-premises storage is owned by you, there is no additional cost for that.

Multiple Redundancy Options   Azure Backup supports LRS, ZRS, and GRS redundancy. It's recommended to have different vaults for backing up your production and testing machines. Production machines are supposed to use GRS for higher durability, while development and testing machines can use LRS.

Creating Recovery Services Vault

When you configure Backup, the data gets stored inside an entity called Recovery Services *vaults*. You can back up data for various Azure services like Azure Virtual Machines (Linux or Windows) and Azure SQL Databases. For on-premises, Recovery Services vaults support System Center DPM, Windows Server, Azure Backup Server, and other services. Backing up to Recovery Services vaults helps you track, audit, organize, and manage multiple servers in a centralized console, while reducing the management overhead.

In the Azure portal, you can search for *Recovery Services vault*, and you can create a vault by following these steps:

1.   Search for *Recovery Services vaults* in the Azure portal and click Recovery Services Vaults. Click Create.

2.   To create the vault, all you need to provide is the subscription, resource group, vault name, and region, as shown in Figure 10.1. The region selection is crucial as you cannot back up VMs that are deployed in a different region.

3.   Click Review + Create and wait for the validation to get completed. Once the validation is done, you can click Create to create the vault.

FIGURE 10.1 Creating a Recovery Services vault

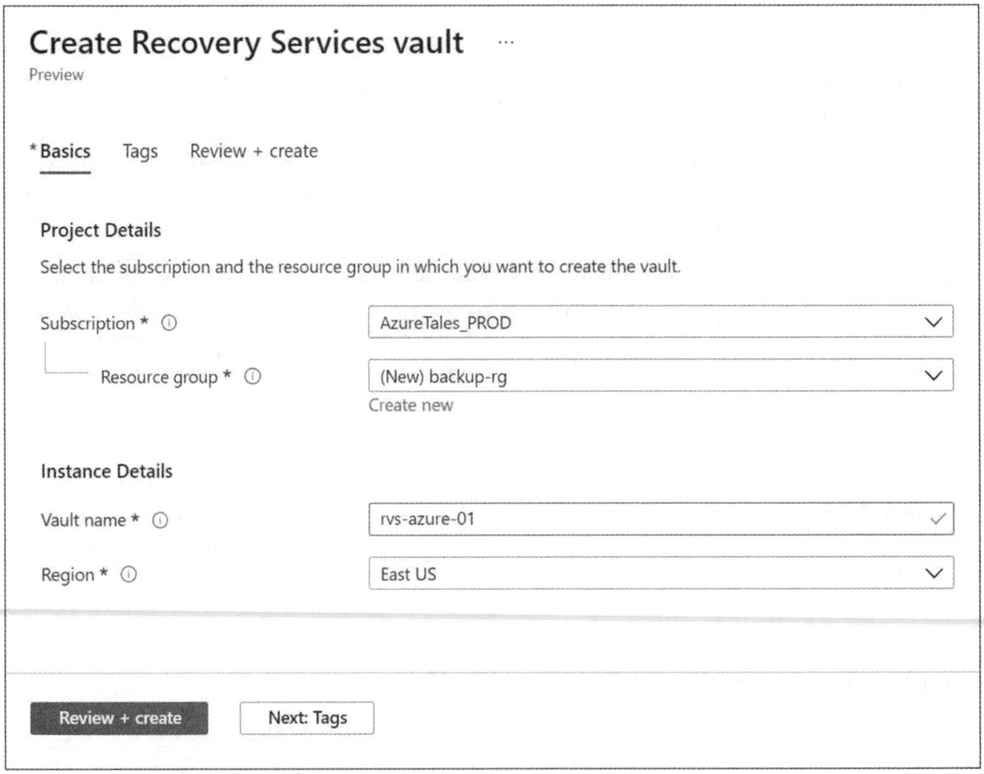

One thing to note here is that when a new Recovery Services vault is created, it's created with georedundant storage. If you are not planning to use this redundancy and would like to optimize the cost, then consider changing the redundancy before you back up any service. Once you onboard any solution, then you cannot alter the redundancy. Now that you have created the vault, let's see the set of services or offerings that can be backed up to this vault. The solutions can span the cloud and on-premises.

Configuring a Recovery Services Vault

Though you can use the Recovery Services vault for backing up several solutions, since we are exploring file and folder backup, we will focus only on those offerings.

Talking about Azure services, to back up files and folders stored in Azure Files, you can use Recovery Service vaults. Along with file shares, you can see other options (refer to Figure 10.2); however, we will talk about this when we discuss virtual machine backups.

When you switch your source to On-Premises, you see a longer list (refer to Figure 10.3) than just options for Azure. You can see Files And Folders, along with other supported services.

FIGURE 10.2   Backup options for Azure

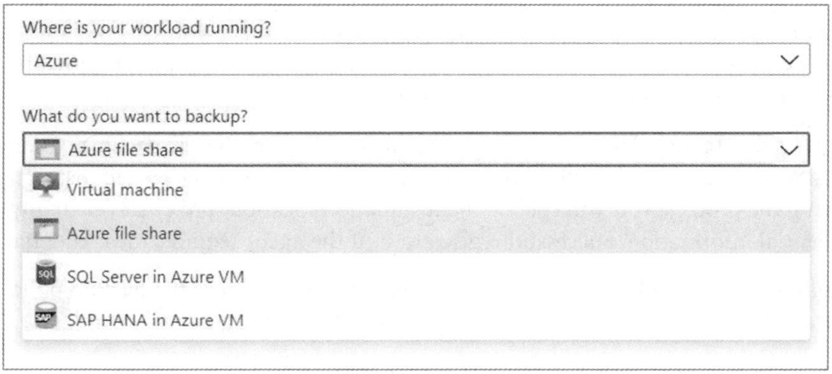

Where is your workload running?

Azure   ∨

What do you want to backup?

🖼 Azure file share   ∨

🖥 Virtual machine

🖼 Azure file share

▦ SQL Server in Azure VM

▦ SAP HANA in Azure VM

FIGURE 10.3   Backup options for on-premises

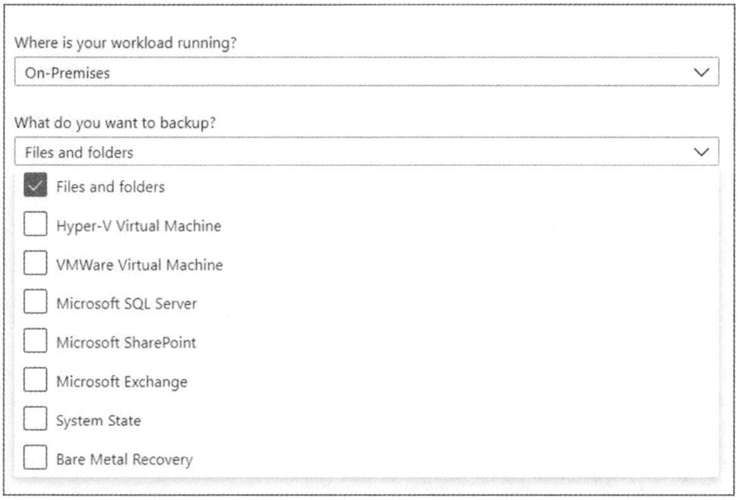

Where is your workload running?

On-Premises   ∨

What do you want to backup?

Files and folders   ∨

☑ Files and folders

☐ Hyper-V Virtual Machine

☐ VMWare Virtual Machine

☐ Microsoft SQL Server

☐ Microsoft SharePoint

☐ Microsoft Exchange

☐ System State

☐ Bare Metal Recovery

Within an Azure subscription, you can create up to 25 Recovery Services vaults per region. When you are working with backups for solutions in Azure, it's seamless as the solutions are natively deployed in Azure. However, working with on-premises may require a couple more steps for implementation. For example, configuring a backup for on-premises files and folders requires multiple steps. The following are the steps required to back up on-premises files and folders to an Azure Recovery Services vault:

Deploy a Recovery Service Vault   Because you need to store the data in Azure, you need to create a Recovery Service vault.

Download the Agent and Credentials File   The Azure Backup agent needs to be installed on-premises on any Windows Server VM or physical server. The agent is responsible for executing the backup from the on-premises infrastructure. Along with the agent, you need to download a credentials file. The credentials file is used by the agent to identify the vault to which it needs to back up. Once you select File And Folders, as shown in Figure 10.3, the next screen gives you the option to download the agent and credentials (refer to Figure 10.4).

Register the Agent After installing the agent on the on-premises machine, you need to register the agent. The installer provides a wizard that gives step-by-step instructions. During the process, you will specify the installation location, proxy server (if any), and credential information. Successful registration of the agent requires the credential file.

Configure a Backup Policy You can use the agent to configure the backup policy that contain details such as when to back up, what to back up, retention period, etc.

FIGURE 10.4 Downloading the agent and credentials

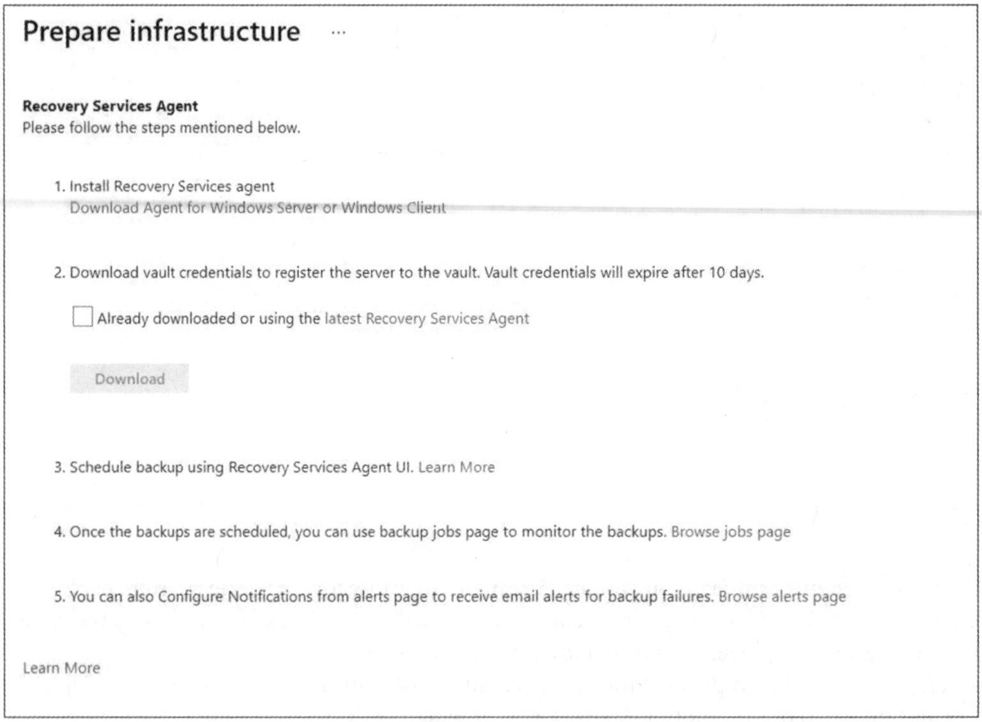

As you can see, the backup is orchestrated using the agent. The agent is called the Microsoft Recovery Services agent (MARS agent), and this needs to be installed on the Windows server or client. At the time of writing this book, Linux machines are not supported. The following are the features of the MARS agent:

- Backup files and folders on Windows physical or virtual machines. These VMs can be in Azure, on-premises, or in other cloud provider.

- No additional backup servers are required.

- Volume-level restore only, not aware of application.

- Backup and restore contents are orchestrated using an agent.

Virtual Machine Data Protection

When it comes to data protection of virtual machines, you have multiple options available. The choice here depends on the use-case scenarios. Let's cover a quick introduction to these options. Nevertheless, we will cover them in depth later.

Azure Backup   To back up Azure VMs or servers, you rely on Azure Backup. You can create application-consistent backups for both Windows and Linux computers; then store them in the Recovery Services vault. During the restore process, you can restore the entire VM or specific files.

Azure Site Recovery (ASR)   Azure Site Recovery is a disaster recovery solution that can be used to replicate your VMs to a secondary region and fire them up during a regional outage. You can fail over from the Azure portal, and the infrastructure will be created in a secondary region within a few minutes.

Snapshots   When it comes to development and testing, managed disk snapshots offer a reliable and simple option to back up your VMs. Snapshots are independent read-only copies of the managed disk and can be used to create new managed disks.

Images   You have already learned about images in Chapter 7, "Azure Virtual Machines." Images will contain the OS disk and all the data disks that were part of the VM. Using this custom image, you can create hundreds of VMs. There are two types of images: generalized and specialized.

From an initial impression, specialized images and snapshots may look similar. In specialized images, you take an image of a live virtual machine retaining the hostname, user accounts, and other information. Taking a snapshot of the disk also preserves all the data and configuration. Well, the difference here is the snapshot applies to a single disk; if you have a VM with multiple disks, then you need to create separate snapshots for each of these disks. In the case of images, all disks are taken into consideration while creating the image. Second, the snapshot is not aware of any additional disks other than the one it contains. This creates an issue when you are working with disks that are in coordination, for example, RAID. As of now, the snapshot lacks this coordination with other disks. Images, on the other hand, take the live copy of the VM, so the disks are in coordination.

Apart from Azure Backup, there are more options you can use for backing up VMs.

- If you want to back up files and folders in Azure VM, then you can run the MARS agent and get this done without the need to back up the entire VM.

- Use System Center Data Protection Manager (DPM) or Microsoft Azure Backup Server (MABS) running in Azure. Then you can back up the DPM/MABS server to a Recovery Services vault using Azure Backup.

- Use third-party backup solutions like Commvault, Veeam, etc., available in Azure Marketplace.

Since we talked about MARS earlier, we will skip that. Nonetheless, we will cover MABS in depth later in this chapter. Let's start with virtual machine snapshots.

Virtual Machine Snapshots

You can use snapshots as a point-in-time backup or to troubleshoot VM issues. The snapshot will be a full, read-only copy of the disk or incremental copies of the disk based on the snapshot type you select. You will be able to snapshot the OS disk and data disks as separate tasks. Creating a snapshot is straightforward and can be performed from the Azure portal, Azure PowerShell, or the CLI. You can simply provide the name of the snapshot, source disk, and tier to create a snapshot (refer to Figure 10.5). Additionally, you will be able to specify the storage type, networking, and encryption.

FIGURE 10.5   Creating snapshots

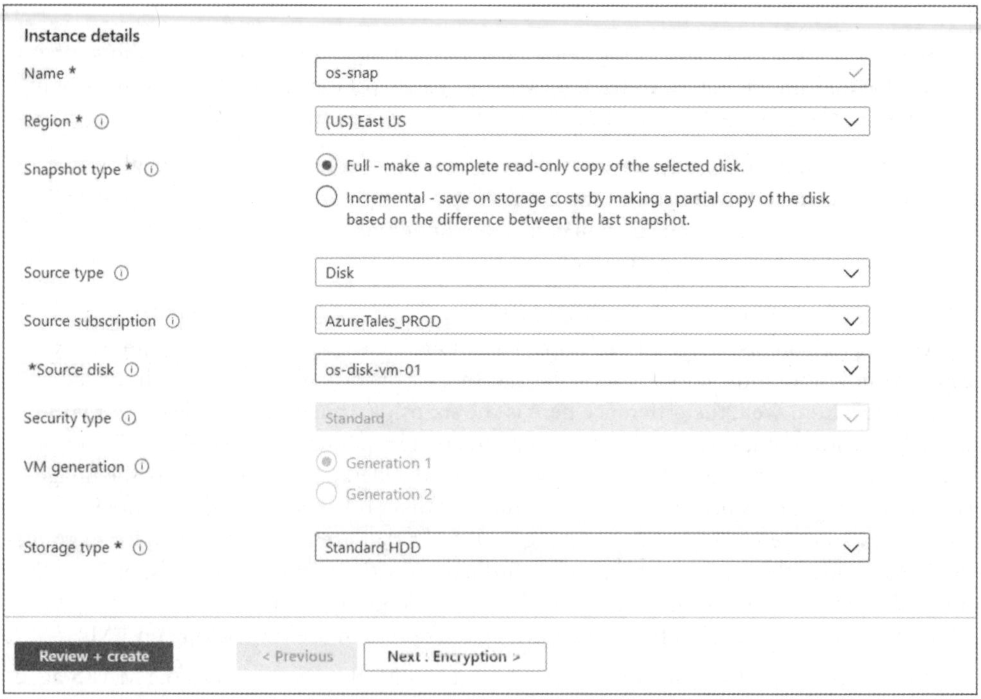

In Figure 10.5, you can see that the snapshot type includes Full and Incremental. Also, the storage types are Standard HDD, Premium SSD, and Zone-Redundant. Standard HDD and Premium SSD use LRS redundancy. Once the snapshot is created, as shown in Figure 10.6, you can see that you have the option to create a new disk from the snapshot.

FIGURE 10.6   Reviewing snapshots

Next, we will talk about Azure Backup, which will help you to back up virtual machines that are deployed in Azure.

Azure Backup

Azure Backup offers a reliable solution to back up virtual machines that are deployed in Azure and also on-premises servers with the help of MABS. The backed-up data will be stored in the Recovery Services vault. Let's take a look at the architecture of Azure IaaS VM Backup (refer to Figure 10.7).

FIGURE 10.7   Azure IaaS VM Backup architecture

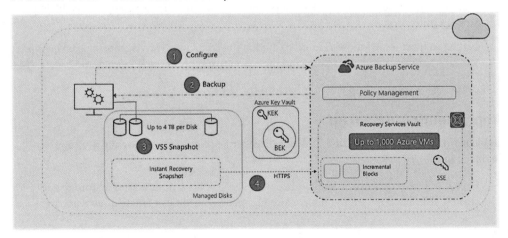

The following steps happen during an end-to-end implementation of Azure Backup:

1. Inside every Azure VM, Microsoft has an extension that can be used to configure and execute Azure Backup. The extension is responsible for communicating with Azure Backup and attaches to a backup policy.

2. According to the backup policy, when the schedule time comes, Microsoft will send a command to the extension. Then, VSS Snapshot will be orchestrated by Azure Backup.

3. The VSS snapshot will be stored in the local storage, and this will act as an instant recovery point. Since the snapshot is stored locally, the recovery process is quick.

4. In the interim, the snapshot will be compared to previous snapshots. Based on the comparison, only the incremental blocks will be transferred to the Recovery Services vault via HTTPS.

5. The backup is encrypted at rest and in transit as the Recovery Services vault is encrypted using SSE.

6. If you are using Azure Disk Encryption to encrypt the disk, the keys are also backed up to the Recovery Services vault. This will help us to restore to any restore point without worrying about the encryption keys.

Now that you know the architecture of Azure IaaS VM Backup, let's understand the benefits of using Azure Backup.

Incremental Backups at the Block Level   As you have seen the architecture, the agent makes a comparison with the existing snapshot and performs an incremental backup. This means that only the changes blocks are transferred to the Recovery Services vault, thus reducing the bandwidth and storage costs. The Recovery Services vault will store different point-in-time restore points representing changed blocks during each backup.

Automatic Data Integrity Check   Along with secured backups, Azure Backup ensures the data integrity of the backed-up data. The integrity check is done in the cloud, and any corruptions caused due to data transfer will be identified and mitigated.

Retention Policies   You can configure retention policies in your Azure Backup policy to decide how long you want to retain the backed-up data. The policy will also make sure that any data exceeding the retention period is automatically recycled, thus reducing storage utilization.

Native Support for Windows/Linux   You don't need to install any agents for backing up virtual machines running in Azure, and there is native support for Windows and Linux VMs.

Let's see how you can implement a backup for your Azure VMs.

Implementing a Backup

Implementing a backup for Azure VM is a three-step process. The following are the steps involved in the process:

Create a Recovery Services Vault   The Recovery Services vault acts as a storage entity for storing your backups, and you have already seen how you can create a recovery services vault. As mentioned earlier, by default the vault gets created with the GRS redundancy. If GRS is not required, you need to change that to LRS before backing up any data or VM.

Define the Policy   Once the vault is created, you need to define the policy. There will be a default policy that will be used; if that requires customization, you can do that. The policy is responsible for defining when the snapshot needs to be taken and how long the backups should be retained.

Back Up the Virtual Machine   Any VMs created using images in the gallery don't require the Backup extension as it is already present on the VM. Any VMs that you create from custom images or migrate from on-premises to Azure will require the installation of the extension. While we discussed the architecture of Azure Backup, you saw the role of the agent in the backup process.

Now that you are familiar with the steps involved in the implementation of the backup, let's perform an exercise to learn the process (see Exercise 10.1). To implement a backup, you need to create a Recovery Services vault and VM (Windows or Linux). The plan is to enable and configure a backup on the VM. Since we have already covered the creation of virtual machines and Recovery Services vault, we will not cover that again. Make sure you have VM and the Recovery Services vault deployed in the same region before you start the exercise.

EXERCISE 10.1

Implementing a VM Backup

1.   Sign in to the Azure portal and navigate to the Recovery Services vault you created for this exercise. From the Overview blade, click + Backup to configure the backup.

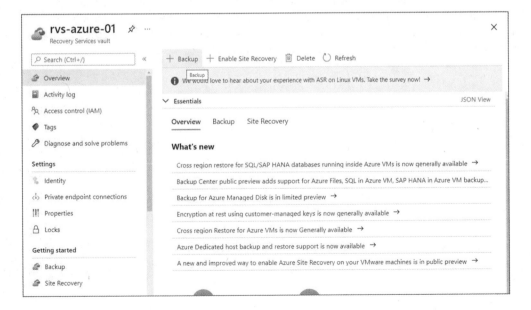

2. Clicking the Backup button will ask you to select the source and the type of workload you want to back up. By default, Azure will be selected as the source, and the type will be Virtual Machine. You don't have to make any changes here, so click the Backup button.

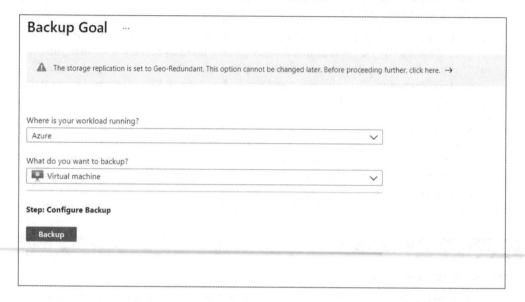

3. On the next screen, you can see that you have the option to select the policy. The default policy will be automatically selected; if needed, you can create a new policy with the preferred time and retention period for the backup. The Azure portal will give a summary of the policy under Policy Details, helping us to understand the schedule and retention. For now, you will go with the default policy.

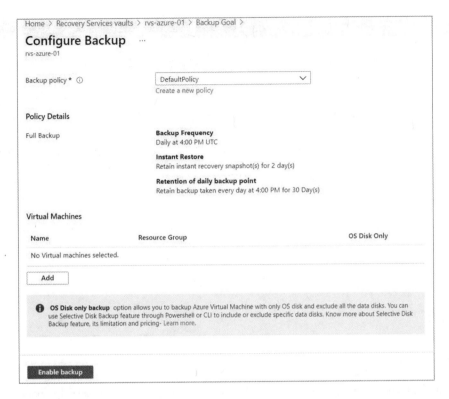

4. You can see that you have an option to add virtual machines. Click Add to configure the backup for VMs.

5. Clicking Add will list the set of VMs available in the region. This list is limited to the VMs deployed in the same region as selected for the vault and the ones that are not backed up yet. You can check the ones you need and click OK. Since you have only the VM, the selection process is easy.

6. Once you click OK, the VM gets added to the Virtual Machines section. You can find a check box called OS Disks Only. Enabling this option will exclude data disks attached to the VM, and the backup will be performed only on the OS disk. To finalize the backup configuration, you can click Enable Backup.

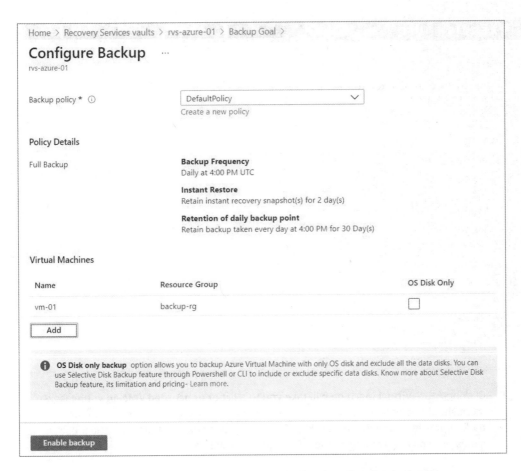

Home > Recovery Services vaults > rvs-azure-01 > Backup Goal >

Configure Backup ...
rvs-azure-01

Backup policy * ⓘ | DefaultPolicy   ∨ |
                       Create a new policy

Policy Details

Full Backup   **Backup Frequency**
                               Daily at 4:00 PM UTC

                               Instant Restore
                               Retain instant recovery snapshot(s) for 2 day(s)

                               Retention of daily backup point
                               Retain backup taken every day at 4:00 PM for 30 Day(s)

Virtual Machines

Name	Resource Group	OS Disk Only
vm-01	backup-rg	☐

[Add]

ⓘ **OS Disk only backup** option allows you to backup Azure Virtual Machine with only OS disk and exclude all the data disks. You can use Selective Disk Backup feature through Powershell or CLI to include or exclude specific data disks. Know more about Selective Disk Backup feature, its limitation and pricing- Learn more.

[Enable backup]

7. Enabling the process may take some time to complete. Once the deployment is completed, you can navigate back to Recovery Services Vault ➤ Backup Items. Out of all the services supported by the vault, you can see the item count as 1 for Azure Virtual Machine.

EXERCISE 10.1 *(continued)*

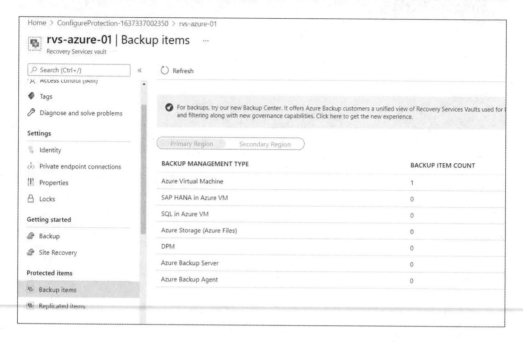

8. Clicking Azure Virtual Machine will take you to a list of onboarded VMs. In your case, there should be only one, as shown here. You will be able to see the status of the backup pre-check and the last backup. Since you have enabled the VM, the last backup status will show a warning as the initial backup is still pending.

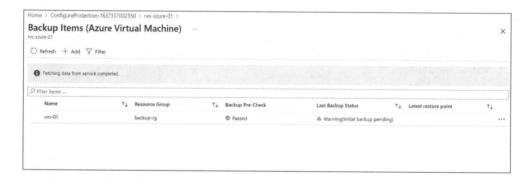

9. If you click the VM, the portal will take you to a new page where can get more insights about the backup and options to control the backup. Per your policy, the backup will be triggered at 4 a.m. UTC, and a full backup will be taken. Click Backup Now to trigger the backup.

10. You will be asked to provide the retention as you are taking this backup outside the policy; you can choose a date in the future and click OK. It may take some time to complete the backup. Once the backup is finished, the warning symbol in the last backup status should disappear as you have completed the initial backup. You can click the View All Jobs option on the same page to track the progress of the backup.

Implementing Restore

If you completed Exercise 10.1, then your virtual machine snapshot is successfully saved to the vault. As of now, you will have only one restore point that was created as part of the backup you triggered earlier, but in real-world scenarios you will probably have multiple restore points created by the scheduled backup. In Figure 10.8, you will be able to see the restore point and also the Restore VM option.

FIGURE 10.8   Restoring a VM

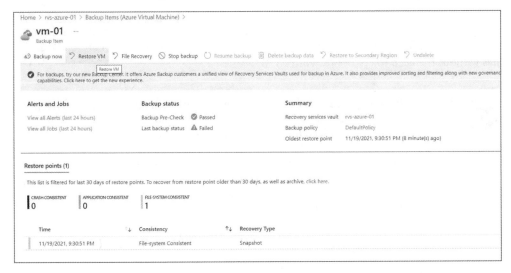

Clicking Restore VM will let you choose the restore point. After selecting the restore point, you can either create a new one or replace an existing one, as shown in Figure 10.9.

FIGURE 10.9   VM restore options

Home > rvs-azure-01 > Backup Items (Azure Virtual Machine) > vm-01 >

Restore Virtual Machine   ...
vm-01

Restore point *	11/19/2021, 9:30:51 PM
	Select
Data Store	Snapshot

Restore Configuration

- ⦿ Create new
- ◯ Replace existing

> ⓘ To create an alternate configuration when restoring your VM (from the following menus), use PowerShell cmdlets.

Restore Type * ⓘ	Create new virtual machine ⌄
Virtual machine name * ⓘ	Enter a name
Resource group * ⓘ	backup-rg ⌄
Virtual network * ⓘ	Select an option ⌄
Subnet * ⓘ	Select an option ⌄
Staging Location * ⓘ	Select an option ⌄
	Can't find your storage account ?

[Restore]

If you take a second look at Figure 10.8, you can see an option to perform file recovery. Using this you will be able to mount the restore point as a drive to your VM and recover the files without the need to restore the entire VM.

NOTE   After completing the exercise, make sure you stop the backup and delete the vault. You cannot directly delete the vault because of the soft delete option. You can read more about this here:

```
https://docs.microsoft.com/en-us/azure/backup/
backup-azure-security-feature-cloud
```

Failing to delete the vault will incur additional charges.

We hope this brings clarity on how to back up and restore virtual machines that are deployed in the cloud. Tracking these backups and monitoring them can be tricky sometimes when you are dealing with thousands of servers. Azure offers a solution called Azure Backup Center to track the backup taken by Azure Backup in a holistic manner. Azure Backup Center can provide insights into the backup jobs, the number of instances you are backing up, and any alerts triggered. With the help of filters, you can fine-tune and monitor a subset of vaults and machines. You can find the Backup Center by searching in the Azure portal. Figure 10.10 shows a sample dashboard from the Azure Backup Center.

FIGURE 10.10   Azure Backup Center

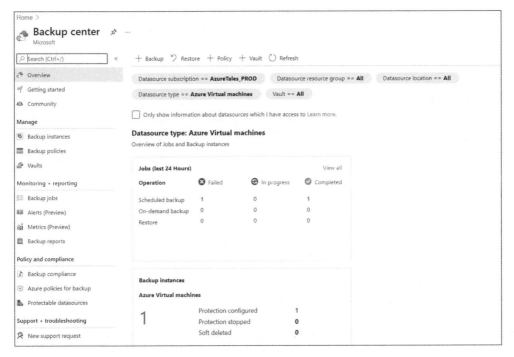

Earlier, when we were discussing different options available for backup, we discussed Azure Backup Server. Let's talk about this in detail.

Azure Backup Server

As mentioned earlier, this is another method to back up your virtual machines with the help of Data Protection Manager (DPM) or Microsoft Azure Backup Server (MABS). This method is ideal for backing up specialized workloads such as SharePoint, Exchange, and SQL Server.

The backup will be taken by DPM/MABS, and then you will back up the DPM/MABS storage to a vault. There are several advantages of doing so.

- You will get support for app-aware backups optimized for applications like SharePoint, Exchange, and SQL Server. Also, you will get support for file/folder/volume backups and machine state backup including bare-metal or system state backups.

- In the case of on-premises servers, you don't have to run the MARS agent on each of the servers. Instead, you will be running the DPM/MABS agent on each VM, and the MARS agent runs only on the DPM/MABS.

- This offers granularity and flexibility in terms of scheduling backups.

- You can group machines under protection groups and back them up together. This is helpful when application tiers are running on different servers and you want to back up them up together.

Let's see how you can implement a backup using DPM/MABS.

Implementing a Backup

The following steps will give you a high-level understanding about the steps involved in the implementation of a backup in DPM/MABS.

1. The DPM/MABS agent needs to be installed on the machines you want to protect and then you add these machines to a DPM protection group.

2. To protect Azure VMs, the MABS server must be deployed in Azure. Similarly, for on-premises servers you need to deploy the DPM/MABS server in the on-premises infrastructure.

3. While setting up the protection, you need to select a local disk for local backup and Azure for online protection. You will be able to configure individual policies for local and Azure protection separately.

4. The disks of the VMs added to the protection group will be automatically backed up based on the schedule to the DPM/MABS local disks.

5. These local disks are replicated to the Azure Recovery Services vault with the help of a MARS agent installed on the DPM/MABS server.

In the Recovery Services vault, you need to select the source as On-Premises and select the workload, as shown in Figure 10.11.

After that, you will be able to see the link to download the Azure Backup Server, which you need to install on-premises (refer to Figure 10.12). If you check the box Already Using System Center Data Protection Manager Or Any Other System Center Product, you will be presented with the steps to perform for DPM configuration.

For beginners, MARS and MABS can be confusing. At the end of the day, both of them are agents for orchestrating the backup; however, with respect to the limits, benefits, and workload type, they differ. Let's see the difference between MARS and MABS.

FIGURE 10.11   Enrolling on-premise workloads

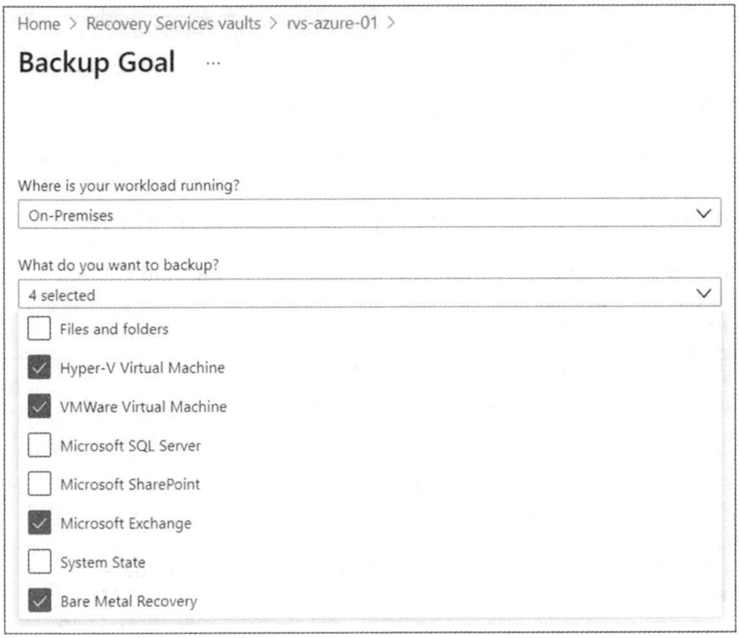

Home > Recovery Services vaults > rvs-azure-01 >

Backup Goal   ...

Where is your workload running?

| On-Premises   ∨ |

What do you want to backup?

| 4 selected   ∨ |

☐ Files and folders

☑ Hyper-V Virtual Machine

☑ VMWare Virtual Machine

☐ Microsoft SQL Server

☐ Microsoft SharePoint

☑ Microsoft Exchange

☐ System State

☑ Bare Metal Recovery

FIGURE 10.12   Downloading MABS

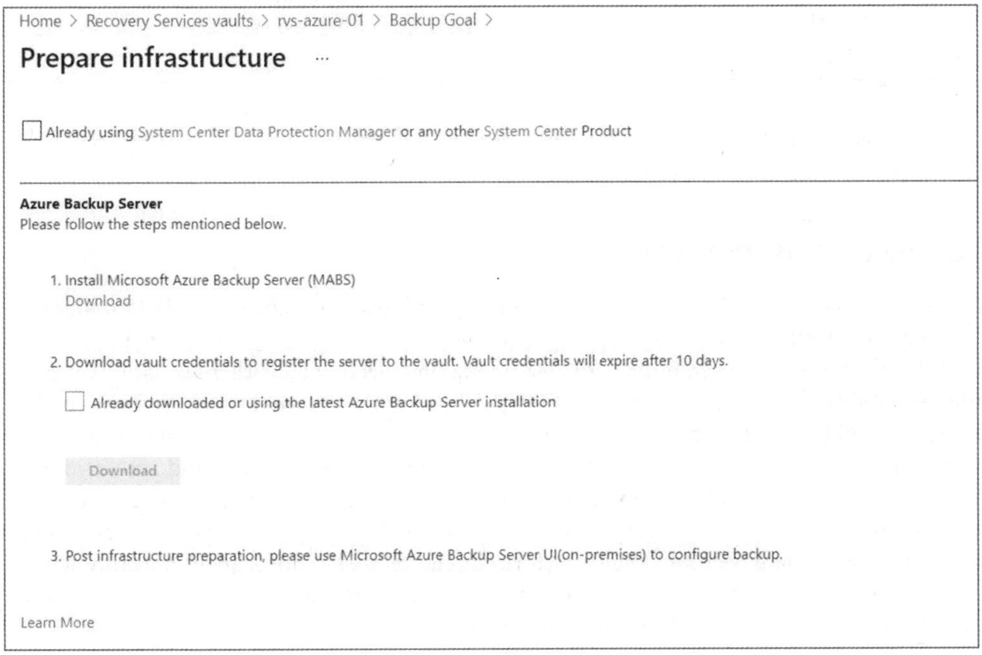

Home > Recovery Services vaults > rvs-azure-01 > Backup Goal >

Prepare infrastructure   ...

☐ Already using System Center Data Protection Manager or any other System Center Product

Azure Backup Server
Please follow the steps mentioned below.

1. Install Microsoft Azure Backup Server (MABS)
   Download

2. Download vault credentials to register the server to the vault. Vault credentials will expire after 10 days.

   ☐ Already downloaded or using the latest Azure Backup Server installation

   Download

3. Post infrastructure preparation, please use Microsoft Azure Backup Server UI(on-premises) to configure backup.

Learn More

Comparison

Table 10.1 summarizes the difference between the Microsoft Azure Backup (MARS) agent and Microsoft Azure Backup Server (MABS).

TABLE 10.1   Comparison Between MARS and MABS

Agent	Benefits	Limits	Workload type	Backup storage
Azure Backup (MARS) agent	File and folder backup solution for physical and virtual Windows servers. No need to deploy Backup Server.	Linux is not supported. Backup is limited to three times per day. Not application aware. File-, folder-, and volume-level restore only.	Files and Folders	Recovery Services vault
Azure Backup Server (MABS)	Linux support on Hyper-V and VMware VMs. Backup and restore for VMware VMs. App-aware snapshots. System Center license is not required.	Oracle workloads are not supported. No support for tape backup.	Files, folders, volumes, VMs, applications, and specialized work-loads like Share-Point, Exchange, and SQL Server.	Recovery Services vault and local storage.

So far, we covered the backup solution. Next, we will cover a disaster recovery solution in Azure. It's none other than Azure Site Recovery.

Azure Site Recovery

Azure Site Recovery (ASR) is a business continuity and disaster recovery (BCDR) solution. You have availability sets and availability zones when you want to implement highly available architectures. However, if the entire Azure region goes down, neither availability sets nor availability zones can help you as they are defined at the region level. With the help of ASR, you will be able to replicate your virtual and physical servers from a primary site to a secondary site. You can initiate a failover during a primary region outage and access your workload from the secondary region. Once the primary location is up and running, you need to fail back to it. One thing to note here is that the failover and failback process is not automated, and you have to manually perform it. Figure 10.13 shows an architecture where a three-tier application is getting replicated to a secondary region. During a failover, the replica of the infrastructure will be created in the secondary region.

FIGURE 10.13   VM replication using ASR

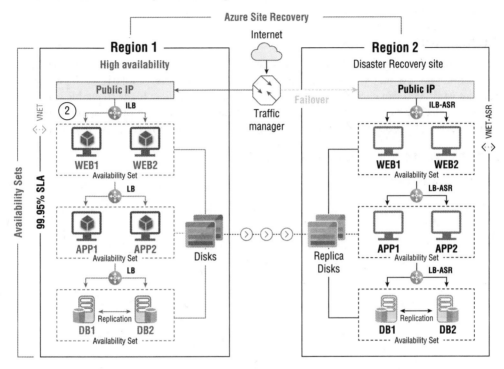

You can use ASR for several replication scenarios as this solution is targeting not only Azure to Azure replication. The following are some other supported scenarios:

- Replicate on-premises VMware VMs, Hyper-V VMs, physical Windows and Linux servers, and Azure Stack VMs to Azure

- Replicate Windows instances running in AWS to Azure

- Replicate on-premises VMware VMs, Hyper-V VMs managed by System Center VMM

  Being a solution for BCDR across platforms, ASR offers the following features:

- Replication, failover, and failback are managed from a single management portal, i.e., the Azure portal.

- Continuous replication is supported for VMware VMs and Azure VMs. For Hyper-VM, the replication frequency is as low as 30 seconds.

- Application consistent recovery points can be created. Disk data, all data in memory, and all transactions will be captured in the snapshot.

- You can execute planned failovers with zero data loss and unplanned failovers with minimal data loss. Once the primary region is online, you can fail back.

- Network management tasks including allocating IP addresses, setting up load balancers, and integrating Azure Traffic Managers can be seamlessly integrated with ASR.

Let's see how the end-to-end replication is done from the primary Azure region to the secondary region.

Architecture

You will be protecting the virtual machines inside a Recovery Services vault. In the backup discussion, you saw that you have an option to back up instances. Similarly, in the Recovery Services vault, you can click Enable Site Recovery in the Overview blade to enable site recovery. Selecting this option will show you the different replication options, as shown in Figure 10.14. The process will take you through a wizard, which is very easy to configure.

FIGURE 10.14 Enabling Azure Site Recovery

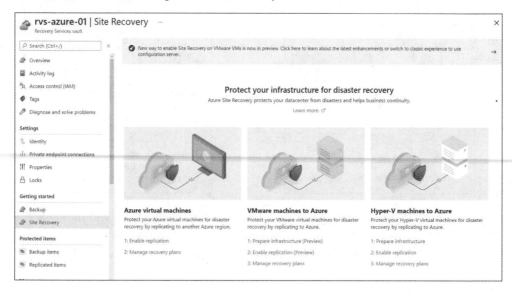

Now that you know how to enable Site Recovery, let's understand what happens under the hood when you enable replication on an Azure VM.

- The site recovery is orchestrated using an agent called the Site Recovery Mobility service extension. When you enable replication, the agent will be installed on all target machines.

- The extension will register the VM with Site Recovery. Continuous replication of the data stored in the disk (storage account) will begin. There will be a cache storage account in the primary region, and it will receive all the disk write operations immediately.

- The data is then processed in the cache storage by Site Recovery and will be transferred to the storage account which is in the secondary region.

- Once the data is processed, every five minutes crash consistent recovery points are created. Based on the policy configured in the replication policy, app-consistent recovery points are created.

- When you perform the failover, the VMs are created in the target resource group, target virtual network, target subnet, and target availability set (if any). These target resources are created beforehand when you onboard the VM. You will be able to see any restore points during the failover process.

Figure 10.15 outlines the ASR architecture.

FIGURE 10.15 ASR architecture

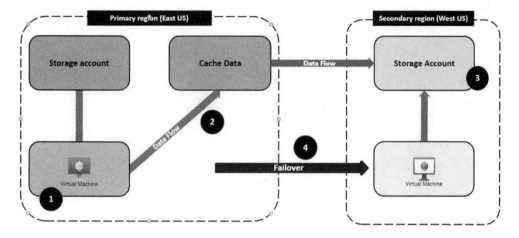

Summary

In this chapter, we discussed two main concepts: file and folder backups and virtual machine data protection. For files and folders, you can back up Azure Files using Azure Backup, and for on-premises you can use the Microsoft Azure Recovery Services agent. In both scenarios, the data is stored in the Recovery Services vault. Depending upon the source of the data, the portal will provide further steps to enable backup.

Second, we covered virtual machine data protection; this includes backup and BCDR strategy. As you saw in the case of files and folders, you have multiple options for backing up virtual machines. For Azure Virtual Machines, you can use Azure Backup. For on-premises servers, you can use DPM/MABS for backing up virtual machines. In Azure, you can use Azure Site Recovery for disaster recovery. Using ASR, you can replicate the virtual machine to a secondary region. When there is a regional outage, you can fail over to the second region.

In Chapter 11, "Monitoring Resources," you will be learning Azure Monitor. Azure Monitor plays a vital role in monitoring Azure resources, thus ensuring the reliability and availability of the services.

Exam Essentials

Learn about the backing up files and folders.   Learn about file and folder backup using Azure Backup and the role of the MARS agent.

Learn about the VM backup methods.   Learn about different methods available for backing up virtual machines. Understand how Azure Backup, DPM, and MABS work.

Learn about the Site Recovery solution.   Understand Azure Site Recovery and its architecture.

Review Questions

1. Your organization would like to back up Azure files. Which of the following solutions should be created for storing the backup?

    A. Virtual machine

    B. Azure Backup

    C. Recovery Services vault

    D. Snapshot

2. Which is the default redundancy when you create a Recovery Services vault?

    A. LRS

    B. ZRS

    C. GRS

    D. RA-GRS

3. You created a Recovery Services vault and started backing up files and folder. You noticed that you are storing data in GRS and would like to change this to LRS as part of cost optimization. However, you are not able to change the redundancy. What could be the reason?

    A. You need to have Recovery Services vault Owner permission to perform this action.

    B. You cannot change the configuration when there are active backup items.

    C. You cannot change this once you start backing up any resource; you should have changed this right after creation.

    D. You don't have access to the file share.

4. Which agent is used for backing up on-premises files and folders to a vault?

    A. MABS

    B. MMA

    C. WAAGENT

    D. MARS

5. You are planning to back up on-premises virtual machines to Azure. Where should you install the MARS agent? (Select all that apply.)

    A. On all servers that you plan to back up

    B. On the domain controller

    C. On the DPM server

    D. On the MABS

6. Which of the following statements is false? (Select all that apply.)

    A. MABS cannot back up Oracle workloads.

    B. MABS supports files and folders.

    C. MABS cannot perform app-aware snapshots.

    D. MABS data is stored in the vault only.

7. Which tool can provide a single unified management experience in Azure for enterprises to govern, monitor, operate, and analyze backups at scale?

    A. Microsoft Backup Server

    B. DPM

    C. Backup Center

    D. Azure Site Recovery Manager

8. Which of the following statements is false?

    A. Azure Linux VM is supported in Azure Backup.

    B. MARS agent is supported only on Linux EXT4 filesystems.

    C. Specialized workloads can be backed up using DPM/MABS.

    D. MARS takes a backup three times per day.

9. When the backups are deleted, how long are they preserved under soft delete?

    A. 10 days

    B. 14 days

    C. 7 days

    D. 1 day

10. While setting up Azure Site Recovery, in which region do you have to deploy the cache storage account?

    A. Primary region

    B. Secondary region

    C. Primary and secondary regions

    D. Secondary region with RA-GRS

11. Which of the following extensions is responsible for orchestrating Azure Site Recovery?

    A. ASR mobility extension

    B. ASR MMA extension

    C. ASR backup extension

    D. ASR replication controller

12. You need to back up files and folders to Azure. Which three steps must you perform? (Select three.)

    A. Download, install, and register the backup agent

    B. Sync the configuration

    C. Back up files and folders

    D. Create a backup vault

    E. Create a recovery services vault

13. You are responsible for creating a disaster recovery plan for your datacenter. You must be able to re-create the virtual machines from scratch. This includes the operating system, its configuration/settings, and patches. Which of the following will provide a bare-metal backup of your machines?

A. MARS

B. MABS

C. Snapshots

D. Images

14. You have several Azure VMs that are currently running production workloads. You have a mix of Windows Server and Linux servers, and you need to implement a backup strategy for your production workloads. Which feature should you use in this case?

A. Managed snapshots

B. Azure Site Recovery

C. Azure Migrate

D. Azure Backup

15. You plan to use Azure Backup to protect your virtual machines and data and are ready to create a backup. What is the first thing you need to do?

A. Define a backup policy

B. Create a Recovery Services vault

C. Install a backup agent

D. Schedule a backup

16. You deploy several virtual machines (VMs) to Azure. You are responsible for backing up all the data processed by the VMs. In the event of a failure, you need to restore the data as quickly as possible. Which of these options would you recommend for restoring a database used for development on a data disk?

A. VM Backup

B. ASR

C. Disk imaging

D. Disk snapshot

17. You deploy several virtual machines (VMs) to Azure. You are responsible for backing up all data processed by the VMs. In the event of a failure, you need to restore the data as quickly as possible. Which of these options would you recommend for restoring the entire virtual machine or files on the virtual machine?

A. Azure Site Recovery

B. VM Backup

C. Disk image backup

D. Snapshot

18. What is the maximum number of Recovery Services vaults that can be created in each region?

   A. 10

   B. 100

   C. 500

   D. 1000

19. What is the limit of data that can be backed up to a vault?

   A. 10 TB

   B. 10 PB

   C. 100 PB

   D. No limit

20. Which of the following workloads can be protected using Azure Site Recovery? (Select all that apply.)

   A. Virtual machines

   B. Active Directory

   C. Dynamics

   D. Exchange

Chapter

11

Monitoring Resources

MONITOR RESOURCES BY USING AZURE MONITOR

✓ Configure and interpret metrics

✓ Configure Azure Monitor logs

✓ Query and analyze logs

✓ Setup alerts and actions

✓ Configure Application Insights

You need to collect various data points from your resources including health, performance, and availability. The process or act of collecting this dataset is called *monitoring*. The process doesn't end with the collection; you should have tools or options for analyzing the collected data. With the help of a proper monitoring system, you will be able to understand the state and operational status of your solution. If there are any issues with the status of the system, monitoring systems can alert administrators and help them to rectify issues before they impact production.

In Azure, with the help of Azure Monitor, you will be able to collect data from various levels of your solution. Azure Monitor offers a platform to collect, analyze, and alert on the data you collect. With the help of agents, you can further expand the monitoring scope to on-premises and other cloud providers. The key to implement the right monitoring system is to learn the available tools. In this chapter, you will be focusing on implementing an end-to-end monitoring solution with the help of Azure Monitor.

Azure Monitor

Azure Monitor is the centralized solution for any monitoring requirements in Azure. It offers the following capabilities:

Monitoring and Visualization In Azure Monitor, you have metrics. These are numerical values collected from Azure resources automatically without any user configuration to convey the state of the system. The state includes the health, operation, and performance of the system. These values can be monitored and plotted on a time axis in real time.

Analyze and Query Logs Logs include various types of logging data from Azure subscriptions, tenants, platforms, and applications. This can be analyzed and queried in Azure Monitor.

Alerts and Actions Alerting is crucial in any monitoring system, as you need to have a solution by which you will be able to notify the administrator proactively. With the help of actions, you will be able to automate corrective measures when a particular alert is triggered.

Figure 11.1 gives a high-level view of Azure Monitor.

In Figure 11.1, the left side represents data sources from which Azure Monitor can pull data. The data ingested from these sources will be classified and stored into two data types: metrics and logs. On the right side, you can see a plethora of functions that Azure Monitor can execute on top of this collection. These functions provide various capabilities such as insights, visualizations, analysis, alerting, and integration with third-party solutions as well. Now that you know about data types, let's understand the difference between metrics and logs.

FIGURE 11.1 Azure Monitor

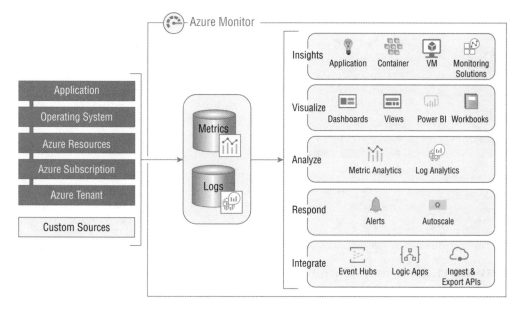

Metrics

Metrics are numerical values that are ingested from Azure resources used to represent the state of the system at a particular point in time. They are lightweight, and the metrics collected will vary from resource to resource. For example, for a virtual machine, the metrics available will be CPU Percentage, Network In, Network Out, Memory, etc. On the other hand, if you take a storage account, the available metrics will be Number Of Requests, Number Of Failed Requests, Number Of API Calls, etc. You can analyze the metrics from the Metrics Explorer; however, for most of the resources, the common metrics are available in the Overview ➢ Monitoring section.

For example, in Figure 11.2, you can see that the Overview ➢ Monitoring section shows different metrics such as CPU (Average), Network (Total), Disk Bytes (Total), etc. Though it is not visible in the figure, there are more metrics like Disk Operations/Sec (Average) and Disk Operations/Sec (Average).

Clicking any of these tiles will take you to the Metrics Explorer, which will help you plot multiple values in a chart and track them. In Figure 11.3, you can see that CPU, Network Out, and Memory are plotted on the same graph. This will help you to analyze different aspects of the system at the same time.

Currently, we are plotting metrics of a single VM on the chart. If needed, you can pull metrics from different VMs and plot them on the same chart. If you take a closer look at Figure 11.3, you can see more options such as changing the timeframe, changing the chart type, sharing the chart, and also pinning it to the dashboard. Further, if needed, you can pull this data into Power BI or any other visualization tool to build business analytics. Without any additional cost, the metrics are retained by Azure for 93 days.

Now that you are familiar with metrics, let's learn about logs.

FIGURE 11.2   Viewing metrics

FIGURE 11.3   Metrics Explorer

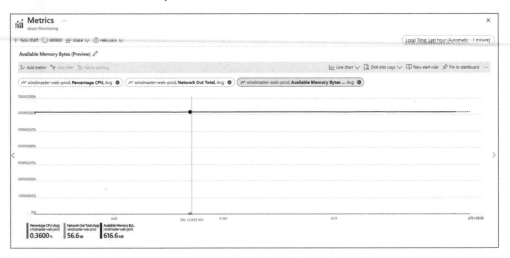

Logs

Azure Log Analytics is responsible for storing the log data that you collect from different Azure resources. The stored data can be queried, analyzed, and filtered with the help of a rich query language called the Kusto Query Language (KQL). The reason why we call this language *rich* is because it offers simple queries as well as complex joins, aggregations, and analytics. Learning this language is easy if you have already worked with SQL or Splunk queries.

Metrics are numerical in nature. But logs are mainly text that comprise information relevant to the operation of the system. The best examples for log content are the data you see in Windows Event Viewer, while the data that you see in Task Manager is more like metrics. Syslog in Linux is an example of a log, as the log data is not consistent and the format may vary from source to source.

In the "Log Analytics" section, you will see how you can retrieve logs from a VM and analyze it in the Log Analytics workspace using KQL. For now, you will explore the different data sources supported by Azure Monitor.

Data Sources

If you recall from Figure 11.1, you can see that Azure Monitor can ingest data from multiple data sources. These data sources represent logs from different tiers starting from the platform all the way to the application itself. The following are the different tiers from which Azure Monitor collects data:

Application Monitoring Data   With the help of Application Insights, you will be able to pull the logs from the application level regardless of which platform you are using. The advantage is that you will be able to analyze the issues that are happening at the application level.

Guest OS Monitoring   Operating system data on which the application is installed can be ingested into Azure Monitor. The scope collection can be expanded to VMs on-premises and other cloud providers as well.

Resource Monitoring Data   Any operation done on the resource will be logged and can be used for auditing purposes. This can be ingested with the help of diagnostic settings.

Subscription Monitoring   The activity log works at the subscription level. This pulls all the operations taking place at the subscription level.

Tenant Monitoring Data   Azure Active Directory–related logs can be ingested into Azure Monitor to log the tenant-level activities including sign-ins, conditional access, and MFA.

Some of these datasets will be ingested as soon as you create the Azure subscription and resources; they are free of cost as well. For example, an activity log will be logged every time you make an operation to a subscription or resource, and these logs will be retained for 90 days free of cost. Other sources like guest OS monitoring and application monitoring require diagnostic settings to be configured. You will be charged for the amount of data you ingest.

Let's explore activity logs as they're crucial in conducting audits.

Activity Log

With the help of an activity log, you can get insights into different operations occurring at the subscription level. The logs include data from Azure Resource Manager, Azure Policy, Service Health, autoscaling, Azure Alerts, and recommendations from Azure Advisor and Azure Security Center (now known as Microsoft Defender for Cloud). The insight is helpful to find out who committed the operation, what operation was committed, and when it was committed. Any PUT, POST, or DELETE operations will be logged in the activity log. Read operations (GET) are not logged in activity logs.

You can navigate to an activity log by searching for *Activity Log* in the Azure portal. You could also open the activity log from the subscription, resource group, and resource levels. Accessing an activity log from these scopes will query the log from the selected scope, making it easier to narrow down the search. Using the activity log, you can find answers to the following:

- What operations were committed?

- Who performed the operation?

- When did the operation occur?

- What is the status of the operation?

- What information does the JSON metadata provide?

As mentioned earlier, the activity log will be automatically enabled from the moment you sign up for Azure Subscription, and it is free. The ingested logs will be stored for 90 days. If you need to retain the data for more than 90 days, you have several options to store the data. As this is an extra configuration, you need to pay for the storage. By default, any data older than 90 days will not be retained. Let's see the different event categories available in activity logs.

Event Categories

As Azure Activity Log is a subscription-wide logging system, Azure has divided the logs ingested into different categories. This will help us in narrowing down your search. The following are the event categories available in activity logs:

Administrative   This includes records of all create, update, and delete operations via Azure Resource Manager. Examples of events in this category are Create Or Update Virtual Machine, Create Storage Account, Add Role Assignment, etc.

Service Health   This is a record of all service health events that have occurred in Azure. An example is "Virtual Machines in West US is experiencing downtime." This event comes in five types: Action Required, Assisted Recovery, Incident, Maintenance, Information, or Security.

Resource Health   Service Health focuses on any health events in Azure, while Resource Health comprises any health events that happened to your resources. The status includes Available, Degraded, Unavailable, and Unknown. Here is an example: "SQL Database health status changed to unavailable."

Alert Whenever alerts are triggered, that will be logged in this category. Here is an example: "Alert triggered - Memory% on VM has been over 60% for the past 10 minutes."

Autoscale All the autoscaling events will be logged whenever an autoscaling event happens for your resources. Here is an example: "Autoscale scale up action succeeded."

Recommendation The source for these logs is Azure Advisor. The recommendations generated by Azure Advisor for resources will be logged in this category. Here is an example: "Right size or shutdown underutilized resources."

Security This includes any security alerts generated by Azure Defender for Servers. Here is an example: "Endpoint protection needs to be enabled."

Policy Whenever Azure Policy is evaluated, the effect action will be logged in this category. You will see Audit and Deny actions in this one.

Though you will have categories for filtering the logs, the number of entries will still be high. You need more filters by which you will be able to query the logs and streamline your search. Let's see what other query filters are available for you in the activity log apart from event categories.

Querying Logs

As you can pull the logs from the subscription scope, there will be thousands of line items in a real-world scenario. Scrolling through the list will be a hectic task, and here comes the role of query filters. In Figure 11.4, you can see how the query was filtered to find VM creation. Let's understand the filters used here:

- **Management group:** Filter the logs to a specific management group. This is ideal for filtering subscriptions.

- **Subscription:** Select the subscriptions.

- **Event severity:** Event severity levels will be represented as Informational, Warning, Error, or Critical.

- **Timespan:** Select the timeframe for the query. Options include Last 1 Hour, Last 6 Hours, Last 24 Hours, Last Week, Last 2 Weeks, Last Month, and Custom for entering the custom start and end date time.

- **Resource group:** This will display resources that are part of the selected subscriptions, which allows us to further filter the logs to a set of resource groups.

- **Resource:** This is the name of a specific resource that can be selected.

- **Resource type:** This is the type of resource that can be selected.

- **Operation:** You can filter the ARM operations. Examples are Create or Update Virtual Machine.

- **Event initiated by:** Filter using an email address; this will be useful to list all the operations performed by a user.

- **Event category:** These are categories explained in the previous section.

- **Search:** You can also utilize the search box to search using keywords.

FIGURE 11.4   Querying activity logs

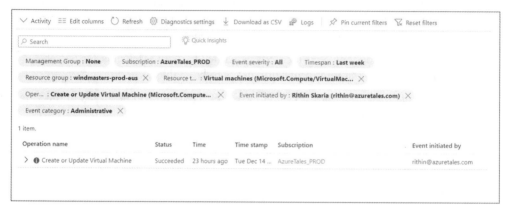

In Figure 11.4, we are trying to list all the virtual machines that were created or updated by user `rithin@azuretales.com` from last week in the selected subscription. As this an administrative task, we have filtered for the event category as well as for demonstration, which is not required as we are sorting on the operation.

Now that you know how the activity log works, let's talk about the service Azure Alerts.

Azure Alerts

Alerting is crucial in any monitoring system as it will help you get notifications automatically before issues turn into bigger problems. In Azure, you use Azure Alerts for alerting. The following are the benefits of using Azure Alerts:

Improved Notifications   With the help of action groups, you can group a set of actions that can be reused in multiple alerts.

Centralized Management   You can create alerts for metrics, activity logs, log analytics, and insights all in a single place.

Alert Management   All alerts can be managed from a common pane, and you can also update the state of the alert.

Workflow Integration   You can integrate Azure Logic Apps, Azure Functions, Azure Automation Runbook, etc., with alerts.

You can create alerts on the following data sources. These include but are not limited to the following:

- Metric values
- Log search queries
- Activity log events
- Service health
- Resource health
- Availability tests

Now you will see how you can create alerts in Azure Alerts.

Creating Alert Rules

Alerts are an inevitable component while building a reliable system as they ensure the reliability by constantly tracking different sources. If there is anything wrong, then alerts are triggered. This way you will be able to review the issues before your end users are affected. Alerts comprise rules, action groups, and monitor conditions. The following are the key attributes of an alert rule:

Target Resource   Define a target resource for which you want to implement alerting. The available metrics or logs will vary depending on the resource you are selecting. Examples include a virtual machine, an app service, etc.

Signal   These are values that are emitted by the target resource. Metrics, logs, and activity log entries are examples of signals.

Criteria   Criteria is more of a condition that can be used to fire the alert. If you combine a signal and logic on a target resource, you get criteria. An example is CPU % > 80 for VM-01; here CPU% is the signal. Greater than 80 is the logic, and VM-01 is the target resource.

Alert Name   This is the name of the alert so that once you get an email for any alert, you can easily recognize the alert.

Alert Description   This is the description for the alert.

Severity   This is to configure the severity of the alert when it's fired. For critical issues, you can set the severity as 0, and for low-priority or informational issues, you can set it to 4. The severity can have a value from 0–4.

Action   This is a specific action that will be executed once the alert is fired.

Once the alerts are fired, you can use the alert states to define the current status of the alert. Let's take a look at the alert states.

Alert States

You can set the state of an alert once it is fired. This gives the stakeholders a holistic view of all alerts fired in their environment and the state of each alert. Alerts are fired whenever a condition is satisfied, and once fired, the state will be set to New. You can change the state to Acknowledged or Closed once you acknowledge and resolve the issue. For better tracking, all these state changes will be logged in the alert history. The following alert states are supported in Azure Alerts, and you cannot create custom states:

New   An alert has been fired, and it is pending review by one of the administrators.

Acknowledged   Transition to this state when an administrator reviews the alert and starts working on it.

Closed   Move to this state once the issue is resolved. If needed, you can always change it back to the Acknowledged state for review.

Now that you are clear about the alerts and alert state, it's important to understand the action groups while creating alerts. Before you move on to the exercise, let's talk about action groups.

Action Groups

An action group is a collection of notification preferences that can be reused in multiple alerts. The notifications and actions that you define inside the action group will be executed when the alert is fired. You can create multiple action groups with different notification preferences, and these can be used across your alerts. Action groups consist of two parts: notifications and actions.

Notifications help us to configure the notification methods to alert users when the alert is fired. You have two options available for notifications, as shown in Figure 11.5.

Email Azure Resource Manager Role   You can send email notifications to Azure RBAC roles like Owner, Contributor, Reader, Monitoring Contributor, and Monitoring Reader that are assigned at the subscription scope. All user principals assigned with any of the aforementioned roles will be notified when the alert is triggered. Azure AD group and service principals are excluded from the email notification.

Email/SMS Message/Push/Voice   Specify any email, SMS, Azure app push notifications, or voice alerts. Email and app notifications require an email address, while SMS and voice require the country code and phone number for sending alerts.

Actions, on the other hand, help us configure the actions that need to be performed when the alert is fired. Action groups support seven actions, as shown in Figure 11.6.

Automation Runbook   You can write automation scripts, and the actions can be executed when an alert is triggered.

Azure Function   Using serverless compute, you can run small chunks of code when the alert is fired.

ITSM   You can integrate your ITSM tools like ServiceNow so that whenever an alert is triggered, the corresponding ticket will be created in the ITSM tool.

FIGURE 11.5   Action group notifications

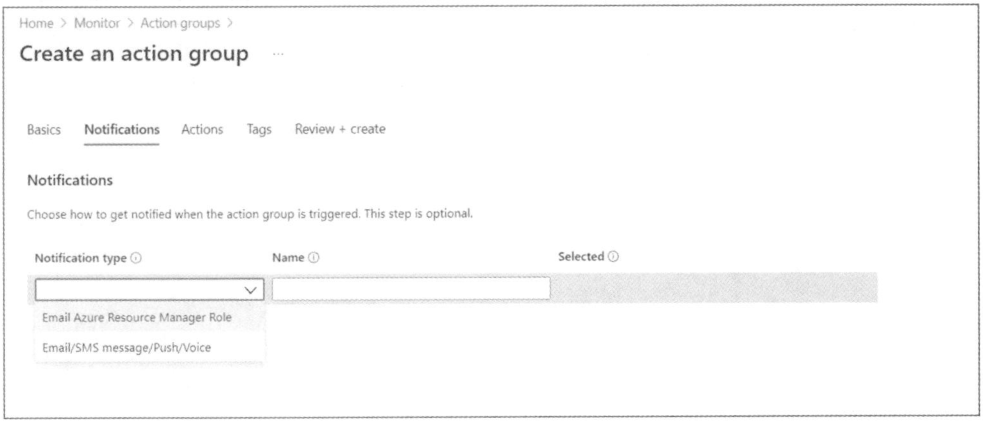

Home > Monitor > Action groups >

Create an action group   ···

Basics   **Notifications**   Actions   Tags   Review + create

Notifications

Choose how to get notified when the action group is triggered. This step is optional.

Notification type ⓘ	Name ⓘ	Selected ⓘ
⌄		
Email Azure Resource Manager Role		
Email/SMS message/Push/Voice		

Logic App   You can connect your business workflows to your alerts.

Secure Webhook/Webhook   This is the HTTPS or HTTP endpoint for an external application to communicate.

Event Hub   You can ingest the event to other systems.

FIGURE 11.6   Action group actions

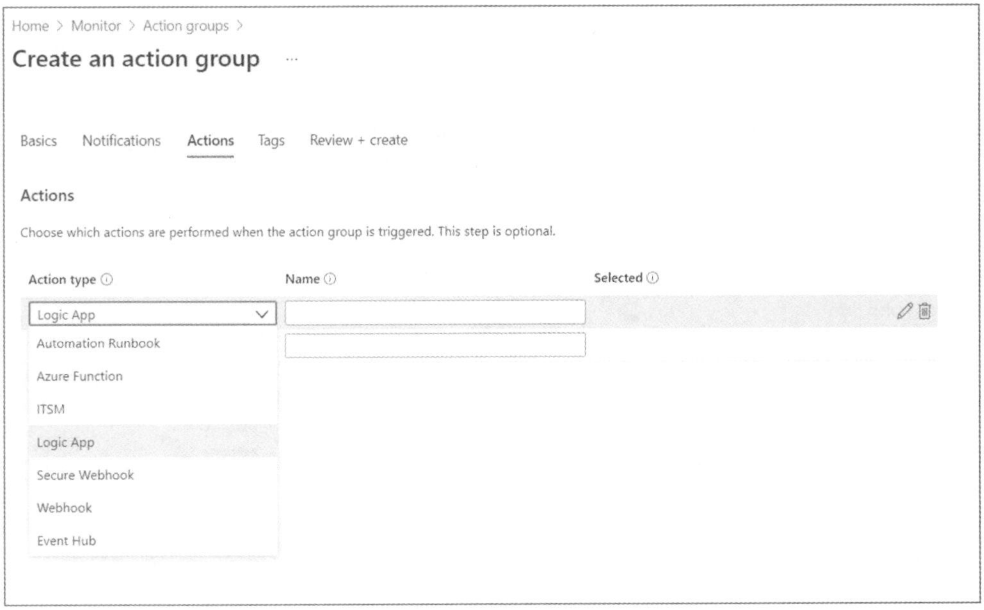

Home > Monitor > Action groups >

Create an action group   ···

Basics   Notifications   **Actions**   Tags   Review + create

Actions

Choose which actions are performed when the action group is triggered. This step is optional.

Action type ⓘ	Name ⓘ	Selected ⓘ
Logic App ⌄		
Automation Runbook		
Azure Function		
ITSM		
Logic App		
Secure Webhook		
Webhook		
Event Hub		

Let's see alerts in action. In Exercise 11.1, you will configure an alert on a VM. When CPU% is greater than 75, you will trigger an alert. Before starting the exercise, please create an Ubuntu virtual machine.

EXERCISE 11.1

Creating Alerts

1. Sign in to the Azure portal and navigate to Azure Monitor ➤ Alerts. Click Create and then select Alert Rule.

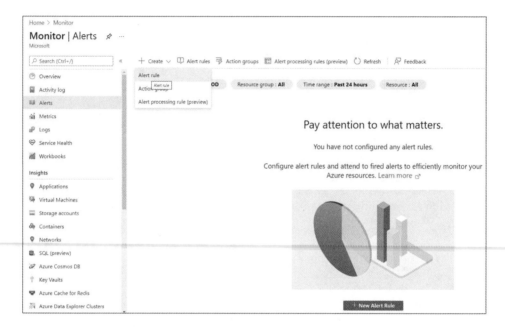

2. Under Scope, click Select Resource to select your target resource. From the side window, select the subscription and set the resource type as Virtual Machines. Select the virtual machine from the list and then click Done. The selection will be populated under the scope.

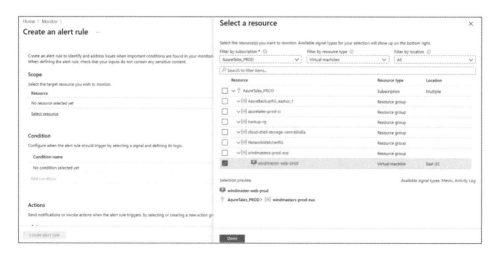

3. To configure the criteria for the alert, click Add Condition. Set the signal type to Metrics, and search for *CPU* in the search bar. From the results, select Percentage CPU.

4. Once you click Percentage CPU, you will be asked to set the criteria and threshold values. Set the operator as Greater Than, the aggregation type as Average, and the threshold value as 70. This means that whenever the average CPU utilization exceeds 70 percent, the alert will be fired. Furthermore, you can configure the aggregation granularity and frequency of evaluation; however, you will go with the default values. The data will be collected per the frequency of evaluation. Click Done.

5. Next is Actions. This is where you select the action group. As of now, you don't have any action groups defined. If you have an existing one, you can use that. In this case, you can create one on the fly and attach it to the alert rule. To create an action group, click Add Action Groups under Actions. From the side pane, select Create Action Group.

EXERCISE 11.1 *(continued)*

6. You will be redirected to a new page to create an action group. To start with the creation, you need to provide basic details such as Subscription, Resource Group, Action Group Name, and Display Name. Click Next: Notifications to configure notifications.

7. On the Notification tab, as we discussed earlier, you can either set up the Email Azure Resource Manager role or use Email/SMS Message/Push/Voice. We will use the second option here. You need to provide an email address to receive the notifications. Click OK to save the configuration. You can add more notification types as required.

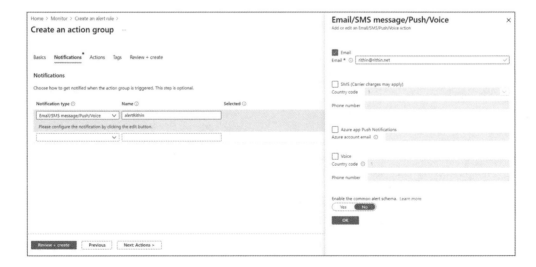

8. Click Next: Actions, and this will take you to the Actions tab. We discussed actions earlier; nevertheless, in this exercise we are not using actions. You can go ahead and click Review + Create. After validation, click Create to create the action group. This is going to take some time.

9. During the creation process, you will be redirected back to the Create Alert Rule page, and the newly created action group will be automatically selected upon completion. You will also receive an email stating that you have been added to the action group.

10. Further, you need to provide additional details such as the alert rule name, description, subscription, resource group, and severity. There will be two check boxes; one is to enable the alert upon creation, and the second one is to automatically resolve alerts once fired. Since you don't want the alerts to be automatically resolved, you will leave the second option unchecked. Click Create Alert Rule to create the alert.

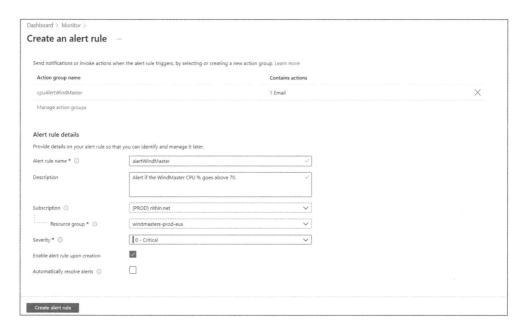

11. Since you checked the option Enable Alert Upon Creation, the alert rule will be enabled as soon as it is created. Now, you will establish an SSH connection to your VM and install the stress tool. The stress tool can be used to simulate load on the VM CPU, and with this you will be able to shoot up the percentage CPU usage of the VM. To connect to the VM, run `ssh <username>@<public-IP>` from your terminal or use any SSH client.

12. Once you are connected to the VM, run the following commands one by one:

```
sudo apt update -y
sudo apt install stress -y
sudo stress -c 2 -v
```

EXERCISE 11.1 *(continued)*

```
rithin@windmaster-web-prod:~$ stress -c 2 -v
stress: info: [13910] dispatching hogs: 2 cpu, 0 io, 0 vm, 0 hdd
stress: dbug: [13910] using backoff sleep of 6000us
stress: dbug: [13910] --> hogcpu worker 2 [13911] forked
stress: dbug: [13910] using backoff sleep of 3000us
stress: dbug: [13910] --> hogcpu worker 1 [13912] forked
```

13. This will start the stress process, and you will leave it running for more than five minutes because we set the aggregation granularity period as five minutes while creating the alert. Azure Monitor will evaluate the value every one minute, and if the average value exceeds the threshold in the last five minutes, the alert will be fired. You will receive an alert similar to the one shown here.

14. If you navigate back to the Azure Monitor's Alerts blade, you will be able to see the fired alerts and the status of the alerts fired.

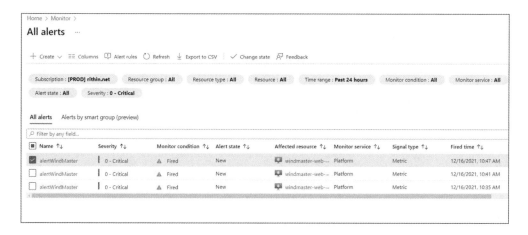

15. Clicking any of the alerts will show you the reason for the alert along with the graph. Also, it will help you change the state of the alert to Acknowledged or Closed.

So, you have successfully created an alert in Azure Monitor and tested it to see if it is working as expected. Similarly, you can create alerts for events that are logged in the Azure Activity Log. You can open any log item in the Azure Activity Log and use the New Alert Rule option to create the alert. The workflow is the same; the only difference is you are using the Activity Log event instead of metrics. Figure 11.7 shows where you can find the Alert Rule Creation option in the activity log.

FIGURE 11.7   Creating alert for the activity log event

As you know, Azure Monitor ingests data from data sources to datastores; one is metrics, and the other is logs. You have seen how metrics work and how they can be used to trigger alerts in your past example. The logs you collect are stored inside the Azure Log Analytics workspace. In the next section, we will cover Azure Log Analytics.

Log Analytics

Using Log Analytics, the logs generated by your cloud and on-premises resources can be collected, and they can be analyzed. As you saw in Figure 11.1, data collected by Azure Monitor is ingested into Log Analytics. On the collected data, with the help of the rich query language, you will be able to build analytics. KQL can be used to analyze the data, and with this you will be able to perform complex operations without the need to write complicated queries.

If you navigate the Azure Monitor ➤ Logs, you will be able to select a scope, and all the logs are collected from the scope. However, if you haven't configured any collection, then you will not be able to see any data. You will see how you can connect resources at a later point in this chapter. To collect data, you need to create a workspace first. Let's see how that is done.

Workspace

Each workspace is an environment that will be used for the ingestion of Azure Monitor logs. The connected sources, configuration, and the repository are managed per workspace. Creating a workspace is mandatory if you are planning to ingest data from the following sources:

- Azure resources

- Logs from on-premises resources

- Logs from machines that are monitored by System Center Operations Manager

- Configuration manager device collections

- Logs from Azure Storage

- Diagnostic logs from Azure AD

Creating a Log Analytics workspace can be accomplished from the Azure portal, the CLI, or PowerShell. From the Azure portal, you can search for *Log Analytics* from the search results and click Log Analytics Workspaces to create a new workspace. Once you are on the Workspaces page, click the Create option to create a workspace. Creation requires the following inputs (refer to Figure 11.8):

- **Subscription:** Select a subscription.

- **Resource group:** Create or select a resource group to place the workspace.

- **Name:** Set the name of the workspace.

- **Region:** Select the Azure region.

Click Review + Create to start the validation. Once the validation is done, click Create to create the workspace. When it comes to the pricing for the workspace, you will be charged for the amount of data that you ingest to the workspace (per gigabyte) and for the data retention. Thirty-one days of log retention is free of cost; any retention more than that is billable. Now that you have created the workspace, you will explore the workspace data sources.

Data Sources

Workspace data sources are the set of resources that are onboarded to the Log Analytics workspace for data collection. As you can see in Figure 11.9, you can collect logs from virtual machines, storage account logs, System Center, and the Azure Activity log.

FIGURE 11.8   Creating a Log Analytics workspace

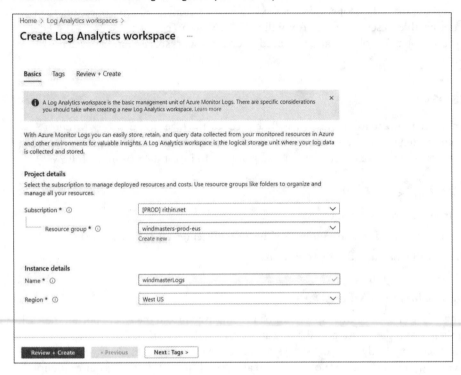

FIGURE 11.9   Connected data sources

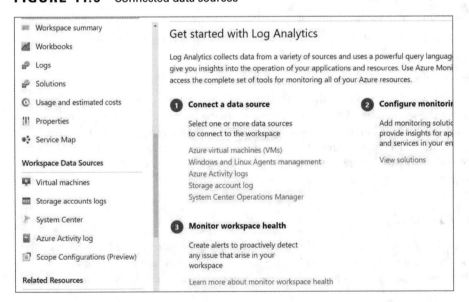

Clicking any of the data sources, for example, virtual machines, you will be able to see all the virtual machines. Also, you will be able to see if the VM is connected to the workspace. In Azure, the onboarding process is easy. Once you connect the resource, Azure will automatically install the agent for data collection in the resource. As you can see in Figure 11.10, you can simply click Connect to onboard the virtual machine.

FIGURE 11.10   Onboarding VM

If you are planning to onboard on-premises or virtual machines deployed in other cloud providers, you need to install the Log Analytics agent in these machines. The agent is available for both Windows and Linux servers. If you navigate to Agents Management, you will be able to download the agent and the keys that are required for configuring the agent (refer to Figure 11.11).

FIGURE 11.11   Downloading agent

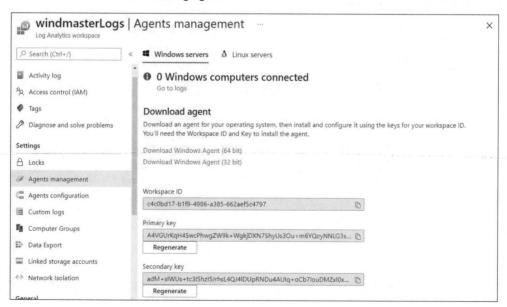

In Exercise 11.2, you will see how you can onboard Azure VM to Log Analytics. Now that you know how to connect the source, you also need to select which logs you plan to ingest. Let's take a look at agent configuration.

Agents Configuration

As you are getting charged for the data you are ingesting, it's important to make sure that you are ingesting only the logs that you require, not everything. With the help of the agents configuration, you will be able to declare what logs you want to collect using the agents and what level of logging information you need. In this way, you will have granular control over what is getting ingested into your workspace.

Using agent configuration, you will be able to configure the following logs:

Windows Event Logs   This helps you to select which event log items you want to ingest to the workspace.

Windows Performance Counters   You can select performance counters and the sample rate.

Linux Performance Counters   These are performance counters for Linux servers and their sample rate.

Syslog   Control which facilities in Syslog you want to ingest.

IIS Logs   This enables collection of W3C format log files from IIS server.

For example, if you take Syslog (refer to Figure 11.12), you can select the facilities and the level of logging that you need to ingest to the workspace.

FIGURE 11.12   Agents configuration

We will cover this during an exercise. Before you move on to the exercise, it is crucial that you understand the query language so that once you complete the exercise, you will be able to query the logs. So, now let's learn the query language. Unfortunately, we will not be able to cover the query language in detail; nevertheless, we will explore some basic queries.

Query Language

Using the query language, you will be able to consolidate and retrieve data. The data you ingest will be saved to multiple tables. The first step in writing queries is to understand which table contains the information you need. Some examples include Event, Syslog, Heartbeat, and Alert. Once you figure out the table, you need to pipe the data and use other operators.

These are some of the common operators:

- **count**: Counts the number of records and returns it.

    Example: `Syslog | count`

- **limit**: Limits the output to specific number of rows.

    Example: `Syslog | limit 10`

- **summarize**: Aggregates or summarizes the content.

    Example: `Syslog | summarize by field.`

- **top**: Returns the top N number of rows.

    Example: `Syslog | top 10 by name`

- **where**: Filters a table using different logical operators.

    Example: `Syslog | where computerName contains "web"`

You can also render charts using the render operation. Microsoft offers a playground with sample ingested data to play with the queries and test your queries. The sandbox environment is available at `https://aka.ms/lademo`. Now that you know how to connect the source, configure the agent, and query the data, you will do Exercise 11.2. For this exercise, you will be connecting one of the Linux VMs and ingesting Syslog and Linux performance counters to the workspace.

EXERCISE 11.2

Ingesting Logs to the Log Analytics Workspace

1. Sign in to the Azure portal and navigate to the Log Analytics workspaces. If you haven't created a workspace, you can create one using the steps mentioned in the "Workspace" section.

2. Navigate to Workspace Data Sources and select Virtual Machines. You will be presented with the list of virtual machines.

EXERCISE 11.2 *(continued)*

3. Select the virtual machine you want to onboard, and you will see the Connect button. Clicking Connect will install the agents in the VM and will enable log ingestion.

4. Once the virtual machine is connected, you will see that the status has been updated to "This workspace" instead of "Not connected."

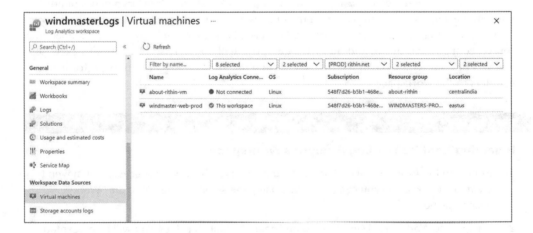

5. Now that you have onboarded the VM, you need to navigate to Agents Configuration and enable the Syslog facilities and Linux performance counters. Navigate to Agents Configuration ➢ Linux Performance Counters and select Add Recommended Counters.

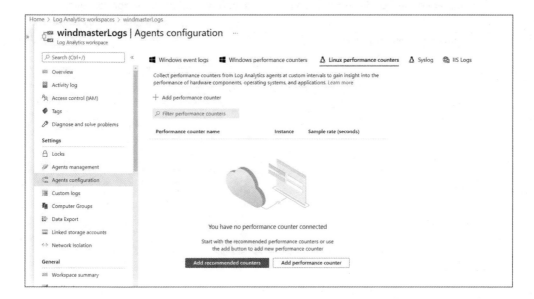

6. You will be prompted with the set of recommended performance counters. Click Apply to save the changes.

EXERCISE 11.2 *(continued)*

7. Navigate to the Syslog tab and facilities one by one by clicking Add Facility. Click Apply once you are done. For demonstration purposes, you will collect logs from all levels.

8. Now you have onboarded the VM and selected the data that you need to ingest. It may take 10 to 15 minutes for the VM to start ingesting the data. You will start querying the data once it's ingested.

9. After waiting for 10 to 15 minutes, you can navigate to the Log Analytics workspaces and open the workspace. Click Logs, and some sample queries will be shown to you. For the time being, you can close that, and you will be presented with a screen where you can write queries. If the data is collected, you will be able to see tables such as Heartbeat, Perf, and Syslog tables under LogManagement.

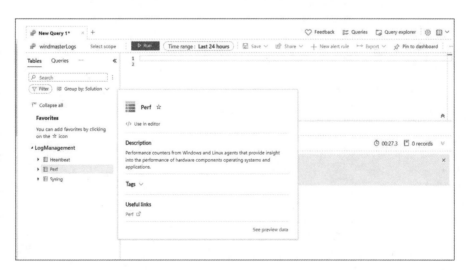

10. In the query editor, write `Perf` and run the query. You will see the contents of the Perf table.

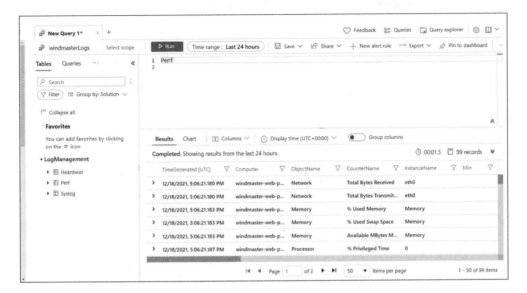

11. Let's try a complicated query; for example, you want to find the Used Memory % and display only the time and value instead of showing all the columns and then sort by time in descending order. Try the following query:

```
Perf
| where CounterName == "% Used Memory"
| project TimeGenerated,CounterValue
| sort by TimeGenerated desc
```

12. The output of the query will only show the time and value in a sorted order. Now in this query, the time generated is in UTC. Let's say I want to convert that to Eastern Standard Time and project the values in the graph. Let's modify the query to the following:

```
Perf
| where CounterName == "% Used Memory"
| extend ESTTime = TimeGenerated - 5h
| project ESTTime,CounterValue
| sort by ESTTime desc
| render timechart
```

13. This will convert the table to a time chart and render it.

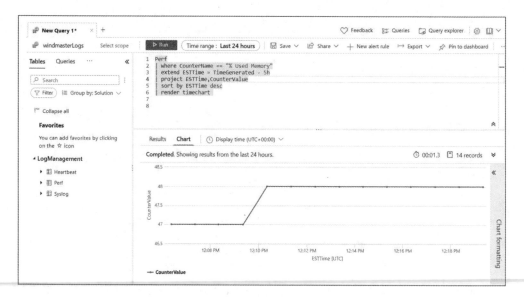

14. Now that you know how to work with the Perf table, you can do similar operations in the Syslog table as well. For example, you can create alert rules when a query returns a certain value.

In this exercise, you onboarded a VM to Log Analytics and queried the data using the query language. Next, you will take a look at the networking monitoring tools that are available in Azure.

Network Watcher

With the help of Network Watcher, you will be able to monitor, diagnose, and analyze metrics, as well as enable logging for resources that are deployed in the virtual network. Network Watcher is a regional service, and it is capable of delivering the following:

Enable Packet Capture for VMs   You can automate packet capture in a virtual machine when a condition is met. This will be helpful in troubleshooting network-related issues by administrators.

Network Insights   With the help of flow logs, you will be able to build deeper insights into the traffic pattern flowing through the network security groups. This data can be used for compliance, auditing, and security purposes.

Diagnose VPN Connections   Maintaining connectivity to on-premises and other sites is important in hybrid scenarios. Using VPN diagnostics, you can collect logs that will be helpful for troubleshooting VPN connections.

Network Watcher comprises a set of tools that can be used for various monitoring and troubleshooting purposes. The following are the tools that you need to be aware of.

IP Flow Verify

IP Flow Verify can be used to quickly troubleshoot connectivity issues from or to a remote IP address from a local IP address. For example, when you create a VM, there will be a default NSG that will be assigned to the VM. Let's assume that even after opening the ports you are not able to connect to the VM remotely via RDP. Chances are that the rule that you added has a lower priority than a deny rule or maybe a misconfiguration. To understand which rule is blocking the connectivity from the remote IP to the VM, you can use IP Flow Verify.

You can access IP Flow Verify by navigating to Network Watcher ➤ IP Flow Verify in the Azure portal. You need to provide the subscription, resource group, and details of the virtual machines so that the local IP address gets autopopulated in the field. In the destination you can put in any public IP address and see if the connection is there, as shown in Figure 11.13. By clicking Check, you will be able to confirm if the connectivity is there or not. If Network Watcher is not enabled for the region, Azure will enable it during the check process.

As you can see in Figure 11.13, connectivity is blocked because of the rule DenyAllIn-Bound. Now you can circle back to your NSG and make the appropriate changes to allow the traffic.

Next Hop

Next Hop is used to ensure if the traffic is getting routed to the expected destination. Ideally, this will be useful in scenarios where you will be using user-defined routes (UDRs) to verify if the routing rules are working. In Azure, as we discussed earlier in this book, when you create a resource in Azure, there will be a set of routes created by Azure called the *system routes*. System routes help in the resources in the same virtual network to communicate with each other and also outbound connections to the Internet without the need for any gateways. Sometimes you want to route the traffic via a network virtual appliance or firewall to make sure the firewall evaluates all the traffic before it hits your virtual network resources. By using Next Hop, you can easily find which route table is used for routing the traffic from a source to destination, as shown in Figure 11.14.

As indicated in Figure 11.14, you can see that the system route is used for the connection from the VM to the public IP address you provided.

FIGURE 11.13   IP Flow Verify

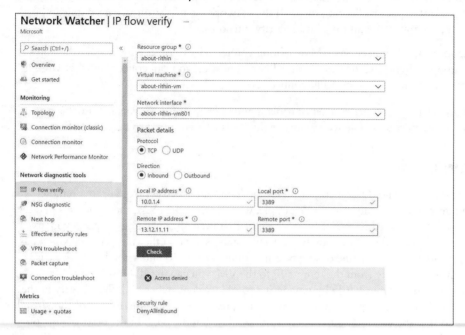

FIGURE 11.14   Next Hop

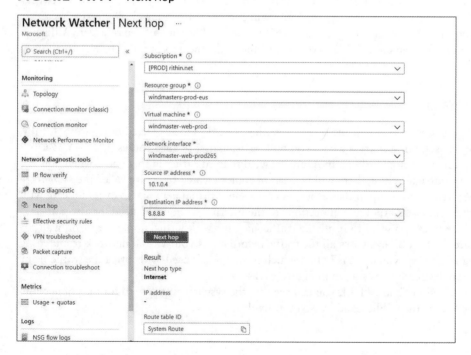

Effective Security Rules

As you know, you can apply an NSG at the subnet level and at the NIC level. Sometimes this can get complicated and with the help of effective security rules will be capable of finding the effective rules applied on the traffic (refer to Figure 11.15).

FIGURE 11.15   Effective security rules

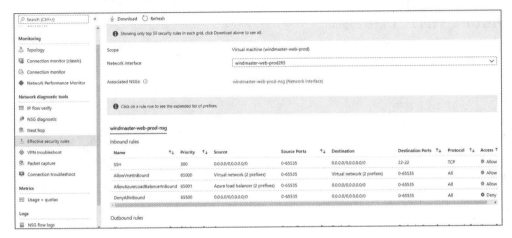

The view will show all the security rules including the name of the rule, priority, source, source ports, destination, destination ports, protocol, and access.

VPN Troubleshoot

In hybrid scenarios, you need to make sure VPN connectivity is always on. Using VPN troubleshoot, you will be able to troubleshoot the connections as well as the gateways. Detailed logs will be generated along with the health metrics of the connection and gateway. This is a long-running task and may require some time to complete the diagnosis.

The collected data will be stored in a storage account you select, as shown in Figure 11.16. The log files include connection statistics, IKE security errors, packet drops, etc. You can also run diagnosis on multiple gateways at the same time if required.

FIGURE 11.16   Effective security rules

	Subscription ⓘ	Resource group ⓘ	Location ⓘ	
	[PROD] rithin.net	Demo	East US	

Select storage account

https://dangleropes.blob.core.windows.net/$logs

	Name ↑↓	Troubleshooting s...↑↓	Resource status ↑↓	Resource Group ↑↓	Location ↑↓
☑	∨ vng01	⊕ Running	Succeeded	Demo	East US
☑	⊙ cn01	-	Succeeded	Demo	East US

Packet Capture

If you have done network troubleshooting, you know the relevance of packet capture. Using packet capture, you can capture network traffic from the VM (Figure 11.17). Further, you can filter and capture specific packets. Packet capture features are handy as you can trigger the packet capture automatically, and they are ideal for diagnosing network issues. The capture file can be stored in a directory within the VM or in a storage account or both.

FIGURE 11.17   Packet capture

As you can see, you will be able to specify the maximum bytes per packet, the maximum bytes per session, and the time limit of the capture. If you don't fill in these values, Azure will go with the default values.

Connection Troubleshoot

When you are designing network architecture for your virtual machines, you will be using NSGs, firewalls, user-defined routes, etc., which makes the troubleshooting tougher. Using Connection Troubleshoot, you can check the connectivity from a virtual machine to another VM, fully qualified domain name, URI, or IPv4 address (Figure 11.18). From the insights generated by the connection troubleshoot, you can understand what is causing the connectivity issue. Connection troubleshoot is handy in the following scenarios:

- Checking connectivity and latency from the virtual machine, application gateway, or Bastion host to remote endpoints such as websites, webapps, storage, etc.

- Checking connectivity between Azure VM and other resources such as Azure Storage or Azure SQL Server

- Checking connectivity for networks that are connected using peering

FIGURE 11.18   Connection troubleshoot

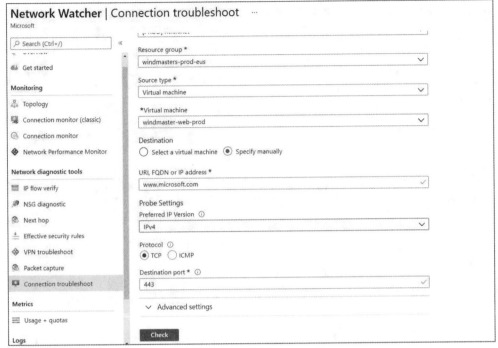

Once you click Check, Connection Troubleshoot will verify if the destination is reachable. It will also show the hops taken to reach the destination and latency, as shown in Figure 11.19.

The source of the request can be the virtual machine, application gateway, or Bastion host. The destination can be either a virtual machine or URI, FQDN, or IPv4 address. Under Advanced Settings, you can also configure the source port.

NSG Flow Logs

With the help of NSG, you will be able to filter the inbound and outbound traffic in a virtual network. Using NSG flow logs, you will be able to view information about inbound and outbound IP traffic through the NSG. The flow logs are in JSON format, and the logs will show inbound and outbound flows on a per-rule basis. Connecting NSGs to flow logs is easy; you just need to specify a storage account to store the logs (Figure 11.20).

The data collected from NSG logs can be sent to Power BI or any visualization tool for easier representation.

FIGURE 11.19   Checking the results

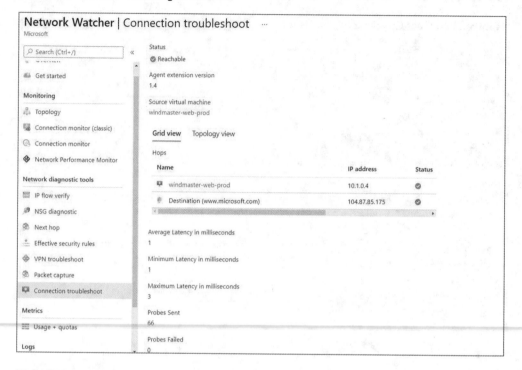

FIGURE 11.20   NSG flow logs

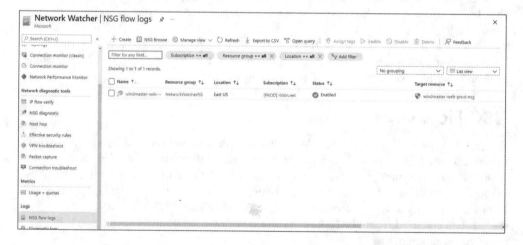

Topology

Network architecture can get complex. Unless you are part of the architecture design, it will be hard to understand the architecture. Using the Topology tool, you will be able to generate the topology of virtual network resources that are deployed. The topology can represent virtual machines, public IPs, route tables, NSGs, virtual network, subnets, and the relationship between them. Topology is always generated at the virtual network level. Figure 11.21 shows the topology of the VM, which you used throughout this chapter.

FIGURE 11.21   Topology

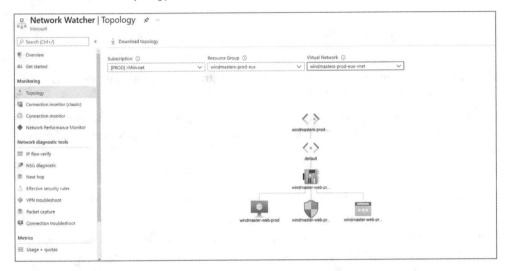

Using the download option, you will be able to download the SVG format and export it to tools like Microsoft Visio. One prerequisite for generating a topology is to have an instance of Network Watcher in the same region that the virtual network is deployed.

Summary

In the chapter, we discussed Azure Monitor, which includes different tools that can be used to perform the diagnosis, audit, and monitoring of your Azure resources as well as on-premises resources. You started with the architecture of Azure Monitor comprising the data sources, dataset, and actions that Azure Monitor can perform on the collected data. All data collected by Azure Monitor will be stored in two datastores: metrics and logs. We covered the difference between metrics and logs, and we discussed the Azure Activity Log, which contains all the operations that you perform in an Azure subscription.

We also covered Azure Alerts, including the alert states and action groups. Action groups play a vital role in notifying users and also in automating actions when an alert is fired.

The next service we covered was Log Analytics. For demonstration, we connected one of the Linux VMs to Log Analytics and ingested performance counters and Syslog from the machine. With the help of the query language, you filtered the data and also rendered charts.

Lastly, we covered Network Watcher, which is a set of tools that can be used to troubleshoot network-related issues. The tools included diagnostic tools such as IP Flow Verify, Next Hop, Effective Security Rules, VPN Troubleshoot, Packet Capture, and Connection Troubleshoot. Further we covered NSG flow logs and topology.

As this is the last chapter of this book, I wish you all the best and hope this book helps you excel as an Azure administrator.

Exam Essentials

Learn about Azure Monitor.   Understand Azure Monitor data sources, data stores, and the operations that can be performed on the collected data.

Understand Azure Activity Log.   Activity Log querying is important for administrators to audit events happening in the subscription. Learn about Activity Log categories and how you can query the logs.

Learn about Azure Alert.   Understand alert design and action groups.

Understand Log Analytics.   Learn how to connect sources to Log Analytics and configure the agents.

Learn about Network Watcher.   Learn all the tools that are described in the book and also their use cases, including Network Watcher.

Review Questions

1. Which of the data stores are used by Azure Monitor to ingest the data collected from the sources?

   A. Storage account

   B. Metrics

   C. Logs

   D. Activity Log

2. Which data store will be used for the performance counters of a Linux virtual machine?

   A. Metrics

   B. Logs

   C. Services

   D. Activity Log

3. Your organization has a very large web farm with more than 100 virtual machines. You would like to use Log Analytics to ensure these machines are responding to requests. You plan to automate the process, so you create a search query. You begin the query by identifying the source table. Which source table do you use?

   A. Event

   B. Syslog

   C. Heartbeat

   D. Alert

4. Your organization has an app that is used across the business. The performance of this app is critical to day-to-day operations. Because the app is so important, four IT administrators have been identified to address any issues. You have configured an alert and need to ensure the administrators are notified if there is a problem. In which area of the portal will you provide the administrator's email addresses?

   A. Activity log

   B. Notification group

   C. Azure Alerts

   D. Action group

5. Your organization has several Linux virtual machines. You would like to use Log Analytics to retrieve auth messages from syslog of these machines. You begin the query by identifying the source table. Which source table do you use?

   A. Event

   B. Syslog

   C. Heartbeat

   D. Alert

6. You are analyzing the company virtual network and think it would be helpful to get a visual representation of the networking elements. Which feature can you use?

   A. Topology

   B. Connection diagram

   C. Network views

   D. NSG flow logs

7. Your company has a website, and users are reporting connectivity errors and timeouts. You suspect that a security rule may be blocking traffic to or from one of the virtual machines. You need to quickly troubleshoot the problem, so which of the following do you do?

   A. Configure IIS logging and review the connection errors

   B. Turn on virtual machine diagnostic logging and use Log Analytics

   C. Use Network Watcher's IP Flow Verify feature

   D. Configure Windows performance counters and use Performance Monitor

8. You are interested in finding a single tool to help identify high VM CPU utilization, DNS resolution failures, firewall rules that are blocking traffic, and misconfigured routes. Which tool can you use?

   A. Network Watcher Auditing

   B. Network Watcher Connection Troubleshoot

   C. Network Watcher Flows

   D. Network Watcher Views

9. You are reviewing the Alerts page and notice an alert has been acknowledged. What does this mean?

   A. The issue has just been detected and has not yet been reviewed.

   B. An administrator has reviewed the alert and started working on it.

   C. Issue resolved.

   D. Ignore alert.

10. You need to determine who deleted a network security group through Resource Manager. You are viewing the Activity Log when another Azure administrator says you should use this event category to narrow your search.

    A. Administrative

    B. Service Health

    C. Alert

    D. Resource Health

11. What is the retention period offered by Azure Activity Log?

    A. 90 days

    B. 180 days

    C. 240 days

    D. 7 days

12. You have onboarded 100 virtual machines to the Azure Log Analytics workspace and started ingesting performance counters. Fifty VM names are in production, starting with the suffix VM-PROD, and the remaining 50 are development machines starting with VM-DEV. Which of the following queries should be used to display the Free Memory counter values for production machines? (Select all that apply.)

    A. `Syslog | where Computer startswith "VM-PROD" and CounterName == "Free Memory"`

    B. `Heartbeat | where Computer contains "VM-PROD" and CounterName != "Free Memory"`

    C. `Perf | where Computer startswith "VM-PROD" and CounterName != "Free Memory"`

    D. `Perf | where Computer startswith "VM-PROD" and CounterName == "Free Memory"`

13. Which of the following charts is not supported by the query language? (Select all that apply.)

    A. `linechart`

    B. `barchart`

    C. `areachart`

    D. `piechart`

14. You plan to calculate the billable data ingestion of your Log Analytics workspace. Which of the following tables should be queried to find the billable data ingestion?

    A. Heartbeat

    B. Usage

    C. Consumption

    D. CostAnalysis

15. You plan to calculate the cost for Log Analytics. Which of the following meters are billed to Log Analytics? (Select all that apply.)

    A. Data ingestion

    B. Number of VMs

    C. Number of data sources

    D. Data retention

16. How many days of data retention is free for Log Analytics, which stores the Linux Syslog?

    A. 30

    B. 31

    C. 60

    D. 90

17. Which of the following options can be used to store the packet capture taken from the virtual machine? (Select all that apply.)

    A. Blob storage

    B. File storage

    C. Table storage

    D. Local storage

18. In which format are NSG flow logs stored?

    A. XML

    B. JSON

    C. YAML

    D. Markdown

19. You would like to determine if the packets are hitting the firewall before they reach the Internet. Which of the following Network Watcher tools can be used to sort this?

    A. IP Flow Verify

    B. Next Hop

    C. VPN Troubleshoot

    D. Network Performance Monitor

20. Which of the following actions are not supported by action groups? (Select all that apply.)

    A. Automation runbook

    B. Function app

    C. Logic app

    D. Webapp

Appendix

Answers to the
Review Questions

Chapter 1: Identity: Azure Active Directory

1. D. Joining a device to Azure AD is an extension of registration. It changes the local state of the device and also helps admins to disable/enable devices. Changing the local state enables users to leverage SSO and sign in using a work or school account.

2. B, D. User administrators cannot reset the password of Global Administrators; only Global Administrator can reset the password of a Global Administrator. Since SSPR is enabled by default for admins, they can leverage the self-service options. If the admin has no access to the authentication devices, they can reach out to another Global Administrator of the tenant.

3. A. Fax is not a supported method for SSPR. SSPR supports email, text, or code to user's mobile or office phone, security questions, and authenticator app.

4. B. Guest users can be invited to the tenant via an invitation redemption process.

5. C. Azure AD uses REST API over HTTP/HTTPS, and queries are made via these protocols. So, Azure AD cannot be queried through LDAP.

6. D. If a non-admin user of a tenant creates a new tenant, the non-admin user will become the Global Administrator of the new tenant.

7. B. An application proxy can be used to enable access to on-premises applications via secured endpoints.

8. D. Azure AD requires a TXT/MX record to be added to your DNS zone. Once the record is added, Azure AD will make a DNS query to make sure that the record is added. If the record is not added, the domain will remain unverified, and you cannot create users with your custom domain name.

9. A. Identity protection and identity governance are available only on the Premium P2 license.

10. B. Each user has a unique object ID and is used by Azure AD to identify the user. This field cannot be modified and is managed by Azure AD.

11. D. Azure AD supports bulk operations to create, delete, or list users in your tenant.

12. C. Deleted users can be restored within 30 days from the Deleted Users blade.

13. A. Devices can be grouped based on their attributes using dynamic devices. Dynamic devices can be created only with security groups.

14. D. The department equal to HR and the location equal to GB scopes the users User 2, User 3, and User 4, and they are grouped together in parentheses. The next expression uses the AND operation, and the condition we have here is that the location is not equal to US. This will omit User 2. Hence, the answer is User 3 and User 4.

15. B. Microsoft 365 groups offer a shared mailbox, calendar, and other Office 365 apps for collaboration.

16. C. Office 365 uses Azure AD for authentication. All users and groups created in the Office 365 Admin panel are automatically synchronized with Azure AD.

17. B. Windows Hello for Business provides you with biometric authentication using facial recognition or fingerprints to access corporate resources and sign in to devices. The devices should have hardware that supports Windows Hello for Business to use this feature.

18. A. Only the global administrator can manage groups and assign necessary roles to other users.

19. A, C, and D. Although the list is by no means conclusive and you may identify others not listed, here are several characteristics of Azure AD that make it different from AD DS: Azure AD is primarily an identity solution, and it is designed for Internet-based applications by using HTTP and HTTPS communications. Because Azure AD is HTTP/HTTPS based, it cannot be queried through LDAP. Instead, Azure AD uses the REST API over HTTP and HTTPS. Because Azure AD is HTTP/HTTPS based, it does not use Kerberos authentication. Instead, it uses the HTTP and HTTPS protocols such as SAML, WS-Federation, and OpenID Connect for authentication (and OAuth for authorization). Azure AD users and groups are created in a flat structure, and there are no organizational units (OUs) or Group Policy objects (GPOs). While Azure AD includes Federation Services and many third-party services (such as Facebook), AD DS supports federation.

20. D. Conditional access can be used to grant access, block access, and grant access after completing MFA based on several signals such as location, device, application, and risk events.

Chapter 2: Compliance and Cloud Governance

1. C. Management groups can be used to group and organize subscriptions.

2. B. You can use Azure Policy to enforce tags during resource creation and also to validate if the tag values are present.

3. D. Budgets can be used to alert users using action groups when the spending crosses the threshold value.

4. A. Initiatives can be used to chain all policies of interest. Once created, they can be assigned to a scope for evaluation.

5. A. The hierarchy is Root ➤ Marketing ➤ EMEA so that the role will be assigned to the EMEA management group.

6. B. Assign the user to the Contributor role on VM-C. This means the user will not have access to VM-A or VM-B. The Contributor role will allow the user to change the settings on VM-C. We can also move the VM to another resource group and grant access to that resource group; however, the task was to minimize administrative overhead.

7. A, C. Create tags for the respective departments and then create an Azure policy. You should create a tag with a key-value pair like the department, such as Finance. You can then create an Azure policy that requires that the tag be applied before a resource is created.

8. A. Since all resources in the subscription should be protected, we can implement a lock at the subscription scope. Second, since we want to restrict only the deletion, we will go with the CanNotDelete lock. This lock will allow modifications.

9. B. A policy cannot restrict user access; this is taken care of by RBAC.

10. C, D. `Get-AzRoleDefinition` can show the definition; however, the output needs to be passed to `ConvertTo-JSON` to appear in JSON format. In the Azure CLI, you can see the JSON output directly using the `az role definition` command.

11. A, C. Tags applied to the resource groups that are not automatically inherited can be inherited by using scripting or policies. Tags applied at the resource group level cannot be used for cost analysis as Azure billing is done at the instance level.

12. C. Locks can prevent activities only on the control plane and data plane, and actions cannot be restricted.

13. A. The User Access Administrator role allows you to delegate access without the need to manage resources.

14. C. The user will have the Owner role. Also, if there are multiple assignments (direct and inherited), the combined permissions are assigned to the user.

15. B. Checking the error message will clearly show if there are any policy restrictions.

16. A, B. You can use the Azure Cost Management API, the connector, or the export functionality to build dashboards in Power BI.

17. C, D. The Account Administrator and Service Administrator roles will be assigned to the user who signs up for the Azure subscription. Service administration can be handed over to another user if needed.

18. C. Service administrators can be modified only by the account admin. No other user will be able to update this information.

19. A, D. Azure Reservations and Azure Hybrid Benefit can bring in potential savings.

20. D. `NotDataActions` can be used to define the set of not allowed data actions.

Chapter 3: Virtual Networking

1. B. Your clients need to make the DNS query to the Azure-provided name servers for the name resolution of zones created in Azure DNS.

2. A. 192.168.0.0/23 contains IP addresses from 192.168.0.1 to 192.168.1.254, which includes the on-premises address space 192.168.1.0/24. As the address spaces are overlapping, it's not possible to set up the connectivity.

3. D. Public IP addresses are required for the clients across the Internet to access the website. Since you need to reserve the IP address, you will go with static assignment.

4. C. The communication from the VM to all resources within the virtual network and to the Internet is allowed by default using the system routes.

5. A. A record can be added to resolve the hostname of the domain controller to an IP address. A CNAME can be added to resolve `files.firbish.com` to `ftp.firbish.com`.

6. C. Records will be propagated to the Internet name servers only if you have registered the domain with a domain registrar. After registration, you can delegate the domain to Azure for managing the records. Unless this process is completed, the records will not get propagated to the Internet name servers. However, we can still point our queries to Azure-provided name servers for name resolution.

7. C. When we are using service endpoint, Azure VM will be using the private IP address to communicate with the Azure service.

8. B. A private endpoint creates a private IP address in your virtual network, and the private link service can be used to connect to the storage account.

9. B. By default, traffic between subnets in a virtual network is allowed. You can use NSG to allow or deny specific traffic.

10. D. Linking the virtual network to the private DNS zone will update the DNS servers of the virtual network. All requests from the virtual machines will be resolved.

11. A. NTP used port 123 for communication; this traffic is allowed to the subnet by the rule Rule03. Since you have another NSG assigned at the NIC level, you will take the effective security rule. Port 123 traffic is allowed by NICRule01; however, NICRule03 has higher priority, and the action is set to deny. Hence, the 123 traffic will be denied.

12. D. Service tags are IP addresses representing different Azure services. Microsoft will automatically update the service tag if there is a change in the service IP address. You can use service tags for supported services without the need to manage the IP address to the services.

13. C. We can use application rule and add the FQDNs used by the Linux servers for updating the firewall.

14. C. The NAT rule can be used to configure DNAT.

15. B. For outgoing traffic, the traffic is first evaluated with the NIC NSG rules and followed by the NSG rules set at the subnet level.

16. A. Azure Kubernetes Service is not supported yet.

17. D. The service endpoint is used for communication between Azure virtual network resources and Azure services and cannot be used for on-premises connectivity.

18. D. NSGs and virtual networks support the TCP, UDP, and ICMP protocols.

19. D. In Azure Firewall, network rules are evaluated first, and then application rules are evaluated. If none of the rules allows the traffic, then it's dropped.

20. A, B. You can have one or zero NSGs assigned to a NIC. In the case of a subnet, you can have zero or one NSG.

Chapter 4: Intersite Connectivity

1. C. Peering is not transitive in nature; you need to create an explicit connection to each virtual network that you want to peer with.

2. A. A local network gateway is created in Azure as a reference to the on-premises VPN device.

3. A, C, E. The prerequisites for a site-to-site VPN are having a compatible VPN device on-premises, having a public IPv4 IP without NAT on the on-premises VPN device, and creating a VPN gateway and local network gateway in Azure. IPv6 is not supported for VPNs. ExpressRoute is a different setup and not part of a site-to-site VPN.

4. B. In this scenario, only one of the answers provides persistent connectivity to Azure, the site-to-site VPN. A virtual network to virtual network connects two Azure virtual networks together. A point-to-site VPN is used for individual connections (such as for a developer).

5. A. Select Allow Gateway Transit on VNET1 and use remote gateways on VNET2. VNET1 will allow VNET2 to transit external resources, and VNET2 will expect to use a remote gateway.

6. B, D. You will need two things: the shared key and the public IP address of your virtual network gateway. The shared key was provided when you created the site-to-site VPN connection.

7. D. ExpressRoute is the best choice for extending the datacenter, as it can use an any-to-any (IPVPN) connectivity model. An MPLS VPN, as typically provided by an IPVPN network, enables connectivity between the Microsoft cloud and your branch offices and datacenters.

8. D. The Gateway SKU selection directly affects performance. Gateway SKUs control the number of tunnels and connections that are available. This affects the overall aggregate throughput of the connection.

9. A. VPN gateways takes around 30 to 45 minutes to deploy. On the other hand, virtual network peering can be configured in minutes.

10. A. Azure Virtual WAN comes in two types: Basic and Standard. The Basic version is cheaper than Standard and supports S2S connections.

11. B. As there is already a gateway configured in the virtual network, there is no need to add additional gateways. In fact, you can have only one VPN gateway per virtual network. To accomplish the requirement, you can add a new S2S connection to the existing gateway.

12. C. Microsoft peering can be used to establish connectivity from an on-premises network to Azure. Azure public peering is not available for new ExpressRoute circuits.

13. C. TACACS authentication is not supported in a P2S VPN.

14. A. The service key, or s-key, is shared with you, the service provider, and Microsoft to identify the ExpressRoute circuit.

15. D. Up to 500 peering connections are supported to a virtual network.

16. A. In unlimited tier, the charges will be fixed, and the bandwidth charges are included in the fixed fee.

17. D. Along with Office 365, Dynamics 365, and Azure public services, Azure DevOps is also supported through the Microsoft peering configuration.

18. D. A gateway type cannot be changed from policy-based to route-based or from route-based to policy-based. To change a gateway type, the gateway must be deleted and re-created.

19. B. You can create a gateway subnet as small as /29, Microsoft recommends that you create a gateway subnet of /27 or larger (/27, /26, /25, etc.).

20. A, B. If your peering connection is in an Initiated state, this means you have created only one link. A bidirectional link must be created to establish a successful connection. For example, to peer virtual network A to virtual network B, a link must be created from virtual network A to virtual network B and from virtual network B to virtual network A. Creating both links will change the state to Connected.

Chapter 5: Network Traffic Management

1. D. Install an internal load balancer. Azure has two types of load balancers: public and internal. An internal load balancer directs traffic only to resources that are inside a virtual network or that use a VPN to access Azure infrastructure.

2. A. NTP runs on TCP/123, and Azure Load Balancer is the ideal solution for working with the TCP and UDP protocols other than web protocols.

3. B, C. By default, Azure Load Balancer checks the endpoint every 30 seconds. The health probe threshold can be configured.

4.   C. Application Gateway uses the hostname, port, and path in the URL of the request to route the request.

5.   A. The Application Gateway distributes requests to each available server in the backend pool using the round-robin method.

6.   C. Path-based rules can be handled by Application Gateway.

7.   C. Installing WAF would inspect the requests and will be used to check for common security threats like cross-site scripting and crawlers.

8.   B. Five-tuple hash is the default routing method used in Azure Load Balancer.

9.   A. A three-tuple hash uses the source IP, destination IP, and protocol for hashing.

10. D. Only Standard SKU provides an SLA and is recommended for any production workloads.

11. A. An HTTPS health probe is supported only in the Standard SKU of Azure Load Balancer.

12. B. Enabling session persistence while configuring Azure Load Balancer will let users connect to the same backend server every time a new session is initiated.

13. D. App Service is not supported in Azure Load Balancer.

14. C. Application Gateway supports both private and public IP addresses.

15. A. Azure Traffic Manager doesn't support internal network connectivity.

16. B. Azure Front Door works at layer 7 or HTTP/HTTPS.

17. A. The web application firewall checks each request for many common threats, based on the Open Web Application Security Project (OWASP).

18. D. Any codes between 200–399 are considered as healthy.

19. C. Supported distribution modes are none (five-tuple hash), client IP, or client IP and protocol.

20. B. The Standard load balancer can use any virtual machines or virtual machine scale sets in a single virtual network.

Chapter 6: Azure Storage

1.   C. In this scenario, you need to reconfigure 50 containers. While you can do that, it goes against the requirements to reduce the administrative overhead of future access changes. A shared access signature could work here, but not with the settings outlined in the options. An access key is meant for use by your apps when communicating internally in Azure to the storage. In this scenario, you should create a new container, move the existing blobs, and then set the public access level to Blob. In the future, when access changes are required, you can configure a single container (which would contain all the blobs).

2. A. Azure Files supports SMB 3.0, is reachable via File Explorer, and supports quotas. The other storage types do not support the requirements. While Blob Storage is good for unstructured data, it cannot be accessed over SMB 3.0.

3. D. The Append blobs optimize append operations (writes adding onto a log file, for example). In this scenario, the company needs to write data to log files, most often appending data (until a new log file is generated). Block blobs are cost efficient but not designed specifically for append operations, so performance isn't as high. Queue Storage is used for apps to communicate. Table Storage is a NoSQL database but not optimized for this scenario. Azure Files is geared for SMB storage, such as from Windows Servers but doesn't offer the optimized solution that append blobs do.

4. C. Azure Blob Storage is the right solution for serving videos and images on websites.

5. B. You should generate a SAS token for the container that provides access to either entire containers or blobs. You should not share the Etag with the contingent staff member. Azure uses Etags to control concurrent access to resources and does not deliver the appropriate security controls. Setting the public access level to Container would not conform to the principle of least privilege as the container now becomes open to public connections with no time limitation. CORS is a Hypertext Transfer Protocol (HTTP) mechanism that enables cross-domain resource access but does not provide security-based resource access control.

6. D. You can switch between performance tiers at any time. Changing the account storage tier from Cool to Hot incurs a charge equal to reading all the data existing in the storage account. However, changing the account storage tier from Hot to Cool incurs a charge equal to writing all the data into the Cool tier (GPv2 accounts only).

7. A, D. Shared access signatures provide more granular storage access than access keys. For example, you can limit access to "read only," and you can limit the services and types of resources. Shared access signatures can be configured for a specified amount of time that meets the scenario's requirements. Access keys provide unrestricted access to the storage resources, which is the requirement for production apps in this scenario.

8. C. In this scenario, only Azure File sync can keep FS01 and Azure synced up and maintaining the same data. While AzCopy can copy data, it isn't a sync solution to have both sources maintain the same files. Storage tiering is used for internal tiering (SSD and HDD, for example). While DFS replication could fit here, DFS namespaces don't offer the replication component. Storage Explorer is a tool for managing different storage platforms.

9. C. Read-access georedundant storage (RA-GRS) is the default replication option.

10. D. The key in this scenario is that you need to move data between storage accounts. The AzCopy tool can work with two different storage accounts. The other tools do not copy data between storage accounts. Alternatively, although not one of the answer choices, you can use Storage Explorer to copy data between storage accounts.

11. A. RA-GRS will store three copies of data within the same datacenter in the primary region and replicate the data to the secondary region. There also are three copies of data within the same datacenter. GRS, GZRS, and RA-GZRS make use of the availability zones.

12. C. `https://diagstorage01.blob.core.windows.net` would be the right endpoint to access the blob storage.

13. C. Blob lifecycle management can be used to transition access tiers and to delete blobs automatically based on the last modified date.

14. B. Azure File Backup can be used to automate the backup using a backup policy. Azure Snapshots can be used to take manual snapshots of your file share.

15. A, B. File Storage premium tier only supports LRS and ZRS.

16. D. SSE cannot be disabled; however, you can opt to bring your own keys for encryption instead of Microsoft-managed keys.

17. C. Super SSD is not a supported tier for Azure disks. Tiers supported are Standard HDD, Standard SSD, Premium SSD, and Ultra SSD.

18. D. Intermediary mapping with asverify will have zero downtime. Refer to the following:

`https://docs.microsoft.com/en-us/azure/storage/blobs/storage-custom-domain-name?tabs=azure-portal#map-a-custom-domain-with-zero-downtime`

19. A. Only StorageV2 or General Purpose v2 accounts support GZRS and RA-GZRS.

20. C. Bearer token is not a supported method for Storage Explorer.

Chapter 7: Azure Virtual Machines

1. A and B. To minimize the impact, put the virtual machines in an availability set and add a load balancer.

2. A, D, E, and G. In this scenario, you need to document which of the options presented is likely to save the company money for their Azure VMs. While this isn't an exhaustive list, the correct money-saving configuration options are to use HDDs instead of SSDs, use different Azure regions, use the least powerful VMs that meet your requirements, and bring your own Windows license (instead of paying for a license with the VM). The other options usually increase cost.

3. A. Azure supports two authentication methods for Linux VMs: passwords and SSH (via an SSH key pair). Access keys and shared access signatures are access methods for Azure storage, not for Azure VMs. In this scenario, you need to use an SSH key pair to meet the requirement.

4. C. When you have a scale set, you can enable automatic scaling with the autoscale option. When you enable the option, you define the parameters for when to scale. To meet the requirements of this scenario, you need to enable the autoscale option so that additional VMs are created when the CPU is 75 percent consumed. Note that the automation script is used to automate the deployment of scale sets and not related to automating the building of additional VMs in the scale set.

5.   B. In this scenario, you should use a scale set for the VMs. Scale sets can scale up or down, based on defined criteria (such as the existing set of VMs using a large percentage of the available CPU). This meets the scenario's requirements.

6.   B. An availability set should hold VMs in the same tier because that ensures the VMs are not dependent on the same physical hardware. If you deploy VMs in a single tier across multiple availability sets, then you have a chance of a tier becoming unavailable due to a hardware issue. In this scenario, each tier should have a dedicated availability set (web availability set, app availability set, database availability set).

7.   A. Configure the Bastion service. The Azure Bastion service is a new fully platform-managed PaaS service that you provision inside your virtual network. It provides secure and seamless RDP and SSH connectivity to your virtual machines directly in the Azure portal over SSL. When you connect via Azure Bastion, your virtual machines do not need a public IP address. Bastion provides secure RDP and SSH connectivity to all VMs in the virtual network in which it is provisioned. Using Azure Bastion protects your virtual machines from exposing RDP and SSH ports to the outside world while still providing secure access using RDP and SSH. With Azure Bastion, you connect to the virtual machine directly from the Azure portal. You don't need an additional client, agent, or piece of software.

8.   A. By default, you can connect Linux VMs using SSH. Nevertheless, you can install GUI and RDP to the Linux machine; this requires further configuration.

9.   C. Premium SSD offers better performance. You also have the Ultra disk option available, which offers better performance than Premium SSD; however, the supported SKUs are very limited.

10. A, B. The Reset Password option in the Azure portal can create users with passwords, and this can be injected into the VM. The second option is to log in with the key pair and enable Password Authentication in the SSH configuration of the VM.

11. C. Azure Bastion is a platform-as-a-service (PaaS) solution; this means that Microsoft will take care of the underlying OS updates and other management tasks.

12. D. Single VMs don't support autoscaling. If you require autoscaling for your VMs, then deploy a virtual machine scale set.

13. C. During vertical scaling, the virtual machine needs to stop and restart to apply the hardware changes. This process will lead to downtime.

14. D. Managed disk storage accounts are managed by Microsoft; therefore, no access can be granted. If you require access and control over the underlying storage account, then you should use unmanaged disks in lieu of managed disks.

15. B. Six hundred instances are supported for custom images, meaning the images you bring to Azure.

16. C. Private keys should not be shared publicly; this key should be secured and should be used by clients that are supposed to connect to the Linux VM.

17. D. WinRM uses TCP: 5986 by default; however, you can customize this and choose a different port.

18. D. A high CPU to memory ratio is offered by compute-optimized machines. It is ideal for medium traffic web servers, network appliances, parallel processing, and application servers.

19. A, B, and C. Scale sets support manual scaling and scaling based on metric or schedule. A scale set is scoped at the regional level and cannot be scaled across regions.

20. A, C. Scale sets are supported by Azure Load Balancer and Azure Application Gateway.

Chapter 8: Automation, Deployment, and Configuration of Resources

1. C. ARM templates are written in JSON format.

2. A, E. An ARM template will be deployed as a subscription-level template, and successful deployment requires `location` and `name` values. A sample template is given here:

```
{
    "name": "resourceGroup",
    "type": "Microsoft.Resources/resourceGroups",
    "apiVersion": "2021-05-01",
    "location": "eastus",
}
```

3. D. There is no resource-level ARM template deployment. If you would like to deploy resources using an ARM template, it will be scoped to a resource group.

4. C. In complete mode, existing resources are destroyed, and resources described in the ARM template are deployed.

5. A. Use the what-if feature. It evaluates the current state of your environment and compares it to the state that will exist after deployment. You can examine the summarized changes to make sure the template doesn't have any unexpected results.

6. A. You can use parameters. Parameters can be used to provide values when the template is running.

7. A. The −Resource parameter accepts the resource ID of the resource. To export, you need to pass the resource ID instead of the resource name.

8. C. The DSC extension can be used to achieve this state. DSC can resume the state management even after reboot.

9. B. In New-AzResourceGroupDeployment, you can use the `TemplateParamterFile` parameter to provide the parameter file.

10. B. The default selected region is East US, and it's not included in the allowed values list. If you are using Visual Studio Code with the ARM extension, you will get the following error message:

```
Template validation failed: The provided value 'Microsoft.WindowsAzure
.ResourceStack.Frontdoor.Common.Entities.TemplateGenericProperty`1[Newtonsoft
.Json.Linq.JToken]' for the template parameter 'location' at line '8' and
column '30' is not valid. The parameter value is not part of the allowed
value(s): 'westus,centralus,northcentralus'
```

11. B, C. `minValue` and `maxValue` are used for an integer. If you want to specify the length of the string, you need to use `maxLength` and `minLength`.

12. C. `output` can be used to display attributes post-deployment.

13. A. When deploying resources, you may need to make sure some resources exist before other resources. For example, you need a logical SQL Server before deploying a database. You establish this relationship by marking one resource as dependent on the other resource. Use the `dependsOn` element to define an explicit dependency. Refer to `https://docs.microsoft.com/en-us/azure/azure-resource-manager/templates/resource-dependency`.

14. B. ARM templates allow you to create and deploy an entire Azure infrastructure declaratively. For example, you can deploy not only virtual machines but also the network infrastructure, storage systems, and any other resources you may need.

15. A, B, C, and D. To deploy a template, use any of the following options: the Azure portal, the Azure CLI, PowerShell, the REST API, the button in the GitHub repository, and the Azure cloud shell.

16. C. Creating a generalized VM creates an image of the VM with existing configuration without user accounts, hostname, etc. This is ideal for virtual machine scale sets.

17. B. Custom Script Extension can be used to run shell scripts post-deployment in Linux machines. You could achieve the desired state using a DSC extension, but it's not written in the shell script.

18. A, B, and G. Only `$schema`, `contentVersion`, and `resources` are required to write an ARM template. The rest of the elements are used for maintaining a neater code. Refer to the following:

`https://docs.microsoft.com/en-us/azure/azure-resource-manager/templates/syntax#template-format`

19. D. Variables are referenced in this format:

`"[variables('variableName')]"`

20. D. The resource group location can be accessed in the ARM template using `"[resourceGroup().location]"`.

Chapter 9: PaaS Compute Options

1. A. Since you are not able to see the scaling option, it means that you are currently in a tier that doesn't support scaling. Though Standard and Premium support manual and auto-scaling, the solution requires the cheapest option; you will have to upgrade the current tier to Basic.

2. D. Free Tier can run for only 60 minutes/day; the next cheapest option is Shared Tier.

3. C. Only Standard, Premium, and Isolated tiers support autoscaling. Out of this, Standard can scale up to 10 instances only, and Premium can scale up to maximum of 30 instances. The cheapest option is to go with Premium.

4. D. Standard is recommended for running production workloads.

5. C, D. Continuous deployment is supported by Azure DevOps, GitHub, BitBucket, or your local Git. To leverage continuous deployment, you should use a source control program.

6. D. Virtual network integration is not swapped during the slot swap.

7. A, D. A and CNAME records can be used to map an Azure App Service to a custom domain.

8. A. LinkedIn is not supported out of the box.

9. C. The Basic tier doesn't support deployment slots.

10. B. A service principal will be created for reading the user information during sign-in.

11. A, B. The App Service can back up the app configuration, file content, and a database connected to your app (SQL Database, Azure Database for MySQL, Azure Database for PostgreSQL, MySQL in-app). Backups can be up to 10 GB of app and database content. Using a firewall-enabled storage account as the destination for your backups is not supported. SSL-enabled Azure Database for MySQL does not get backed up.

12. A. Container groups are scheduled on the same host.

13. C. You pay for only the virtual machine instances, storage, and networking resources consumed by your Kubernetes cluster.

14. A. Yes, you can host multiple applications in a single App Service plan.

15. D. The orchestration requests and schedules running the requested containers.

16. B. NodePort maps incoming direct traffic to the pods using the port mapped on the node.

17. A. The horizontal pod autoscaler should be used to increase or decrease the replicas of the pod based on demand.

18. B. The PV should be created, and the PVC will claim the storage in the PV. Later this PVC can be mentioned in the pod manifest.

19. C. Virtual Kubelet is an open source Kubernetes kubelet implementation that masquerades as a Kubelet. The Virtual Kubelet component installed in your AKS cluster presents ACI as a virtual Kubernetes node.

20. B. With Azure CNI, pods and nodes receive IP addresses from the Azure virtual network.

Chapter 10: Data Protection

1. C. The Recovery Services vault is used to store a backup.

2. C. The default replication used in the Azure Recovery Services vault is GRS.

3. C. You can only change the redundancy before backing up any items to the vault. Once you start backing up, you cannot change this. The only option is to create a new vault with LRS and reconfigure the backup to that vault.

4. D. The MARS agent is used for backing up files and folders to a vault.

5. C, D. MARS needs to be installed on the DPM/MABS servers.

6. C, D. MABS supports files, folders, volumes, VMs, applications, and workloads. The backups are stored in the vault, and the local disk is attached to the MABS.

7. C. Backup Center provides a single unified management experience in Azure for enterprises to govern, monitor, operate, and analyze backups at scale.

8. B. MARS doesn't support Linux.

9. B. Even after the backups are deleted, they're preserved in a soft-delete state for 14 additional days.

10. A. The cache storage account is created in the primary region and used to send the replicated data to the secondary region.

11. A. The ASR mobility extension is installed on all the VMs that are onboarded to Azure Site Recovery.

12. E, A, C. First create the recovery services vault, and then download and install the backup agent. Finally, back up the files and folders.

13. B. The Azure Backup server provides bare-metal support.

14. D. For backing up Azure virtual machines running production workloads, use Azure Backup. Azure Backup supports application-consistent backups for both Windows and Linux virtual machines. Azure Site Recovery coordinates virtual-machine and physical-server replication, failover, and failback, but Azure Backup will protect and restore data at a more granular level. Managed snapshots provide a read-only full copy of a managed disk and is an ideal solution in development and test environments, but Azure Backup is the better option for your production workloads.

15. B. When performing a virtual machine backup, you must first create a Recovery Services vault in the region where you want to store the data.

16. D. You can use snapshots to quickly restore the database data disks.

17. B. Use Azure Backup to restore a VM to a specific point in time and to restore individual files. Azure Backup supports application-consistent backups for both Windows and Linux VMs.

18. C. Up to 500 Recovery Services vaults can be created per supported region of Azure Backup.

19. D. There is no limit on the amount of data that can be backed up to a Recovery Services vault.

20. A, B, C, D. ASR-supported VMs, AD, Dynamics, SharePoint, SQL Server, and Exchange can be protected. Read more here:

https://docs.microsoft.com/en-us/azure/site-recovery/site-recovery-faq#what-workloads-can-i-protect-with-site-recovery-

Chapter 11: Monitoring Resources

1. B, C. All data collected from the sources is ingested into two data stores: metrics and logs.

2. B. With the help of waagent, you can send performance counters to the Log Analytics workspace.

3. C. The Heartbeat table will help you identify computers that haven't had a heartbeat in a specific time frame, for example, the last six hours.

4. D. When creating the alert, you will select Email for the Action Type option. You will then be able to provide the administrator email addresses as part of the action group.

5. B. Auth is a facility that is part of the Syslog table.

6. A. The topology feature provides a visual representation of your networking elements.

7. C. Diagnosing connectivity issues is ideal for Network Watcher's IP Flow Verify feature. The IP Flow Verify capability enables you to specify a source and destination IPv4 address, port, protocol (TCP or UDP), and traffic direction (inbound or outbound). IP Flow Verify then tests the communication and informs you if the connection succeeds or fails.

8. B. Azure Network Watcher Connection Troubleshoot is a more recent addition to the Network Watcher suite of networking tools and capabilities. Connection Troubleshoot enables you to troubleshoot network performance and connectivity issues in Azure.

9. B. An alert status of Acknowledged means an administrator has reviewed the alert and started working on it. The alert state is different and independent of the monitor condition. The alert state is set by the user. The monitor condition is set by the system.

10. A. Any PUT, CREATE, and DELETE requests will be logged under the Administrative category.

11. A. The activity log will be stored for 90 days.

12. D. Performance counters are stored in the `Perf` table, and you need machines starting with VM-PROD where the counter name equals Free Memory.

13. A. The query language supports `areachart`, `barchart`, `columnchart`, `piechart`, `scatterchart`, `timechart`, and `treemap`.

14. B. Hourly usage data for each table in the workspace is stored in the Usage table.

15. A, D. Log Analytics is billed for the data ingested and the data retention.

16. B. Thirty-one days of retention are included free.

17. A, D. Capture files can be stored in blob storage, local storage, or both.

18. B. NSG flow logs are stored in JSON format.

19. B. In Next Hop, you can specify the remote IP address. If the route table is in place, you will see that the next hop is the firewall.

20. D. Webapp is not a supported action. Supported actions are webhook, secure webhook, logic app, function app, automation runbook, and ITSM.

Index

K

L

M

Z

Online Test Bank

Register to gain one year of FREE access after activation to the online interactive test bank to help you study for your MCA Azure Administrator certification exam—included with your purchase of this book! All of the chapter review questions and the practice tests in this book are included in the online test bank so you can practice in a timed and graded setting.

Register and Access the Online Test Bank

To register your book and get access to the online test bank, follow these steps:

1. Go to www.wiley.com/go/sybextestprep.
2. Select your book from the list.
3. Complete the required registration information, including answering the security verification to prove book ownership. You will be emailed a pin code.
4. Follow the directions in the email or go to www.wiley.com/go/sybextestprep.
5. Find your book on that page and click the "Register or Login" link with it. Then enter the pin code you received and click the "Activate PIN" button.
6. On the Create an Account or Login page, enter your username and password, and click Login or, if you don't have an account already, create a new account.
7. At this point, you should be in the test bank site with your new test bank listed at the top of the page. If you do not see it there, please refresh the page or log out and log back in.